PREPARED, READY TO ROLL

Evacuation, Safe-Haven Selection, and Shelter-in-Place Guidebook.

Danger is on Your Doorstep

Book 2 & 3
Consolidated in One Volume

A Preparedness Manual By
SIG SWANSTROM

Part of the 36READY Preparedness Series

PREPARED: READY TO ROLL - BOOK 2

Cover Photo

The picture on the book cover is of
lightning strikes near a home above Medina Lake,
in the Texas Hill Country near San Antonio.

This photographic image has not been retouched except
for color correction. The composite image was made during
a 6-minute period using four 4-second exposures at ISO1600.

Depicted is multiple negative cloud-to-ground lightning strikes,
perhaps combined with the deadliest type of lightning strike of all,
a positive bolt commonly referred to as an *out-of-the-blue strike*.
In these instances, the lightning can strike an area that is
many miles away, often outside the storm in a zone
where the sky is still blue, as it is in this image.

This out-of-the-blue circumstance is a fitting reminder.
Not only can we discern that there are various dangers
on our doorstep, we also need to remember that disaster
can strike unexpectedly when our skies are
blue and life seems peaceful.

Nature Photographer: MICHAEL TIDWELL
www.MichaelTidwell.com

SIG SWANSTROM

No part of this publication can be reproduced, stored in or introduced into a retrieval system, or transmitted in any form or by any means (electronic, mechanical, photocopying, recording or otherwise), without the prior written permission of the copyright holder cited below. For permissions, as well as discounts on the purchase of more than a dozen books, contact the publisher or the author through their websites:

www.OxbridgePress.com   /   www.SigSwanstrom.com

LIBRARY OF CONGRESS CATALOGING IN PUBLICATION DATA
Swanstrom, Sig
"Prepared: Ready to Roll"
This is Book-2 & 3 in a four-book series using the same title.
Subtitle for this book: "Danger is on our doorstep.
Your step-by-step guide to evacuation, safe-haven selection,
and shelter-in-place.

This book is part of the publisher's series,
36READY Preparedness Guides

ISBN: 978-0-9996455-0-5

⌛

Oxbridge Press
Oxford - Cambridge - Seattle
www.OxbridgePress.com
Copyright 2017 by Sig Swanstrom
All rights reserved.
First Edition
+

Dedication

This book is dedicated to three groups of brave guardians. First, to the selfless oath-keeping Constitution-loving law enforcement officers who daily put themselves in harm's way. These men and women are the thin blue line which separates us from lawlessness.

Second, to the Firefighters and other First Responders who risk their lives fighting fires, helping those who need emergency medical care, and rescuing those who find themselves trapped by a disaster.

Lastly, this book is dedicated to those members of the public who are our "Sheepdogs." These are the ordinary men and women who live life in a state of readiness, equipped and willing to courageously step-in to help neighbors in need (sheep).

It is this informal partnership between professionals and dedicated volunteers where peace is forged, justice is restored, lives and property are safeguarded, and where hope can flourish during times of adversity. Yes, danger is on our doorstep, but these are the people who will help us win the battles we face. Because of their faithful service, we can be optimistic about the future.

God bless them all. Sheepdog-Up.

How to Use this Book

Okay, this is a thick book, but don't be put off by its size. This volume is two books in one. And, it is both a guidebook and a reference resource. By design, each chapter is a self-contained topical unit. Reading it sequentially is ideal, but it also works to jump around to satisfy your needs or interests.

As a guidebook, it can help you gear-up and plan for an emergency situation. It provides step-by-step instructions for successful evacuation, locating a safe-haven retreat location, and what you need to shelter-in-place.

As a reference book, it includes a wealth of relevant, essential information such as how much bleach it takes to purify water, or the Calories and nutritional requirements of a person operating in a high-stress environment.

If you choose to skip over these "reference book" details, at least scan each chapter so you can quickly find this vital information later. You might even want to cut some pages out of this book and add them to your GO-Bag (evacuation bag). To accommodate this practice, some key reference information is repeated in abbreviated form in a different chapter.

As you read, you will notice that the author sometimes uses the pronoun "I" and other times "we." This is because he is sometimes speaking from the viewpoint of his own personal experience ("I"), while on other occasions he is the spokesperson for the team of experts ("we") who reviewed and developed content for the book.

Importantly, the advice contained here, does not merely represent the viewpoint of one person, but rather the combined insights of a group of credentialed experts. As a final step before publishing, it was also peer reviewed by a cadre of scholars and specialists who validated the recommendations it contains.

Before you put this book aside, take the time to examine each chapter—even if you consider yourself an expert on that topic. It's easy to inadvertently miss essential information or a perspective that you may not have previously considered. Such mistakes can be costly when our decisions affect the safety and security of ourselves and those we care about.

Table of Contents

	Foreword	11
	About the Author	13
	The Other Books in this Series	14
	Introduction	15
CHAPTER		
	Planning	
1	Scenarios: The Tactical Approach to Emergency Planning and Training	35
2	Adaptable & Balanced Advance-Planning is Critical	71
3	Escape "From" vs. Escape "To"	75
4	Selection of a "Safe-Haven" Retreat Location	83
5	Maps, Routes, and Navigation	113
6	Transportation for Evacuation	121
7	Communication During Emergency Situations	173
	"Right Now" Evacuation & GO-Bag Essentials	
8	Prepare and Share a 2-3 Page 'Plan Summary'	191
9	GO-Bag: Evacuation Kit (Bug-Out Bag) Overview	197
10	GO-Bag Contents: Food and Water	215
11	GO-Bag Contents: Supplies and Gear	243
12	Clothing and Footwear for Evacuation	261
13	Emergency Kits: Vehicle-based and Home Supplies	265
	Core Necessities (The following is Book-3)	
14	Water Purification Methods, Finding Water, and Safe Water Storage Options	273
15	Emergency Larder: Evaluation of Food Choices	303
	Defense and Safety	
16	Gun Selection and Ammunition Choices	329
17	Tear Gas & Pepper Spray as a Self-Defense Option	357
18	"Prepared" vs. "Prepared and Ready to Roll"	365

- Turn page for the continuation of this Table of Contents -

Table of Contents
- Continued -

CHAPTER

Medical & Health
19	Medical Emergencies: You Will Need More Than a First Aid Kit	373
20	Preparing for a Dental Emergency	395

Misunderstood & Neglected Essentials
21	Flashlights, Emergency Lighting, and Batteries	403
22	Fuel Transport, Stabilization, and Safe Storage	423
23	Backup ID, Encryption, Micro Data Storage for Mobility, Key PDF Reference Documents	433
24	Dogs and Pets: Turning a Problem into an Asset	443
25	Bartering, Sustainability, and Opportunities	447

Postscript
26	Author's Personal Reflections	453

Appendix
A	GO-Bag for Extended Duration Use	479
B	Nutritional Standards for Emergency Food	487
C	"Black Sky" Events: Protecting Electronics and Essential Gear from EMP, Solar Flare/CME, Nuclear, and Other Grid-Down Events. D-I-Y Protection Containers & Faraday Cages	489
D	Summary of Radio Options and 'Quick Reference' Frequency and Radio Guides	495

Foreword

Having started my professional life as a police officer and serving primarily in the Los Angeles area of California, my work life was routinely filled with lots of action. By the age of 30, I had personally experienced numerous deadly force encounters, faced snipers and active shooter incidents, several riots, an assortment of natural and manmade disasters, and lots of violent crime. If police departments issued Purple Hearts, I would have earned four during that decade.

A few years later, after taking an early retirement from law enforcement, I moved my family to Guatemala to follow a different career path. I was no longer a police officer, but my new job involved living in a country that was suffering a bloody civil war, so those experiences added additional breadth to my emergency-situation experience.

> *"While people are saying*, 'Peace and security,' destruction will come upon them suddenly, like labor pains on a pregnant woman, and they will not escape."
>
> Holy Bible
> 1 Thessalonians 5:3

One of the lessons learned during these years was how suddenly life can change. Everything is fine. Then, 1-minute later, everything is very, very different.

While living in the United States and in Central America, I saw people's lives change as the result of calamity. Those who were vigilant and watchful, and aware of their surroundings and circumstances, often did okay. They may have suffered hardship, but usually they were not overcome. Whereas those who were unprepared, often experienced serious harm or devastation. Some didn't survive.

When I speak to various groups and relate stories drawn from my personal experiences, no one is ever surprised to hear that whether the circumstance was violent crime, urban unrest or civil war, those who were physically and mentally prepared, typically experienced a better outcome. Yet, most people still choose to remain unprepared. By default, they are accepting unnecessary pain. Since you are reading this book you are different. You are the one I want to help.

Thankfully, those who live a lifestyle of readiness and personal responsibility can often emerge victorious. Some even thrive.

Today, we have a choice. We can let delusion guide us, or we can get ready for a future which will likely look very different than today. We can act like an adolescent who fails to wear his helmet, yet drives his bicycle recklessly and then complains bitterly after being injured. Or, we can choose to utilize appropriate safety equipment and make informed choices regarding risks and our personal safety.

It's not about living in fear. It's about living a healthy and hope-filled life because we are ready to face the uncertain days ahead. When we are PREPARED: Ready to Roll, we can live fearless, optimistic lives.

If you are willing to think, plan and get ready, this book is for you. Disaster *is* on your doorstep. Sooner or later, serious change will crash into our life. Today is the day to get ready for it.

"Be dressed in readiness, and keep your lamps lit."

Holy Bible
Luke 12:35

About the Author

SIG SWANSTROM has wide-ranging experience with disasters, social unrest, civil war, and emergency operations and preparedness. He has personally lived through, and responded to many natural and manmade calamities.

In addition to his law enforcement career in the Los Angeles area where he dealt with violent crime and civil unrest as a police detective and SWAT team operator, and his time overseas in Guatemala where he lived with asymmetric warfare on a daily basis for several years, SIG has repeatedly been on-scene with various natural disasters, too.

This includes two deadly earthquakes, helping with the evacuation efforts during major storms, and he was onsite immediately after the nuclear bomb-like volcanic eruption of Mount St. Helens. And, he was first on scene and provided aid after the crash of a commercial airliner in a densely populated urban area. As a result, the scope of his experience is unusually broad.

SIG has dedicated his life to help people get prepared and ready to roll into any type of emergency situation. Whether it be an encounter with a lone violent criminal or crowd bent on civil unrest, widescale political upheaval, a local or regional disaster, or an event that is life changing for a nation, SIG's passion is to help people fearlessly get ready for that moment when life suddenly changes.

In addition to founding two firearm defense academies, and authoring several books and many articles on the topics of firearms defense and emergency preparedness, SIG is also a popular speaker and regularly appears on national and international talk shows.

For more about the author, visit: www.SIGSWANSTROM.com

The Other Books in this Series

PREPARED: Ready to Roll – Book 1
Why Responsible People Are Preparing

A great book for family and friends who don't understand why emergency preparations have become so essential, as well as for the informed who want to avoid the time and money-wasting pitfalls which surround these efforts. To add emphasis to the message that we need to be *ready to roll*, this book opens with a motivational fiction story written by best-selling author DAVID CRAWFORD ("Lights Out"). In the pages which follow that story, SIG SWANSTROM documents the U.S. Government's two decades of facilities development and unprecedented preparedness efforts, to provide the reader with a framework on which to build their own personal preparations. Throughout, SWANSTROM uses well-documented facts to expose why a dependence on a government solution is foolhardy and dangerous. And, he provides compelling evidence that the coming era will be disastrous for those who are not prepared to face this new season of unprecedented change. Plus, he shows us how we can live fearlessly as a victor rather than a victim.

PREPARED: Ready to Roll – Book 4
Organizing a Safe-Haven Retreat Location

This last book in the series focuses on selecting and setting up a "safe-haven" retreat location. It includes criteria for selecting people to be part of your retreat community, advice on safe-haven retreat living, co-op development, long-term food options, methods of water purification for small groups, medical care when clinics and hospitals are unavailable, and guidance for community organizers and leaders. Other often forgotten needs are also addressed, such as: How to obtain news during a grid-down crisis; 2-way radio and secure communications options; community security and safety; public health; dealing with refugees; helping family and friends cope with a prolonged disaster; preparing to face the increased violence which often accompanies chaotic incidents; and, gun selection for self-reliance and self-defense. It also includes an overview of highly-specific hazards to address; transportation and travel disruption; changes in government services; widespread disease and pandemics; airborne contaminants; loss of Internet and communications systems; prolonged power outages; and, solar storms and electromagnetic pulse (EMP) incidents.

Introduction

A friend of mine is the Chief Financial Officer in a Fortune 500 company, and recently I had the opportunity to hear him speak at an event. During his presentation, he expressed confidence in our nation's economic recovery, and that he was optimistic about the future of the United States and Europe. He said that he anticipates a bright future for ourselves and for our children. The audience loved it. It was just what they wanted to hear.

My friend is a smart, well-connected guy, so I was surprised. Very surprised by the rosy view he expressed of the future.

After the crowd thinned, and the two of us walked out of the hotel ballroom where the meeting had been held, I expressed to him my astonishment. Explaining to him that based on what I've read and heard from top economic forecasters, the leading long-term economic indicators look bleak. In fact, incredibly depressing, so I asked him, "How can your view be so different from their projections?"

In answer, he said that he does agree with the doomsayers, but privately. He can't acknowledge this publicly. If he and his CFO friends voiced their concerns, the stock market would plummet. He said that their stock price would suffer a huge drop in value if confidence waned, and that would be bad for everyone.

My CFO friend told me that he and his financial expert friends had informally agreed to do what they can to prop-up confidence, to buy time. He said he wasn't lying during his speech. He is truly "hopeful" because he does "hope" that some solution will surface before the "house of cards" collapses. He said a solution must be found because the alternative is too horrendous to contemplate.

At the core, my friend admitted that his motivations are self-serving, but is his "buying time" goal reasonable? Can we still avoid catastrophe?

Yes, we can. At least on a personal level.

Economic collapse is one of the many looming disasters that are on our doorstep. But there are many others. We also need to get ready for various other challenges, too. Any of them can make the future look very different from today.

Nationally and worldwide, we are currently suffering the effects of many serious problems, but these are nothing compared to what is coming. There are many grave dangers on our doorstep, and any one of them has the potential to change our lives—and our world.

Isolated acts of terrorism are a concern but are less of a threat than open warfare, which is also a genuine possibility. The current effects of geoengineering are problematic, but the risk of regional drought and food shortages are even more sobering. Racial strife and immigration are contemporary issues of consequence, but the manipulation of elections and the loss of national sovereignty is society-changing and probably irreversible. Political shenanigans are a corrupting influence on our society to be sure, but far less significant than lawlessness in government agencies, or the effects of courts reinterpreting the U.S. Constitution and Bill of Rights.

Yes, natural disasters can be heartbreaking, and since they are commonplace, they certainly deserve our attention. However, as we prepare for disasters of all sorts, we need to remember that natural disasters are generally far less devastating, long-term, than many of the manmade disasters which are also looming threats.

For example, scores of sane, knowledgeable experts, are warning us about problems such as the collapse of our national power grid, an Internet crash due to cyber warfare, or hacker-anarchy that will cause the failure of financial markets. NASA warns us that we are overdue for an electronics-destroying solar flare (CME), while warfare experts tell us to expect mass casualties in the first year after North Korea, or some other rogue nation like Iran, hits us with an electromagnetic pulse (EMP) weapon—which we know they have.

These, plus various other threats, are long-duration disasters which will change our lives, perhaps permanently. Despite all the money spent and energy expended, national governments will be unable to fix these problems in a timely fashion. These will, therefore, create long-term problems. Due to the magnitude, we need to be able to cope with the effects of these, alone, without outside assistance.

The odds of eventually getting walloped by some incident seems inevitable. Therefore, we need to do what we can now, personally, to mitigate these increasingly-likely scenarios.

Every year, the list of dangers-on-our-doorstep is growing. Many of these have the potential to change life as we know it. Eventually, one of them will do just that.

Momentous upheaval and change will hit us soon, or at least during our lifetime or that of our children. We'd better be ready.

No matter how bad you think things are today, it is going to get worse. Much worse. This isn't a doom-and-gloom attitude. For those who are willing to look at our situation, it's an obvious fact-based conclusion based on our current state of affairs.

What do you think? Are you concerned? I hope so.

Fortunately, we do not need to accept victim status. We have other options than to sit back and suffer a lightning-strike of circumstances. Individually, we can personally prepare for the coming days of unprecedented national and international change. Our efforts today can make a huge difference in our future—and the future of our family.

Personally, I do think that many of these disasters can be averted. It is possible. But can we sidestep all of them? That's unlikely, and it is foolhardy and irresponsible to base our future on vague hope.

Unfortunately, the necessary changes will not come through positive thinking, optimism, or an upbeat attitude. And further, an adequate safety net cannot possibly be provided through the efforts of the Federal Emergency Management Agency (FEMA), the Department of Homeland Security (DHS), or your local government.

The election of the best political leaders and their acceptance of advice given by experts, can do little more than delay the inevitable. Poor decisions will speed the arrival of our day of reckoning, but even highly competent politicians cannot stop the dawning of a new, less pleasant era. It will eventually arrive.

We are facing many life-changing problems, but the core problem resides in the hearts and minds of the citizenry. Unless this fundamental shortcoming changes, disaster is inevitable.

Unfortunately, we're beyond simple, painless solutions. Therefore, disaster and emergency situation preparations have become crucial. Individually, we may not be able to change the world, but we can change our part of the world. We can help our family and friends.

For the United States, the UK, and Europe to avoid what is coming, we need to experience a fundamental change in the hearts and minds of our fellow citizens. The central problem is a citizenry that is self-centered and pleasure-focused, a population that wallows in entitlement and is unwilling to embrace personal responsibility, is delusional in the face of evidence, and suffers from the effects of a normalcy bias and a nihilistic worldview.

Fortunately, these are shortcomings we can address in our own personal life. And, we can work to nurture healthy change in the lives of our family, friends, and through our spheres of influence.

I'm not a cheerleader by nature, but each of us does have the opportunity to change our corner of the world. We can make changes in our own life, and we can encourage and assist others to make these changes, too.

All of us need to get ready for the changes and dangers we face, but the first step in preparation is to focus on our own, personal revival. When we get our own heart and mind and energies refocused, then we can aptly deal with getting prepared, and become ready-to-roll when an emergency situation is upon us.

Local and national governments are preparing for the dangers on our doorstep, but their preparations will not be adequate when it comes to us, personally. Our solutions will not be found in government programs, nor in the efforts of charitable organizations.

Since healthy personal choices are not being made by the masses, nor by their governments, responsible people need to "cowboy up." We need to look to ourselves and do what we can to get ready.

Even if politicians suddenly decide to link arms in an uncharacteristic effort of nonpartisan reform, millions of our fellow citizens would protest and sidetrack these measures before they can be enacted. Regrettably, *austerity* and *personal sacrifice* are terms that are no longer in our lexicon.

Yet, miracles do happen. But absent a miracle from God, it's not going to materialize.

Unfortunately, a significant economic "reset" is just one of the many highly-likely dangers we must face and prepare to endure. There are many others which are equally, and even more severe.

These dangers aren't just hypothetical. There are many real dangers on our doorstep, and some of these are far-reaching. Very. They are credible threats to our way of life. Literally. And the failure to systematically take the steps necessary to prepare for the coming changes is, frankly, irresponsible.

"Yes," we can be hopeful about the future. We can be optimistic. We can. Yet, hope and optimism can only be considered a rational response under one condition: *When we are personally prepared for the changes that are coming.*

I need to be blunt. If you are optimistic about the future but you aren't getting ready for the coming changes, you are delusional. If you say, "I'm a Christian and God will protect me," you don't know your Bible.[1] On the other hand, if you are fatalistic and think you can't do anything about what's coming, you are just as wrong.

It's true that the United States and other Western countries are suffering social, cultural, and moral decay. Observant people acknowledge this fact. Sadly, this moral decline is additionally germane to this discussion because, during hard times, a large number of people will resort to criminal conduct to get what they need or think they need.

Even those who in normal circumstances live like law abiding citizens, may, during disastrous times, resort to violence to get what they want. Many will probably succumb to this temptation. Therefore, we need to expect widespread violence. Fortunately, we do have the capacity to plan a proactive response.

If things stay calm and people are helpful and selfless during a disaster, that's fabulous. But if things turn nasty, we need to be prepared to cope with that aspect of an emergency, too.

We need to face reality. If we suffer a disaster that is widespread or continues for an extended time, we need to expect social strife. We need to anticipate what will happen if the thin veneer of civilized conduct melts away. Then, we need to develop a personal plan to deal with it, alongside a plan for living without outside help.

We the people have been living like a binge-drinking college student. As a result, our irresponsibility is dumping crapulence into every corner of our society. And just like an impenitent college student, many refuse to acknowledge that this lack of sobriety will adversely affect our future—and the future of our children.

We can't ignore the inevitable repercussions. Personal action and preparedness, aren't optional. They are our duty.

---

[1] Proverbs 6:6-11, Proverbs 12:3, Matthew 16:2-4, et al.

Danger is on our doorstep.
Both problem-solving and hazard-reduction
need to be a top priority.

During the Great Depression, a majority of the U.S. population had an ingrained moral fiber based on biblical principles, and this guided the behavior of even the non-religious. Also, though most of the population lived in cities, most of the citizenry was only one generation removed from life on the farm, so they knew how to plant a garden and grow food.

When we compare that era to today, we recognize that morality has sharply declined. Behavior is now guided by a belief that moral absolutes don't exist, and conduct is a matter of personal choice. As to self-reliance, most don't know how to grow food. They can't even differentiate between a carrot and a potato when they are still buried in the ground.

These two factors alone suggest that the public's response to another Great Depression or some other largescale problem, will be very different from what it was in the 1930s. Though these examples are shortcomings that can be corrected, there is no evidence that the transformation of society has started.

Regardless, for us individually, knowing how to grow healthy food is a tremendous asset. Today our grocery store varieties of fruits and vegetables, and even our fresh-frozen prepared foods are notorious for having little nutritional value. Whereas homegrown fruits and vegetables, grown from non-GMO "heirloom" seeds, are often far healthier. A diverse diet of these homegrown foods may even reduce the number of the ailments and health problems which seem to plague modern society. In the future, these same skills may prove to be invaluable.

This is but one example of how our disaster preparations can also enrich our lives today, even when life is routine. Importantly, these preparations can be used to teach the next generation self-sufficiency.

Having a backyard garden, and learning independence-producing skills such as gardening, are of value to us today. Plus, at some future point when the grocery store shelves are empty or filled with food that is too expensive for us to purchase, having a family garden may prove to be a necessity. Unfortunately, when that happens, it will be too late for most people to start learning.

Benefits of preparing include healthier living for today, *and* being ready to adapt to future changes.

Thankfully, many of our preparations are generic in nature, so they are beneficial to us for an assortment of potential dangers. Minor or major, slow to develop or instantaneous, many threats share the same after-effects. This means that those who are willing to take the steps needed to prepare, can be ready to respond to most emergency situations. This makes preparation a manageable task.

> By our actions, or our failure to act, we are making a choice.
>
> Today, each of us is choosing to be either a victim or a victor.

Safety and the ability to get to a safe-haven location, produce pure water, nutritious food, and the knowledge and skill-sets required for self-sufficiency, are the foundational needs of any emergency situation. Therefore, these are the focus of this book.

Living Fearlessly

Another key benefit of being prepared and *ready to roll* with our preparations is that we can learn how to put fear in its place. Readiness can help us overcome fear.

As we proactively prepare, we have the opportunity to redirect any anxiety or fear we may feel. If we are intentional, we can transform these debilitating emotions into healthy motivation. Once redirected, these can become enthusiasms which produce fruitful, productive action.

As we get ready for the dangers and changes that will make life difficult in the future, which may even threaten our survival, we can learn how to live life more fully today and tomorrow. If we let fear motivate us—but not control us, we embark on a pathway which can lead us to a more fulfilling and vibrant life; a life that is driven by purpose. Self-reliance is gratifying and freeing.

So "yes," we should hope for the best and work to stimulate positive change in our world today. However, it is foolhardy to make this our only plan of action. We need to recognize that we are facing many dangers, and that threats are increasing in both quantity and magnitude.

The trends have been going the wrong direction for many years. It's now time for personal action.

The world is teetering. Our nations and Western culture are headed in the wrong direction. While many people are aggressively working for positive change, these efforts, at best, are now only a delaying action. Unfortunately, these activities are not enough to turn things around. Nevertheless, I applaud these initiatives, and I will continue to help wherever I can.

On another front, I am preparing for trouble. That's what open-eyed discerning people do, too.

The uncomfortable truth is that we need to spend more and more of our time preparing for what is coming. To be clear, I'm not saying abandon ship. Rather, realizing that we are probably not going to get the ship of State safely to port, I'm saying it's time to caulk the sinking ship so that we can delay the inevitable as long as possible.

Like my Chief Financial Officer friend, we can retain a hopeful attitude. But unlike him, we need to acknowledge that our hope needs to be anchored in something more than wishful thinking. We can be hopeful if we prepare for what's coming by getting ready physically, mentally, relationally, and spiritually.

During this time, we need to build lifeboats for ourselves, our families, and friends. Though the ship may not make it to safety, *WE* can, if we are diligent.

Change Brings New Opportunities

> *"If you prepare yourself... you will be able to grasp opportunity for broader experience when it appears. Without preparation, you cannot do it."*
> - Eleanor Roosevelt
> Autobiography
> U.S. First Lady, 1933-45

For these reasons and others, responsible people are now making disaster and emergency-situation preparedness a top priority. If you are one of them, this book is designed to help you take the step-by-step measures necessary for getting prepared and ready to roll. Together, we can prepare for a future that is increasingly volatile and uncertain—and filled with opportunities.

And as we prepare, let's keep in mind that preparing for these changes also means that we will be able to seize new opportunities. These will only be available to those who are ready for them.

'Watchers' see that non-trivial change is now inevitable. Those who are perceptive, recognize that some of these changes will bring some positive side effects. Nonetheless, most of the repercussions will be exceedingly negative, especially for the millions who are unprepared. We can be different.

How? This is not the time to sit back, wring our hands, and whine about it amongst our friends. It is foolish to just wait for this wave of change to sweep over us. It's a time for discerning action.

Most of us are not in a position to help solve the problems of our world or our nation, but we can be a positive influence, and we can be an asset to our family, friends, and community. In effect, we can figuratively build lifeboats for ourselves and for those we love. So, when those stormy days come, we can help others stay afloat, too.

Step-by-step, we can get ready for the epoch period of change that is coming. On an individual level, we can learn how to mitigate the adverse effects. This is the task at hand.

You are currently reading one book in a series on disaster preparedness. Each volume in this series focuses on a different aspect of disaster and emergency situation preparedness. All were written to help you get ready for what is coming.

You may be frustrated because you can't afford to do more or buy more. Don't be. Do what you can. That is all that God expects of us.

The most important tool we own is our brain. Let's use it to think, plan, and avoid future problems.

Be creative. Be a problem solver. Seek out other like-minded people, and be in community with them.

It's with a sigh of relief that I acknowledge that we're not in this alone. If you are alone, do what you can to change that, but even with this task, find solace in doing what you can. Don't bemoan what you don't have the capacity to accomplish. Do what you can.

In Book-1 of this series, the case is made for why responsible people are preparing. In it, the emphasis is on documenting the scope and nature of U.S. Government preparations. As we observe what the government is doing, we can use this information to clarify what we need to do personally.

Those readers who are old enough or are students of history, will note a significant difference between the U.S. Government's action today and those of the Cold War period.

Due to the threat of nuclear war in the 1950s and 1960s, the U.S. Government installed air raid sirens in each major city to warn the public of an imminent attack, and they built neighborhood bomb shelters, too. These they filled with supplies and equipment, and they provided training for both adults and school children.

What Book-1 in this series documents, is that governmental disaster preparations in our modern era are far different. Today, the U.S. Government is building elaborate, massive, underground shelters, but these are for politicians, government workers considered *essential*, and a collection of well-connected civilians.

This isn't a conspiracy theory. It's not even a secret.[2]

Rather than the old program known as "Civil Defense," this current effort is referred to as "Continuity of Government." This transition away from 'civil defense' to 'government survivability' has been going on for years. Though these efforts have recently increased in intensity, these preparations have been underway for several decades—during both Republican and Democrat administrations. The details are underreported by the media, but it is easy to research.[2]

During the Cold War, the primary objective of government preparedness planning was to protect the civilian population. Today, the U.S. Government's efforts are designed to protect a few hundred thousand "select" people. (By the way, if you've not already been contacted by a representative of the government and been given instructions, you have not been selected.)

Okay, so I'm not included. You probably aren't either. What am I going to do about it?

What I'm *not* going to do is whine about it to my senator or congressman. Rather, I am going to take personal responsibility for finding my own solution.

The sobering reality is that the task of protecting myself and my family is up to me. It's my responsibility. The government isn't going to help.

---

[2] For more on this topic, read "PREPARED: Ready to Roll – Book 1 – Why Responsible People are Preparing," by SIG SWANSTROM.

The protection, and preparations needed for my family and me, are totally up to ME. Getting ready is my responsibility, anyway. It is not something I can depend on the government to do for me.

Even if someone *is* willing to help, remember that it's our individual duty to make sure we are prepared. Even if you have a family member, or someone else who has offered to help, take an active role in the effort.

While it is true that the federal government of the United States (and most Western countries) is also engaged in preparations for the general public, frankly, what they are doing isn't very attractive. Their "general public" efforts do not paint a pretty picture of life under their care. Those who are depending on government help are going to be sorely disappointed by what they experience.

Even if the government's planning for civilians looked good on paper (which it doesn't), personally, I wouldn't want to depend on an inefficient bureaucracy for my welfare. This is accentuated when I realize that in the government's current efforts, the civilian population is the lowest-priority for receiving help.

> *"Anyone who thinks he can be happy and prosperous by letting the government take care of him, better take a closer look at the American Indian."*[3]
>
> - Henry Ford
> Founder of the
> Ford Motor Company

In the U.S., the Department of Homeland Security (DHS) and the Federal Emergency Management Agency (FEMA) are preparing shelters for the general public. The U.S. Army is charged with managing these facilities as they become operational. However, U.S. Army publication FM 3-39.40 "Internment and Resettlement Operations" (updated February 2010), which is the handbook for operating these facilities, depicts a prison-like picture of what life will be like in these "camps." At best, it will be unpleasant. If you think that it won't be so bad, I encourage you to search the Internet for an unredacted copy of this confidential (but not Classified) Army publication. It is obtainable.

---

[3] Though universally attributed to Henry Ford, this quote has not been validated by the authoritative resource, the Henry Ford Museum. Notwithstanding, even though they have not been able to find original source validation for this citation, it is consistent with the viewpoint of Henry Ford.

Fortunately, evacuating to a FEMA resettlement center needn't be our fate. We do have another choice. When things get bad, if we have prepared for it, we can go to our own safe-haven location.

If you are ready to take the initiative, this book, along with Book-4 in this series, can help you prepare your own safe-haven retreat location. It's not enough to be prepared to evacuate...

It's not just a matter of escaping *'from'* danger.
We need to evacuate *'to'* a safe place.

In this book, the focus is on evacuation and the physical preparations necessary for coping with both human-caused and natural disasters, particularly in the first hours and days after they occur. Here you will find practical answers to the questions of, *"What do I need to do?"* and *"How should I prepare?"* What you have in your hand is a guidebook to help you stay safe and healthy during those crucial first minutes and first days after an emergency develops.

Keep in mind, often more people are killed and injured in the *aftermath* of a disastrous event, than are harmed by the direct effects of the event itself. By following the straightforward, step-by-step advice offered in this book, you can prepare to be a 'victor' rather than accept 'victim' status.

100% Prepared

Even if you think of yourself as aware and ready for the days ahead, are you sure you're 100% prepared? For those who have already been thinking about these things and have made preparations, this book can help you evaluate what you have already accomplished. Importantly, it can help you identify weak spots in your preparations.

If you're just now starting to think about these issues, don't feel overwhelmed. This book can help you get started. These step-by-step instructions can also help you avoid the time-wasting and money-squandering mistakes that are often made by those who lack practical experience.

Develop a Two-Phase Plan: First, we need to be personally prepared for the period immediately following the onset of an emergency situation. Second, if the disaster becomes protracted, most of us will need to evacuate to a safer place where we can link-up with trusted friends and family.

This is even more important for city dwellers and those who live in the suburbs. If you don't already live at your safe-haven location, you need to be able to evacuate to a prearranged, pre-prepared, safe-haven retreat location.

Now is the time to think about this need: *If it does become prudent to evacuate, where will you go? Will you go to a government "camp" refugee center? On the other hand, if you do have a place to go, is that location equipped with what you will need?* Using the criteria included in Chapter-4, you can find a suitable safe-haven retreat location and begin to prepare it.

Remember, there is more to a successful evacuation than just getting out of town. You need to know where to go, and that location needs to be made physically ready and equipped with supplies, in advance, before you arrive. In other words, now.

- - - - - - -

Use the Table of Contents of this book to move from one topic to another. It is the hub of information.

Each chapter is self-contained. Therefore, it is easy to jump around according to your initial concerns and natural interests.

If you encounter a topic on which you are already an expert, feel free to skip that chapter, but it might be better to continue reading. Since preparations need to be comprehensive and real-world, it can be helpful to look at the topic from a different perspective.

Each facet of preparedness is vital. We can hurt ourselves by ignoring topics we find uninteresting or by thinking our knowledge is already complete. So, at the very least, you might want to skim those chapters you are tempted to skip over.

In my experience, most people who think of themselves as prepared are, at best, only prepared in two or three of the dozen categories that are necessary for readiness and sustainability (Chapter 25). They are wholly *un*prepared in the others.

It is impossible to be an expert in every facet of preparedness, but we can gain some basic knowledge about those things we don't know. This is important.

We also need to know what we don't know. Only then will we be able to successfully recruit others who can buttress our areas of weakness with their skills and expertise.

For example, those who attend our firearm-defense training classes may be ready to protect themselves from violence, but they are often ill-prepared for other important aspects of preparedness. They may be proficient with guns and personal security, but they may not be equipped to purify water, they may not have stockpiled a sufficient quantity of healthy food, and they may not know how to grow and store enough food to meet their long-term nutritional needs.

Similarly, even Master Gardeners and commercial farmers, are often woefully unprepared in many of the required areas of expertise. They may have grown extensive 'organic' vegetable gardens or crops, but they may not know how to maintain a garden when they can't go to a nursery or farm supply store to order supplies. And, rarely do they know how to fully satisfy our need for dietary protein and fat.

Likewise, a medical doctor will need help. A medical professional may be able to set a broken leg, but they probably can't fix a broken piece of machinery or electronic device.

There are many areas of expertise that will become indispensable, that experts, and even top-notch generalists, don't have. Each of us has something to contribute. And, each of us can learn more. We can all refine our skills and become an asset, or a greater asset.

Preparedness needs to be comprehensive.
If our goal is long-term sustainability, we can't achieve it alone.
It's a team effort.

With this need for comprehensive preparations in mind, I encourage you to make sure you are prepared in all facets of emergency situation preparedness. Don't make the common mistake of just working on those topics which interest you.

Lastly, in the immediate aftermath of a disaster, you may be alone, at least for a time. Your spouse and your children might also be alone. So, expect it, and prepare for it. Prepare *them* for it.

It may be necessary to walk a considerable distance to meet up with family or friends—if it's even clear where to go to rendezvous with them. *Do they know what to do? Do they know where to go? Do they know when to wait, and when to head out on their own?*

We need a plan, not just provisions. Moreover, *everyone* in your group needs to know "the plan," and everyone needs to know where to find, and how to use, the group's basic gear and supplies. Every family member and friend we care about, needs to know what to do when disaster strikes. Plus, they need to have ready access to what they will need for evacuation, and the knowledge and skills necessary for starting-up your safe-haven.

By reading this book series and acting on the recommendations contained in it, you will be better off than 99-percent of the population. However, in trying times, it isn't enough to be *better* prepared; you need to be *wholly* prepared. I urge you to start today.

Personal responsibility is a waning virtue, as is self-reliance. When disaster strikes, most of us will not be able to help everyone we would like to help. Yes, we may desire to help, but most of us will not have the resources needed to help others during a protracted period of hardship. If you want to be able to help others, you need to build that into your provisioning plan.

If you are married and your spouse doesn't understand the need to prepare, don't let that stop you. This may limit what you can do, but it doesn't mean that you can't do anything. You love your family, so do what you can.

Don't delay. As Senate chaplain Peter Marshall reminds us, *"Small deeds done are better than great deeds planned."*

Don't let naysayers delay you. Don't let criticism defeat you. Remember the story of Noah and the Ark? When Noah was building his ark, he and his family were alone in making their disaster preparations.[4] None of his neighbors or friends were making preparations. No one was worried about a flood; everyone was preoccupied with living life. Everyone but Noah and his family, had a 'normalcy bias.'

If you are criticized for your preparedness efforts, know that you are in good company. Noah is just one of the many highly-respected people who, throughout history, demonstrated uncommon insight and resolute action in the face of criticism.

---

[4] For the Bible story of Noah, read Genesis 6:8 – 9:29.

Noah didn't start building his ark because it was starting to rain. It took Noah 20-40 years, or more, to build his ark. During that time, we can be confident that he was ridiculed mercilessly—but he remained undaunted. He prepared for what he knew was coming. He ignored his critics.

There are many things we can learn from Noah. We may not be preparing for a worldwide flood, but the risks we face are similarly dangerous for us.

> *"A prudent person foresees danger and takes precautions. The simpleton goes blindly on and suffers the consequences."*
> Holy Bible,
> Proverbs 22:3

Similar to Noah's situation, today most people lack insight regarding what is coming. If they mock you today, rest assured that your vindication will come in the future—just as it did for Noah.

Don't be sidetracked by pessimists, nor blue-sky idealists. When conversations with family and friends become nonproductive, stop talking about it. As the days go by, you can drop hints to indicate that you are still preparing, but don't become a one-topic person. Make methodical progress, quietly, and do the best you can to get ready.

If your family and friends are not supportive, find new, additional friends who are more discerning. Get their help to formulate your plans, and to help you put your plans in motion.

The politically incorrect, real-world lessons taught by Hurricane Harvey and Hurricane Katrina

There is much we can learn from comparing these two disasters. Though Harvey was a more catastrophic event in regard to damage and displaced people, that disaster was mitigated by people being more self-reliant. Regrettably, during Katrina, much of the New Orleans population expected the government to solve their problems for them. If the victims of Harvey had demonstrated a similar expectation, the death toll would have been 100x greater. This was particularly the case during the first 4-days, before state and federal resources were fully mobilized and on the scene.

Yes, thankfully, the Texas Division of Emergency Management was more squared away than was the State of Louisiana during Katrina. Importantly, TDEM had engaged in extensive scenario-based training, and yet they were still willing to adapt their plan on the fly. This made a big difference.

There is a warrior truism, "a battle plan doesn't survive the first engagement" with the enemy. As individuals, we need to apply this sage truism to our own planning and expectations. Just as with a victorious warrior, we, too, need to be resilient and adaptable.

The TDEM leadership also encouraged problem-solving by their leaders in the field, rather than force them to wait for decisions made by a centralized authority (which is what took place during Katrina). This adaptability demonstrated by the State of Texas, improved resiliency, increased response speed, and brought countless benefits to the suffering people of the region.

Whiners and those who are politically motivated, spout unfounded criticisms of President Trump, Governor Abbott, and federal and State responses to the disaster. But the truth is, they pulled off an impressive strategy that quickly subdued what would have become, the disaster that caused the greatest loss of life in U.S. history.

Notwithstanding, what made the biggest difference of all was the actions of tens of thousands of ordinary, self-reliant Texans and Cajun volunteers. The instantaneous involvement of these people, neighbor-to-neighbor and community-to-community, is the single factor which saved the most lives.

Lesson #1: Independence, self-reliance, the willingness to take action, and advance preparation are the key components for overcoming the dangers which surface during an emergency. Moreover, if you aren't adequately prepared, you will not be in a position to help others. As the flooding expanded during Hurricane Harvey, there was an abundance of people who were sufficiently prepared, so they were available to immediately help others.

When these fundamental attributes are combined, the result is a community that is far more resilient. Conversely, when the individuals in an area, like New Orleans, fail to personally prepare because they expect the government and others to solve their problems for them, they are far more likely to become victims. Many of these people not only weren't prepared, they also failed to demonstrate personal initiative. As a result, they needlessly became victims.

Experience teaches us that 9 out of 10 times, becoming a victim is preventable. Those who want to be a victor rather than a victim, will develop a spirit of independence, situation awareness, the skills needed for self-reliance, and they are motivated to be problem-solvers. They are diligent about being prepared and ready for the future.

Lesson# 2: Redundancy is an essential element of preparation. The military adage, *"Two is one, one is none"* is true. We need 2+ flashlights, 2+ spare sets of batteries, 2+ radios, 2+ sources of pure water, etc. When it comes to essential equipment, 'one' is never enough. Things break. Electronics stop working. So, the more critical the function, the more back-ups we need.

Lesson #3: A GO-Bag (for evacuation and shelter-in-place) and other essential supplies are *minimum* requirements. Water, food, safety, shelter, medical supplies and medicines, extra eyeglasses, fuel, and other critical items need to be stockpiled in advance, and kept nearby. If you find that you need to make a trip to the store because an emergency is looming, you are already on the wrong side of the power curve. The activities of the unprepared will sidetrack them from more strategic actions.

It's better to avoid being in harms way than to risk injury. This requires comprehensive advance preparation, situation awareness, and living in a state of readiness—being ready to roll (act).

Lesson #4: Get out early. Have a family (or friends) plan, a rendezvous location, and a safe-haven destination. Have paper maps and know alternate routes. Don't depend on electronics; have backup communication methods. Be ready to walk. Don't delay. *Roll.*

Reflection:

In 2017 when our VFD rescue boat crew volunteered to help with Hurricane Harvey, we had 2-*days* to get ready. I was told by TDEM to prepare for 96-hrs of independent rescue operations in Port Arthur, and that we would be operating outside of supply lines. They said we would not be resupplied for 4 days, a very unusual situation for a fire department. This might not seem like a big deal to you, but it was a race against the clock for us to get ready. Similarly, when it's time for *you* to bug-out, you may be forced to operate independently for many days, as well. Unfortunately, *you* will probably only have *minutes* before needing to depart. At that point, there is no time to shop or locate needed gear.

With this in mind, you need to live life PREPARED, *Ready to Roll.*

Keeping our options open is a strategic choice. When we bug-out early and it turns out it was unnecessary, it is easy to return home. Options remain wide open. But, when we fail to evacuate in time, we may be stuck for the duration. At that point our choices have radically diminished, and this often generates unnecessary, additional dangers.

When we delay evacuation, it can create an unsolvable two-part problem: Either we become trapped or herded by a swollen, agitated and often irrational crowd of evacuees. Or, we lose our options and become trapped at home (or at work).

The primary problem with this scenario is not that we are unable to prepare our homes, but that we will be dealing with neighbors who are completely unprepared, and criminal opportunists who will take advantage of the police being busy elsewhere. When we shelter-in-place we limit our options.

Those who bug-out early retain a host of options, such as: speed, stealth, evade, hide, surprise, escape, confront, negotiate, forming new alliances, violence-of-action, targeted action, etc. When we bug-out early, all of these responses are available to us. Unfortunately, when we wait too long, our options quickly dwindle or evaporate entirely.

When we choose to shelter-in-place in a danger zone, we are de facto accepting that if danger increases to an unexpected level, or we need to fight, we will be doing so from a position of weakness. Those who find themselves needing to shelter-in-place are forced to defend themselves at a fixed location regardless of the threat. No matter how well fortified the site, these people will be responding from a position of weakness because their options are extremely limited.

Key to Success: Bug-out early.

Nevertheless, our reputation should not be as an 'alarmist.' But rather a 'prudent person' (who is spontaneous and occasionally takes unplanned vacations. ☺)

Summary

Both Hurricanes Harvey and Katrina are examples of disasters which were massive in scope, yet these were still only regional disasters. Unfortunately, as we look to the future, informed people see many harbingers which suggest that a national disaster is, sooner or later, inevitable. When this does happen, the combined resources of even a well-prepared state and federal government will, nevertheless, be wholly inadequate when this happens. We should expect to be on our own for an extended period of time.

If individuals, families, and groups of friends are not prepared to face a wide-scale emergency situation independently, empowered by self-reliance rather than government-dependence, *and,* provisioned by personal preparations that are beyond what was needed for Harvey and Katrina *(which includes our own safe-haven retreat location)*, success will be haphazard.

This book is designed to help you get ready to face minor, major, and in between emergency situations. As the author, my goal is to help you join ranks with the top 1% of those responsible people who are actually ready to face the future.

No one is ever 100% prepared.
We can all learn and improve.
Let's do it now, before it's too late.

This isn't just a nicety to accomplish someday, when we have the time. It is our moral responsibility, now, today.

Chapter 1

Scenarios: The Tactical Approach to Emergency Planning & Training

"Running scenarios" is the key to unlocking the tactical, and real-world practical, approach to preparing for disasters and emergency situations. Unfortunately, most people fail to start their planning and training sessions with both short-term and long-term objectives in mind.

For our planning to be useful, we first need to ask two foundational questions. The answers need to underpin our efforts:

1. What emergency situation events should I be prepared to face? (i.e. hurricane, earthquake, terrorist bombing, pandemic, economic collapse, failure of the power grid, etc.)

2. In these situations, what are the circumstances that I am likely to encounter? (i.e. loss of communication, transportation shut down, empty stores, contaminated water, looting and rampant violence, etc.)

How do we figure this out? As we think about the threats we face today, we quickly observe that many planners concentrate on one specific threat and give only a superficial nod to others. Of course, they may be right in identifying the threat we will face, but astute preparations need to be more comprehensive since other threats may emerge.

We can't know with any certainty the particular emergency situation we will face, so we need to prepare generally as well as specifically. Yet, since there are effects and problems which are common to most catastrophic events, this is a good place to start.

At the same time, we can also prepare for the needs inherent to a particular type of disaster. For example, if a flood is something you are likely to encounter, you might want to have a boat. However, if your prime concern is an earthquake, then it probably isn't helpful to spend money on a watercraft. But, since the need for a supply of food and water is something you are likely to encounter after both a flood and an earthquake, these two topics should be a top priority.

It is to our advantage to undertake comprehensive "general" preparations on a parallel path with those which relate to a particular threat. If you are mainly motivated by a specific threat like a grid-down situation, that is appropriate, but just because "general" needs are more routine and mundane, don't be sidetracked from taking a comprehensive approach.

In other words, we need to address the needs created by the threats which concern us most. And, we need to prepare for the life-threatening circumstances which we are likely to encounter during *any* emergency situation.

Since the aftermath of an incident will often have many similarities, no matter what initiated the emergency, many of our preparations are universal. Thankfully, this makes planning a more straightforward task.

For example, in a weather emergency, or in the aftermath of an earthquake, or even a terrorist incident or power grid failure, the public often respond emotionally. Fear, anger, panic buying, long lines at gas stations and grocery stores, traffic accidents and gridlock, and even violence are all common reactions. Therefore, if we can get home and hunker down with our pre-stocked supplies until the initial panic has passed, we will be safer and more comfortable. And, we won't be adding to the confusion.

However, we can only sidestep these issues, and those suddenly perceived needs of the public, if we are adequately prepared with our own supply of pure water, food, shelter, sanitation, energy and light, medical resources, and a safe environment. If these requirements have already been met, then we may be able to escape the cacophony.

Running Scenarios

However, to determine what we will need and how to best respond to an emergency situation, we need more than food, water, and gear. We also need discernment and an understanding of the situations, *scenarios*, we are likely to face.

These scenarios need to be identified in advance so that our preparations can take these factors into account. Expressed in popular terms, we need to be *tactical* in our preparedness efforts, as being tacticians (people who develop sound strategies). We need to identify the circumstances that we will likely face, and develop well-thought-out responses which take the details of these circumstances into account.

The military engages in elaborate "war games" to help them prepare for the next war. As civilians, we can achieve similar "tactical scenario" insights by doing something far less arduous—we can engage in a mental exercise referred to as *running scenarios*.

At its most basic level of implementation, running scenarios is a mental exercise which is kept practical and real-world in its scope. This is the simplest and most straightforward way to start the personal planning process.

These problem-solving drills are simply a mental process in which we conceive a story, or scenario, of a potential disaster or emergency incident. Then, once we have this framework, we put ourselves into the story, placing ourselves at an assortment of locations such as our place of employment, home, grocery store, at a friend's house, favorite restaurant, and other places we frequent.

Next, we add to this scenario the various circumstances which we might encounter. This will first include fundamental problems such as being unable to use your usual route to get home, your car breaking down, needing to help an injured friend, having children at school or alone at home, etc.

As we use these scenarios as a backdrop to analyze potential problems, we can clarify what "needs" we expect to encounter. Whether it be gear, training, or the need to communicate in advance with loved ones, this exercise leads us to practical planning.

Next, we change-up the scenario, or conceive a new one based on a real-life incident from the past, the personal experiences of someone we know, or something we read about in the newspaper or saw on television. However, in all these scenarios, we need to keep the details practical and the problems real-world.

The "mental exercise" aspect kicks in as we use these scenarios to ask ourselves "what if" questions that relate to the story. "What if 'X' happens, what would I do?"

Questions such as, "If that was the circumstance I was facing, how would I handle it?" "Is there a better way?" "How would I solve that problem?" "What would be my other options?" "Which of these would be my best choice, and why?" "What can I do now, to be ready for such a situation?" "What will I need?"

The answers to these questions will involve more than identifying supplies needed and personal actions. The answers will likely also include training which would be useful, skills to hone, physical fitness or medical needs to tackle, coordination with family and friends which must be accomplished in advance, reference materials that you will need to have, communication plans and methods to establish, home or vehicle repairs to be undertaken, etc.

Use scenarios to expose both broad and specific needs. There is far more to getting ready than purchasing supplies.

In the context of weather-initiated emergencies, most of us have had a measure of practical experiences to make our scenarios more real-world practical. We hardly think of them as running scenarios, but that is what we are doing when we ask ourselves questions such as: "What will I do if the snow gets deep while I'm at work?" Or, "How will I know if the flood waters are rising during the night while I'm sleeping?"

We need to apply a similar form of *situation analysis* to other types of emergencies, too, especially those which are different from anything we have previously encountered. Only then can we match our preparations with our anticipated needs.

Identifying anticipated needs and corresponding tactics is Phase-1 of making a disaster preparedness plan. This phase helps us identify the gear we need, clarifies the quantities of supplies required for ourselves and others we may need to care for, helps us select alternate travel routes, storage locations, provides for our anticipated communication and transportation needs, exposes safety and training gaps, and identifies physical and human resources we need to recruit.

Without identifying, and understanding the problems we expect to face, it is impossible to fully and adequately prepare.

Phase-1: A Seven-Step Process for Effective Use of Scenarios

1. Identify the threats which represent viable risks. (Take notes)

2. Explore the likely ramifications of each threat to you personally, and to your family and friends.

3. Next, develop your response options to each threat, and

4. Determine the needs associated with each option. This makes it possible for us to…

5. Test the viability and desirability of each prospective path of action.

6. Once the above has been accomplished, use your notes to make a list of gear, supplies, training, coordination efforts, etc. Assign a priority rating to each. (#1, high priority; #2 priority, etc.)

7. Implementation priorities are based on: a) the risks and threats that are the most viable; those which are most probable, that we are more likely to encounter, and b) those that would have the most catastrophic effect on our well-being. Mitigation of all threats is an admirable goal, but the place to start our planning and implementation efforts is with these two categories.

* We can bring together essential gear, water and food, and a generic GO-Bag (evacuation bag), without undertaking this "scenario" exercise. However, an effective and comprehensive emergency plan requires us to set the stage before we can begin acting on it. Running scenarios and developing tactics can help you personalize your contingency plan, and improve your GO-Bag and provisions plan.

Does this process sound complex? It needn't be. This undertaking can be started today. The easiest way is to get together with your spouse or a friend for an hour or two and do a little brainstorming. Scan news stories. Let your creative juices flow. First, identify the threats you are most concerned about. Let that naturally expand into a discussion on how that disastrous situation might affect you, personally. Then, address the topic of the resources (supplies, skills, etc.) you will need to overcome each anticipated adversity.

Prioritize. Keep it real-world. Keep it simple.

Brainstorm Scenario Storylines. Repeat.

As you periodically repeat this brainstorming session, aided by additional research accomplished during the intervening period, your planning will progressively become more comprehensive and viable. The best planning process is one that is ongoing.

No matter what mechanism you choose to use for your situation analysis and your scenario-driven planning, these sequential steps must be taken first. This needs to happen before you travel very far down the road of emergency planning and provisioning.

It is commendable to stockpile food, but where should it be stored? How should it be stored? Should it be easy to transport? It is helpful to plant a Liberty Garden? If you do, how are you going to protect it when your neighbors are hungry?

It is questions like these that are often not asked. Yet, the failure to plan for these cause-and-effect problems can bring about unintended, and sometimes very negative consequences.

Most people lack wide-ranging experience with different forms of disasters, so they fail to ask the right questions. It is for this reason that most people orient their emergency preparations around a previous experience, or, a type of disaster they have been exposed to through friends or news reports. This myopic approach may still be useful, but if your preparations are not sufficiently comprehensive to meet your needs during a different type of disaster, you may find yourself woefully unprepared.

The Rule of Unintended Consequences

Running scenarios can help offset this lack of experience. However, just identifying solutions to problems is not enough. Our scenarios need to also expose the effects that each solution may bring with it. This is the 'Rule of Unintended Consequences.'

This cause-and-effect, and the reality that solving one problem may create yet another, is real. For example, having a generator is useful when the power goes out, but if your lights are "on" when everyone else is in darkness, this will likely cause new problems. Your neighbors, and even criminals, will be attracted to your location. Your lights, or even the sound of your generator, announce that you are prepared, and more than likely, you have other supplies, too.

Use scenarios to help you plan on both 'micro' and 'macro' levels: Having a generator on hand is an example of a "macro" planned response to preparedness planning. Whereas a "micro" (detail level) approach incorporates additional effects such as attracting unwanted attention. Our planning needs to address both.

A micro approach will address important, additional details that are not always as obvious as the need for a generator. For example, "If the storm lasts longer than usual, will I have enough gas to power my new generator?" "How can I safely store this gasoline?" And, "What will I do if I am the only house with power, and my neighbors start showing up, expecting me to feed and care for them?" What will I do if uninvited friends and family show up, because they know I am prepared? How many can I help before I put my family at risk?

In the situation of an anticipated storm, the microanalysis will elicit the possibility of additional problems. However, for us as individuals, we need to plan primarily on the *micro* (individual, small-scale) level.

For us as individuals, we need to avoid dwelling on what caused the disaster and how it might affect our community. It's more critical for us to concentrate on how it will affect us, and then identify our options for reducing the adverse effects on us, our family and our friends.

Practical vs. Foolish: If you want to help your community too, asking these questions may sound selfish, but it's not. Personally, I do hope that you include helping others in your disaster preparedness plan. However, if you fail FIRST to take care of your own needs, you will only be able to help others temporarily.

If you've flown on a commercial airline, you will remember that the flight attendant's pre-flight instructions are specific. Before take-off, she tells the passengers, "If we lose cabin pressure and the oxygen masks drop down from the overhead compartment, put on your own mask FIRST, before you attempt to help others."

This same practice of priority setting is an essential tactic for achieving readiness, too. Prepare for yourself and your family first, and then do what you can to help others.

> Death is easy. It's living that is hard.
>
> Only the living can hope for a better future, and effect the changes needed to benefit others. Heroes respect life.

It is not compassionate, or somehow the "Christian" thing to do, to *needlessly* die because you were helping others. It's far better, and more biblical, to care for yourself and stay alive. Then you can continue to help others. This is the practical vs. foolish response.

This is not just pragmatic. It's wise, prudent—and *practical.*

Moreover, these questions need to be asked and answered in advance, when you can be more logical, less emotional, when you can obtain counsel and undertake research if it's needed. At the core, the issue is, "Where is your primary responsibility?" Is it your spouse, immediate family, friends, distant relatives, friends of your children, neighbors, anyone who knocks on your door; who, and what, is your first responsibility? What is the hierarchy of responsibility? [5]

My first developing world (Third-World) experience was to live for some months in Haiti. It was a rude awakening for me as a 20-year old American, when I realized that if I gave away everything I own, and everything I would ever own, I would not make a dent in the poverty which infected the people of Haiti.

If I were called upon to help the people of Haiti, I would be able to accomplish much more by staying alive and healthy. To make a one-time donation or help temporarily, is not as significant as continuing to help long-term. (Of course, there are occasional exceptions.)

It's the same for a major disaster. You may decide to sacrifice your own well-being or safety for a period of time, to help others, but it makes absolutely no sense to put your family at risk to accommodate a risky lifestyle that makes you feel saintly. To do otherwise is not virtuous martyrdom, it's narcissistic foolishness.

---

[5] Jesus' parable of the Good Samaritan as recorded in the Bible (Luke 10:25-37), is perhaps the premier example of our moral responsibility to extend loving care to strangers, even when it is costly to us. However, it is significant that this story only involves compassion, and the sacrifice of time and financial resources. When the Samaritan took care of the injured and neglected man, he was not putting his own family at risk. Adding that detail would represent a radical change to the story. We do have a responsibility to care for the needs of others, but our first responsibility is to care for the needs (not wants) of our family. This duty surpasses our responsibility to care for others.

When I was a young unmarried police officer, it was not unusual for me to take risks that I didn't take later, when I had a family. I still did the job, and I did take measured risks, but I recognized that my first priority was to come home to my family.

The Bible talks about it being virtuous to lay down one's life for a friend. However, it does not direct parents to lay down their lives for strangers. Unless it is an action that is undertaken to bring about justice or some broader benefit, a sacrificial act to help a stranger might actually be the abandonment of responsibilities to your family.

Furthermore, the Bible condemns thrill-seekers. Among other things, taking unnecessary risks which do not have the potential of delivering vital rewards, is a stewardship failure.

During an emergency situation, you may feel the urge to do something risky. That's another benefit of running scenarios; you can calmly and rationally decide when these risks are reasonable and appropriate, and when they are reckless or injudicious.

In any case, as you develop "what if" scenarios to help inform your preparations, do not give much attention to heroic exploits. It's far better to focus on the normal requirements for living a free and healthy life than to descend into far-out possibilities.

Another core tactic of effective preparedness planning is to identify the effects that you and your family might encounter as a result of various types of disasters. I can't overemphasize this: Consider scenarios which you might actually encounter. Plan responses, and gather equipment and training commensurate with the events which you can expect to face in the real world.

This includes scenarios such as aiding an injured and trapped neighbor when 9-1-1 is overwhelmed and unavailable, what to do if your route home is unpassable, or when toilets don't flush, and fresh water isn't flowing, or radio news reports fail to provide the facts you need for decision making. What are you going to do?

Regardless of what caused the emergency, you need to identify multiple options and various solutions to your problem. And, you need to build versatility into your response, too, and make sure your loved ones know what to do if you aren't around to help.

Only after we have identified the likely scenarios can we develop a targeted response and a plan, which anticipates the scenarios we may encounter. Without this evaluation, and familiarity with the proposed response by everyone involved, we can't secure the cooperation needed for a viable response.

A plan requires more than superficial details. We can quickly identify basic preparations, such as having cash on hand in case electronic commerce is interrupted or credit cards don't work. However, measures such as this are only elementary steps.

What happens when gas stations close because their electric gas pumps no longer work? A problem such as this is not solved by stockpiling provisions at home and having your own generator. For this, we need a flexible plan, and it needs to take into account our geographic location, our neighborhood, and the ongoing needs of our family and friends.

Why? It's because problems, and our solution, can create new challenges. Envision a situation in which you are well equipped, and you have a supply of water, food, and power, but your neighbors do not. What will you do when they come knocking on your door?

Since you may think this tactic of "running scenarios" is unnecessary because you know what to do, and you want to jump into a review of gear and the do-it-yourself skills you'll need, let me set the stage. It's vital for us to get this right.

What is "Tactical"?

"Tactical" is not a word which only applies to the military and paramilitary actions. Nor does it only relate to the use of firearms. It also conveys real-world strategic planning, deft skills, ingenuity and creativity, the application of a calm, problem-solving mindset, and readiness to embrace the unknown.

Those who have done something before are better able to develop appropriate tactics. But if you don't have extensive experience, you can use the power of "story" to think about a scenario, put yourself into the situation, and problem-solve.

Using this mechanism, you can calmly reflect on potential problems and identify the best course of action. You can also do research, and seek wise counsel from those who do have experience.

As I write this, it is important for you to know that I am writing from the vantage point of personal experience. Personally, I have operated in many different types of emergency situations, both as a police officer and civilian. This includes major earthquakes, volcanic eruptions, major storms and floods, the crash of a commercial airliner, urban race riots, crime rampages, violent protests, civil war, guerrilla attacks, and a terrorist bombing.

These were not minor incidents. For example, I personally rode out the land waves of Alaska's 9.2-megathrust "Good Friday Earthquake," the largest in North American history. And, California's 6.9-magnitude Loma Prieta (World Series) Earthquake which killed or injured 3,820 people. Also, I was on scene the day after the volcanic eruption of Mount St. Helens, which produced a nuclear bomb-like effect, including a blast zone 60-miles in diameter.

On and on goes the list. Major and less memorable disasters, natural and manmade, I have personally experienced an assortment of disasters. So I speak from the perspective of experience—and having observed unnecessary pain and hardship.

As you read this book, you will learn about various emergency situations I have personally experienced. Hopefully, these will do more than establish my credibility. I include these details because I want to impress upon you a fact of life:

When disaster strikes, at that point it's often too late to make plans and stockpile supplies. We need to do that now. If we are willing to be proactive, we, and our loved ones can often evade privation and suffering.

When I was a police officer in the Los Angeles area, I often confronted violent crime and criminals. During my life, I have had people try to kill me, survived civil unrest and gang war, and an assortment of other life-or-death natural and manmade emergency situations. So, when I stand on a soapbox and urge you to get prepared, it is not a theoretical topic. Firsthand, I've seen the ravaging effects.

In the process, one of the things I've learned is that serious emergency situations are often a surprise. Even when we train for them, the actual circumstance, the event itself, often comes as a surprise.

Even when we know it's coming, what develops is often different from what we anticipated. I've found that there is a certain element of surprise to every emergency situation. Therefore, our plans need to expect the unexpected.

Our plans, and we ourselves, need to be flexible.
We need to be resilient.

I've also learned that once a major problem begins to develop, it's momentum forges a widening path of disaster. This can make the situation harder for us when it doesn't follow our plan and we are rigid rather than adaptive.

Once an emergency starts to roll, we need to roll with it. At that point, it is too late to prepare contingency plans; all you can do is respond. The momentum of an incident cannot be stopped, but it can often be directed—or better yet, sidestepped.

Resiliency and adaptability are paramount.

Contingency planning needs to be done in advance. These resilient, adaptable plans need to be made now when we can think clearly, when we have time to problem solve—when we have time to develop skills, network with friends, plant a garden, etc.—and, while there is still inventory on store shelves.

The better your advance preparations, the better you can handle the emergency, and the less likely it is that you will become a victim. It's that simple.

Yet, don't think that your preparations will ever be complete. To be prepared is to live our life aware, always preparing, and in readiness. By routinely asking the "what if?" question as we move through life, we can continually improve and expand our preparations.

Moreover, we should not trap ourselves by just using lists of items, and focusing on sequentially assembling a checklist of supplies. It's a mistake to pursue a goal of stockpiling a 1-year supply of food before making plans to store and purify water. It's foolhardy to prepare for defense without also getting ready for medical emergencies.

Our preparations need to be parallel, not sequential. And, they need to be complete and well rounded, not just in alignment with our hot-button personal interests.

To the best of our ability, we need to make-ready all fronts simultaneously. We also need to routinely revisit each of the twelve pathways (tracks) which lead to sustainability (see Book-4 for details). We need to refresh and expand our stockpile of supplies regularly, train, develop useful skills, nurture mutually beneficial relationships, and together, improve our readiness as we have new insights, time and financial resources.

We need to prepare as if a disaster of some sort will strike tomorrow. And also, for the "BIG ONE" that might hit in 20-days or 20-years. We need to be ready for a disaster strike tomorrow, next week, next month, and in the next decade.

Since various life-altering events might happen in the more distant future, we need to use our time wisely, so that we can secure more extensive preparations. And, we need to use the time we have to prepare the next generation for the changes that are coming.

Prepare for tomorrow. Prepare your children for the future. All of us need to be prepared for the coming changes.

Start Now

We cannot count on having years to prepare, but if that is what happens, we still need to start now. At some point, a catastrophic event will descend on us or the next generation. Our needs will be extensive, so we can't afford to waste the intervening time.

Our lifestyle needs to be one of readiness and personal responsibility. We keep preparing; we methodically work on it. We continuously strive to improve, and to be intentional about keeping our preparations balanced. We live life joyfully today, but we also get ready for tomorrow.

If you have children, teach them the skills of preparation, self-reliance, and personal responsibility. Don't conjure fear. Teach them to be forward thinking. Whether they are young or old, teach them by your example to live by the Boy Scout motto, *Be Prepared*. Show them how to be strong, resilient, and adaptable.

If you have children, join the Scouts or an organization which teaches preparedness skills. Teach your kids, family and friends, the broad array of competencies needed to be self-sufficient. If you don't have these skills, learn together.

With these goals in mind, if you don't have a GO-Bag (evacuation bag), put one together as best you can, as soon as you finish reading this chapter.

Don't wait until you have bought the ultimate knapsack and have assembled ultra-lightweight backpacking gear and freeze-dried food. Pull together some basic supplies now. Having something is better than nothing.

If you don't have a knapsack, at the very least, grab a couple of grocery sacks and fill them with a few necessary items. Add as many of these things as you have on hand: a few cans of food, a small can opener, a pocket knife, a few bottles of water, a flashlight with spare batteries, a cigarette lighter (or matches), a large trash bag, some duct tape, 10' of string, a washcloth and sliver of soap, first aid kit items, prescription medicine and extra glasses if you need them, one outfit of functional clothing (cool in summer, warm clothes in winter, rain gear if you're in that season), athletic socks and durable shoes. Close each bag with string, and put these bags in the trunk of your car.

If you do this, in just 30-minutes you can be far better prepared than you are right now. During the upcoming week, try to find a knapsack to use, replacing the less durable plastic bags, and add what extra items you can on your next trip to the grocery store. As you read more of this book, add additional items to your GO-Bag. Once that's done, start preparing your home and workplace, and then start looking for a safe haven. Throughout the process, think about the possibilities, and use these "what if?" scenarios as the framework for your planning.

If you already have a GO-Bag, get it out and check its contents. Determine if anything needs to be replaced, and take care of it today. If you have kids, go over the contents with them, and show them how things work.

We may not be able to control an emergency event, but we can control our response.

It is important to remember that the greatest threat to our safety and well-being is often not the initiating event, but rather the public's response to the incident. Hurricane Katrina is a good example.

It wasn't the high winds and flooding of Katrina which caused the most suffering. Most of the injuries, death, and hardship came during the following weeks. The biggest problem wasn't the force of the storm, it was the forces of evil and the lack of preparation which brought harm to so many.

What is going to happen to them when something even bigger happens, when emergency services are stretched thin, and no one is able to help the public? What will they do? What will you do?

Unfortunately, even those who are considered "responsible" members of our society often have an unhealthy dependence on emergency services. The police are known as "the thin blue line," and the fire department as "the thin red line." Why? Because these services are a like a thin veneer protecting society. These thin lines of services are often stretched thin during normal times, but they can quickly snap during a large-scale emergency situation.

When the general public experiences a problem, they routinely call on the government to solve *their* problem. We must be different.

I'm now a volunteer firefighter, and I'm appalled by the nature of many of the 9-1-1 calls. When people should be driving themselves to an emergency care clinic or hospital, or waiting until the next day when a family member, neighbor or a friend can take them to their doctor, many telephone 9-1-1 for help. They expect the government to fix their problem.

Today, most people are unable to handle even a minor emergency on their own, while others look to the government to solve even minor health, safety, and life-maintenance needs. As they habitually look to someone else, whether it be a government agency, First Responders, a nonprofit organization, church or a neighbor, they develop a habit of dependency. They establish a lifestyle of expectancy— they expect someone else to fix their problems.

This not only leads to a dangerous level of dependency, it often produces lazy, unhealthy living and the loss of problem-solving skills. Increasingly, it also creates such a magnified emotional dependency that they become livid, sometimes violently angry, when no one steps up to solve their problems for them. This is true even when the situation is one which they created.

Why do I bother to mention this attitude of entitlement? I'm bringing it up because it is a subtle, often subliminal problem that we all need to face. Even those of us who disdain the "entitlement generation" are infected by it.

If you lack the skills needed to splint your broken arm, if you can't grow your own food and preserve it, if you aren't prepared to defend yourself, if you can't walk a half dozen miles to a store and then carry your purchases home without help, then you have become a dependent person. For most of us, our grandparents would have been able to accomplish these four things without a second thought.

We have two problems. No, three.

These complications are made even worse if we live in an urban or suburban area. The first problem is that most of our neighbors can't take care of themselves. The second problem is that we can expect some of them to become violently angry when they lose the services they currently enjoy.

The third problem is that those of us who think of ourselves as *basically* ready and *mostly* capable, are not genuinely self-reliant. We're not really prepared for what's coming. We might be better prepared than our neighbors, but we are not truly ready. Our life isn't sustainable without outside help or resources.

The days when self-reliance and self-sufficiency were commonly held virtues have disappeared. Today, this creates a huge problem when we encounter a prolonged emergency situation.

I'm not suggesting that we shouldn't call for help if we need it. That would be foolish. If help is available, it is appropriate to summon assistance. Notwithstanding, we need to embrace the possibility that government-sponsored aid may not be available, so we need to be ready to respond on three levels: First, we need to be able to take care of ourselves. Second, we need to be ready to help others. Third, we need to anticipate that some people will become irrationally angry if they don't get what they think they deserve. We must be ready to both avoid and contend with these violent people.

Plus, we need to also keep in mind that when we call 9-1-1, those who respond are our fellow citizens. They may be trained, and they may have some specialty equipment, but First Responders are just people, too. And, they are a limited resource, and someone else may need them more desperately.

When I was a police officer, I had the opportunity to be part of an advanced-training transfer program. In it we were switched around to different metropolitan areas. The objective was for us to become familiar with the law enforcement problems, and the policing techniques used, in these various areas. One of the areas I was assigned was Los Angeles's 77th-Division (precinct), which at that time, had the highest crime rate in California.

This division, more commonly known as Watts, was plagued by out-of-control violence. It was not unusual for there to be several different crimes of violence—in progress—all at the same time, with no police officers available to send! So, though these cries for help were eventually answered, the response wasn't always timely.

As this truism reminds us,

*"When **seconds** count, the police are only **minutes** away."*

When disaster strikes we need to keep this in mind. During a large-scale catastrophic event, the authorities may not be minutes away, they may be *hours* or *days* or *weeks* away. This isn't a hypothetical problem. It's real. Ask anyone who's been in a regional disaster.

You may be on your own. Therefore, every adult in your family and all of our friends, need to be able to take care of themselves. If this isn't the case, things need to change.

Being able to care for our own needs is the most basic level of personal responsibility. We need to be prepared to be on our own, and we need to help others become self-reliant, too.

Most police officers are acquainted with the snobby saying…

"When the public is in trouble, they call the cops.
When the police are in trouble, they call SWAT."

So, for me, it was a matter of intense pride to be both a police officer and a member of an elite SWAT Team (Special Weapons and Tactics Team). Being part of an elite unit was invigorating.

Southern California routinely experiences serious law enforcement problems, as well as civil unrest and terrorism, so I wasn't disappointed when I transferred from a police department in Washington to one in the Los Angeles area of California. Unmarried at the time, I was drawn by a desire for professionalism and serious action. I wasn't disappointed on either front.

After spending some years in a patrol car and then as a crime scene investigator (CSI), I was able to join the SWAT team. The SWAT team was used to counter the most violent of threats, and it got the best training and equipment. It's no surprise that this was an exciting assignment, but I found that my gratification actually came from forging peace in times of violent chaos. I was a peace-*maker*.

What many people don't understand is that the SWAT team's elite status didn't come from just being good with a gun, nor was it the expensive gear and "special weapons" we were issued. There was a lot more to it. It was our training and *tactical* skill which made us uniquely capable.

The reason I'm bringing this up is that there is a practical application to this skill set that can benefit all of us. My goal with this book is to accomplish more than help you gain knowledge. I want to help you get prepared so that you can roll into a disastrous time with confidence; armed with readiness. I want you to be truly ready for what's coming, and this doesn't automatically come with the purchase of food and gear.

Yes, this book will get into equipment and training, but it also provides you with the opportunity to move beyond getting equipped with *stuff*, to being PREPARED: ready to roll. It's about developing skills, discernment, real-world practical plans, resiliency, adaptability, and true *readiness*.

This is more than a book of lists, and it includes more than survival "tips" and "how-to" instructions. These things are valuable, but we need more. Just as owning a football doesn't make you a football player, having gear doesn't make you prepared.

So, before we get into discussions of gear and instructions, I want to explain what I mean by the tactics of preparedness. If you want to be ready for an emergency situation, this understanding is a necessity.

Having the gear and technical knowledge required to survive a calamity isn't enough. My goal is to help you thrive during the coming difficult times, not just survive them. Why? Because I want you to emerge as a victor, not victim. And, I want you to be capable, so you can help your family, friends, and neighbors.

It's also about moving beyond anxiety and fear, to a mindset of assurance and even courage. Today we have the opportunity to get ready for the uncertain future that is going to force the passenger train of society onto a different track.

Change is coming. It may be a destination we don't want, but it looks like we won't have a choice. If we aren't ready for this change in destination, the train will run over us like a pedestrian hit at an unmarked intersection.

Conversely, if we are prepared for it, and we are looking for the figurative railroad-switch that lies ahead, which will shift us to a different track of life, we might be able to reach the new destination without serious injury. At the very least, we can grab a safety strap and brace ourselves, so we don't get thrown around by the wild ride.

On the SWAT team, in addition to our firearms and physical training, every month we participated in a major drill which was designed to test and hone our skills. With each of these scenarios, we focused on meshing our individual skills with tactics, so that we could solve the serious law enforcement problem presented in the drill.

On those occasions, just as for us today, we can't expect future problems to look exactly the same as the scenarios we develop for our planning and training. We can't achieve total clarity. Even the experts don't have prophetic skills for seeing into the future. Nevertheless, we can learn from the past, consider current trends, equip ourselves, and learn how to problem-solve and adapt.

As a SWAT operator, through a slew of different drills, we gained the skills we needed to be resilient and adaptable during times of chaos. We learned how to adapt to future events which would look different from those we had seen in the past. In more recent years, I have used this same framework for training expatriates overseas.

In today's rapidly changing world, we need to be adaptable. How do we hone this skill?

Gear is important. Training is necessary. Knowledge is valuable. However, effective tactics are those developed as the result of discernment – knowing how to apply forward-thinking and problem-solving skills to achieve a positive outcome.

For our SWAT team, one of the mechanisms for developing these abilities was also "running scenarios." Though we actually engaged in training activities based on them, it is essentially the same mental exercise that started the process. By adding this procedure to the development of your preparedness plan, you will be better equipped to weather the coming storm.

Fortunately, this is a simple technique. It's easy to learn, and you can begin using it today.

Wrong actions and the failure to act, are the chief cause of having regrets in life. By contemplating "what if" scenarios we can minimize regrets brought about by both inappropriate action, and, the often equally painful response, inaction. As well as the inability to act because we were not prepared.

I recently provided a listening ear to a father who was grieving over his daughter's severe but preventable injuries. She was grievously injured because he was not prepared to intervene. If he had been equipped, he could have easily saved her. Unfortunately, he wasn't, and his daughter paid the price for his failure.

For most civilians, *"running scenarios"* is only a mental exercise. I'm not suggesting that you obsess with this activity, nor that you can eliminate every potential problem by running scenarios and problem solving with them in advance. What I am suggesting, is that if you regularly 'run scenarios' with sufficient depth of thought, you can create your own learning experiences.

When applied to preparedness, this will help you formulate plans, select supplies, train, problem solve, and learn to make rapid decisions. Plus, help others get ready, too, and prepare to help others at their hour of greatest need.

For example, you might be watching the news on television, and hear a story about a sudden storm that struck some other region of the country. As you listen to the report, you learn that people were forced to stay at their workplace because a flood made it unsafe to venture out. Moreover, the floodwaters were not expected to recede for a week.

If you are using this to run a scenario, you will ask yourself, *"If I was trapped at work, how would I fare? Would I have bottled water to drink? Food? A way to stay warm? What about my coworkers?"* If after running this simple scenario you realize that you would not be ready for such an event, the next day you can take the steps needed to become ready for such a scenario.

Something like this happened to me a few years ago. In downtown Seattle, I was working alone in a large, empty office building at night. Since the region is known for having moderate winter weather, I hadn't anticipated any problems. But without warning, the city was suddenly hit by an unexpected and unusually severe, snow storm. In just a few hours, downtown Seattle had become a ghost town.

It was close to midnight when, realizing I had missed dinner and was hungry, I took a break and ventured outside to find a restaurant where I could get a late-night meal. But everything was closed. Not a soul was on the street.

The weather had deteriorated quickly. By the time I became aware of the situation, the ground was covered by two feet of slippery, wet snow.

The streets were clogged with abandoned cars. Like a scene from an apocalyptic movie, hundreds of unoccupied vehicles lay buried under a blanket of snow, blocking the roadway and obstructing each intersection. As I stood alone on the empty sidewalk, the traffic signals clicked, and their colored lights cycled and reflected brightly off of the snow.

As I walked back into the empty office building, I realized that the computerized heating and ventilation system had shut down. The automatic programming had turned the system off because the building was usually unoccupied at night.

No heat. No phones. No one else around. I was unexpectedly alone and the temperature was dropping.

Chilled from being outside without proper clothing, I got back into the office where I was working, only to find that it was on the side of the building exposed to the wind, and it was beginning to feel like an icebox. Within an hour, the indoor temperature fell to 45-degrees. For those equipped for such temperatures, not a problem, but I was wearing a lightweight suit.

Too cold and hungry to keep working, I used newspapers for a blanket and spent the night awake and shivering, trying to sleep. By the time morning came, I was miserable.

This circumstance never did devolve into a "survival" situation, but what I experienced was nevertheless unnecessary. Importantly, it could have become a more serious problem. Freak storms do sometimes last for days. Yet, both minor inconveniences and more severe problems, can often be wholly averted.

Steps to take…

a) **Be aware of circumstances, potential problems, and your surroundings.**

If I had been watchful and left for home as soon as it became evident that there was a potential problem brewing, I could have arrived home not only before the storm, but even before traffic became snarled. The storm would have been a non-issue.

b) **Keep a knapsack GO-Bag and other supplies nearby.**

If I had maintained a duffle bag of necessary supplies at my office and had a GO-Bag in the trunk of my car, I would have had food to eat, bottled water to drink, and a sleeping bag to keep me warm. It would have been a non-issue.

c) **Keep season-appropriate clothing and boots in your vehicle, and at your place of employment.**

If I had made it part of my routine to keep a waterproof jacket, seasonal clothing, a hat, and boots in my vehicle (and at work if my car isn't parked close to my place of employment), then I would have been ready for even a "surprise" storm. Even if I had decided to stay in my office, I would have been comfortable. The storm would have simply been an inconvenience; a non-issue.

The Nitty-Gritty of Running Scenarios

This is where these "running scenario" exercises kicks in. We ask ourselves "what if?" questions based on potential real-world problems.

Let's trade places. If you were the one to experience the surprise storm situation rather than me, would you have been ready for it? What would you have done?

> When you are ready for adversity, minor emergencies disappear, and major problems become manageable.

No matter where you live, a freak storm can suddenly strike. Would you be prepared for such a development? What if some event happened and you found yourself stranded, would you be ready for such an occurrence?

If you experienced the situation which I described, would you have tried to drive home anyway, irrespective of the many stuck cars? What if you had been unable to contact your family, and knew they would be worried about you? Would you risk getting stuck and having to spend the night in a cold car, stranded at some location that was too far to walk home, and also too far to return to work?

Or, would you have been prepared to face the situation? Would you have spent the night inconvenienced, but warm and comfortable?

Beyond this, would your family know what to do if an emergency situation developed when you, or they, are away from home? Are they ready for an unexpected problem such as this?

An additional advantage of being prepared: One of the other benefits of using scenarios to inform our preparations, is that minor incidents are not even a problem. Events like my sleepless night in Seattle are merely inconvenient.

In my Seattle story, what would have happened if the unexpected storm had also become life-threatening? What if the snowstorm had lasted several days and the electric power to the entire downtown area had gone out? How would I have managed? I'm embarrassed, but I need to acknowledge that though it would have been easily survivable, I probably would have needed to break into vending machines and other businesses in the building to find water, food, and other supplies. Restitution would have been embarrassing and very costly.

Delusional "hope" vs. legitimate "optimism"

Most people live in "hope," thinking that the government, or someone, will save them. And, perhaps that's what will happen. But, what if no one arrives to bail you out? After all, my scenario involved mild-weather Seattle, not storm-savvy Boston. In Seattle, the government is not prepared to rescue hundreds of people during a freak snowstorm. Yet, even if they were, would I want to depend on their largess?

In a city like Boston, government agencies are prepared to rescue scores of people during a snow storm, but would they be able to come to the aid of thousands, or tens of thousands? What if the disaster was far more significant than a winter storm? What if the situation was massive in scope, and the needs were monumental?

Whether your "what if?" scenarios come from expanding on your personal experiences or those of your friends, or from television news, or the storyline of a movie, "running scenarios" consists of likely, potential problems which you might someday face.

Two Examples of 'Running Scenarios'

Scenario #1

Picture this... Tomorrow you get in your car and head off down the road. You've arranged to have lunch with a friend. It's a bit of a trek to the restaurant, but it's a favorite spot and worth the extra miles.

The weather is a bit iffy, and the roads are still wet from an earlier rain, but otherwise, it seems to be an ordinary day. Traffic is light. As you drive, your thoughts drift to the other things you need to accomplish today.

As you enter an intersection, you hear the hiss of tires. Suddenly, the right side of your car crushes inward as your vehicle is catapulted to the left. From out of nowhere you've been struck broadside by an old pickup truck that failed to stop at a red light.

You don't remember your car's airbag deploying but it obviously did. There is talc-like dust in the air, and the remnants of the airbag are hanging from your steering wheel. Your nose is bleeding, and your left wrist hurts, but other than that, you are unharmed.

You unbuckle your seatbelt and get out of the car. The unkempt driver of the truck is uninjured and on her mobile phone. You hope she has insurance. You thank God that you had the foresight to add uninsured motorist protection to your vehicle insurance policy—just in case.

- - - - - - -

What do you think? Is this a plausible scenario? Could something like this happen to you? Yes, of course it could.

Many people carry more insurance than the law requires because if an accident does happen, the added protection might be a godsend. They don't make this purchase decision because they are looking for ways to spend more money, but because it makes sense. Responsible people protect themselves from credible potential problems.

Example of Possible 'Actionable Conclusions' for Scenario #1

1. Verify that I have uninsured motorist insurance and that my coverage is adequate.

2. Work at becoming a more defensive driver, and stop assuming that other drivers are going to stop at traffic signals and stop/yield signs.

3. Make sure that the next car I purchase has a good safety rating for side impacts as well as front/rear collisions.

Scenario #2

Now picture a different scenario; one that starts exactly the same. But in this new hypothetical situation, what you experience is not a collision with a truck, but something else.

As you drive through the intersection you aren't hit by another vehicle, but rather your car's engine suddenly stops running. The radio in the car's dash becomes silent, and the flashing yellow traffic signal goes dark. The only noise you hear is the sigh of your tires as your car coasts to a stop.

As you look around, you realize that all the other drivers who are nearby, have experienced the same problem. Everyone gets out of their vehicles; some open the hood to view the engine, while others grab their mobile phones only to discover that they are dead, too. A few seconds later, strangers are congregating together to talk. Everyone is asking, "What's going on?" Everyone is mystified, except you.

You know about two dangers which can cause this type of systemic failure. You understand that modern cars, radios, computers, cell phones, and everything else containing electronic micro-circuits, can be irreparably damaged by two dangers we are currently facing.

Possible Cause / Effect: The problem could have been created by a naturally occurring solar phenomenon, commonly referred to as a *solar flare*. This is a sudden burst of energy, a pulse of magnetic and plasma power that is periodically generated by the sun. Scientists refer to these as a Coronal Mass Ejection (CME). For years, NASA has been warning us that this could happen. It is a credible threat.

Typically, these power-pulses only create temporary, minor problems, such as static noise heard on radios and televisions. However, occasionally they generate severe problems.

For example, in September 1859, an era which was before the development of our damage-prone modern electronics, a solar flare commonly referred to as the *Carrington Event*, hit the United States. Though invisible and unfelt by humans, it had sufficient power to cause telegraph wires to catch fire.

Similarly, four decades later, in September 1898 the telegraph communication system in Chicago totally collapsed after being hit by a solar flare that was less powerful than the Carrington Event. At the same time, in Nebraska, Tennessee, and Washington, this same pulse destroyed many of the low-voltage telegraph systems. Their 1.14-volt devices were suddenly fried when struck by a 280-volt electrical surge.

A few decades later, in May 1921, Eastern Canada was hit by an even smaller yet similar solar flare. It caused, among other things, the entire power grid to fail. With this incident, even many nonelectric railroad train engines quit working.

In more recent times, a solar flare of a similar magnitude to the Carrington Event narrowly missed hitting Earth. If that July 2012 solar event had struck the planet when your part of the world was facing the sun, even now, years later, you would probably still be suffering from the catastrophic effects because this wouldn't be a short-term quick-to-recover calamity.

Regrettably, our modern electronics are susceptible to damage from a solar flare. Today, our electronic devices are far more sensitive than the old telegraph systems—and yet even those failed.

How would we fare if hit by a Carrington Event today? Much, much worse. It would cause catastrophic failures in electronics and many electrical systems. Most power grids would fail.

Yet these examples, which I've drawn from historical accounts, did not have severe consequences. Why? There is a noteworthy reason for this. When they occurred, society was not yet dependent on electric and electronic technologies. Today, the developed world is very different.

So, we need to recognize that even though massive solar flares are not frequent occurrences, they are not rare. Further, though the other solar flares that hit North America in the last century were not as massive as the 1859 Carrington Event, the 2012 incident reminds us that it was not a never-to-be-repeated anomaly. It is a repeatable event, and it can strike any part of the world.

Lastly, we need to embrace the fact that our technology-driven society is literally dependent on electronics to function, and that these devices are prone to failure if they are exposed to a major solar flare. Therefore, we must conclude that the danger posed by a massive solar flare does pose a clear and present danger, and that an event such as this can hit at any time, without warning.

Possible Cause / Effect: Another possible cause of this problem is a similar-in-effect but man-made threat. This includes a cyber-attack, or the detonation of an electromagnetic pulse device, more commonly referred to as an EMP weapon. Several rogue nations and terrorist groups now have the technology to make, and deliver to the U.S., Europe, or anywhere else in the world, a device commonly referred to as an electromagnetic pulse (EMP) weapon.

North Korea has repeatedly threatened to launch this type of attack against the United States. The U.S. Congress task force charged with assessing this threat, has concluded that it is credible. Their report concludes that we are vulnerable and they are capable of initiating this type of attack—and their leader is crazy enough to do it.

Just one medium-sized EMP device has the potential to cause extensive damage to half of the United States. Or, throughout the entirety of Western Europe or any developed country.

Oddly, these weapons don't directly harm people. Nevertheless, since they can create catastrophic effects over a large geographic region, people will be injured and killed as a side effect.

As the device takes down the national electrical power grid, locally, it permanently destroys the microcircuitry in private and public computers and electrical equipment of all sorts. As a result, all nonmilitary communication is interrupted, transportation grinds to a halt, emergency services are disabled, commerce is stalled, and the economy goes into a tailspin. In response, the public falls into the grip of debilitating fear.

Within weeks after such a detonation, a technologically advanced society will crumble. Within months, it will be catapulted into a new stone age.

Cars and most trucks won't work, and replacement parts will be similarly damaged. Not that it will matter much since gas stations won't be able to draw fuel out of their underground tanks.

Radio and TV stations will be damaged beyond repair, unprotected 2-way radios will be inoperable, and both landline and mobile phones will cease to work. Most businesses will close, and paychecks will stop coming.

In many areas, water systems will stop flowing water to faucets, and sewage systems will stop pumping effluent to treatment plants. Traffic signals, street lights, and many of the lights in our homes will stop working, as will LED flashlights, newer kitchen appliances, fans and heaters, air conditioning systems, and even gasoline-powered emergency generators.

Almost everything electrical, electronic, most battery-operated devices and most modern mechanical equipment will stop working. Permanently. Most consumer electronics will be irreparable.

Is this really a credible danger? Well, we know that Iran has been testing missiles for this purpose and that North Korea, China, and Russia, already have these weapons and the delivery systems.

Additionally sobering, is that the use of an EMP weapon is less risky for the perpetrator. This is because it can provide both anonymity and disguise the severity of the attack.

Delivered shrewdly, such as launching it from a tramp cargo ship off the coast of the United States, followed by blowing up the ship after the missile launch, would make it very difficult to trace its origin. Plus, since a device detonated in the upper atmosphere would not cause carnage on the ground, news broadcasts would not show injuries resulting from the weapon, so people who are outside the affected area would not understand the severity of the attack.

These factors make the weapon less risky to use. Therefore, retaliation is unlikely if no one can quickly prove who initiated the attack.

It is even more troubling that North Korea and China have been caught selling this technology to terrorist groups. An EMP weapon is not a "future" technology. It's available, now.

This danger isn't theoretical. It is a clear and present danger.

Most government officials avoid talking about this threat because we have no effective countermeasures in place.[6] They don't want to incite panic. But whatever the reason, experts, all agree that this type of strike is a viable threat.

Back to Scenario #2...

As you sit in your inoperable car, you thank God that you are aware of what's happening and you are prepared for it. You know that either a naturally occurring solar flare or an EMP attack has happened. Yet, as helpful as that information is, what caused the failure doesn't really matter at this point. What matters is that your vehicle, your phone, everything electronic, and almost everything powered by electricity, will have stopped working and probably won't restart.

Example of 'Actionable Conclusions' for Scenario #2

1. Keep a GO-Bag in my car, along with walking shoes, etc.
2. Make sure my family and friends know about this danger, and help them understand what they need to do.
3. Establish a rendezvous location (home, or elsewhere) to link-up with family or friends. (Define who is in this group.)
4. Establish a walking plan from various locations I frequent, and identify various routes for hiking from each, so that I can safely and quickly reach my rendezvous location. Assemble maps and refine my map reading and compass-use skills.

What is relevant at this point is that unless you have a bicycle or horse with you, you will need to start walking. Your car isn't going to be repaired anytime soon; maybe never, as replacement parts will have been damaged, along with the manufacturing equipment.

Not only has your vehicle, phone, and radio stopped working, these items have stopped working for the police and fire department, too. Moreover, your credit cards won't work.

---

[6] There are notable exceptions such as former CIA Director, Admiral James Woolsey, and government expert Dr. Peter Vincent Pry, who have been very outspoken about this threat.

At this point, what matters most to you is that you are unable to communicate with family and friends—or anyone, and you can't summon help. And, you understand that it's pointless to search for a payphone because it won't be working. Since the Internet is down, you can't use a Wi-Fi hotspot either.

You will not be able to contact family, friends, or anyone else. And, you won't be able to purchase supplies unless you have cash. You will be on your own. Your plans need to take this into account.

Hopefully, you have a GO-Bag. And a well-thought-out plan.

Problems that are common to an assortment of disasters: Keep in mind, in Scenario #2 as well as in many other emergency situations that are far less severe, public transportation may not be running, restaurants may not be serving food, and grocery stores may not be selling food or water. Even street lights may have stopped working. Many stores will lock their doors, at least initially.

Some mom-n-pop stores may be open but many will only accept cash payment. Since ATMs may not be working, most people won't be able to buy much because they don't carry much cash.

If the problem is widespread, and the social situation declines, stores will begin to get looted, businesses and people robbed, and a general sense of lawlessness will prevail. The police will fail to respond because their communication systems will also be affected, and/or because they are busy elsewhere with bigger problems. Once criminals realize this and understand that they can rampage with impunity, acts of criminal violence will soar.

You don't want to be around when this happens. This is why you can't afford to delay evacuation. You need to get to your rendezvous location, or at least to a predetermined place of safety where you can hole-up for a few days. If you don't show up at your rendezvous location, others need to know where to look for you.

Personally, several times in my life, I have experienced serious, disruptive events. So, this circumstance is not an abstract threat. It's a credible danger that is on our doorstep. If you encounter an incident such as this you'd better be prepared and ready to roll.

If you planned ahead, you have a pair of boots or good walking shoes in the trunk of your car. You need to put them on, sling your GO-Bag over your shoulder, and start walking down the road at a quick, but not attention generating, resolute pace.

Hopefully you have a gun, too, or at least pepper spray, because it is possible that you'll need it. Without a firearm your ability to defend yourself is limited.

You'll need to get to a place of safety as soon as possible. You can't waste time talking with other stranded people, fuming or fussing. At this point you're on a mission—your objective is to get to a safe place in case the situation decays.

If you want to be able to help people, do it from a position of strength, not when you are operating alone. Be circumspect, not impetuous. You need to wait to take action until others are available to help if needed. This means that acts of service should generally be launched from your rendezvous point or your safe-haven retreat location, not undertaken when you are alone.

If you have the choice, it's *not* a time to hunker down and hide, either. Even if you have a gun, you don't want to be foolhardy and take unnecessary risks.

You need to get going. You need to hurry to your pre-determined rendezvous point or your safe-haven retreat location. No delays, no side missions unless it's to pick-up a member of your party.

Once the thin veneer which separates social order from anarchy has been breached, society is going to change rapidly. This change may be radical and quick, or progressive, but change is imminent. In our modern world, a catastrophic event can plunge society back to the Stone Age. At the very least, the Wild West.

If an annual "sale" at a Walmart store is enough to cause a riot, what do you think will happen if the police are busy elsewhere and the entire community is gripped by fear and reeling under the adverse effects of a disaster? Even if most people remain calm and helpful, what will happen if just 2% of the population panics? In a city of one million inhabitants, this equates to 20,000 out-of-control people.

Two-Stage Danger

If a calamity develops, the effects will be twofold. First, the dangers caused by the disastrous event itself. Second, by the public's response to the event. This will include fear, anger, desperate hopelessness, irrational actions and emotions, and opportunist criminals who will pillage and rule many streets. I've seen it.

If the problem were caused by a solar flare or EMP device as in this scenario, it would have caused irreparable damage to nearly everything electronic, and most things which use electrical power. Granted, this is a worst-case scenario, but it isn't far-fetched. So, what should you do?

Hope for the best. Plan for the worst.

If there is a failure in the power grid, even if something else caused it such as an equipment failure or a system overload, and the outage is protracted, serious problems will develop. Once battery backup systems run out of juice, and emergency-power generators run out of fuel, expect problems to flair and quickly compound.

If there is a deliberate cause behind a power grid failure, such as a hacker attack or cyber warfare, it is likely that computers, banking, communication systems, and electrical devices will be damaged by the same malicious attack. This will make the difficulties even more arduous for the public to endure.

It doesn't take a solar flare or EMP attack to create a protracted emergency situation. The effect of another cause might not be as long-lasting, but the short and mid-term severity can still be devastating and life-threatening.

The second stage of any major incident is the effect it will have on a clueless and unprepared population. Most people have never heard of a solar flare or an EMP weapon, and even if they have, they are ill-equipped to deal with the after effect. Most people can't even comprehend a power grid failure that lasts more than a few hours, even though the energy companies have been talking about their vulnerability for years.

Panic and fear are emotions which cripple most people; irrational behavior will often follow within minutes. In a widespread incident, sooner or later, civility will vaporize.

What do you think the effect will be when people realize they are stranded? What will they do when it sinks in that they are cut-off from government help? How will they react to being unable to contact their loved ones? What will be their response to being hungry and thirsty, and scared?

What if this incident happens at night, or the lights don't come on as darkness sets in? What happens when they find themselves in the dark and the flashlight app on their phone no longer works?

How will people respond when they find they are alone and on their own, and that help isn't coming? How will they react if airplanes start falling out of the sky and they don't know the cause? (Which may happen after a solar flare or EMP.)

These are just a few of the effects of a major solar flare, EMP attack, or another disruptive grid-down event. Most of us can't get our mind around the massive scope of this kind of disaster.

For most people, a scenario such as this is so far beyond their personal experience, that they assume it won't happen. At least not to them. Is this a reasonable assumption, or is it the dangerous effect of a normalcy bias?

In a major disaster or emergency situation, within minutes, most people will be overwhelmed by panic. If we lose power, our society which is electricity dependent, will quickly descend into total chaos.

More to the point, what will you do if this happens? How will you react? Are you ready to face a major event?

Knowledge of the cause and an understanding of the effects are helpful, but physical preparations at home, at work, and having a GO-Bag stored in your vehicle or nearby, is the insurance policy that you will need to cope with a sudden emergency.

Unfortunately, solar flares and EMP attacks aren't the only threats we face today. We also need to be ready for the growing number of other forms of natural and man-made disasters which are on our doorstep. Hurricanes, tornados, floods, extreme cold, protracted hot weather with acute water shortages, earthquakes, volcanic eruptions, tsunamis, the arrival of radioactive sea water and fish, and other natural disasters are now striking with unnerving regularity.

Plus, we now live with many man-made threats that are increasing in frequency and in magnitude. Terrorism, Islamic extremism and the rapid growth of the Madrasas school movement which is training millions of young people to hate non-Muslims, immigrants who don't want to be in their host country and are refusing to obey local laws, porous borders and rampant illegal immigration, increases in corruption and loss of trust in government and its officials, loss of personal freedoms, intrusion of government, social unrest, increasing racial strife, underemployment which throws hardworking people into poverty, regulations which make it difficult to start a business or which force existing businesses to close, increases in food cost, the growing number of retirement-age people without retirement funds, as well as bankrupt retirement funds, the insolvency of the social security and Medicare systems, new untreatable diseases, an increasingly unhealthy and physically unfit population, skyrocketing health costs, schools which don't prepare people for jobs and fail to inculcate a work ethic, Agenda 21 redux, loss of national sovereignty, one out of every three working age people receiving government welfare aid, a federal government that is printing fiat money to pay a national debt that is now $1 million per tax payer, the Department of Justice's predictions that we can expect a major increase in violent crime, prisons which are so overcrowded that violent offenders are being released early, plus the intended and unintended effects of advances in genetics, robotics, artificial intelligence, nanotechnology, and synthetic biology. The results of geoengineering, genetic DNA manipulation in food, animals, and people, expanding water contamination, new threats of strikes and transportation disruption, the deferred maintenance and decay of our roads, bridges, and rail systems, electrical outages and our aging power grid, economic disasters in various forms... and the list goes on, and on, and on.

Each of the problems listed here is like a leaking fuel container. Together they surround us with a ring of dangers, and a lit candle is burning in the middle. As the leaks grow and the flammable vapors combine and saturate the air, danger mounts. No one can say when it will happen, but at some point, even a small breeze will be enough to bring the gas-saturated air into contact with the candle's small flame. A sudden explosion will follow.

A major event like a solar flare or an EMP may happen first. But if not, there are plenty of other leaky gas cans surrounding us. Eventually one of them will fuel a conflagration.

Whether caused by an individual event or the combined effect of several incendiary causes, either way, we can expect to eventually experience the explosive force of a widespread natural or man-made disaster. This is what we are facing.

The facts are in plain sight. It's delusional to think otherwise.

We can debate when it will happen, but informed people realize that sooner-or-later, we can expect either an explosion or a fire that will consume our comfortable life. Life-altering change is coming.

If you're not sure that this is an accurate statement, read Book-1 in this "PREPARED: Ready to Roll" series. In addition to other evidence, in it, you will be exposed to ample proof that the U.S. Government is getting ready for major, widespread disaster of unprecedented scope. For more than two decades the federal government has been feverously getting ready. Don't take my word for it, use the hundreds of footnotes to test my conclusion.

Whatever causes the coming disaster, the result will not be pleasant. Nor will it be short-lived. More to the point, if you aren't ready for it, life will become difficult, extremely difficult.

Experts do debate the likelihood of a complete collapse as the result of a solar flare or EMP attack. On the other hand, a "confluence event" is universally regarded as a ticking time bomb. It is obvious to any serious observer that several of these lesser problems will eventually intersect. Once that happens, it can quickly snowball, and roll us into a period that is rife with social and economic disruption.

If we aren't prepared, it won't make much difference to us if this new era was caused by a solar flare, an EMP attack, a natural disaster, pandemic, or if it came about as a result of a series of lesser events that converged to create a domino effect.

For us, the cause is actually less important than the effect. Therefore, to habitually rant or concentrate on a problem is a dangerous distraction if it sidetracks us from pursuing solutions for ourselves, our family and friends. We need to get ready for what's coming, not just whine about it.

Granted, we don't know when we will be hammered by one of the dangers on our doorstep. What we do know is that we can expect both manageable disasters, and more severe life-altering changes, in the months and years ahead.

It is likely that these changes will happen in our lifetime. But if not during our life, we can depend on a life-altering event or series of life-changing circumstances, to adversely affect our children. So, we need to get ready for it. And, we need to help the next generation prepare for a difficult future.

We need to teach the next generation the skills needed to overcome these problems, how to be resilient and ready for change, and how to be fearless. It's not some weird Freudian "survival of the fittest" dogma, it's simply imbuing them with *strength of will* and the life *purpose* that our Creator provides to us. This brings the ability to face adversity and not give up.

Thankfully, we don't need to fear these changes. We just need to prepare for it—and we need to prepare our children. This mission is attainable.

We need to teach them to expect change, and to be resilient and adaptable. And, we also need to teach them the skills they need for self-reliance, so they can attack adversity and overcome it.

To help them succeed, we will need to model these same characteristics. In alliance with other insightful family members or friends, we need to live our lives in a way that clearly and intentionally demonstrates these same priorities and character traits. We need to infuse their spirits with a zest for life and a love for liberty, teach them discernment and creative problem-solving skills, and explain the value of running scenarios as a tool to anticipate difficulties and design real-world solutions.

> *"In reality, we cannot build a better future for our children, but we can train them to be flexible, and we can prepare them for a future that will look different from today."*
>
> Translation of an ancient Greek proverb

Chapter 2

Adaptable & Balanced Advance-Planning is Critical

1. **Decide now that you will get out early.**
   In advance, anticipate causes of delay and find solutions.

2. **Pre-plan your evacuation routes and details.**
   Have a Plan-A, Plan-B, and Plan-C, as contingency planning and resiliency is essential.

3. **Make sure your family and friends know the plan.**
   Practice your plan. Confirm that they remember the details. Include a 2-3-page plan summary in each GO-Bag.

4. **Have your evacuation supplies packed and ready to go.**
   Keep a GO-Bag(s) in each vehicle, or nearby.

Routing, navigation, timing of departure, and predetermined locations to meet-up with family and/or friends, are critically important elements of every personal emergency plan. Unfortunately, in an emergency, nothing seems to go exactly according to the plan. Never. So, develop contingencies. Flexibility is essential.

Evacuation routes are often thought to be obvious, and yet the obvious routes are often a poor choice when disaster strikes because they become crowded or unsafe. Pre-plan now with alternate routes.

In the major cities and suburban areas of the United States, as well as rural locations where major storms are a part of life, evacuation routes have been established. These are generally marked with special signage, and maps of these 'official' evacuation routes are typically available online at the website for your local government's Emergency Management Planning office.

> "GO-Bag" is an acronym for a "Get Out" evacuation bag. Typically, it is a knapsack containing water, food, essential supplies and gear. This emergency supplies kit is sometimes also called a "GOOD Bag" (Get-Out-of-Dodge Bag), a "Bug-Out Bag" (old military term), "Urban Survival Kit," "Evacuation Bag," or by various other terms.
>
> Whichever name you choose to use, the concept is the same. It's a portable collection of essential items that you are likely to need when you are away from home, or traveling from one place to another after or during a disaster. It is a bag suitable for carrying on a long walk.
>
> A GO-Bag needs to be portable and easy to carry, so a knapsack with shoulder straps is the best choice for a container. It needs to be comfortable to carry, so 15-26 pounds (7-12 kg) of essential supplies is maximum for a multipurpose GO-Bag. At a minimum, this will include drinking water and other supplies that you may desperately need for safe evacuation and sustenance for 3-5 days.
>
> In this chapter and in the appendix of this book, you will find lists of recommended contents for GO-Bags. Gathering the provisions and gear yourself, and assembling your own bag, is generally less expensive and produces a better result than buying a prepackaged kit.

Notwithstanding, it may be more prudent to review these 'official' routes and then use them as a reference when you decide on your own evacuation route. Actually, several routes. Multiple ways to the rendezvous location where you intend to meet your family or friends, and from that site to a more distant safe-haven. You need to identify direct routes, and 'Plan-B' and 'Plan-C" routes to use when your first-choice route is compromised.

In a danger-is-imminent situation, you may need to skip the rendezvous location and immediately flee to a nearby safe (or safer) location. Make this part of your plan, too, and make sure everyone understands this detail.

Once the initial danger is past, the maps and other items in your GO-Bag will make it possible for you to get to the prearranged rendezvous location so you can reconnect with family and friends. Everyone needs to understand how they are to respond in different circumstances, and where to go.

Adaptability is essential, so is an understanding of evacuation route options. Each member of your group needs to have complete clarity on what they are to do. Each member needs to have printed directions, a good map(s), a compass, and they need to be familiar with these items and how to use them. Having food, water, and gear in your GO-Bags isn't enough.

Planning more than one evacuation or travel route is important. Nevertheless, don't forget to pack detailed street maps even if you have identified routes and backup routes. You may still need to adjust your plan on the fly.

Though part of your pre-planned route may be the same, you need alternate routes not only for travel to your final destination, but also from your home, work, and the other areas you frequent. You need to plan for traffic bottlenecks, congestion, roadways blocked by traffic accidents, fires, and damaged buildings—and social disturbances. You need options. You need places to regroup and relax, and you need to remain flexible.

If disaster strikes when you are on vacation or traveling for work, you have hopefully planned for that eventuality, as well. Most people won't take the time to make a detailed plan for every eventuality, but we nevertheless need to keep this potential need in mind while we travel.

Disasters never happen at a convenient time. And, disasters and emergency situations are often even more catastrophic for those who are far from home. Therefore, don't neglect this possibility. You may not be able to take your GO-Bag with you on a commercial airlines flight, but you can include a few essential items in your suitcase.

Since you might be far from home or in an unfamiliar place when disaster strikes, you also need highway maps, and ideally topographic maps which show terrain and land features in greater detail. Beyond this, acquaint yourself with roadway choke points which impede travel, as well as local dangers and high-crime areas to be avoided.

Moreover, for most of us, it's not just about getting out of the area, it's about getting out and being able to quickly rendezvous with our loved ones. This acknowledged, your plan needs to articulate when, and under what conditions, you should abandon the local meeting place and travel to your 'Plan-B' location. Safety and the reality of extenuating circumstances may make it necessary for you to head out alone, and meet your family and friends at your 'safe haven' retreat location.

How do you know when to switch to 'Plan-B'? How do you know how long you should wait before abandoning the local rendezvous site and heading out to a Plan-B location or your more distant safe-haven? How do you decide when to go looking for a missing family member vs. getting the rest of the family to safety?

The answers to these questions need to be in your plan. Moreover, each family member and every other member of your group, need to be aware of the plan. In case they forget or are rattled by circumstances, a short summary needs to be included in the top section of each GO-Bag.

Emergency situations create confusion. Expect it. Plan for it.

This is why it's so important to develop your own, personalized, evacuation plan. And, why it is so important for each family member and friend involved, to understand the plan, so that they know what to do (and when to do it).

Developing route options and establishing a distant safe-haven isn't enough. You also need to answer "if, then…" questions, because adaptability and resiliency are essential for a safe evacuation. You, your family and friends, need to know how to respond. Everyone also needs to know what to do when some circumstance makes following the plan impossible or unsafe.

It isn't practical to put every possible contingency into your plan. Notwithstanding, you can develop guidelines which are adaptable.

As you formulate your plan, build into it a structure which provides flexibility, so that a separated family member or friend, can reconnect with the group.

If each GO-Bag contains a 2-way radio, you can also include in your plan the radio frequency to use, and the time when a separated member of your group should try to establish radio contact. For example, high noon, dusk, and first light. Then, the group and the separated person can, if possible, get to a higher location at that predetermined time. Being at a higher elevation, or a place that is not obstructed by buildings or hills, makes it possible to communicate at a greater distance. (See Chapter-7 for more on this topic.) It is details such as this that should be included in your plan.

"The plans of the diligent lead surely to advantage."
Holy Bible, Proverbs 21:5a

Chapter 3

Escape "From" vs. Escape "To"

It's not enough to evacuate *'from'* a danger area. You need to flee *'to'* a safe place where you can ride out the threat.

Oftentimes more people are harmed or killed in the aftermath of an emergency incident than by the actual event. So, we need to keep this in mind as we consider evacuation to a safe haven.

As important as timely evacuation is for safety, it's only one component of the equation. The formula for personal safety includes not only pre-planned evacuation routes, but also a quick departure, readily accessible emergency supplies, and selection and preparation in advance, of a safe-haven retreat location.

Unlike the masses who will travel the evacuation routes prescribed by the government plan, your own pre-planning gives you the opportunity to choose different routing options and destinations. Don't just select one rendezvous point for your family, and only one evacuation route. Provide several options as circumstances may require a change.

As you plan, identify multiple destinations. First, a nearby, central meet-up location. Next, an intermediate rendezvous site if the first place becomes untenable. Third, a final destination, a well thought out location of safety, a safe-haven, that will not be inundated by other evacuees.

Many who failed to pre-plan, will still be looking for a safe destination that is different than the government's evacuation plan. Therefore, your safe-haven needs to be someplace that is not an obvious destination. Campgrounds and parks are obvious destinations, so these locations should be avoided.

Where do you want your evacuation route to take you? Ideally, to a pre-planned 'safe-haven' retreat location that provides safety and is pre-stocked with emergency supplies.

Even if you don't have a safe-haven, it may be to your advantage to go somewhere that is 20+ miles away from an urban area and the displaced crowds who are fleeing the danger zone. Ideally, pick a location that is not on or near a highway. Your retreat location should not be easily stumbled upon by those who become frustrated and leave the pack of escaping people.

Increased violence, erratic behavior, and a shortage of supplies are attributes of displaced people. By preplanning, you have the opportunity to avoid this fate.

Remember too, though you may need to evacuate alone, or just with your immediate family, it is unlikely that you will be able to sustain a protracted emergency situation alone. Even if you are extremely proficient and well equipped, being part of a team is generally a huge boost to sustainability. So, as part of pre-planning, seek to develop or join a team; create your own 'community' to deal with an extended emergency.

Those who depend on community 'camps' established by government agencies or relief organizations, generally don't fare as well, especially during the aftermath of a major disaster.

Recent history has demonstrated again and again that government-sponsored refugee centers are often places where mistreatment and violence are rampant. Too often those who enter these "Camps," "Shelters," or "Centers," simply trade one bad situation for another.

On the other hand, those who pre-plan, prepare, and retreat to a well-selected safe-haven, can often avoid internment in a jail-like refugee or FEMA (Federal Emergency Management Agency) camp.

It makes no sense to trade one form of disaster for another, so in my view, it makes sense to find a retreat location that is not operated by a government agency. If you have "private" options, such as a shelter run by a community church, check them out. There may be a much better alternative than a government or Red Cross refugee camp.

Or, develop your own makeshift shelter. Working with neighbors and friends to establish a private retreat, may be a far better choice than what the government has to offer.

Keep in mind, too, that when you enter a government-sponsored shelter or refugee camp, you may not be allowed to leave. When you enter these *camps* you not only give up privacy, you often lose your freedom, as well. If you doubt this, talk to someone who has used these government services during a major disaster.

A private retreat is additionally important if you have a dog, cat, or some other pet that you care about. Many shelters do not allow pets. Furthermore, a federally mandated protocol for government shelters during a major disaster, calls for forced euthanizing of domestic animals (killing of pets) at these shelters.

It's far better to maintain your independence by retreating with a group of trusted friends and family to a private location. Ideally, a place you prepared in advance, where you stockpiled supplies. A place that paves the way for independent and self-reliant living; where you can depend on each other for mutual care, safety and security.

Take the time to select and prepare a safe-haven, now. At the very least, develop a retreat site at, or near, your home with the help of friends or family members. Plus, a safe-haven at an out-of-the-way rural location.

No matter what location you plan to retreat to, when the emergency situation is upon you, the best evacuation advice is…

Get out early. Don't delay.

Even if you act on this with foresight and establish a safe-haven retreat location, and plan to evacuate together, this doesn't guarantee safety. It's not unusual for an individual, or part of the group, to not arrive at the rendezvous point promptly. Consider this possibility now. Plan for it.

How long will you wait? Your plan needs to include this detail. If not, the delayed person may waste valuable time trying to get to you when they should be opting for 'Plan-B' and a different rendezvous location.

Moreover, when you wait for the missing person, your window of opportunity for a safe escape may close. You may become trapped by circumstances. Don't let this happen needlessly.

In advance, build into your plan the amount of time you will wait at your first rendezvous location. Then, when disaster strikes, stick to your established plan. That way everyone knows what to expect, and what is expected of them. Due to circumstances, it may not be practical to say you will wait a prescribed amount of time, such as two hours, since it may be unclear when the countdown started. However, you can indicate a deadline such as "two-hours before dusk."

For those who are elderly or with physical limitations, there is an even greater tendency to wait. Yet, this natural inclination can make escape even more challenging. There is a fine line between waiting for family and friends who can help mitigate your mobility issues, and waiting too long and losing the opportunity to get to safety. This is yet another reason why it is advantageous to have pre-arranged routes and secondary rendezvous locations along the way to your safe-haven retreat area.

If you delay your departure because you are waiting for someone. Or because you need to gather more supplies, as was the situation in short story by best-selling author David Crawford which is included at the beginning of Book-1 of this series, you are asking for trouble. At the very least, you will likely get bogged down with the thousands of other people who also waited too long to evacuate.

This doesn't just represent a time delay. It translates into increased danger. Every minute you delay introduces new threats and increased risk.

Identifying sound evacuation route options and rendezvous locations is foundational to every personal emergency plan. Regrettably, in surveys taken among both adults and children regarding disaster preparedness, most were unable to recall the details of their family's plan, even when they remembered that a family plan had been established. This is a solemn reminder that an outstanding emergency plan is only a vapor if the participants can't remember the details.

Adaptability
Resiliency is a core attribute that must be included.

Unfortunately, this quality is also often neglected. This can render the plan irrelevant at the time when it is desperately needed.

Complexity hampers memory and the retention of details. Furthermore, an emergency plan which lacks adaptability can make a plan ineffective. So, what do we do?

We identify likely problems, we make contingency plans for these developments, and we build flexibility into our plan. We don't burden ourselves with unnecessary complexity, but we do include essential details and information on Plan-A, Plan-B, etc. Plus, we specify what circumstance(s) will dictate a change from one plan to another.

We anticipate, and we build flexibility into a simple, straightforward plan of action. Then we clearly communicate the details to everyone involved.

Destination
Is your destination your home, or is it another location?

The best answer is both. But each member of your family (or group) needs to know where they should be heading, and the conditions or timing which will redirect them from the primary to a secondary destination. And, what route to take.

Invariably, when someone fails to arrive at the predetermined location, it is tempting to organize a search party to look for the missing person. Unfortunately, if you aren't confident of the route which would have been taken, this may not just be a futile exercise, it may also be extremely hazardous.

Make decisions such as this in advance. In your Plan Summary document, be detailed regarding timing, and under what conditions you will move to Plan-B.

Plan-A - Your 'First-Choice' Plan: Evacuation to a safer, less-populated rural location.

If you live or work in an urban or suburban area and disaster strikes, the best plan may be to get to a less populated area where self-sufficiency is possible. If the emergency situation affects thousands of people, and it looks like it may last more than a few days, then you need to get out early, while you still can. You need to evacuate to a safe rural location.

If you wait until the masses of people arrive at the same conclusion, it may be too late. You may be trapped by traffic congestion, blocked roads or crowds; conditions which are often followed by violence.

Where will you go?

How will you get there?

What will you take with you?

> *Last minute decisions of this magnitude are often disastrous because they are poorly conceived.*
>
> *Making plans in advance is imperative.*

Ideally, the selection of a retreat location is a decision to be made in advance, as part of your emergency plan. With advance planning, you have the opportunity to select a suitable location, stockpile supplies, and identify routing and transportation options for safe and expeditious travel. Plus, you have the chance to relocate to this place via a small caravan. This cooperative venture provides for shared labor, mutual aid, and increased security.

Plan-B - An intermediate destination or a friend's house.

If your primary retreat location is many miles away, be sure to select a "Plan-B" location that is on the way, within 1-2 days (or 1-2 nights) walking distance. For those who live in a major city, this Plan-B retreat may not be in a rural location, but rather a better place within the city; a place where you can congregate with other family and friends for mutual aid and improved safety.

Irrespective of whether your retreat location is rural or urban, *'community'* is essential for surviving an emergency situation that lasts more than a few days. If you can avoid it, don't try to go it alone.

Invariably those who bug-out early, before the rest of the population realizes their plight, are far more likely to reach safety. Delay can be deadly. But to leave for a non-specific location may also be deadly. Make your plans now, before you need them.

> *"The ways of the lazy are filled with sorrows, and the ways of the upright are clear [like an open highway]."*
>
> Holy Bible
> Proverbs 15:19

Chapter 4

Selection of a "Safe-Haven" Retreat Location

Why is a safe-haven essential?

In a disaster or emergency situation, agencies of local, state and federal governments, and non-profit groups (NGOs) such as the Red Cross and churches, rush to establish shelters. These have often been a godsend to a community, but they don't constitute a "safe-haven."

They are important, but they are often not adequate, especially in our modern world. There is a big difference between a *shelter* or *refugee camp* and a private *safe-haven* which is a pre-prepared retreat location.

When people are forced to flee from their damaged homes or from communities threatened with danger, those who are displaced need help. This is a legitimate need. It has often been the selfless, charitable acts of shelter organizers and workers who have saved the day. We must acknowledge and support these short-term solutions and the volunteers who make them work.

Notwithstanding, as we think about *our* future and the well-being of our family and friends, there is more to consider. When an emergency situation is widespread and severe, community shelters are quickly overwhelmed. And, if the calamity lasts for more than a few days, these temporary facilities are drained of their resources. At that point, these bastions of safety can become encampments of misery.

Even when supplies of water and food remain available, recent history is replete with examples of community shelters becoming enclaves of hopelessness, suffering, violence, and the loss of safety and even basic liberties. In Chapter-3, "Escape *From* vs. Escape *To*," as well as in the last chapter of this book, the Hurricane Katrina debacle is summarized, but there are many other recent examples which could have been used.

The bottom-line is that community shelters and government refugee camps are necessary, but they are often not a pleasant solution. At best, they provide a workable solution for a few days.

We can do better. We must do better.

Government and NGO shelters and encampments are designed to serve the general "unprepared" and "unmotivated" population. As a result, when these facilities are operated for more than a couple of days, serious problems of all sorts quickly develop.

Though the news media likes to blame the Federal Emergency Management Agency (FEMA) and the Department of Homeland Security (DHS) and other agencies for ineptitude, in fairness, these problems cannot be solved by politically-correct planning. At the core, the problem is inherent to the people being served.

Self-reliant people develop their own, better solutions. That's the group we need to be a part of because independence, and self-reliance can provide us with freedom of action, as well as a safer, healthier environment.

Even if our goal is to serve needy people, this laudable objective is best accomplished from a position of strength. Our ability to help will be sorely limited if we, too, must rely on others to meet our basic needs.

Moreover, what may appear at the onset to be a temporary emergency situation, may develop into one that is protracted. So, if we can avoid it, we don't want to be trapped in a refugee camp, short-term or long-term.

The heart of the problem: Those who choose to go to shelters or refugee camps for longer duration emergency situations, tend to be 'dependent' people. These aid-seekers often bring with them attitudes of entitlement, dependence on others to solve their problems, the orientation that they are a victim and don't have personal responsibilities, a lack of motivation and an unwillingness to work, and an assortment of other social and behavioral problems including criminal conduct and a lifestyle of violence.

More to the point, these are not good neighbors. They are not problem solvers. They are problem-creators or problem-exacerbators, who suck resources but fail to help restore community health.

Therefore, you don't want to be in one of these shelters if it can be avoided. Regrettably, it is not unusual for good people to become trapped in these encampments, a problem which becomes more serious if the quest for short-term aid transitions into longer-term need.

Therefore, the only true safe-haven is one that is privately established and populated with participants who are selected for involvement. These are intentional retreat locations and intentional communities, suitable for both short and long-term safe, healthy living. For those who are interested in serving others, a safe-haven is also necessary as it forms the base of operations.

Lastly, when a natural disaster occurs, the advantage of evacuating to an established, private safe-haven is obvious, but this circumstance is not the only time when you might be thankful that you have it. The time may also come when you want to get away from political turmoil, terror threats, a consequential labor strike, violent protests, transportation disruption, food shortage, racial or social unrest, lockdowns, economic instability, power grid failure, weather shift, a public health danger such as a spreading pandemic, fallout, a period of oppression, fear-mongering or persecution, or some other danger that has arrived on your doorstep. In our modern world, like having an insurance policy, it is prudent to have a safe-haven.

Location, Location, Location.

Just as with buying real estate, location is everything. You need to be even pickier when it comes to selecting your retreat location (aka/safe-haven). Whether you are fleeing the city for a few days, weeks, or the few weeks turn into months or years, your location needs to have specific attributes for it to qualify as a safe-haven location.

When safety, defense and being able to sustain healthy life are the goal, we need to acknowledge an uncomfortable truth. When things get difficult, a retreat site located in an urban setting will be overrun quickly, followed within days by suburban sites. Unless fortified and guarded like a military camp, the next to fall will be upscale gated neighborhoods that are in, or near, a city. This includes those communities which are "gated" and have their own security force.

While each of these is progressively better than the previously mentioned site, none of these can provide the safety, sustainability, and healthy living conditions of a safe-haven. Important, too, is that these metropolitan sites are unsatisfactory for achieving sustainability.

As a temporary retreat location for a couple of weeks, these other evacuation sites might be okay, but they will not be adequate if the emergency situation degrades and becomes protracted. In other words, they are a risky choice.

If you have the option, your best retreat location is certainly not behind the gate of an estate or luxury home. A neighborhood populated by those who expect others to serve them, and come to their aid, will quickly crumble.

Also, these enclaves of affluence will be obvious targets for criminal opportunists. As a result, within a week or two, most of them will fall prey to the relentless pounding of wave after wave of criminals and street gang thugs. Communities which are ostensibly "protected" by rent-a-cop security forces are still vulnerable.

History confirms my personal experience: During a long duration emergency, security officers (and police officers) whose loyalty is based solely on a paycheck, who are stressed by the threat of violence and have loved ones living in an unsafe location elsewhere, will soon abandon their posts. This transforms these bastions of wealth into sand castles which are not only easily crushed, but also far more vulnerable than their less-noticeable neighboring communities.

If miscreants are aware of the enclave, an affluent community will always be a prime target; all the more in a disaster scenario which includes looting and social unrest. Security that is effective in normal times will not be adequate during a period of turmoil. Both the previously-good citizen and the criminal will see a wealthy community as one with an abundance of needed (or desirable) resources. Absent prison-like walls and battlements, even the best security force cannot stop hordes of desperate people or armed gangs.

Since opulent homes and estates are often separated by acres of space, a community-based security force will be stretched thin in these luxury neighborhoods. This makes it easy for criminal gangs to breach security, while the privacy makes each home ripe for unhurried plunder, and the residents the easy victims of pent-up class warfare rage. These weaknesses, as well as possible vehicular breach-points in the walled perimeter, must be remedied if this type of community is to withstand even the first wave of looting.

Alarm systems and safe rooms are great, but these measures will not stop a conflagration or endure weeks of protracted siege. A well selected, remote, rural farm or ranch can provide better safety as well as sustainability.

Unfortunately, many close-to-the-city farms or ranches are similarly vulnerable. City dwellers will rightly perceive that farms and ranches produce food, and therein they will be seen as the place to go when the grocery store shelves are empty. So, these rural locations are not automatically a good choice, either.

'Good people' will quickly identify these places as potential retreat locations for their families. When their city or suburban home life is threatened, droves of these people will flee their neighborhoods in search of a safer place. When this happens, rural homes, ranches, and farms that are visible from primary and secondary roadways will become a target.

On an emotional level, it will be difficult to turn these desperate people away. But since this entourage will have many mouths to feed and bring with them only a few days of food at best, it must be acknowledged that these ranchers and farmers will be unable to solve the problem.

These unfortunate people saw the signs of the times, and just like us, they had the opportunity to prepare. Yet, they were nevertheless surprised by the circumstance and were unprepared to deal with it. They will be desperate for help.

Some rural landowners will welcome these people into their homes. Others will try to help by distributing groceries. But at some point, even the most kind-hearted will realize that they can't personally solve the crisis. The circumstance will far exceed their capacity to help.

When I was 20-years old, and about to graduate from college, I had the opportunity to live in Haiti for part of a year, to help a friend who was writing an article on Haitian folklore. For me, it was my first experience in an undeveloped country. It was a rude awakening.

One day while sitting on a hill above the marketplace, where I could view the squalor of my surroundings, I had an ah-ha moment. An epiphany. I realized that if I gave away everything I owned, and everything I would ever own, I would still not be able to stop the widespread hunger in Haiti—at least not for more than a few days.

In a protracted emergency situation in the United States, or any developed country experiencing a widespread disaster, this is what you can expect to encounter. This will be what the residents of these close-to-the-city homesteads, farms, and ranches will experience.

If the emergency situation is protracted, at some point, likely when it is too late, kind people will realize that even if they take in everyone and give away all their food and supplies, they will not solve these people's problems. This is yet another reason why even rural landowners may want to evacuate to a safe-haven.

What are the characteristics of a safe-haven site?

The general location: Traditionally, the rule of thumb has been to pick a retreat site that is more than one tank of gas, or even further, from any town or populated area. While this makes sense, this isn't practical for most of us. Though not ideal, real-world considerations of employment suggest a compromise. Without a doubt, a closer location will not be nearly as safe, but a place you can get to is better than an ideal safe-haven you can't reach.

If you are a mechanic or have the money, you might rebuild a pre-electronics Jeep or 4-wheel drive pickup truck that will hold sufficient fuel to drive to a more distant location. But most of us need a simpler solution. In a pinch, we need to be able to walk to it. We need to pick a place where we can, if necessary, reach by walking.

The *"How far can you walk in a day?"* principle: Since you may find it necessary to hike to your retreat location, consider what it will take to walk the route before you finalize your decision. Consider the *worst case* scenario.

What might pleasantly surprise you is that most people can walk a considerable distance in just a couple of days. When circumstances require it, you can accomplish much more than you think you can.

A neighbor who lives near me is substantially overweight and is, impressively, doing something about it. She is walking a dozen miles a day, up hills and down, to help lose weight. On an average day, it takes her 3-1/2 hours to walk 12 miles.

If you're not sure what distance you can walk in a day, determine this before you start looking for a location. It's easy; consider it a "healthy exercise day."

If you are in good health, schedule an appointment with yourself and spend a morning walking with your GO-Bag, or a knapsack that weighs around 20-pounds (9 kg). Pick your route in advance, and walk for 6-hours, taking short breaks as needed to drink water and snack. Then, turn around and walk back to where you started. Total walking time, 12-hours. If you don't have a pedometer, drive the same route so you can measure the distance you walked. If you're having motivation problems, pick a fun destination.

Now you have your per-day distance. In an emergency, you may choose to walk nonstop, but day or night, rain or shine, a 12-hour walk can be accomplished by most reasonably-fit adults.

Multiply the distance you walked by two, and then by four. The two sums will represent 2-4 days of walking. It is reasonable to spend 2-4 days, or nights, walking your evacuation route if you find it necessary to bug-out on foot.

This exercise will help you identify a reasonable distance to travel from your workplace to your safe-haven, which in turn, will help you determine the areas to search as you try to find a suitable retreat location. This exercise will help you to keep your quest practical.

You may opt for a safe-haven retreat location that is further away. That's fine. But if that is the desirable option you select, then you will need to more diligently plan for alternative transportation since, when the time comes, your first-choice may not be viable. Either way, it's still worth considering what it would take to walk to your destination.

When the time comes and you need to bug-out, at that point, hopefully, you will be able to drive, pedal a bike, hitch a ride, or take public transportation at least part of the way. But if you find that you need to walk, you need to know what to expect.

Your 'experiment' day of walking may produce different results since your health, stamina, and terrain will be different. Nonetheless, it's worth noting that the brisk walking speed of moderately fit adults[7]

---

[7] Don't just guess. A walking 'experiment' will help make your planning real-world. Even a 4-hr walk can help you evaluate the distance you can walk in 12-hrs.

is 3–4½ MPH. So if you assiduously walk at a brisk pace for 12-hours, you will be able to travel 36-48 miles (58-77 km).

When you multiply that distance by 2 to determine how far you can walk in two days, and again by 4, for four days, you will gain a better understanding of what speed and distance is attainable. Since 2-4 days is the maximum most people are willing to hike to reach their safe-haven, these calculations will provide useful parameters.

If you conduct your own experiment, you will be able to do the math using more accurate numbers. Notwithstanding, my example of 36-48 miles/day suggests that many will need to either compromise when it comes to distance, embark on a fitness regimen, or establish a resilient transportation plan with reliable back-up options.

This compromise may be required when you consider the improved safety of being further from an urban area, and compare it with the reality of how far you can reasonably walk. For most people, this suggests finding a safe-haven that is 100-200 miles (161-322 km) from their home and workplace.

Those who are willing to move or develop more than one mode of alternative transportation may redasonably select a more distant location. But for those who opt to use the *"How far can you walk in a day?"* principle, and the criteria of 100-200 miles from your home and workplace, start your search by drawing two circles on a map.

With your home as the center, draw two circles. The first circle to represent a 2-day walk (or the radius of 100 miles from your home). Then draw a second circle which represents the distance of a 4-day hike (or a radius of 200 miles). Start your search for a safe-haven retreat location in the area that is between these two circles.

Of course, since street routing and terrain will prevent you from taking a direct route, the actual mileage will need to be taken into account before you settle on a site. This mapping exercise is just to help you get the process started. When you plug-in your actual walking speed and route mileage, the results will be more useful.

The parameters for site selection will need to be further modified by your health and physical impairments, the terrain and geographic obstacles, and if you will have out-of-shape friends or young children in tow, or other impediments.

Fortunately, when danger is on your doorstep, you will probably be able to walk further and faster than you think. Conversely, the circumstances of the emergency might make travel more difficult. Therefore, it's usually best to be conservative when you establish your minimum and maximum-distance parameters for site selection.

After drawing the two circles on your map, consider obstacles and choke points such as bridges and parts of town you will want to avoid. These potential *"danger zones"* need to be taken into account if any of your direct evacuation routes will take you through them. You need to identify a way around these areas or avoid them altogether.

It is to your advantage to select a safe-haven site that can be easily reached via alternate routes. One or two secondary routes that are entirely different from your first-choice route, but add less than a dozen miles, will help improve your adaptability to change.

Armed with the results of this 2nd exercise, you will have further narrowed where you should begin to look for a safe-haven location. At this point, the general vicinity for your site search should become apparent.

Don't be ambushed by an unattainable quest for perfection. As mentioned earlier, compromise is often necessary. Nonetheless, be circumspect about your compromises. Finding the "perfect" location may be impossible but be wise in the concessions you make. For example, it may be acceptable to choose a place that is on the other side of a choke-point such as a bridge, but it may not be prudent to pick a site that would force you to evacuate by traveling through a high-crime area.

Even if you don't undertake this full exercise, at least keep these factors in mind. And remember, too, that you may be forced to walk to your destination. Don't assume that you will be able to drive.

For me and the city where I live, when I undertook this process, it became apparent where I should look for a safe-haven location. It needed to be either North or West of my home and workplace.

Other compass directions would be a foolish choice. If I were to walk East, I would need to traverse the central core of the city. This would require travel on 40-miles of city streets before I even reached the city limits. Not a good plan.

If I were to travel SE, it would create a different set of problems. This route would take me through a high-crime neighborhood. And, if I walked South, it would funnel me toward the densely populated downtown. All of these other directions would be a poor choice.

Yes, there may have been some viable safe-haven locations 100-200 miles in those directions, but since the route to get to those areas involved traversing *danger zones*, I didn't include them in my search. Instead, I chose to confine my search to areas which were North and West of where I live and work, because the routing was safer.

This made sense as I already live and work in the NW corner of the city. So by traveling in an NW direction, I would get out of the city environs faster since I was already on that edge of the city.

With this in mind, using my map with circles drawn on it, I examined the quadrants which are N, NW, and W, of my workplace. These areas would be the most obvious place to find a safe-haven retreat location.

For me, my residence and my business are near each other, so the center of my circles was the same. Your situation may be different. Your best solution may include moving your place of residence or changing jobs, so your workplace is more conducive to evacuation. Or, a more straightforward solution may be to draw two pairs of circles, one with a center at your home and the other your workplace, and concentrate your search in the zone where the circles intersect.

As I perused my map and the circles I had drawn on it, I was reminded that there are several small towns and a major highway in the North quadrant of my city. These are nice communities, but that direction is, of course, more populated, plus the freeway which runs through this area is an interstate route. With these details in mind, I elected to further limit my search to the geographic regions which are NW and W of my home and workplace.

At that point, on the following weekend, I started exploring by car, beginning with the two quadrants that I had identified. I decided to initiate my search by concentrating on the areas I didn't know, that I had not previously visited.

These locales were places I'd not already visited because they are not on the way to anywhere interesting, and there are no "destination" sites in these geographic areas. This anonymity was an additional indicator that I might find a suitable place in these locales.

Not only were they unfamiliar to me, but they were also unlikely to be considered by others, too. Importantly, these areas wouldn't come to mind when city dwellers were looking for an evacuation destination, nor would they be considered by marauding criminals. No one would be quick to travel to these areas.

So these areas seemed to be the best locales to start my on-the-ground exploration, but I still needed to identify what I was hoping to find. My next task was to clarify what I was looking for regarding the site itself. I needed to do this before starting my search, so I wouldn't be unduly enticed by a place that was beautiful or a bargain.

Evaluating an actual property: Find an established farm, ranch, rancho, or vacation property with acres of land (or like-minded neighbors), in a sparsely populated, nondescript rural, agricultural or wilderness area. Or, raw land in a place that is geographically isolated.

Some features are essential while others are merely advantageous. For example, the property *must* have a reliable water well or its own private source of water which is suitable for both drinking and irrigation. Conversely, if the ground is unsuitable for gardening, planting soil can be trucked in to solve the problem. Nevertheless, it is far easier if the land is already arable for planting food crops. Likewise, security systems can be built, but natural terrain features such as the site being invisible from the road, will make security improvements easier. So, even though many attributes are not required, they may represent a huge plus.

Though existing housing, structures, and equipment are not a requirement, either, these can make a safe-haven site less expensive to develop. As a result, these land, structure, and equipment features can make operational readiness a much faster process.

When considering both a locale and an individual site, there is an inescapable need to evaluate both the financial resources and time it will take to transform the location into a safe-haven. The expense of acquiring a property is only one aspect of the selection process.

Note: If you are going to ignore the "walking" aspect of these recommendations, at least look for an isolated area that is at least a 2-hour drive from a metropolitan area, and ideally 4-hours from a city or metroplex with a population that is larger than one million.

At the very least, the sited needs to be far away from any main roadway, and beyond an easy walk from any village. These are minimums that can be overruled if the route to the proposed location is very circuitous or the geography inhibits travel.

If you choose to live full-time at the location: If you want to live at the site and still work in the city, at least pick a place that is accessed from a rural roadway that doesn't lead anywhere. When wandering marauders visit in search of places to plunder, you want them to think the area is uninteresting and bereft of value.

Moving your home to an intermediate location that is en route to your safe-haven: Once you have selected the site for your safe-haven, consider moving your place of residence to a location that is between your workplace and your retreat. This is additionally beneficial if you have a spouse or children, as regardless of whether they are walking or driving, this will take family members past your home.

Whether you are rendezvousing with family or friends, using your home as a part-way-to-your-retreat location has many advantages. Not only is your home easy to find by friends and family alike, but it also gives you the opportunity to grab extra gear or supplies before you head off to your safe-haven.

Rural areas can still be a problem: Unless very distant from a city, rural areas will not be without problems, either. Roaming livestock and cultivated fields which have food crops planted or already growing, are tempting targets for anyone seeking food. Do some sleuthing to learn about the crime rate and criminal activities in the area, the reputation of the community and other potential problems, before you make your decision.

Demographics: The characteristics of the human population of the area is significant, too. If the region has features such as a population that is nearly balanced between men and women, a high percentage of the children living in two-parent families, high school educated adults (higher education is irrelevant for the purpose of this evaluation), substantial church attendance, high employment, low crime rates, and other features you deem to be relevant, these may indicate a community that will be more stable during hard times.

In the United States, this information is available free of charge from the Census Bureau (on the Internet, visit: factfinder.census.gov). In other countries, similar information is generally available and perhaps even more current. If you are thinking about settling in another country, be sure to check-out the CIA's

World Fact Book. This free publication of the U.S. Central Intelligence Agency can be found on the Internet by visiting: www.cia.gov/library/publications/the-world-factbook/.

Sites in low-income rural areas: Areas populated by poor people are not inherently a bad choice, as long as the population is mostly hard working and not plagued with an attitude of entitlement. In fact, they might be the best. Poor people know how to be poor.

They know how to go without, can be very resourceful, and the rural poor know how to repair things. Importantly, they often have extensive vegetable gardens, and, because they can't afford to hire help, they often have many self-sufficiency skills.

Salt-of-the-earth people make great neighbors in a grid-down situation, especially if the community is spiritually vibrant. Visit local churches to learn about the area, its people, and to take the spiritual temperature of the community.

Invasion of city gangs: Even when gasoline is in short supply, gangs will still find a way to reach semi-rural areas and "claim" new turf. Even a well-armed family of farmers or ranchers will be unable to defend their home from these marauders. Homesteads located near cities, or close to highways, will be ripe for appropriation.

Community **is essential** for sharing the labor load, for acquiring the necessary skills needed for sustainability, and for defense.

The Best Safe-Haven "Community" Option: IC / ICE

If a more distant rural farm or ranch has suitable terrain, and its own source of water and other needed features, it might be an okay choice. If it is well positioned, away from main roads and highways which city dwellers will use to flee the city, it might be a great choice. It has the potential to become the location of an *Intentional Community (IC)* or a *Intentional Community Enterprise (ICE)* safe-haven. These structures provide the best and most sustainable solution for both long-term sustainability and safety.

If you can't afford to purchase such a property, don't despair. This can be a win-win for the landowner in addition to the IC/ICE members. Unlike the "IC" structure which is largely based on existing relationships, the "IC *Enterprise*" (ICE) is a commercial endeavor, but both utilize a similar operational structure.

With both the IC and ICE planned communities, the landowner gets the benefits of a support community for defense, additional labor, and increased sustainability. At the same time, the other community members get the benefit of a safe place to retreat, where they can wait out the emergency situation, and flourish while they wait.

> For more on the different community models which work for safe-haven retreats, see Book-4 in this series.

On a practical level, even a farm or ranch which has operated for many years and already has a loyal and well-armed staff, its resident population will generally be insufficient for both defense and the work required for independent living. No matter how self-sufficient they think they are, they will probably not be able to sustain themselves during a protracted grid-down situation.

Short term, it may not be a problem. Maybe. But long term, the landowner will need to either develop their own IC or ICE, or welcome one into their midst. Preferably, this will be accomplished well in advance of an emergency incident so organizers can be more selective, but after-the-fact is better than nothing.

Though a large farm or ranch may have on-hand, sufficient family and staff members to thwart the efforts of a poorly trained group of marauding attackers, it will likely not possess the right mix of skills and resources for long-term defense and sustainability. Thankfully, motivated landowners can utilize their property, facilities, and equipment as the nucleus for establishing an IC or ICE.

Though an independent organizer may not be required, most landowners will want to develop their community in partnership with an organizer who is already looking for an appropriate site. The property owner keeps doing what they do best, and the organizer recruits suitable participants and develops the community. It's a strategic alliance.

In any case, unlike raw land, an established farm or ranch can be quickly converted into an Intentional Community. Unless you have buckets of money to pour into the effort, an existing agricultural hub provides a much faster, and ultimately less expensive, implementation solution.

If the landowner is willing to cede some control over his land to facilitate the creation of a mutually beneficial community, a symbiotic partnership between the landowner and the Intentional Community (IC) can work well for both parties. But regardless of the contractual details, to be successful, this needs to be considered an equal partnership; a cooperative, a collaborative effort that is mutually beneficial.

Whatever structure is used, documentation is necessary. At the very least, a Letter of Understanding accompanying an Operating Plan can specify the duration of the agreement, roles, responsibilities, remedies, and other details.

Clarity is paramount to avoid future problems, especially those which will arise during high-stress periods. You don't want to get bogged down in details, but clarity and structure will eliminate many future problems.

It is important for the landowner, *and their family*, to perceive the IC members as leaseholders, not squatters or interlopers. At the very least, the details of this relationship, including rights, responsibilities, and remedies, must be spelled out before the community is established. This is not so much an issue of protecting interests in a lawsuit, it's to ensure that everyone understands roles, rights, expectations, and agrees to both a path for problem-solving and binding arbitration.

Reality Check

There isn't a perfect location. The best you should hope for is a safe-haven retreat location that works for you and your situation.

Once selected, don't relocate from an established IC or ICE absent a compelling reason. Relational and other problems will develop wherever you go. Just as in a family, it's often better to deal with this head-on but with grace, patience, and forgiveness, rather than float from one 'marriage' to another, looking for the always-elusive 'perfect' community.

Most of us will not be able to find and secure the use of a perfect retreat location, either. Compromises will, therefore, be required since it is of paramount importance to establish a safe-haven without undue delay. Whether you live in a city, a suburban community, or a rural village, in an emergency situation you need to be able to bug-out "to" a safer place, not just flee "from" the looming dangers of your own area.

If you don't readily find a 'perfect' location, at least identify a better-than-nothing temporary location, but keep in mind that it is temporary. Don't invest a lot of time and money in fixed, non-portable infrastructure.

Basic Site Selection Criteria: These are our recommendations, but your situation may dictate different criteria.

Both permanent and temporary locations will ideally be at least 150 miles from a major population center, and accessed by travel on a low-traffic volume country road that is at least a dozen miles from a major freeway and 20 miles from a public evacuation route.

If your safe-haven is more than 200 miles from your home and workplace, you may need more fuel than what is in your car to reach it. If the gas stations aren't open, or if your bug-out location is further away, you will need to have the ability to refuel.

Carrying extra gas is not necessarily a problem, but it is something you will need to incorporate into your inventory of supplies that you will be transporting. Extra fuel is heavy and space consuming, but it is something you will need to carry in your vehicle along with your other supplies. This is yet another reason why most of your supplies need to be stockpiled at your safe-haven, rather than kept at your home or in a storage locker. (For more on transporting fuel, see Chapter-22.)

You also need to ask yourself how often your gas tank is less than half full, or nearly empty? The further away from your retreat location, the more fuel you will need to stockpile at your home or rendezvous site. Worth noting, this assumes that you will be able to get to that fuel before you need to flee from the city.

Additionally, it will take more driving time to get to a distant retreat location, which means an extended period of vulnerability during travel and roadway conditions that you can't control. Look at what happened to 'Joe' in David Crawford's short story, "PREPARED: Ready to Roll – The Bug Out," which is included at the beginning of Book-1 in this series. How well did that work out for him?

Conversely, the downside of a closer retreat location (<150 miles) is that it will not give you as much space between your retreat location and a burning out-of-control city. Nor, the marauding gangs who will pillage the region in the aftermath, a la Hurricane Katrina. But, you aren't as vulnerable during your evacuation, either.

As explained earlier in this chapter, a physically fit person can walk 150-200 miles in four days if they stay focused, persevere, and keep walking even when they are tired.

If a constant, brisk pace is maintained, a healthy person can actually hike 150 miles in two long days. (Based on 16-hours of walking per day at slightly more than 4.5 MPH / 7 kph.) You may not be able to maintain this pace for more than a few days, but the point is, you can probably walk further than you think you can if you are motivated by danger and urgency.

> Your search for a safe-haven retreat site should not pivot on finding the perfect place. Rather, find the BEST site available to YOU and your group. Finding a 'perfect' location can be elusive. Don't let your quest for perfection obstruct timely implementation.

Greater distance from your city to your safe-haven vs. longer travel time. You pick the priority. Either way, it's a compromise. That's my point. With all locations, there are positive and negative aspects. Moreover, every geographic location will pose additional problems.

As mentioned in the earlier chapter, the concept of bugging-out "To" vs. escape "From" a location, is important to keep in mind. Even if you prepare a safe-haven retreat site, you may not be able to get to it, at least not right away. You need a Plan-B destination.

Wherever you bug-out to, remember that at the very least, the location needs to be *20+ miles away from the routes traveled by the displaced crowds who are fleeing the danger zone.*

Invisibility: Your best security asset may not be the result of building elaborate fortifications or forming a well-armed and a tactically trained security team. Your best security asset may be *invisibility*.

Pick a location that is on a light-duty road. Find a site that is at least several miles from a rural highway, and away from primary country roads. Pick your spot well, so that it is not easily discovered by wandering travelers.

Especially important is to avoid selecting a retreat site that might be stumbled upon by frustrated travelers who have exited a clogged highway or evacuation route. Whether they are seeking a detour path or a place to squat, evacuees often create a crime wave.

Displaced people routinely steal gasoline and vehicles, pilfer food from gardens, burglarize homes and storage buildings, kill animal life, damage fences and property, ignite wildland fires due to poor campfire management, contaminate water supplies, and they often exhibit dangerous, erratic behaviors and engage in predatory violence. It's not unusual for them to bring disease, too.

Whether their impact is major or minor, you don't want to be near such a crowd. It's simply too risky.

The Topography of Your Site: In addition to location, topographic features can be a substantial asset or a detriment. Since invisibility and limiting access provide a significant strategic advantage, land features such as dense trees and undergrowth around the perimeter, hills and valleys, or a body of water, cannot only be beautiful, these features can make your safe-haven less noticeable, attack more difficult and defense easier. Conversely, the lack of such features will make your site more vulnerable.

Just like in Medieval times, certain land features and challenging terrain can be beneficial for security. Cliffs and uphill approaches, lack of ancillary roads, limited access, and driveways and structures hidden by hills, rocks or foliage, can make a location safer from both ne'er-do-well wanderers as well as from marauding gangs of thieves.

Equally important is your ability to observe the approach of people who are entering your domain on foot, as well as those who are driving on nearby access roads or approaching via off-road paths. You want to have early warning of threats, while at the same time denying visibility, and making access more difficult for both potential adversaries and panhandlers alike.

If you are compassionate and want to help the unfortunate, do so from an off-site location such as a church or food bank. Your own property should remain unseen and your resources unknown.

Even if you think you'll only need the safe-haven for a few weeks or months, circumstances may change. You may need to be there much longer, so plan for it.

If retreat buildings or outbuildings are visible from the road, efforts must be made to make them look ramshackle and unpromising to marauders. Since the community probably won't have the time and money to turn the location into an impenetrable fortress, its best to make the place look like it's not worth the effort to plunder. At the very least, the site needs to look far less desirable than surrounding properties. This is true even if your safe-haven is rural and remote.

The best safe-haven location will not only be somewhat remote, but it will also have arable soil for planting food, a year-round source of water, and will have land features which aid in its defense. These four attributes are essential. Even if you are not concerned about long-term sustainability, pick a location which is conducive to it.

Your Safe-Haven as a Vacation Property: If your safe-haven is far from the people and pressures of city life, is suitable for cultivation (or you bring in planting soil), has favorable sun exposure and rainfall, has a reliable and uninterruptable source of water and is made attractive by its terrain or setting, then you have a winning combination.

A location such as this can not only serve as a safe-haven during your time of need, it can also be a vacation property that you, your family and friends will enjoy during the good times. It can be a legacy that you hand down to your children.

As you look for a place to establish your safe-haven, it's worth remembering that when you combine desirable security attributes, sustainability features, and pleasant vacation property attributes, you have found a prime location. It is a place worthy of the investment of your time and money.

Beyond your need for a safe-haven, such a property can also be a sound financial investment. It can be a threefold asset.

Your safe-haven needn't be only an "emergency" retreat location. Chosen well, it can be a financial *and* relationship-building asset, too.

Moreover, if your mindset and the outlook of your family and friends is that it is a fun place to visit, you will likely get more help, and cooperative attitudes, when it comes to spending time and money developing the site.

Cooperation and Community: Compromises in both security and sustainability will generally be necessary when looking for a safe-haven site, as well as in the selection of the individuals who will bring the diverse skills needed to form an Intentional Community (IC). Regardless of community structure, every adult and older teen must have an attitude of cooperation and community spirit.

Furthermore, each person needs to feel like they are part of the security team, whether they are an official member of it or not. And, each member must see themselves as an active participant in the broader relationship-based community, as well. Some individuals will be outgoing, while others will be shy by nature, but all must think of the Community as *their* team; *their family*. Healthy IC communities are highly relational.

Discernment in knowing when to compromise, the willingness to get dirty and work hard at manual labor, a disposition geared toward helping others, being adaptable with a problem-solving orientation, and a commitment to unity and collegial life, are required character traits for building a successful community. Everyone needs to embody a commitment to unity and friendly cooperation.

If you are the IC founder and this doesn't describe your personality, work on developing these attributes. In the meantime, recruit a winsome community leader, and team members, who personify these characteristics.

If you are considering joining an IC, keep these factors in mind, and remember that those who have done the work to establish the safe-haven deserve your enthusiastic appreciation and support. If you can't provide this, you're not ready to join.

If you have the opportunity to join an established community, you need to be discerning. Before enrolling, validate that the community has a satisfactory physical location and that the community structure and members are compatible with you and your needs.

You are not signing up for a condo association. It's more like adoption into a family. Or, like being inducted into a club you've wanted to join, or a semi-pro sports team you've always admired.

As such, you need to get to know your teammates, learn to work together cooperatively, and eagerly accept the responsibilities which come with being part of the team. And as a team player, you must also develop a healthy pride in association with both the community project itself and with your fellow team members.

As a strategic decision, you will probably choose to avoid telling clueless friends about this community affiliation. Yet, this should be a strategic decision; not one which reflects a lack of pride.

Your association with a safe-haven community shouldn't be just about you and meeting your needs. That's part of it, of course. But an IC safe-haven should be regarded as a co-op that is a mutually beneficial asset for you and your entire team.

Therefore, you need to be committed to developing relationships in your community, and to expanding your personal skills, particularly those which will benefit the community. And, committed to helping others develop their community-building skills and relationships. You need to be oriented to becoming increasingly self-reliant, and to be increasingly community minded.

It's about helping build a flourishing community. It's not just about solving your need for a personal retreat location.

A spirit of cooperation, a commitment to unity, mutual respect, support, and relational health, all packaged in patience and an attitude of forgiveness. This is the foundational commitment. Organizers and members alike need to exhibit these virtues.

What is the optimal size of an Intentional Community?

There is no universal answer to the question of how many people it takes to maintain a successful safe-haven retreat community. Notwithstanding, at a bare minimum, you will need at least a dozen able-bodied adults for an emergency situation which lasts more than a week or two. If young children, elderly or infirm people are part of the community, additional adults will be required.

When evaluating a property as a potential safe-haven for security, functional invisibility is absolutely necessary if the community is smaller than 80 adult defenders. There is no reliable shortcut.

The 12/60 Rule: A dozen adults is the minimum number of people required for a small, invisible community. This is especially true if you will be dealing with an emergency situation that lasts for 1-12 months. Of course, this assumes that the group has also stockpiled a year's supply of water and food, has adequate shelter, and sufficient energy and other supplies for a full year.

However, 60+ well-selected adults are generally needed for sustainability. To achieve physical security, and to assemble a group of people which has the diverse skills required for long-term viability, 60 well-selected adults seems to be the minimum requirement.

This is the same as what developed for wagon trains, and also by pioneer communities in the U.S. In our modern era, this has been validated by the kibbutz communities in Israel which strive for agricultural self-sufficiency and safety.

So, 12-adults are needed to maintain safety during short-term emergency situations, and a minimum of 60-adults is necessary if the environment is dangerous, or if the community will be operational for a longer period of time. Again, the 12/60 rule relates to minimums.

When I lived in Guatemala during that country's civil war, I observed the same 12/60 outcomes. In that environment, a squad of 12 armed adults was the minimum needed for safe travel in rural areas. And, communities which survived the ravages of guerilla warfare seemed to always consist of at least 60-adults. If the community was isolated, or the terrain was not helpful to its defense, the communities needed to be larger.

Unfortunately, most people will not heed this advice. Most will establish a safe-haven which consists of extended family and a few friends. If you fall into this category, at the very least, get to know your neighbors and determine which are honest and trustworthy, and learn about their skills, vocation, and hobbies.

Once you know who you can trust, formally develop a 'Community Watch' with them, and establish a 2-way radio communication network. It's fine to use telephones when they work, but don't depend on third-party electronics.

In addition to establishing a mutual-aid agreement consisting of a promise to help each other in an emergency, work at developing relationships with them, too. Make it a habit to help each other with the needs of daily living.

This "small" IC approach does not equal the benefits of a standard Intentional Community. Nevertheless, it is far superior to trying to do it on your own as an isolated, insular, small group.

No matter how you decide to move forward, understand that, on average and over time, the typical size of a successful Intentional Community (IC) is 60-120 motivated adults. For an Intentional Community Enterprise (ICE) which also has a service or entrepreneurial component, such as growing food for barter or to sell in a farmers market, or to provide regional medical services, the number is larger.

If your group is small, don't rush to populate it. Wait for the right people. In the mean time, find ways to compensate. Don't just ignore the time-tested experience of those who have done this before. "Safe-haven" may be our contemporary name for a rural, independent, safe community, but the concept is as old as civilization.

Whether we look at the pioneer communities of the Wild West, the rural kibbutz communities of Israel, or the recent civil war period of Guatemala, the group-size numbers seem to be the same. Long-term survivability requires an intentional community, and our community needs to be big enough to provide for its own defense, and diverse enough to include the various skills needed for healthy, independent living.

Your situation may be different, especially if your IC community is populated with experienced off-grid people. However, don't be quick to settle on a smaller size without justification.

Irrespective of the size of your safe-haven community, avoiding being a target is a more feasible approach to security than staffing-up to build a non-trivial security force. Invisibility is not the only mechanism to accomplish this, but it may be the best. Notwithstanding, a trained well-armed security force is still necessary.

Security Staffing: In my experience, a bare-bones but credible security force that is well-armed and has 2-way radios and other force multipliers, still needs to have a minimum of three people on duty, 24-hours each day, seven days each week. This provides an absolute minimum level of coverage, yet it still equates to a relatively large security team.

The efficient use of scouts and strategically located observation posts can be useful, as can electronic force multipliers. But these do not take the place of vigilant security patrols, particularly at night.

If each member of the security team works a 6-hour shift and has one day off each week to relax, a necessity for long-term effectiveness, then 24 security personnel will be needed to staff the smallest-size security team. Moreover, to maintain focus and an attentive edge, the members of the team cannot be assigned much in the way of other community duties.

A smaller security team, or one whose members have other responsibilities they perceive to be a higher priority, or which drains mindshare or increases fatigue as a result of physical labor, is dangerous. Security needs to be the first priority for those who are part of a security team. Other, additional assignments, need to be of secondary importance.

Relegating security, or participation with the security team as a lower priority duty is dangerous. Yes, maintaining water, food, shelter, and community health are all "top" priority endeavors, too. Notwithstanding, any community which might fall victim to violence needs to make security its highest priority. Similarly, any community which faces the rapid spread of disease or an epidemic, or dangerous weather extremes, needs to make that risk its top priority.

Serious Need = *High* Priority. Critical Risk = *Top* Priority. If a community is overrun by violent criminals or ravaged by a deadly epidemic, other "high" priorities will quickly become almost irrelevant. Therefore, all "high" priorities need to be ranked based on both short-term and long-term threat levels, and the risks they represent for community survival.

Of course, only one endeavor can truly be the top priority, but others can still be critically important. If priorities conflict, the leadership team must step up and make hard decisions, but that does not necessarily mean that other critical risks and high priorities must be ignored. It just means a reallocation of staff, extending the work day, or doubling up on duties.

When it comes to site security and susceptibility to epidemics, a perimeter that has gaps, or which can be breached even by a single person, can result in irreparable and immediate harm. Though compromises in the other "high" priority endeavors can be damaging, these failures are usually correctable, less urgent, and not as catastrophic. Whereas strong security, maintained 24-hours a day and 7-days a week, is typically at the heart of community well-being.

When it's not possible to staff a standard security team: Utilization of force multipliers, such as motion detectors and slaved video security cameras, can perhaps justify a size reduction of a security team short-term, but electronics cannot be relied upon as even a semi-permanent solution. Electronics fail. Batteries die. When there is an overreliance on technology, security becomes an illusion.

Therefore, a robust security operation is necessary even when an unrelated crisis has become paramount. During that period, if a security team only consist of part-time participants under the leadership of 2-3 experienced people, it still needs to be fully operational, 24-hours each day, 7-days each week.

If this reduced staffing is normal, as in a small-community safehaven, these part-timers need to take their security role very seriously. They had better be trained, armed, and keep their weapon and extra ammunition with them at all times, no matter what they are doing.

Still, the best security plan during a period of crisis, as well as during regular times, is to avoid the need to pull a gun's trigger. When site security is well-designed and properly implemented, aggressors will often pass you by because they didn't see you, or they have concluded that their success is unlikely. If they do see a community member, they also need to note that he/she is armed, looks competent, has the ability to summon help quickly, and is vigilant.

Ideally, if an opposing force does notice your community, they will conclude that it is not worth the bother, or the risk, to attack. But better yet is for them to not see your enclave at all. Remember, invisibility is the best defense, so design it into your community.

Do what you can to increase your safe-haven community's invisibility, and then do what you can to make it look like it is an undesirable target. At the same time, prepare physical defenses. Then equip every able-bodied mentally stable adult to fight as a unit to protect your safe-haven. If prevention fails, be ready to fight.

Security isn't the only priority: Of course, in addition to security operations, your community will also need to have people who cook meals, grow food, care for animals, prepare food for storage, perform maintenance and accomplish repairs, provide medical care, build and maintain systems for sanitation, potable water, irrigation, acquire energy, and to construct site improvements, as well as to teach children, provide child care for the young, etc. Altogether, this can quickly add up to a community of 80 people, so if you have less, each member must be cross trained.

If it is unrealistic to have 60-80 people in your community, you will still need to develop a team that has diverse practical skills; hopefully, multiple skills embodied in each individual. Plus, a location which makes some tasks easy, such as growing food or getting water.

There are different types of ICs, so select a model that works for you and your situation. The key attribute is being *intentional*. (There are various forms and structures for safe-haven communities. This topic is beyond the scope of this book, but is addressed in Book-4 of this *PREPARED: Ready to Roll* series.)

A safe-haven that is well-stocked with gear and adequately provisioned is still not ready for use until it is populated with an enthusiastic team; an intentional community. This group might include family, but ordinarily, it will not be limited to a single family.

It may be natural, and more comfortable, to limit participants in your safe-haven to your immediate family, but unless your family is large and possesses unusually diverse skills, this isn't adequate. For safety and sustainability, even a small encampment needs a broad assortment of skills, experience, and competencies.

Even a small safe-haven needs at least a dozen responsible adults who are trained to work together for security, and who also possess a variety of other needed skills. In addition to the "commune" or "village" model of a traditional Intentional Community (IC), this can also be accomplished using a rural neighborhood or "colony" model.

The *Colony* IC: In this alternative variation of an Intentional Community, participants live nearby each other in a rural area, but not together at one encampment. Leadership, therefore, becomes more difficult, and relationship-building and coordination must be even more *intentional.*

This neighborhood model of an Intentional Community is appropriately also referred to as a "Texas Ranger" community. In the early days (1823) of what later became an official State law enforcement agency, Rangers were not government employees. They were ordinary community members who worked full-time as farmers, ranchers, school teachers, doctors, and shopkeepers, who came together as a group of volunteers because they cared about their community.

These individuals were so committed to the welfare of their neighbors that they were willing to put their lives on the line. When needed, they fought to protect their neighbors from criminals, as well as from violent, marauding tribal gangs of Comanches, Tonkawas, and Karankawas.

Though these Rangers were fellow neighbors, they were still vetted before being accepted into service. Acceptance wasn't automatic.

In recognition of their service, they received a gift of land if they were not already property owners. They also received other gifts of appreciation from their neighbors, but remuneration was not the prime motivation of these servant-leaders.

When mobilized, Rangers dropped what they were doing to come to the aid of their neighbors. They risked their lives for their friends. For the Rangers, it was all about loving their community, loving their neighbors, and serving unmet needs during periods of danger.

Community Leadership: Needing structure to operate efficiently, Rangers elected officers annually to lead them, and to coordinate their activities. Today, this same leadership model is often used to govern Intentional Community safe-havens. Each landowner and leaseholder in the IC have a position on the Leadership Council

(1-adult per tract of land), which in turn elects three Commissioners who provide day-to-day leadership of the community.

However, those who risk their lives as members of the security team, elect their own security team Officers. Each adult member of the security team, property owner or not, has a place on the Leadership Council. And, the senior Officer of the security team, who also serves as the community "Sheriff," is always one of the three Commissioners.

As with the early Texas Rangers, the rural neighborhood "Colony" IC is based on community service, mutual aid, is barter-oriented and based on ability-to-pay, and the recognition that every hard-working community member has value, and is entitled to respect, assistance, and equal justice. It's a model that recognizes inter-dependence, and yet it accommodates greater privacy and independence, too.

Regardless of the IC model used, each type of Intentional Community has a similar foundation. One based on "loving your neighbor as yourself,"[8] and an operating philosophy based on personal responsibility and mutual aid.

Operationally, the IC rural neighborhood "Colony" model, is the most difficult type to develop and maintain. It only works if a fraternal sense of *community* can be established. Since members are separated by distance, they need to feel close as a result of shared relationships, shared core values, and the common goals which they hold in common. A church community with members who are individually committed to the precepts of the Bible is ideally suited for this purpose.

All Intentional Community participants must link arms, intentionally, and make a sincere commitment to each other and to the community's well-being. This is facilitated when the members understand and make three practical commitments to each other.

---

[8] Holy Bible, Galatians 5:14

The 3-Commitment "Triangle Pledge"

- When needed, I will work diligently, and do what is necessary to meet the needs of my community. I will maintain its safety and take an active role in providing essential community services.

- As a community member, I will endeavor to become cross-trained with others, so that together we can achieve and maintain community health. If a necessary skill-set is missing or inadequately met, I am willing to stretch myself, acquire new skills and accept additional responsibilities to satisfy that unmet community need.

- Since unity and relational health are such a high priority, I enthusiastically accept the obligations of being a part of this community. [For those with children] I will insist that my children exhibit a similar commitment in both attitude and action. I [we] willingly accept the requirements of community affiliation and will accept the decisions of the community's leaders according to our group's organizational documents.

Whether this pledge is used or another simple promise is developed, the individual members of an Intentional Community must have a deep commitment to each other; mutual aid, a willingness to help others, and a desire to strive for unity within the community. These attributes are necessary for defense and sustainability, and ongoing attitudes of divisiveness must be throttled early.

In practice, it is easiest to achieve unity when there is an underlying relational link, such as the spiritual bond developed through regular participation in the same community church, or a fraternal organization which the participants hold in high esteem. Notwithstanding, success comes when the affiliation is based on something deeper than proximity and need, something more analogous to kinship; a perceived sense of family, a Band of Brothers (and sisters).

> For additional information on safe-haven site selection, community development and administration, see Book-4 of this series.

Chapter 5

Maps, Routes, and Navigation

In an emergency situation, the shortest distance between two points may not be the best route to travel. Environmental factors, such as the effects of a storm and storm damage, traffic congestion, traffic signals not working, accidents and choke points created by bridges and tunnels, new dangers such as social unrest, lawlessness or the expansion of high-crime areas, may make a circuitous (and longer) route far more prudent.

Remember, a multitude of factors may make highway travel, subway, and commuter travel impossible. Therefore, you need a backup plan which includes alternate routes, and also alternative modes of transportation. And, you need paper maps, and a non-electronic compass, in case your battery-operated devices do not work.

What is your best route if you find yourself walking instead of riding? Identify alternate routes now. Freeway routes may be too dangerous for foot travel. Major thoroughfares may offer the shortest travel time by vehicle, but they may not be the fastest or safest choice in an emergency situation.

Importantly, your usual routes which utilize major roadways or freeways are often miles longer than a more direct route which can be used by those who are walking or riding a bike.

Keep in mind that railroad tracks and above ground subway tracks may be more direct but not included on maps. Tracks and power line right-of-way areas may be fine for walking, but these routes may be more tiring as your walking-stride may be adversely affected by railroad tie spacing, terrain, and plant growth.

In any case, factors such as these must be taken into account. It may seem like a bother, but when legal and possible, it is better to walk these routes in advance so that you know what to expect.

It is to your advantage to walk, or at least drive each alternative route as maps never provide all the details you need. An emergency situation is not the time to find that your selected route has become inaccessible due to road changes, construction, new security fences, or the emergence of unsafe neighborhoods.

Mark your maps with routing and relevant route details. After you have traveled each route, produce an updated set of maps for the GO-Bag belonging to each member of your group. Treat each map with "AquaSeal Map Seal" to protect it and make it more durable. At the very least, store each map in a separate Hefty Slider plastic bag.

Don't just select multiple evacuation routes, make the route selection process integral to developing a practical, real-world *Emergency Plan*.

Anyone who has been in combat is acquainted with the adage, *"No plan survives contact with the enemy."* And the saying, *"The plan is nothing, but planning is everything."* These military truisms, which emphasize the importance of adaptability, are valid for our personal emergency plans, as well. Awareness, and an orientation to problem-solving based on prior planning is necessary for timely decision making, prudent action, and resiliency.

Developing an emergency plan has enormous benefits. It provides advantages such as the ability to make strategic decisions unhampered by stress, it gives you time to do research, the opportunity to obtain expert advice, and to select and get buy-in from participants. Importantly, it gives you the chance to work on the plan together, and to obtain agreement on the details. By taking the time to develop a plan, many problems can be solved in advance.

Anticipate potential problems.
Identify solutions.
Build-in adaptability and resiliency.

Your *Emergency Plan* doesn't need to be an elaborate document. Bullet-point details that are discussed can be enough—especially if the concept of writing a plan is so daunting that you won't do it.

Every thinking person knows that an emergency plan is necessary. Unfortunately, the tyranny of the urgent often keeps us from completing tasks which are truly important.

So, start now; don't wait until you have the time to make an exhaustive or "wow" plan. It's far better to take a few minutes to outline a personal plan as soon as you read this chapter. Then tomorrow, get a collection of maps to evaluate and select which maps are best. Get a set for each member of your group.

A personal or family-and-friends plan needs to be simple yet precise, and at the same time, resilient and adaptable.

Adaptability needs to be built into your Plan. *If-Then* decision-making coupled with a description of the necessary action must be clear to each participant. (*If* I encounter this…, *Then* I will …)

For example, if your Plan includes what route your spouse should use to get home from work after an emergency, then it will be possible to search for them if they don't arrive home within a reasonable timeframe. Conversely, without knowledge of this most simple detail, a timely and effective search is probably impossible. Furthermore, any search effort may actually result in compounding your problems rather than solve them.

Making Alternate Plans (Plan-A, Plan-B, etc.)

When 'Plan-A' isn't possible, everyone needs to know when to switch to 'Plan-B.' Or, 'Plan-C.' Adaptability isn't just an attitude; it needs to be an attribute of your plan.

Take a few minutes now to make a list of the problems you will likely face, and add to this list over the next few days.

Make sure your plan addresses each potential problem that has serious ramifications. A quick-and-dirty plan is better than nothing. A basic plan can be developed using a simple outline format, with bullet-point details. In its most basic form, a written Plan can consist of a bullet-point list of potential problems that might be encountered, followed by the action-steps which relate to that particular scenario.

Maps

For evacuation route planning, the use of Google Maps or a similar, free online mapping program is a good place to start. Many of these offer the quickest driving, biking, and walking routes, along with second- and third-choice alternative routes. They even include time estimates for each. This computer-based information is helpful, but it is only a place to start.

The next step is to determine if your local government has established evacuation routes for your community. If so, review them closely as these maps have probably been developed after extensive research on traffic patterns and flow, land features, and elevations (flooding). This information can save you a lot of time and research, so be sure to build on the work of your community's Emergency Management Planning Department, and the work of national agencies such as the FEMA (Federal Emergency Management Agency: www.fema.gov) rather than starting from scratch.

Even with these tools, at the very least you will need to transfer this information onto your own paper maps. The maps you download from sites like Google Maps, as well as government emergency management and planning departments, do not contain sufficient detail.

There are at least three types of maps that you will want to buy:

1. Regional highway map,

2. Local street maps for each municipality you may need to traverse, and

3. Detailed topographic maps, such as those produced by U.S. Geological Survey (www.usgs.gov) or the equivalent in the country where you are living or will be traveling.

The regional highway map should help you orient yourself and others to an illustrated summary of your entire evacuation route, including the locations of towns, rivers, and various hazards and helps. Whether contained in a map book or a large foldable paper map, this will help you orient yourself and others to the big picture.

Second, you will need detailed street maps for any metropolitan area you may need to traverse. You will need to include a detailed roadmap for any community you might find yourself in when your journey starts, as well any town that may need to be crossed, or detoured through, as you make your way to safety.

It's easy to develop a primary route, but rarely does it go according to plan, especially in an emergency situation. These maps can help you adapt.

Lastly, and often forgotten, is the need for detailed topographic maps. Most of us are so conditioned to driving on the main roadways that we forget that in an emergency, it may be necessary to utilize alternate routes, including dirt roads, paths, and even make your own trail across the rural terrain. A topographic map shows land features and elevations, trails, footbridges, and in the countryside, even buildings. These detailed maps can save time and increase safety.

Map Source: Though there are many companies which produce topographic maps, the best ones usually come from the least expensive source, the U.S. Government. The USGS (United States Geological Survey – www.usgs.gov) creates maps which are used by federal, state, and local governments, and also the U.S. military. Their 'Map Locator and Downloader' software is available free of charge, and high-resolution USGS topographic and satellite maps can be downloaded for free from their website, as well.

However, for most of us it's easier to identify the maps we need on the USGS website, and then order paper maps directly from the USGS online store. In addition to maps of the United States, USGS has topographic maps for other parts of the world.

Which Topo Maps are Best? For selecting and navigating evacuation routes, high detail topographic (topo) maps, or combination maps which overlay topographic lines on top of a satellite image.

Maps which utilize the "**7.5-minute**" scale provide high-detail terrain information. On these maps, 1-inch (2.5 cm) equates to 2,000 ft. of distance (approximately 1/3 mile or .6 km).

Whereas a "**15-minute**" topo map packs a similar amount of detail in half the space (½ inch / 1.3 cm) of space. With this in mind, for complicated or complex terrain, a 7.5-minute map is usually the best choice. Whereas for nearly featureless areas such as a prairie or desert where there is little change in elevation and few roads, a 15-minute map is often adequate.

If you have never used a topographic map, spend a little time with a tutorial before you buy your maps. It's not complex, but a few minutes spent educating yourself will accelerate your progress.

In addition to your maps, you will need a decent non-electronic compass, a simple plastic protractor that also has a straight edge, and a pencil with an eraser. After you have learned how to use these tools, keep them in your GO-Bag.

Selecting a Compass

The U.S. Military '3H' Lensatic compass with tritium dial, made in the United States or Japan by Cammenga, Inc., is what the soldiers of many countries use for navigation. However, a less expensive but still quality compass is a viable option. A basic compass, such as the SUUNTO A-30 NH USGS Compass, is still an excellent choice and has added features for using USGS topographic maps.

Both the 3H Military Compass and the far less expensive compasses made by quality manufacturers such as SUUNTO, can be found online and in sporting goods stores which cater to serious backpackers. Expect to pay $25+ for a decent compass.

Don't store or use your compass near anything magnetic, such as a radio or speaker. To obtain accurate readings, don't use your compass inside a vehicle or near metal objects, either, as they can disrupt the magnetic needle.

If you are inexperienced with map reading or compass use, buy an illustrated short book such as, "Be Expert with Map and Compass: The Complete Orienteering Handbook" by Bjorn Kjellstrom and Carina Elgin. Or, search online for a free PDF copy of the U.S. military training Field Manual, "Map Reading and Land Navigation, FM 3-25.26."

Note on Maps and Map Software

Maps created by the U.S. government can be freely duplicated, so there are many commercial printers who adapt these maps and use them in their software and paper-map products. These are usually more expensive than buying directly from USGS, but they do occasionally include extra features. However, these "enhancements" may not be worth the added cost. Importantly, with these commercial map products, it is often difficult to verify that it is the most recent version of the government-produced map.

If you elect to print maps from software using your own printer, use a weatherproof tear-resistant synthetic paper, such as the product made by Casanova's (CasanovasAdventures.com).

Practice:

Take the time needed to practice with the maps and compass you select. If you have children, consider making a game out of it, so that you can teach them how to use these non-electronic tools.

Search the Internet using the term "geocaching" to find game ideas. Though most of the existing geocaching websites are designed for participants who are using electronic GPS hardware, the same principles can be used to develop your own treasure hunting game for your family and friends.

Footnotes for this chapter:

1. Map Cases and Map Seal

A map case may seem like an unnecessary item but is nevertheless worth considering since paper maps are easily damaged by use, as well as exposure to rain. At the very least, use a large Hefty Slider bag to store your maps in your GO-Bag, and also include an additional extra-large Slider bag to use for the map you will be actively using.

The use of a map case or an extra-large clear plastic Hefty Slider bag will help protect the map you are using from moisture and tearing the paper. Fold the map to match the interior size of the case or Slider bag, and only remove the paper map from the bag to refold it.

For important maps, in addition to using a map case or a clear plastic bag for protection, paint the map front and back with AquaSeal (or similar product) to waterproof the paper and make it tear resistant. The product "Map Seal," made by AquaSeal, is the most popular product for this purpose. It can be found online and through marine product stores, and also at retailers who serve the backpacking community.

2. Compass examples used in this chapter:

Cammenga 3H Military Compass

Though more expensive, a military compass as utilized by the U.S. military (military specification mil-prf-10436n) is a durable and reliable choice. The selection of a military-style compass will be additionally beneficial if you plan to use military training materials such as the Field Manual mentioned on the prior page. Unlike the many knock-off versions of this style of compass, a true military compass is extremely durable, waterproof, and has tritium microlights, an illumination source that does not require batteries.

SUUNTO A-30

Products such as this SUUNTO A-30 model are designed for serious backpacking, so these are also excellent options. Though not as durable or feature-packed as a military compass, they have the advantage of being lighter in weight and less expensive. The SUUNTO line of compasses are accurate and reasonably durable, features which are not found on many lower-cost compasses. They are also perfect for use with the "Orienteering Handbook" mentioned earlier in this chapter. (Avoid models that require a battery.)

For additional details on products, links to manufacturer's websites, and other details which are periodically updated to keep them current, visit the author's website. On the "Resources" page, look for "Book 2 – Supplemental Information."

www.SigSwanstrom.com

Chapter 6

Transportation for Evacuation

Our modern world takes ease of transportation for granted. These expectations will be forced to change once we are hit by a widespread disaster or emergency situation.

Since roadways become clogged and impassable during even a relatively minor storm, the question we all need to consider is, "What transportation disruptions can I expect when a disaster in my area is severe, or even monumental in scope?"

What will you do if your usual transportation method is no longer available to you? If you are at work and your kids are at school, how will you get together? What about your spouse or friends? How will you all get home? How will you get to your safe-haven evacuation location?

When planning for an emergency, assumptions are the enemy of success. If we are to avoid unnecessary problems, we must question all of our regular routines and expectations, and test them for adaptability.

For example, we can't assume that we will be able to drive home, or that we will be able to pick up our children from school. Nor can we expect that we will be able to use our car to evacuate to a safer place. We need backup plans.

If you live in an urban or suburban area and your government is well run, they will have an emergency transportation plan. It probably involves using city buses, school buses, reconfiguring mass transit, and changing certain highways into one-way thoroughfares to increase traffic flow out of the city. All of this is very helpful. If you fail to get out in time, in advance of the general population, you may not have another choice but to use these government-provided services.

Sounds okay, right? Maybe not.

The more profound question which comes with this assistance is: *"Where will their route take me?"* The answer, *"Probably not where you want to go."* And equally important, *"Perhaps not to the location of your family and friends."*

This is another reason why it is so important to ask more penetrating questions. And, why it is so vital to get-out-early, at the first sign of trouble.

Still, even if you are prepared to get out at the first indication of trouble, you still need to have transportation backup plans. Some emergency situations, such as a hacker attack on the power grid, an EMP detonation, or even a naturally occurring solar flare, can instantly turn-off traffic signals, stop commuter trains, and render vehicles inoperable.

When a grid-down situation like these occurs, everyone will feel panicky, tempers will flare, mobile phones won't work, or the circuits will be clogged, and emergency services like police and fire will be without adequate communication. Therefore, you will need to act quickly.

You need to be self-reliant. If you find yourself alone or with clueless colleagues, you need to seize the initiative even if you aren't ordinarily a leader. You need to get out of the high-danger zone. Now. ASAP.

Quick, decisive action is even more urgent if you are in an urban or suburban population center. For this evacuation to go smoothly, you need to get out as fast as possible, before others awaken to the same need.

This is a genuine concern even if you don't work in a major city, and even if you don't live in an urban area. If you ever visit such a place, you need to have a plan to get out. Disasters don't wait to happen until you are on your home turf.

For commuters and city dwellers: If you commute to work in an American city, unlike Europe, the typical U.S. commuter travels 15 miles (24 km) between their home and job, and 1 in 10 commutes more than 30-miles (48 km). If you fit into the 10+ mile category, you need to give particular attention to your transportation needs since driving, and public transit, may not be viable during an emergency.

The rule of thumb is that if you are in good health and reasonably fit, and you have a commute distance greater than 10 miles (16 km), you need to give extra attention to emergency transportation planning. This is because in an *urban setting*, during a crisis, even walkers with decent shoes and in reasonably good health, cannot travel nearly as far; often only 10 miles in 4 hours. And, because after approximately 4-hours following the onset of an acute emergency, or if darkness comes before getting home, travel becomes more dangerous.

Of course, we are citing averages here, and lessons learned from practical experiences. Your situation may be different. Still, these statistics provide an important point of reference, and this topic is one we all need to consider.

Timing: Unfortunately, if the emergency situation is significant in scope or grave, you may have less time. You may not have 4-hours. Plus, you not only need to think about how to get home from work, but you may also find that you need to find a missing friend or family member. Furthermore, you may not only need to get home, but you may also need to rapidly get out of the area and get to your safe-haven retreat location.

For all three of these transportation needs, you will want to explore your options for alternative transportation. We need to do this now, in advance of the need.

In the U.S., coast-to-coast walking clubs expect to be able to walk across the country in 280 days (although they usually plan a 12-month trek to accommodate rest periods). These seasoned walkers average 15-20 miles per day, day after day, but the distance they travel during a particular 24-hour period depends on terrain and weather.

So, though you may not be excited by the prospect of walking 50, or even 250 miles (80-400 km) to get to a safe-haven retreat location, it is something you can probably accomplish. It may not be pleasant. It may not be fast. But for most people, it is doable. If truly necessary, it can be accomplished.

The Central Problem: Unfortunately, the chief problem isn't the distance we need to travel. It's being able to carry enough water, food, shelter, and to make the trek safely. During an emergency, necessities may not be available along the way. So, you need to bring them along. This is the limiting factor. For most people, the daunting problem isn't the long walk, it is being able to make the trek during turbulent times when the world has been turned upside-down. And, if the weather is adverse, finding adequate shelter along the way.

If you live in an urban or suburban area, you need to develop an alternative travel plan that will get you home from work—and other places you frequent—in under four hours. Within the timeframe of an additional two hours, you and your group of traveling companions, need to be out of the urban sprawl. That's six hours total. Maximum. That's my team's recommendation.

If this isn't practical for you, then at the very least, don't doddle. Don't waste a minute of time. Get going. This means you need to decide to evacuate long before you are told to do so.

For me, personally, I consider 6-hours to be WAY too long. Way too long!

My wife and I have organized our family life so that we can evacuate and be out-of-town in under an hour. That's our self-imposed deadline. Importantly, we've done it more than once, so we know it's a reasonable goal.

Your goal may need to be different. But regardless of where you choose to live and work, in addition to being oriented to bugging out early, and in addition to developing alternative travel *routes*, be sure to consider alternative travel *methods*, too.

Alternate Modes of Transportation: Your usual travel method may be unavailable, so don't count on using it. Develop a plan which includes several alternative modes of transportation. Walk if you must, but investigate other, more rapid transportation options now, in advance of the need.

Your mode of transportation needn't be exotic or expensive. If weather conditions are conducive to riding a bicycle, this mundane conveyance is a better option than walking. Even if your bike gets stolen from you before you get out of town, at least you had the advantage of greater speed for part of your journey.

To make the trek on foot should be your plan of last resort. Nevertheless, in your car or at work, store a pair of hiking socks and durable walking shoes or boots which provide stability, traction, and support. In other words, be prepared to walk, but make it your last option.

Why is walking a problem? Because unless the distance you need to travel is relatively short, walking isn't fast enough. And, because in most circumstances, unless you are incredibly stealthy and vigilant, foot-travel makes you more vulnerable to robbery, assault, and worse.

If you are fleeing from a weather problem, such as a hurricane or flood, an extended time of walking may subject you to additional storm-related problems. New hazards develop as weather decays.

This vulnerability may be lessened by walking with a group of people. Nonetheless, foot travel can still be risky.

If you are physically able, walking should certainly be one of your alternate modes. In some circumstances, it will be your best option. But generally, speed is an essential element for safe evacuation, and walking may not provide adequate speed.

This is true for making a speedy decision to evacuate. And, your transportation speed as you leave the area.

The Need for Speed: Speed is a fundamental element of defense for avoiding weather-induced problems, encounters which can range from unsavory harassment and simple theft to more serious assaults which include physical harm. Or, speed can be fundamental to timely escape from a danger zone that is becoming increasingly chaotic.

When I moved from the U.S. to a new job in Central America, I needed a vehicle for getting around. Since I couldn't find a suitable vehicle in-country, I decided to buy a Jeep in the United States and drive it the 1,800 miles to Guatemala. To ship the vehicle would have taken weeks that I didn't have, so I decided to make the road trip.

The trek would require 37-hours of driving to get from my cousin's house in Dallas, Texas, through Mexico, down the Pan-American Highway, into Guatemala and then to Guatemala City. That's 3-4 long days of driving and a few nights in motels along the way. No problem.

Unfortunately, it wasn't as easy as it was supposed to be. Along the way, we encountered various challenges. Flood damage from a recent storm, combined with our highway route, was a veritable Wild West of lawlessness; individual thieves, marauding gangs of criminals, drug cartels, political upheaval and social unrest, rogue police and military units, and guerrilla soldiers.

Even if we were able to avoid robbery and carjacking, we found that it was unsafe to leave the Jeep unattended. After the first night, it became apparent that we couldn't risk parking the Jeep overnight, even in a high-end hotel's walled and guarded parking lot. So, my friend and I decided that we would take turns at the wheel and drive straight through to Guatemala.

Along the way, we found it necessary to ford five rivers; three because bridges had been washed out by a storm, and two because the bridges had been blown up by guerrillas. Thankfully, only one river fording was at night.

Since we were driving an off-road equipped 4-wheel drive Jeep, this wasn't a daunting impediment as we were able to find reasonably shallow areas to make the crossings. What quickly became evident as a more formidable challenge was the violence-prone opportunistic gangs of thieves. These quickly became our greatest concern, as they seemed to be lurking behind every curve in the highway.

The problem was solved with speed. We learned that by driving down the road at 80-90 miles per hour, it was possible for us to get past the gang member's cars that were waiting to waylay unsuspecting travelers. We were past them before they could react. Even if they tried to follow us, they couldn't catch us because of the lead we were able to maintain as a result of our speed.

Most of the highway was in good repair, but it was still risky to drive at these high speeds. However, in this situation, it was even more hazardous to drive slow. These are the types of decisions we must be prepared to make. It's a question of risk vs. reward.

In our case, the gang members were lounging next to their vehicles which were partially blocking the roadway. Though they were armed and ready to barricade the road, we were able to move in and out so fast, that we were beyond them before they even knew we were coming.

We weren't racing at a reckless, indiscriminate speed. We used under-control speed. That was the key.

Because we were in a Jeep equipped for off-road travel, we were often able to use our topographic maps to identify, and then avoid, the areas which were likely points of attack. While in other high-threat areas, we had no option but to blast through the choke point at high speed.

We drove fast enough to get past these inexpert roadblocks before they even knew we were coming, blasting our air horn to help further disorient our would-be attackers. (Since we were in Mexico, we were unarmed.)

If we had been walking, we would have experienced a very different fate. Our bodies would now be skeletons resting in an unmarked shallow grave. It was vigilance and speed (and the good Lord) that saved us.

In telling this story, I want to make one thing clear. While you may not be able to evacuate at 80-90 MPH, the same principles still apply. Find ways to go around areas that pose a discernable risk, and if possible, select a transportation method that is fast.

Your mode of transport may not be freeway fast, but even rapid pedaling of a bicycle is faster than running on foot. First vigilance, then speed.

Children: This isn't a forum to consider the merits of encouraging children to be involved in physically challenging sports, but it is worth noting that even very young children are capable of learning how to ride a 2-wheel bicycle. I taught my son to ride a 2-wheel bike when he was 3-1/2 years old. My daughter wasn't interested until she was 5. But both were capable of long bike rides before they turned 6-years old. They weren't motivated by "disaster preparedness." They were motivated by "fun."

So it is for us today. Our young children should not fear the future, nor should they worry about needing to evacuate, but we can sub rosa help them prepare for both the future and evacuation. When we encourage them to engage in rigorous physical activities such as action sports, we are cultivating the development of physical strength and stamina, and we are also quietly preparing them for adversity.

If parents select bicycles or motorcycles as an alternative transportation method, they can involve their children in sports such as motocross to help them develop and refine their bike riding skills. Not only can this be a healthy activity for these kids, but it also helps the parents get their family ready for evacuation if that becomes necessary. It's a win-win.

Walking is a legitimate option: As mentioned earlier, our last-choice alternate transportation method is walking. This is because slow speed makes us vulnerable. This doesn't mean we shouldn't be ready to walk, but rather, walking should be a 3rd option which follows at least one alternative transportation method. It should follow other choices. By the way, this doesn't apply to all emergency-situation circumstances, but it does apply to evacuation.

If you need to evacuate on foot, compensate by using extra vigilance. If you sense that lawlessness may be increasing, consider a new route that looks safer. Either way, it may be time to employ stealth. You may need to move with a group of people, or if alone, quickly from one place of concealment to another. Both will slow your progress, but increased safety may justify the delay.

In some situations, traveling at night is safer because you can be somewhat invisible, while in others the danger increases during hours of darkness. Therefore, we need to analyze our circumstances; discernment is critical to success.

Avoiding Violence: Experience teaches us a valuable lesson: Once lawlessness begins to set in, during the hours that follow, violence tends to increase exponentially.

In America and in Western society, civility and morality are now but a thin veneer. It sounds harsh, and perhaps a bit dramatic, but don't expect anyone to be trustworthy. When people who are ordinarily law-abiding become afraid, some respond with uncharacteristic kindness, while others do horrible things they would never even consider during normal times.

Prudence may suggest that we reduce our speed of travel, but it is likely that during an evacuation, "speed" will still be necessary. If there are indications that lawlessness is increasing, it may be advisable for us to take some added risks to avoid the even greater risks that may soon surface.

Though traveling by bicycle isn't fast when compared to a car, it is still faster than walking. If confronted by an assailant who is on foot, you can pedal hard and put on a burst of speed, and fly past them. If they follow you in a car, you can take your mountain bike off-road, or squeeze through a narrow route that the car can't follow. These emergency diversions are yet another example of why pre-planning alternate routes are so important.

When I was learning to fly a plane, my instructor beat into my head that I needed to always have an emergency landing site in mind. At some point, I might need it. If that day came, I wouldn't want to waste precious seconds looking for a place to land.

We need to do something similar. When we ask ourselves the question, "What would I do if…?" We are sharpening our *readiness* skills for that moment when a new predicament arises.

Hopefully, you won't need these active measures, but I include them here to provoke your thinking and spur you to plan for a circumstance that is different from a summer drive to a picnic. As with my trek through Mexico, due to our proactive measures, we never had to stand face-to-face with any of the adversaries who punctuated our route. We avoided the encounters.

This should be our goal. Having a firearm does provide a distinct advantage, but even if armed, it is generally better to avoid a confrontation. During an evacuation, being armed with "speed" may prove to be more important than having a gun.

Think outside the box. When it comes to alternate forms of transportation, we need to pre-plan. As we make these plans, we need to be creative, and we also need to be real-world practical.

If your usual transportation method and the primary route are operational, and you are able to use them to get home or to your meet-up place, and then to your safe-haven retreat location, unencumbered, that's great. If not, you need a Plan-B (and "C"). The rest of this chapter is dedicated to various "Plan-B" transportation alternatives. They are included here to help you evaluate your personal options, and to spur your creativity.

When possible, select alternative transportation methods that you can also enjoy. Whether it be motorcycle riding, mountain biking, off-road 4WD, RV vacationing, backpacking or hiking, or some other useful method of transportation, try to make it enjoyable or interesting, too.

When you use your alternate transportation for recreation or some other, additional purpose, this provides us with an added advantage. When we use it more, this equates to more practice, increased skill, and practical improvements to our transportation. It can also inject a little fun into our lives, too.

If you select modes of transportation that you also learn to enjoy, you can reap a triple benefit. It can be therapeutic recreation, practical training for an emergency situation, and you will find that you practice more frequently.

The importance of training with your equipment can't be overstated. Therefore, try to incorporate the transportation modes you select into a sporting or leisure activity you enjoy. If you do this, you will find that your capabilities will soar when operating in a stressful, emergency situation.

Perhaps you can think of a better method of transportation than those which are contained on the following pages. But whether you select transportation modes from the following recaps, or you identify others that are more appropriate for you, be sure to select at least two alternate forms of transportation. Then, do what needs to be done to get them ready, and practice their use.

Modes of Transportation

Public Transportation

Even if you ordinarily drive a car, check out your public transportation options. If you typically use public transportation, investigate other routes and other forms of public conveyance.

If you usually drive or fly to where you want to go, still examine your public transportation options. If for some reason you can't drive your car, but public transportation is still functioning, public transportation may be your fasted way out of town. Don't automatically discount the value of public transit.

Different forms of public transportation have their own inherent problems. On the plus side, subway travel is rarely impeded by vehicular traffic congestion. Yet, it is harder to get out of a stranded subway train and make to the surface, than it is to exit a stranded bus. So, fit your transportation solution to the problems you are likely to encounter.

Since departure times and the routes of trains and buses are outside of your control and tend to change during an emergency, don't count on schedules. Build flexibility into your plan.

Also, whether it be the enclosed space of a commuter train, a subway car, or bus, since public transportation requires us to step into what is essentially a box, and we can't get out of it whenever we want, it has an inherent danger. To minimize this risk, locate the emergency exits and emergency equipment built into the conveyance. Learn how to get out and back onto the street.

Public transportation is rarely an ideal choice. Yet, sometimes it is still the best option.

Cars and Trucks

Maintaining your vehicle so that it is reliable, and keeping the gas tank at least half-full, is a given. But there are other important motor vehicle considerations, too.

For example, the fuel efficiency of your vehicle, and having a stockpile of extra fuel stored at your home or some nearby place, is important. Since gas stations may run out of gas or diesel, or may not be able to pump fuel out of their underground tanks during a power outage, having a vehicle which is able to travel a considerable distance before refueling, is an advantage. (Refer to the chapter on fuel and fuel storage for important details.)

We need to keep in mind, too, that even gas station owners who have installed generators may be forced to stop dispensing fuel during crisis situations. If their generator hasn't been adequately maintained, it may fail. And, in a grid-down situation, their electronic cash registers may stop working. Or, if the Internet has crashed, their credit card processing machines may not be able to approve transactions. There are many circumstances which may prevent a gas station's fuel pumps from working.

Though many gas station fuel-delivery systems have a mechanism for overriding this problem, employees may not know how to override the automatic systems. Therefore, obtaining fuel during a crisis may be a problem. So, even if the worry of getting additional fuel is only the prospect of waiting in a long line at a gas station, this time-wasting predicament needs to be solved in advance. Stockpiling extra fuel is the answer.

In contrast to the desirability of owning a fuel-efficient vehicle, is the need for having a damage-resistant vehicle. During an emergency situation, many motorists are emotionally distraught, impatient, distracted, or driving too fast, so accidents occur more frequently. Since most fuel-efficient cars are quickly rendered inoperable in a traffic accident, it may be more advantageous to utilize a larger vehicle that is damage resistant, even though it is less fuel efficient.

For example, a full-size pickup truck is more resilient to damage and has the added advantage of being able to haul more supplies. Both of these features are beneficial attributes.

Further, a 4-wheel drive pickup truck has the advantage of being able to exit roadways and drive around accident scenes and gridlocked roads. Therefore, this capability provides yet another strategic advantage.

However, if your supplies are already stockpiled at your safe-haven location, then the 'hauling' benefits of the pickup truck may be academic. In this situation, payload capacity may be irrelevant. If this is your situation, then a 4-wheel drive (4WD) Jeep-like vehicle that has been adapted for off-road driving, will be more versatile.

What do you anticipate encountering? What is the terrain in your area? If you are going to purchase a vehicle, choose one that aligns with your needs and your operating environment.

Or, you may not be able to replace your car right now. If that's the case, then do what you can to keep it in good repair and the gas tank at least half full. And, when the time comes that you need to bug-out, don't overfill your car with "stuff." Overloaded vehicles are more likely to break down, and reduced visibility is a recipe for a traffic accident.

If you are thinking about purchasing an EMP-resistant vehicle, you will quickly learn that cars and trucks which are older than 20-years tend to be considered "classics," and the prices start to climb again. For example, a 1960s era (pre-electronics) Ford pickup truck in fair condition, will sell for more now than when it was new. So, you may want to consider getting a pre-2000 truck or 4WD and then have the electronic systems removed. A self-employed "small shop" mechanic can help you eliminate all the electronics on an older car that has not yet reached "classic" status.

Regardless of how you choose to proceed, be sure to get expert advice before you make your purchase decision. Even within the same year of manufacture, vehicles are not all the same when it comes to eliminating electronic systems.

Vehicles which are popular among those who want to avoid EMP problems are usually trucks or sport utility vehicles manufactured before 1971. These include old Jeep Wranglers and Cherokees, old Dodge Power Wagons, Chevy/GMC Blazers, Ford Broncos, and Ford, Chevy and Dodge pickup trucks. Vehicles which have a diesel engine tend to be even more EMP-resistant.

If you live in North America, you probably want to avoid purchasing a Land Rover or other foreign-made Jeep-like vehicles because parts are difficult to find. A multi-purpose truck such as the Unimog (MOG) may be an excellent EMP-resistant off-road vehicle, but if it breaks down and you don't have the needed spare parts, it is a useless piece of machinery. However, if you live in Europe or South America, it might be a viable choice.

No matter what vehicle you choose, be sure to have a collection of essential spare parts. This includes mechanical and electrical components, including electrical wiring.

RVs: Motorhomes, 5th Wheels, and House Trailers (Caravans)

Being able to take both your shelter and gear with you, unobtrusively in an RV, provides a distinct advantage—but only if your RV can be stored near your home or at a nearby rallying point, or at a site that is on the way to your safe-haven.

An RV not only provides you with shelter en route to your retreat location, but it also makes it possible for you to switch destinations. If for some reason your safe-haven becomes untenable, or the road is blocked, having an RV makes other options viable.

Or, if you've not yet been able to establish a safe-haven, an RV provides you with well-designed shelter wherever you choose to go. If you don't have a retreat property, an RV can partially offset that disadvantage by offering unparalleled flexibility.

And, when you do find a safe-haven, even if it's just raw land, you already have temporary housing. This frees you to concentrate on other site-development priorities rather than be distracted by the need for housing.

Even if you have a house or cabin at your retreat location, an RV can provide housing for friends or family that show up. And, if you have an RV at your safe-haven, you also have the option to move to a more strategic location if that becomes advantageous. Plus, you can use it to set up an ancillary encampment for security, quarantine, or some other purpose.

If you opt to use an RV for transportation, if possible, keep it protected in an enclosed storage building, or at a safe location that you regularly visit. Regardless of the storage method, you need to check it periodically to make sure everything is operating correctly. In cold climates, these rigs need to be winterized.

Two factors change an RV from a good to a bad choice:

1. If you are going to bug-out in an RV, it's not just important to get out early, it is absolutely imperative. If you are able to exit an urban area before others are evacuating, then an RV may be an excellent choice for you. If not, this option can be a nightmare

If you're trying to flee town on a congested roadway with one of these rigs, you're probably going to have a tough time. On the other hand, if you already live near the outskirts of a suburban area, your experience may be trouble-free.

2. The other issue is the weather. Snow, rain, flooding, and other weather-related problems make driving a motorhome or towing a house trailer far more challenging, and getting stuck far more likely. And, if you intend to use it for lodging when the weather is cold, you will still need cold weather clothing and sleeping bags. This is true even if the rig has a high BTU heater and air conditioner. The insulation in the walls, ceiling, and floor of an RV is inadequate for extreme cold and hot weather.

While far, far better than a tent, an RV doesn't necessarily provide comfortable living conditions when it is subjected to weather extremes. Yet, steps that can be taken to mitigate these problems. This is another reason why "practice" is so valuable.

*** Despite these inherent problems, if you don't have a suitable house or cabin at your safe-haven retreat location, an RV may be a godsend. Per square foot of space, these are usually highly functional. The forethought put into the design of an RV by an experienced manufacturer who has listened to years of customer input, will usually exceed even the best "small house" design. Plus, even a new house trailer (caravan) is far less expensive than building a cabin. (In the long run, they are less durable than a cabin, but perhaps a good choice if finances are tight or you may need to change locations.)

Nevertheless, since you're probably not going to use a motorhome to commute to work, you will still need an alternative transportation method, even if it's just to get you to your RV. (For stored vehicles, be sure to read the chapter on fuel treatment and storage.)

Motorhome vs. house trailer hauled by a truck: If you don't already have a truck that has a towing package and is rated to pull the weight of a trailer, consider buying a motorhome. These are essentially a trailer built on top of a truck chassis. Plus, most motorhomes can haul a small vehicle such as a Jeep or a motorcycle trailer (referred to as a "Towed," pronounced, "Toad"), which means you can also have backup transportation.

Surprisingly, it is usually cheaper to buy a new-looking Class-A luxury motorhome with a gasoline engine that has more than 50,000 miles (80,000 km) on it, than it is to buy a modest truck and a barebones house trailer. Prices often vary widely from seller-to-seller, but great deals can be found by those who are willing to search for them.

Used motorhomes and used house trailers can both be found at surprisingly low prices, especially off-season. Or, if purchased from an elderly person who is no longer able to travel, or a family with children who no longer want to go RV-ing. Worth noting, too, is that when purchasing a used RV direct from the seller, they are often willing to include extra gear that would be very expensive to buy new.

If you are doing a lot of up and down driving in the mountains, you may want a diesel motorhome or diesel pickup truck, but otherwise, a gasoline-fueled engine is probably adequate—as well as far cheaper to purchase.

Vacationing with your RV can be an enjoyable byproduct of this transportation choice. These journeys also have another spin-off benefit. Each holiday jaunt serves as a practice run, too.

An RV vacation lets you learn how to use your equipment, identify what else you might need, and practice safe-haven retreat living. It gives you the chance to drive your RV on different types of roads and in various traffic conditions, the opportunity to use specialized equipment such as electricity generators, marine toilets and black water tanks, 12v lighting, solar rechargers, and to experience small-kitchen cooking and close living. It's the perfect combination; practical training that is also fun.

Utility Trailers & Rooftop Carriers

An impressive example of preparedness is that some people store a utility trailer in their garage that is pre-loaded with emergency gear. If you don't have a safe-haven retreat location where these items can be pre-positioned, this may be a sound choice. But you do need to have a suitable vehicle that has a towing package. And, of course, you need to evacuate early, as described in the prior section on motorhomes and house trailers.

Towing a trailer in heavy traffic is a difficult task, and is an accident-prone choice especially when other drivers are panicky. And, if you are forced to stop on the roadway, your trailer is ripe for pilfering. Hauling a trailer loaded with supplies makes you a target for armed robbery and carjacking, too. If it is evident that you have emergency supplies at a time when others are feeling unprepared, this makes you vulnerable. Therefore, if you select this option, cover your trailer contents with a well-secured opaque tarp. This is essential.

Disguise your load. If your trailer's contents are masked or at least covered, and observers think you work for a lawn maintenance company or your cargo is similarly uninteresting, you might be okay.

Even then, if you plan to haul a trailer, even a small one, get out early. If others are already evacuating, take a route which will help you avoid getting stuck in traffic, and don't stop unless necessary. Even if you are in an area that is ordinarily safe, don't park your vehicle, or leave your valuables unattended even for a minute, even if your supplies are concealed by a tarp.

If it is time to bug-out and you've not yet loaded your trailer, or you intend to use a rooftop carrier, this can be a problem if it delays your departure. So, if you can't store your trailer pre-loaded, have everything ready in one section of your garage.

This is the same for a roof-top carrier, too. It would be too heavy to lift into place if it was stored pre-packed.

With both an empty utility trailer and a roof-top carrier, practice loading it, in advance of your need. When you're in a hurry, rarely does everything fit unless you've recently drilled and previously solved the problems which seem to always surface.

Hitch Carriers and Bike Racks

It is much easier to weave your way through traffic with a hitch rack or bike rack on your vehicle than to tow a trailer. The downside is that they don't hold much and your load is exposed.

Bicycles and motorcycles are hard to hide, but if you're not evacuating early, unlike the situation with a trailer, you may not want to conceal your load. Since these 'carriers' are rarely covered with a tarp for ordinary use, to do so during an evacuation will communicate concealment, and therefore high value.

Disguise is also challenging and may not be practical. Therefore, you will need to make a judgment call based on the circumstance. However, in most cases, inexpensive-looking storage bins are often the best way to disguise hitch-carried supplies.

Bicycles

For many people, a bicycle is the best choice. An easy-to-operate mountain bike made by a reliable manufacturer is a durable, reliable, low-tech solution that travel twice the miles of walking in the same amount of time.

Since a bicycle doesn't need a motor or fuel, and since it can also be used as a pack mule to walk alongside, as well as to pedal and ride, it can be an excellent choice. Even if you lack the physical fitness needed to ride a bike up a hill, you can push it up and then ride it when you have the opportunity to coast downhill. On level ground, you can probably pedal your bike faster than a fit pursuer can run.

For adults over 5-feet tall, a bicycle with 26-inch wheels is generally best for traveling. For tall riders, 29-inch models are becoming popular, but since finding tires and tire tubes is a bit more difficult, especially when traveling, we still prefer the 26-inch models for most adults. If children are too small to ride a 20-inch bike without training wheels and pedal it themselves over the distance that needs to be traveled, then they should be transported in a child carrier behind a rider, or in a bike trailer. Only a muscular and aerobically fit adult can carry both gear and a child.

In all cases, "mountain bikes" or "fat tire" bikes should be used if toting a GO-bag or equipment of any kind, as these bikes are designed to be ridden on non-paved surfaces and even cross country on wilderness trails. Further, though knobby tires do not provide as comfortable a ride, they do afford better traction on uneven pavement, dirt, sand, grass, rocks, and gravel.

A multi-geared bike is recommended, but a 3-speed "mountain bike" is adequate for amateur riders. Further, bikes with shock absorbing suspension are much more comfortable to ride than solid-frame bikes. In addition to reducing rider fatigue, the suspension can also improve control, so it provides two advantages.

Notwithstanding, for bikes which will be used for evacuation, durability is more important than comfort. A used-but-in-excellent-condition high-quality bike is a better investment than a cheap, new Walmart bike.

Since even experienced bike riders are often thrown off balance by riding with a GO-Bag on their back, we do not recommend carrying more on your back than a water bladder, such as a 100-ounce (2.5 liters) Camelbak. If you insist on wearing a GO-Bag on your back rather than carrying it on the bike's cargo carrier, at least keep the knapsack weight to under 20-pounds (9 kg) and use the waist strap to keep the bag from shifting and throwing you off balance.

It is easier to ride, or even push a bicycle with gear attached, so there is a temptation to transport more than the contents of a standard GO-Bag. That's fine, but unless you are an experienced bike rider and physically fit, about 50-pounds of gear is still a reasonable maximum weight if you intend to pedal the bike. If you are using large well-designed panniers (saddlebags), this can be increased to 100-pounds if the rider is physically fit.

Even more important than weight, is that the weight of your gear is distributed evenly on both sides of the rear tire. Only a small amount of the weight should be carried above the top of the rear tire. Distributed accordingly, you will be able to maintain greater stability and balance while riding. If you will be using the bike as a pack mule and not riding it, this weight distribution is not as critical.

Packing gear in panniers next to the front tire, or in a basket or bag above the front tire, can also be accomplished in addition to using rear panniers. However, the use of front panniers will make the bike harder to steer and will reduce stability. If you intend to carry gear on top of the handlebars, or above the front tire, it is best to limit it to something lightweight such as a sleeping bag.

Make sure your supplies and equipment are solidly in place, that it will not shift after riding on a bumpy road, and that you are able to consistently maintain plenty of clearance between moving parts such as the bicycle brakes, tires, spokes, chain, and sprockets. Unstable loads are the cause of many bike-related accidents and injuries.

If you don't want to purchase specialty bike accessories like panniers, at the very least add a "carrier" rack above your rear tire. If your carrier doesn't provide at least three support struts on each side of your bike, perform a do-it-yourself (DIY) solution to keep carried items from touching the tire or swinging into the spokes. You can use a stout string like paracord, wire, or duct tape for this purpose.

This DIY solution is accomplished by stringing paracord (or wire, or duct tape) from the axle area and chain-stay bar of the rear tire, to the cargo carrier which is above the rear tire. The paracord should be looped up and down to form a screen that protects the spoke area. This makeshift shield can help keep your gear bags from swinging into the moving tire and spinning spokes.

Of course, a helmet is a good idea, too, but make sure it does not inhibit your hearing or visibility. You will also need a small, lightweight bicycle tool, tire-tube repair supplies to fix a flat tire, a small hand pump to refill your tire with air, and a tire pressure gauge. Puncture-resistant tire tubes or no-puncture solid foam tube replacements, are a worthwhile investment, even if you only plan to use your bike as a pack mule. Pushing a bike with a flat tire is fatiguing.

Since you may need to operate your bicycle at night, be sure to either have a headlight on your bike, or a headlamp worn on your forehead. For roadway light, the advantage of using a headlamp is that it provides light in whichever direction you look, and is still useful when you dismount from your bike. For more on headlamps, see the chapter on flashlights and emergency lighting.

A red taillight is necessary if you are operating your bike in traffic, but may be a disadvantage if you want to stay invisible to others. Therefore, a helmet mounted tail light, or a wired tail light with an off-on switch on the handlebars that can be quickly turned off while riding, is best.

Folding Bicycles & Pocket Bikes

Designed to fold and fit into the trunk of a car, these bicycles cost about the same as a standard bike. Though not as comfortable to ride, especially long distances, they do offer a unique advantage: They can be hidden in the trunk of your vehicle alongside your GO-Bag.

This makes them far more secure from theft than a bike carried on the outside of your vehicle. For those who drive a car to work, this may be the best backup transportation alternative.

Pocket bikes are not really pocket-sized, but they are smaller than a folding bike. Therefore, if a folding bike won't fit in the trunk of your car, or a folding bike is too heavy or awkward for you to handle, then a pocket-bike may be your best alternative. Operationally, a folding bike is more useful for transportation and more comfortable to ride, but a pocket-bike may get you out of town faster than walking, so it's still worth having.

With these small bikes, you will need to wear your GO-Bag on your back. This is not ideal for stability and comfort, but panniers and other gear-transport accessories will rarely fit on a folding bike or pocket-bike. If this is the backup transportation option you choose, use your bike at least twice a year to make sure it fully operational, and that the tires are full of air. You'll still need the same repair kit and safety equipment as mentioned in the prior section.

Electric Bicycles

Since electric bikes tend to be heavy to lift and expensive to purchase, this option isn't for everyone. If you have a long way to travel, it may not be for you, either. Technological advances are rapidly emerging to make this option viable, but many of the lower-cost electric bikes only have a 10-mile (16 km) operational range on level ground, so they aren't adequate for most of us.

There probably isn't time for even a quick-charge along the way, and carrying an extra battery isn't usually viable, either. Yet, for some, an electric bike is worth considering. Just keep in mind that distance estimates offered by the manufacturer of these bikes are usually overly optimistic and concocted using a smooth, level road surface, and a 100-pound (45 kg) rider.

To help the rider evade unnecessary confrontations, at the very least, we recommend that an electric bike is able to operate at a speed that is faster than a person runs. If not, your electric bike may soon be someone else's ride.

Folding Electric Bicycles

Though often lighter than their full-size counterpart, folding bicycles which can fit in the trunk of a car usually have a smaller battery. Therefore, most models won't last for even 10-miles. Yet, for some, this relatively short range may be adequate. Just be sure to test the bike on the various routes you might take, to make sure it does meet your needs. Remember, it's not just transporting your weight. It also needs to be adequate to carry you and your GO-Bag.

Mopeds and Add-on Gas Motors for Conventional Bicycles

Mopeds, or motorized pedal bikes, are readily available in Japan and throughout Asia, but not in the United States except in kit form. With these kits, an add-on gasoline engine is installed on a 1-speed, 3-speed, or 10-speed wide-tire bicycle such as a mountain bike. If you are interested and can't find a moped, look online for a kit.

Not only can a motorized bicycle kit be less expensive to buy than a motorcycle, but they also provide transportation that is lighter weight, more fuel efficient, and easier to operate. In many places, these low-powered motorized bikes do not require a driver's license. In the U.S., most states don't require a driver's license if the engine is 50cc or smaller in size, and not operated at speeds above 25 MPH.

Most front-wheel and rear-wheel "friction roller" kits can be added to an ordinary bike in about an hour. However, center frame-mounted and chain-drive engine kits require more installation effort.

The better add-on kits do not interfere with the pedal mechanism, so the bike can still be pedaled normally, or powered by the motor, or by both pedaling and the motor. However, on any moderate-to-steep grade, expect to pedal in addition to using the engine.

Most of these kits are designed to be mounted on the frame between the rider's legs. This can be awkward for the rider, and this design can also result in burns to the legs if the rider isn't careful. Whereas the rear-mount chain-drive and belt-drive units can be safer and tend to be easier to install.

Conversely, models which are installed in front of the handlebars, above the front tire, can make the bike less stable to operate. While models which place the motor behind the seat are safer to operate, they do eliminate the "carrier" space that many bikers use for transporting supplies. However, with many of these engine-above-the-rear-wheel models, panniers (saddlebags) can still be used. On the downside, when a motor larger than 40ccs is mounted above either tire, the bicycle often becomes noticeably top heavy.

For maximum power and reasonably easy installation, select a rear-mount chain-drive or belt-drive unit with a 60cc or larger motor. A 37cc engine can also be used, but it will require more pedaling. With both a 60cc and 37cc engine, flat-land speed will be nearly the same if the rider, plus gear, is under 200-pounds—but a smaller motor will definitely require more pedaling, especially when traveling up a grade or hill. On the plus side, a rear tire chain-drive (or friction-roller) kit can be installed on either a men's or women's bike.

For the easiest to install kit, choose a rear wheel friction-roller kit. It will deliver 30% less power than a chain-drive kit which uses the same motor, but reliability is often better.

For an aesthetically more pleasing look, select a center-mount chain-drive unit. These kits are harder to install, but when a larger engine is used, the bike looks more natural and has the appearance of a lightweight motorcycle. Adding a "flex" muffler can further improve the "look" and reduce the burn hazard. Whereas when an engine larger than 37cc is mounted above the rear tire, the bike looks ungainly, and it can be difficult for the rider to mount the bike.

Note: Engines with the same displacement (same power) made by different manufacturers will not be the same height and width. Therefore, investigate the motor's physical dimensions before you make your purchase decision.

Why is this an issue? For example, a *tall* engine may not be a problem when used for a center frame-mount installation, whereas a *wide* engine mounted in the same location might get in the way of pedaling the bike.

Conversely, when a *wide* same-power engine is used for an above-the-rear-tire installation, it will have a lower center of gravity (good), and it may be easier to mount the bike. (A *tall* engine mounted above the rear tire, might make it difficult to swing your leg over the engine when it's time to mount your bike.) Message: Select the best engine for your application.

Worth noting is that center frame-mount kits provide a lower center of gravity, and their chain-drive mechanism delivers better more positive power. Unfortunately, these do-it-yourself units are considerably harder to install, and the sprockets engaged by the chain must be in precise alignment. And, a men's style bike is usually necessary due to the space requirements.

Whereas with the easier to install, front- and rear-wheel "friction roller" models, the engine powers a small wheel or a spindle/friction roller that presses against the tire, using friction to force the tire to turn. Therefore, installation is much simpler and less prone to mechanical problems. On the downside, in addition to less power, these front and rear tire-drive friction-roller units can lose even more power if the tires become wet or muddy.

With both the friction-roller, belt-drive, and chain-driven designs, the gas engines are relatively lightweight (20-25 pounds), so they all have limited power. They do not convert a bicycle into a motorcycle.

When traveling up a hill, the rider often needs to pedal, to assist the underpowered motor. Still, this can represent less work than pedaling a bike without motorized assistance.

4-cycle vs. 2-cycle engines: We recommend selecting a 4-cycle OHC engine because they are quieter, and you can select a model/size which does not require the operator to mix oil with the gasoline. (Fuel mixing is necessary with 2-cycle engines.)

Mufflers: With most kits, a muffler is included to reduce engine noise, but if an optional muffler is available which makes the engine quieter, this is a worthwhile addition. A good muffler will not only make your bike more pleasant to ride, it will also help you avoid unwanted attention.

Motorized Bike vs. Motorcycle: A portly rider, or a person who is carrying more gear, will need to pedal a motorized bicycle on any incline. Yet, despite this labor, for some individuals and situations, a motorized bike may still be a better choice than a motorcycle. Perhaps additionally so since a motorized bike under 50cc (approximately 3 hp) can, in most areas, be legally driven on not just roadways, but also on dedicated bike lanes and urban bike paths.

For others, a motorized bike will be a better choice because motorcycles are heavier and harder to transport, require a drivers license or license endorsement and vehicle insurance, they can be difficult to learn to ride safely, cost more to purchase, and for most people, motorcycle repairs require a mechanic.

Those considering a motorized bicycle should keep in mind that riders who weigh more than 200-pounds, and those who may carry a combined rider-gear weight of 200+ pounds, will be happier with a larger engine. Small engines, such as the popular 37cc motor, will still work but the rider will need to pedal a lot more.

Gearing/Sprocket Size: It's not just a matter of engine size that counts, but rather that you gear the bike to optimize engine size, tire size, and the weight the bike will be transporting.

For motorized bikes which will be carrying a heavy rider or a rider + gear, or, will be operating in a rugged or hilly environment, opt for a 48-tooth or larger sprocket on the rear wheel. The more teeth on the rear sprocket, the better the take-off and climbing ability of the bike. A larger rear sprocket (gear) will reduce the top-end speed of the motorized bike, but this may be a necessary compromise.

Even a small 37cc engine that is chain-driven, and mounted on a bike equipped with a 48-tooth rear sprocket, can become a low-cost yet remarkable form of transportation.

Gas Tank: By adding a larger gas tank (recommended), these diminutive add-on bike engine kits can be great, long-distance performers. They can deliver 100-miles per gallon fuel efficiency, labor efficient speed, and extended traveling range (distance) if a large gas tank is added.

Range & Speed: Distance and top-end speed depend on the size of the motor, the terrain where the bike is ridden, the weight of the operator plus gear, bike tire size, and how much the rider assists the motor by pedaling. But even without pedaling, speeds of 25+ MPH, and an operating range of more than 100 miles before needing to refill the tank can be attained on level ground. And, if you carry a small extra gas can (2 gallons), operating range can be dramatically increased.

An important attribute of a motorized bicycle is that if you run out of gas, you can keep going because you can pedal the bike. This provides a distinct advantage over motorcycles and other forms of motorized transportation.

Before purchasing, be sure to check buyer-ratings. Some motorized-bike kit brands are far more reliable, as well as easier to repair.

EMP-Protection: Since most of these add-on bike motor kits use simple engines without electronics, use carburetors rather than computerized fuel injection, and a pull-cord to start rather than an electronic ignition, they are EMP-resistant from the onset. No modifications are needed.

Recommendation: If this is the transportation mode you select, use a 26" men's mountain bike in good condition, and add a 49cc center mount chain-drive motor kit. This maximizes power, but in most places, qualifies the rider for operation on secondary roadways as well as bike lanes and bike paths. It also eliminates the need for a driver's license and vehicle insurance. (Check your local laws.)

To attain maximum range, install the largest-size optional fuel tank that will fit your bicycle. Also a flex muffler, a clamshell sprocket adapter, a spring-loaded chain tensioner to reduce vibration, and a 48-tooth (or larger) sprocket for the rear wheel. In our opinion, this combination provides the ideal balance between performance, reliability, speed, fuel efficiency, traveler safety, and maximizes the distance that the bike can travel without refueling.

Where to shop? The oldest and largest company which sells motorized bike kits in the United States is Live Fast Motors, located in Arizona. Website: www.LiveFastMotors.com

Bicycle Trailers & Bike Racks

Even when bikes are locked to bike trailers or to a hitch or bumper/trunk-mounted bike rack, bicycle theft is still relatively easy for thieves to accomplish. If you evacuate early, this may not translate into a problem for you.

However, if you've been delayed, and others have begun their long walk of evacuation, then theft, or at least attempted theft which may damage your bike, becomes more likely. Plan for it.

While roof-mounted bike racks make your cargo more visible, they do tend to reduce the likelihood of theft, at least while the vehicle is moving. For those transporting bicycles on a trailer or hitch rack, covering the bikes with a tarp which both conceals the bikes and disguises their distinctive shape, may prove to be beneficial.

In all cases, it is just as important to securely lock the rack or trailer to the vehicle, as it is to padlock the bike to its carrier. Keep the key to these locks handy, in case you need to abandon the bike rack or remove the bike quickly.

Despite these problems, having a bicycle for each passenger can be very advantageous. If your vehicle breaks down or becomes undrivable due to a traffic accident, or choking traffic congestion or abandoned cars block your progress, you can switch your mode of transportation. As discussed above, in most evacuation situations, riding a bike is far better than walking.

Even if you don't have a bicycle for each passenger in the vehicle, having even one bike can be useful as it can be used to scout the road ahead, or as a pack mule to transport additional supplies. It is possible to carry a larger and heavier load on a bike, even if it is only used as a pack mule; one that you walk alongside and push rather than a burden that you carry on your back or in your hands.

If you do find that you need to abandon your vehicle and its contents, don't delay. Grab your GO-Bag and get going. The exception to this may be if you are not being observed by others. In that situation, you may want to take a few minutes to remove your valuables from your vehicle and find a nearby place to hide them. You may be able to come back for them later.

Foot-Push Scooters and Electric Scooters

Two-wheel scooters, such as the folding, compact, lightweight scooter made by Razor, are popular with young people. Yet, they require considerable energy to operate, and even adult riders who are physically fit will find that scooter operation will quickly fatigue their leg and back muscles. Ridden with one foot on the scooter while the other is used to push it forward is a high-fatigue operating method.

Nevertheless, an ultra-lightweight aluminum model which folds compactly and weighs under 7-pounds (3 kg), can be strapped to a GO-Bag and used to coast downhill. For most people, this will not be a first-choice alternate transportation method, but for teens already accustomed to these toys, and adults in hilly paved terrain, this approach might be worth considering.

Since the operating range of most motorized scooters is limited, the merits of an electric or gas-powered model probably aren't offset by the added weight and transport difficulties. This goes with both small "toy" versions, as well as the heavy-duty models used for transporting adults with mobility problems. The larger "mobility" scooters are designed for getting around a home, neighborhood, or store, and do not have the operating speed or range needed for use in an evacuation scenario.

The exception to this is the Knightrider (military) and ESR-750 Portable Patrol Vehicle (police/security), both made by Go-Ped, and similar commercial-grade products. These often have an operating range of 25⁺-miles and are capable of bursts of speed of 19⁺ MPH. However, with a purchase price equal to that of a small motorcycle or ATV, most people will not be interested unless they are looking for motorized transportation that will fit in the trunk of their car.

Segway Personal Transporters, DTV Shredder, Euno Bolt, and emerging new technologies for personal transportation.

Segway Personal Transporters, made famous in 2002 when they introduced their innovative self-balancing 2-wheel "human transport device," now also produce an off-road version. While other manufacturers sell electric 2-, 3-, and 4-wheel scooters using their own design, it is Segway that has captured the interest of many.

While the standard 2-wheel Segway is popular with those who live in the downtown area of a city, as well as with Messenger companies which serve downtown areas, and with city tour companies who use them to for self-guided tours, Segway also makes an off-road version. It is this off-road model, the x2, and subsequent variants, which may be more conducive to the bug-out transportation needs in rural areas, small towns, or metropolitan areas with hills.

The off-road version, with its larger tires and other enhancements, is capable of going up steeper grades, traversing dirt trails and packed sand, rocky dirt, and grassy hills. Unfortunately, it lacks the extended operating range of its city-bred counterpart. The x2 off-road version has an operating range of only 9-12 miles (14-19 km).

Since the standard version can travel a much greater distance, it may be a better choice for getting home if you live and work in an urban setting that has sidewalks or bike lanes. With its 16-24-mile (26-39 km) range, it can be useful for personal transport, but only if you will be using it on relatively smooth paved surfaces.

Like all electric transport devices, the operating range of the Segway varies greatly according to the weight of the load being carried and the terrain. With both the city and off-road versions, the maximum payload (you and your gear) is 260-pounds (117 kg).

Cargo should be kept low to avoid interference with steering, a task which is accomplished by leaning your body to the left or right. Similarly, speed is controlled by tilting forward or backward. To increase speed, you lean forward. To stop or slow down, you bend your body toward the rear. Knapsacks, bags, and gear can interfere with these processes, so practice is essential for safe operation.

On the practical side, since the off-road Segway (x2) weighs 120-pounds (55 kg), it isn't something that you will want to carry across a stream or lift over a downed log, at least not often. Still, these units may still be worth considering, but only if your use would be in an environment that is conducive.

Since recharging empty batteries takes 8-hours, and a spare set of batteries weighs 23-pounds (10.3 kg), it's hard to extend the range of a Segway in an evacuation situation. Moreover, a 2-wheel Segway can't be used safely in snow or freezing conditions. In emergency evacuation situations involving an EMP or solar flare, a Segway will probably stop working due to its dependence on microcircuitry.

The built-in speed limiter restricts the Segway's operating speed to 12.5 mph (20 km/h), which fails be meet our recommended standard of 20 MPH (32 km/h), but it is still faster than running, and these units do have the capacity to haul a significant amount of weight. They are not recommended for riders weighing less than 100-pounds (45 kg).

DTV Shredder: Similar but designed for serious off-road and military use, is the DTV Shredder (Dual Tracked Vehicle) made in Canada by BPG Werks (bpgwerks.com). Rather than using two wheels, it has two motorized tracks like a military tank or bulldozer, but the user still operates this 280-pound transportation platform from a standing position. Like the Segway, it is steered by leaning the body in the direction you want to travel.

Think of the DTV Shredder as a gas powered all-weather all-terrain snowboard. It does have a handlebar to aid stability, but it is steered by leaning left or right, like a snowboard, and the tightness of the turn is controlled by how far you lean. Casual use and operation are simple and far easier to master than a snowboard.

Powered by a small 4-stroke 14-horsepower gasoline engine, it can go a long way on a gallon of gas. Only slightly wider than its human rider, it can operate on and off trails and on narrow tracks, but in the open, it can attain speeds of nearly 30 mph (40 km/h). Though these cost about the same as a motorcycle, it is more maneuverable. And, when folded for transport, it can fit into the trunk of a car (47x27x25-inches)—but it would be difficult to lift in and out of a vehicle without assistance.

We have not had the opportunity to test the DTV Shredder, but the "Trail Edition" was designed for wilderness use by the Active-Sports community, so it should be relatively durable.

Uno Bolt: (unobolt.com) is an example of the many innovative, new designs which are quickly making their way into the market. Unfortunately, the long-term durability of these personal transportation devices is still unproven.

Like the Segway, the Uno Bolt uses a computerized gyro to maintain the rider's balance, but the Uno Bolt has only one wheel and a seat. The single rubber tire is 18-inches tall and 10-inches wide, reportedly delivering adequate traction for road surfaces up to 45-degrees. Top speed is 22 MPH (35km/h) on a smooth level surface. The most noteworthy features of the Uno Bolt is its claim to provide a 25-mile range (40 km), plus a weight and size which are conducive to carrying it in the trunk of some cars. Battery recharge time is only 45-minutes, and it is feasible to take along an extra battery. Tests conducted by the manufacturer, demonstrate that the Uno Bolt can transport 280 pounds (127kg) maximum total weight.

The Eno Bolt, and many other new, innovative personal transportation devices are quickly expanding the capabilities of electric transportation. The downside is that the manufacturers and reliability of the products are unproven, spare parts and repairs are difficult to obtain, and of course, they are prone to damage if the emergency situation was created by an EMP or CME.

Motorcycles

The safety risks of motorcycle riding are well known. Nevertheless, they are a serious contender as perhaps the best bug-out transportation vehicle for a lone individual. Street bikes and road bikes are less useful for urban evacuation and often worthless off-road, but street-legal dirt bikes are adaptable and versatile.

Older dirt bikes which have been well cared for, and do not have electronic fuel injection but do have a kick-starter (perhaps in addition to an electric starter), can be a bargain to purchase, extremely reliable, and can transport the rider many miles on a single tank of gasoline. Not only is an older, mechanically simple motorcycle easy to repair, many are also EMP resistant.

Thankfully, old street-legal off-road motorcycles are generally inexpensive to purchase, mechanically simple, relatively easy and cheap to fix, and reliable. This makes them an excellent choice.

Before purchasing a motorcycle, make sure you have the body weight and physical strength to use its kick-starter. It also needs to be reasonably quiet, so it may need to be updated with noise-reduction mufflers to mute the snarly sound of the engine.

Some motorcycle owners enjoy drawing attention to themselves and install aftermarket parts which make their bike louder. These changes may need to be reversed. In fact, we need to do what we can to make our bug-out motorcycle as quiet and unobtrusive as possible. When we are evacuating, invisibility, or at least being inconspicuous, is an asset.

Before purchasing a motorcycle, check user ratings for repair history and reliability, talk to several owners of motorcycle repair shops, and then peruse the bike's schematics to look for electronic components. Be sure to purchase a repair manual and the spare parts that may be needed when parts and repair shops are closed.

If this is the transportation method you select, choose a motorcycle which has an engine that is powerful enough to easily carry the combined weight of both you and your gear. If you might need to carry a passenger, be sure to take that into account, too.

If you might carry a passenger, make sure your motorcycle is set up to accommodate them. This includes protection from the burning heat of the exhaust pipe and muffler, pegs to support their feet, and toe guards to keep feet and legs away from gears, spokes, and the spinning tire.

Yet, don't get a motorcycle that is larger than you need, either. Avoid choosing a bike that is too heavy for you to pick up if it has fallen to the ground. You want power, but you also want fuel efficiency.

Check the tires carefully. Tires should not be selected based on ride comfort, but rather on all-weather durability and their ability to work well on all surfaces; street and off-road, dry pavement and mud. Don't forget to add a flat-repair kit and two flat-fix bottles of air, and a mini tool kit.

In an emergency situation, there is a tendency not to wear safety gear, such as a helmet. This is a mistake. Both highly skilled and occasional-use motorcycle riders and their passengers, need to wear clothing and safety gear that will provide some protection in the event of a fall or traffic accident.

When selecting a helmet, look for a model which maximizes your ability to hear, and which does not restrict your peripheral vision. The capacity to hear and see what's happening around us is a way to avoid not only traffic hazards but also non-traffic dangers.

As mentioned previously in the section on bicycles, bug-out gear should be carried on both sides of the rear tire, ideally in panniers (saddlebags). To avoid operational problems, the driver, as well as a passenger if there is one, should not wear a backpack weighing more than 20-pounds (9 kg). Knapsacks and all gear should be secured and able to handle the jostling of off-road operation, even if you anticipate driving exclusively on paved roadways.

Many families have a street-legal off-road motorcycle for each family member, including children, for use in recreational activities today, and for emergency use in the future.

2x2 ATV (All-Terrain Motorcycles) & Midi-Motorcycles

Rokon: The Rokon motorbikes are smaller than a full-size motorcycle but still larger than a mini, and have full-time front/rear wheel drive. The Rokon Trail-Breaker is used by the U.S. Army's Special Forces and has proven itself all over the world, in all sorts of conditions, sand-to-snow. Smaller in size but larger in the purchase price, a new Rokon costs slightly more than a quality off-road motorcycle made by another manufacturer.

Though it is designed primarily for off-road use, the Rokon Mototractor is street legal in all U.S. states except California. Since it is lightweight, it can be transported using a rack mounted to a vehicle using a 2-inch receiver hitch, as well as in the bed of a pickup or on a trailer. At 79x39x30-inches, it is too big to fit into a car's trunk.

With 15-inches of ground clearance, the Rokon can climb over many obstacles and up a jaw-dropping 60% grade. It can also tow a trailer weighing 2,000-lbs, even though the motorcycle itself only weighs 218-lbs.

With one or two riders on board, the Rokon can fjord a stream that is 24-inches deep. And, if deeper water is encountered, the bike can be put on its side and floated across the water obstacle. (Yes, this steel-frame motorcycle floats.)

Since the bike is light and has extremely wide tires, it can traverse terrain that could not be managed by other motorcycles and bikes. And, it can do so without even leaving much of a track.

The Rokon's 3-speed gearbox behind its 7 HP gasoline engine, can propel the bike to a top cruising speed of 35 MPH (56 km/h). It's 2.7-gallon (10 L) fuel tank can operate the bike for 8-hours of continuous use, and the 8 x 25-inch tubeless tires can be used to hold an additional 2.5 gallons of fuel (or water).

There are many other mid-size motorcycles, including combination street-legal off-road models which can be found used, and as such, are much more affordable than a Rokon. Many of these other motorcycles will work well for evacuation, even though they don't compare to the Rokon.

When other similar-size motorized vehicles are compared feature-to-feature and capability-to-capability with the Rokon, they aren't in the same league. Nevertheless, many of the dual-sport motorcycles made by companies such as Honda, Kawasaki, Suzuki, and Yamaha, while not comparable, are still adequate for most evacuation purposes. Plus, many of these are capable of highway speeds, which may be an important feature, especially if evacuating from an urban area.

Since these other motorcycles can be found in excellent condition on the used vehicle market, for a price that is half that of a new Rokon, most of us will compromise and buy a used dual-sport model. (Even though Rokon motorcycles have been manufactured for 50-years, it is unusual to find a used one for sale.)

For those of us who don't have deep pockets, a mid-size motorbike made by another reputable manufacturer can amply meet most of our needs. Perhaps even better, since the Rokon isn't capable of operating at highway speeds. Yet, the Rokon is a stellar performer for off-road use, and quieter than most other motorcycles. It is also an EMP-resistant workhorse which is easy to ride and simple for even a layman to maintain and repair.

Golf Carts and Electric Utility Carts

As the name implies, these small 2-4-person vehicles were invented to transport golfers around the pristine lawns of a golf course. Though these are usually battery-powered (36-volt) and quiet, with the advent of their use for utility purposes, has come the introduction of nearly identical-looking carts which are powered by a small gasoline engine.

In addition to standard fiberglass body styles, it's not unusual to find models which are flamboyant in design or lifted and have large tires and mag wheels to look like an off-road vehicle. However, though some models are street-legal in some communities, and some can attain speeds of 35 MPH or more, these are generally not 4-wheel drive, nor are they optimal for transportation much beyond a neighborhood.

With fresh batteries and a full charge, and driven on flat land by a single occupant, a golf cart can travel as far as 30-miles. However, once additional weight and hills are added to the mix, the operating range declines rapidly.

If you already own a golf cart and plan to use it to evacuate, keep it charged and well maintained. If you are thinking of buying one for this purpose, there may be better options. Yet, a golf cart powered by a gas engine might be a viable alternative if the terrain is conducive and your destination is nearby. However, in most situations, a street-legal ATV or UTV is a better choice.

All-Terrain Vehicles (ATV), Utility Task Vehicle (UTV), Side-by-Side (SxS), and Rugged Terrain Vehicles (RTV)

There is a lot of confusion between these off-road sport and utility vehicles, primarily because the dividing line which separates one from another is blurred. Each manufacturer seems to have a slightly different take on the subject.

Features vary widely, too. Some require manual shifting while others have automatic transmissions. Some have a slow top speed such as 20 MPH, while others can operate at freeway speeds. And, just as with motorcycles, some models are inexpensive while others can cost as much as a car.

Some of these special-purpose vehicles are 2-wheel drive (2WD), and other models made by the same manufacturer might be 4-wheel drive (4WD), 6-wheel drive (6WD), or even 8-wheel drive (8WD). Some can float, while others are amphibious vehicles that can be used for transportation on both water and land. (In our experience, these combo vehicles provide marginal performance on the water, and they are not truly all-terrain vehicles on land, either. But if both a boat and land-vehicle are needed, such as in a marshy area or swamp, these amphibious vehicles can be a godsend.)

The following information is merely an orientation to the topic of these special-purpose vehicles. For inclusion here, we define this category as special-purpose vehicles which are:

a) commercially manufactured,
b) gasoline powered,
c) have 3 or more wheels,
d) have the capacity to transport 2 or more people, and are
e) smaller than a car or truck.

For those looking for simplicity and EMP-resistant transportation, ATVs tend to be less technologically advanced both mechanically and with their electronics than the other vehicles in this category. Plus, ATVs are usually easier to start with a dead battery, and lighter weight if they need to be pushed. Yet as a class, all of the vehicles in this category are simple mechanically and less dependent on electronics than even an economy car or truck.

ATV: When first introduced, these were motorized three-wheel "trikes" with a lower center of gravity than a 3-wheel motorcycle. They came equipped with large knobby tires, and they were designed for off-road and trail use. These "sport" vehicles were designed around having family fun rather than for a utility purpose. Since the tricycle design is inherently unstable, most manufacturers stopped building these ATV trikes in the early 1990s, replacing them with 4-wheel "quads" which were similar in size but had four wheels.

Today, most of these are still made for a single rider, but there are 2-seat ATVs. Perhaps the most distinctive differentiation is that these cannot haul much weight, and the purchase price is often significantly less than the other small vehicles in this category.

UTV and SxS: Though the terminology is different, Utility Task Vehicles (UTV) and Side-by-Side (SxS) vehicles can look and operate the same. Both have configurations which fully enclose the occupants in a loosely-fitting cloth or fiberglass cab, or with a roof only, or with a cab that is open to the weather. Most do not have heating or air conditioning. Most can be equipped with a winch to help extricate the vehicle if it gets stuck.

More expensive than an ATV, these vehicles also tend to be more durable. Plus, they often have additional off-road capabilities, greater capacity to haul cargo and beefy passengers, can carry more people, provide better weather and accident protection for travelers, are easier to drive and more stable, and they routinely have an abundance of accessories available for work-related purposes. A UTV or SxS feels more like a vehicle, whereas an ATV feels more like a toy.

RTV: Rough Terrain Vehicles are basically the same as a UTV, but the manufacturers claim they are more durable, and perform more reliably under harsh use, than a standard UTV. We have not had the opportunity to test these assertions. As with all of these vehicles, quality varies considerably from one manufacturer to another. Nonetheless, UTV and RTV models which are used by the military are usually more durable and worth the added cost.

Dune Buggy, Sand Rail, 3-Wheel Roadsters, Desert Patrol Vehicle (DPV) aka/ Fast Attack Vehicle (FAV), Light Combat Tactical All-Terrain Vehicle (JLTV / L-ATV), and TOMCAR.

Dune Buggies and Sand Rails: Built by specialty shops primarily in California, Dune Buggies are constructed using a fiberglass shell which serves as a topless body for the vehicle. These shells are often mounted on top of a Volkswagen undercarriage and powered by either an air-cooled VW or Porsche engine.

A Sand Rail is similar, but it is built using tubular steel to create the frame and body shape, with axels, steering assemblies, transmission, engine, and other running gear salvaged from a truck or Jeep, or sometimes from a VW Beetle. Since they rarely have a cab to protect the occupants from the weather and road debris, these offer little protection for passengers and gear. Notwithstanding, they can be fast, highly maneuverable and ultra-lightweight.

The key to the success of these vehicles is the simplicity of the design, and the removal of inessential parts not actually required for transportation. There are commercially manufactured versions of both of these vehicle types, as well as many home-built versions. Today it is hard to find these in new condition, and those available on the used market tend to have suffered from hard use. Nevertheless, a used Dune Buggy or Sand Rail in good shape can be a bargain, easy and inexpensive to repair and maintain, and the ones without electronic components are EMP-resistant.

3-Wheel Roadsters: The Polaris Company broke new ground in the 3-wheel motorcycle market with the introduction of the Slingshot, which is a 3-wheel roadster. Other manufacturers are following their lead.

Rather than use the traditional tricycle design of most 3-wheel motorcycles which is inherently unstable in turns, the Slingshot (and clones) have two wheels in front to maintain stability. These front wheels are controlled by a steering wheel like a car. When viewed from the front, these roadsters look like a low-slung sports car. However, when observed from the rear, there is only one wheel.

It is this single rear tire which provides traction to accelerate the 3-wheel roadster, much like a conventional motorcycle. Since this vehicle has no cab to protect the two occupants from the weather, has minimal road clearance so it cannot be taken off-road (at least in its standard configuration), has only limited cargo space, and only one-wheel power (1WD), this is not a versatile vehicle. However, it is fast, far more stable than a motorcycle, and it is more maneuverable than most cars (and it is fun to drive).

Polaris RZR, General, and Ranger: The Polaris company (Polaris.com) has a wide range of off-road vehicles which can be customized by the factory to meet your specific needs. If you want to keep your vehicle street legal, that will limit your options, but the products produced by this company are time-tested and worth considering.

Desert Patrol Vehicle (DPV) / Fast Attack Vehicle (FAV): Both the DPV and FAV are military versions of a Sand Rail that are commercially constructed by a defense contractor for use by spec ops troops in Iraq and Afghanistan. These are all but impossible to find through military surplus outlets and auctions, but off-road shops do sometimes make similar vehicles for customers using GMC or Ford truck parts.

L-ATV: Designed to be more combat capable than the HMMWV (aka/Hummer) but lighter and far nimbler than the MRAP (Mine Resistant Armor Protected, v-hulled tank-like wheeled vehicle), the L-ATV is made by Oshkosh Defense. Though not available to the public, DIY mechanics and specialty shops are producing a similar-looking truck built from the bones of a 4-wheel drive ¾ ton diesel pickup truck. Though not generally armored like the L-ATV, these combine the benefits of easy-to-find parts which are commercially available for off-road 4WD pickup trucks, with the enhancements popular with owners of off-road Baja trophy racing vehicles.

TOMCAR: Designed by the Israel Defense Forces for delivery by parachute, the TOMCAR is now available to the public. Assembled in Arizona for the America markets, these small versatile vehicles are available with either a 110 HP gas engine, diesel, electric, or hybrid gas/electric. The TE6 hybrid has a 600-mile range which includes 60-miles in 'stealth' mode that has zero thermal signature, and is silent because its power comes from the hybrid's 60 HP electric motor. Impressive off-road, 4WD models can climb a near vertical grade, and traverse surfaces that are beyond the capability of a military HUMVEE. Configurations range from a 2-person fast-attack model to a 9-person troop transport, from a firefighting model to one that has an integral water purification system capable of purifying either fresh or salt water. Field repairable, the cost for the basic model is equivalent to the price of a compact car.   www.TOMCAR.com

Horses, Mules, Llamas, Camels, and Other Pack Animals

While useful for transporting people and supplies around the vicinity of a safe-haven retreat location, or for transportation or patrol in a rural area, it would be a rare circumstance when an animal can be used for urban evacuation.

Moreover, the rider or handler needs to be experienced. Though these animals may be well-suited for non-mechanized rural evacuation, the capabilities will nevertheless vary widely according to the capacity and training of the animal, the saddle type, bulk and weight distribution, and the abilities of the rider/handler. Practice is essential, both for the rider or handler, and the animal.

Dogs as Pack Animals

A dog which is one of the working breeds is sometimes used as a pack animal. However, it is cruel to expect even a young healthy dog, to carry a load that exceeds 10-15% of the animal's trim body weight.

Unless you know that the breed is capable, and your dog has undergone the necessary training and conditioning, a dog should not carry a cargo load that is awkward, off-balance, or which weighs more than 15% of the animal's optimal body weight.

Even when a proper harness and a dog-pack is used, this equates to small load capacity. For example, a 60-pound Labrador working dog should only carry about 9-pounds of combined weight (harness, pack, and supplies). Therefore, in most situations, this load needs to be limited to the dog's own 3-day supply of water and dry kibble dog food.

Using this 60-pound dog as an example, the weight of a large but lightweight mesh harness and a side-by-side dog backpack (required for balancing the load), will weigh approximately 2.75-pounds. A 3-day supply (9 cups) of dry kibble dog food contained in Hefty Slider plastic bags, 3.75-pounds. Plus, two water bladders, together containing a 3-day supply of water for this animal, will add an additional 13.25-pounds. Total weight, nearly 20-pounds.

Without adding any additional cargo, this already exceeds the recommended maximum pack weight for this animal. Therefore, at best, a dog should not carry more than the animal's own 3-day supply of water and food. Nothing extra.

Note: The abilities and the food and water needs of your dog will be different from this example. These quantities are included here solely to illustrate that a pet should not be considered a cargo-carrying pack animal.

Walking and Running

Walking: In an urban setting, an adult is usually only able to walk 2.5-miles in an hour due to traffic and other impediments. Whereas on open, level terrain that is paved or has a smooth surface, the average for a healthy adult is 3.5 MPH. Yet, experienced, fit walkers with appropriate boots or shoes can maintain a brisk pace of 4.5 MPH for many miles. The takeaway message? Attend to your health, and purchase good walking shoes for short distances, and hiking boots for longer treks.

Proper hydration en route is necessary for health and to maintain a brisk pace, as well. Therefore, wearing a backpack-style water bladder, such as a Camelbak, is a good idea since it is effortless to sip water hands-free while sustaining your walking pace.

If you plan to walk more than a mile or two, suitable footwear and socks are needed. If you will be walking more than 5-miles, appropriate footwear becomes essential.

Further, if you will be carrying anything, it should be transported on your back using a shoulder strap over each shoulder, backpack-style. The weight of the load also needs to be well distributed inside the backpack to keep you balanced, as an unbalanced load will increase fatigue.

When carrying a load, hiking boots are a better choice than walking shoes. (Not just boots, but *hiking* boots.) Heavy duty socks, or ideally a soft, thin inner sock (sock liner), plus a thick outer sock which provides additional padding and perspiration absorption, and snug, but not tight-fitting boots, will facilitate foot health. Hiking boots, sock liners, and hiking socks are available at large sporting goods stores.

Both walking shoes and boots need to be broken-in before a long walk. With most footwear, three short break-in hikes, each involving a 2-mile walk, is usually sufficient to break-in a lightweight pair of boots. Boots made for backpacking or constructed of stiff leather or plastic may require more time.

How do you know if your footwear is adequately broken in? You should be able to walk for 2-miles without experiencing any hot spots, blisters, or sores on your toes, feet or ankles.

If you routinely get blisters on your feet or ankles in the same places during a long hike, before starting a long walk, cover the affected skin area with Moleskin adhesive foam pads. If you don't have Moleskin, use Band-Aids.

Take care of your feet. A small annoyance can develop into a problem that will slow you down, reduce the distance you can travel, and interfere with maintaining vigilance.

If your feet get wet, and you can safely stop to change into a dry pair of socks, this will help diminish the onset of blisters. Wet feet are prone to blistering, so do what you can to keep your feet dry.

In hot weather, waterproof boots and shoes can prevent perspiration from escaping, and this trapped sweat is another mechanism which increases friction. If you don't need waterproof footwear, select shoes or boots designed to help your feet 'breathe.'

During a long walk, if you stop to rest, do not remove your footwear unless necessary. Feet will typically swell during long walks, so putting your footwear back on your feet after you've rested, may prove to be difficult or even impossible.

Keep your shoes/boots snugly laced while walking. It's fine to loosen laces while taking a break from your hike, but do not remove your boots until you've finished walking for that day.

Running: When I was involved in advanced training for urban SWAT teams, we periodically had Navy SEALs come through the FBI's wilderness operations course. For them, it was just practice. They could have taught this field class, but to their credit, they were always looking for new ways to do what they already do so well. Now to my main point.

Rather than hike the course like police SWAT team operators, they ran the course. They literally ran or jogged the entire mountainous route. They ran continuously for three days. Three days. Daylight hours and through the darkness with headlamps, they ran the unmarked course without pausing to rest or sleep. They ate and drank while they ran. They talked and made their strategy plans while they ran. These guys made the Energizer Bunny look lazy.

These guys were phenomenal. Of course, they had to stop running to engage in the various operator scenarios we had planned for them along the way. This ranged from being hyper-alert when they ran so they could avoid being surprised by booby traps and IEDs set on the trails, to full-blown engagement with terrorists with WMDs, but at all other times, they ran. They ran up the mountains and down. They ran and ran and ran.

I've never encountered anyone else who could accomplish such a feat. So, when Marathon runners tell me they intend to evacuate by running, I appreciate their enthusiasm and skill, but I also understand that their plan is often ill-conceived. Run-walk-run-rest-run-walk-run is a more practical strategy.

If you are a Navy SEAL or a spec-ops soldier, you can engage in all sorts of ancillary activities and still retain combat vigilance while you run. But for most of us, this warrior skill can't be switched "on."

Most marathon runners are entirely consumed with the act of running when they compete, but this focus is detrimental to evacuation running. Evacuation, whether by car or on foot, involves maintaining keen situation awareness, and being able to adapt to changes in conditions instantly.

If you are an accomplished runner, don't consider evacuation as a new Marathon venue. Use your skills to run, walk when appropriate for added vigilance and to eschew detrimental attention, and rest periods to maintain your energy and hydrate. At some point, you may need to transition from marathon runner to sprinter, to Parkour free-runner, or to stop and help someone. Speed is important, but it isn't the only thing that is important.

Baby Strollers, Shopping Carts, and Wheelchairs

Strollers: Jogging strollers are not only an excellent choice for transporting young children, but they are also useful for hauling gear. They can be used for either purpose or both.

If you will be walking with a young child, OR, transporting a load which weighs more than 20% of your body weight, consider using a "jogging stroller" for your gear. These have large wheels and suspension that adapts to uneven roadways and off-road dirt trails, long handles which let you stand in a normal position, and a design that makes it easy to climb curbs. Of course, they are not useful in rough terrain, so consider your routing before purchasing one of these strollers.

Yet another advantage of carrying gear in a jogging stroller is the concealment they can provide. These strollers often have sunscreens or optional rain flaps designed to protect the young rider from the elements. These protective covers can also be used to hide what you are carrying.

Since most thieves aren't interested in stealing children, most won't bother to look behind the flap to inspect your load. As a result, you will often be able to proceed without interference even though you may be carrying a theft-prone cargo.

Adjust the handle of your jogging stroller to match the height of your waist. This will help you maintain a brisk pace and reduce fatigue. If the handle height is a little high, this isn't a big problem, but if it is low and you need to bend forward, it will increase fatigue. Those who are tall may need to adapt the stroller to compensate for the added height, as handle height and having sufficient distance between the operator and the stroller is necessary for maintaining a natural stride.

Though a double jogging stroller (2-child stroller) usually has a stated weight limit of 100-pounds, they can often be adapted to haul a mobility impaired person or an elderly adult weighing twice that amount. Therefore, a large, sturdy, jogging stroller might be a better option than a standard wheelchair.

Since a quality jogging stroller can be expensive, consider finding one at a resale store which specializes in items for children. Or, look on Craig's List or some other discount source which sells used products. If your jogging stroller is old or used, check the tires, and oil the axles and wheel bearings to keep your stroller serviceable.

Jogging strollers are made for speed. Other strollers are not. Standard models, car-seat strollers, classic perambulators and traditional strollers, are difficult to control when walking fast.

The opposite extreme is the ultra lightweight and "umbrella" strollers made for convenience. These lack load capacity and durability, increase operator fatigue and are prone to break down during a long hike. Yet, if you aren't accustomed to carrying a heavy backpack, any stroller may be better than no wheels when you are hauling more than 40-pounds (18 kg) of gear. Carrying all your supplies on your back, mile after mile can be a grueling task.

Lightweight and standard baby strollers are not nearly as desirable as a jogging stroller. They are not adequate for transporting children over long distances, nor are they ideal for hauling supplies. Their frail construction, small tires, mushy suspension and short handles, make it difficult to use them on anything other than smooth pavement. Notwithstanding, they are still an option if you don't have access to a jogging stroller.

Shopping Carts: Often used by homeless people to transport all their worldly possessions, grocery store shopping carts are sometimes also stolen by evacuees during a disaster to accomplish a similar purpose. However, beyond the moral issue, is the fact that these carts are only useful on smooth surfaces. They might work okay on a sidewalk or paved street, but they are wholly unsuited for anything else. Nevertheless, during a disaster scenario, they are often used as a last-resort method for transporting an injured or elderly person.

Wheelchairs: Even the styles which have large rear wheels are not suitable for evacuation when the distance to be traveled is more than a few blocks. The hard rubber tires, lack of suspension to soften the ride, and push-handles which require bending over, make this a less desirable choice. Skilled users of self-propelled wheelchairs may be useful for the experienced user, but motorized transport may be a better choice.

Boats and Boats on Trailers

In coastal communities, boats are often forgotten or not considered viable for evacuation. This is unfortunate. If the need to bug-out is not related to a storm, tsunami or some other event which would make travel by boat dangerous, then a boat may be worth considering.

Boats: However, this isn't a viable option unless specific criteria are met. The watercraft must be seaworthy, and the engine 100% reliable. It must have sufficient fuel aboard plus an extra 20%, a backup power method even if it's just oars in oarlocks. Weather and tides must be favorable. Drinking water, and emergency food for more days than the anticipated duration of the journey must be onboard. Lastly, the selected course needs to be familiar and the destination known to provide the characteristics of a safe-haven. If these requirements are met, then travel by boat is worth considering.

The limiting factors for small boat evacuation are usually lack of speed, inability to transport a sufficient quantity of fuel, space and payload capacity for people and supplies, lack of navigation equipment, and the seaworthiness of the boat for operation more than two miles offshore. Still, these problems can often be overcome.

If the destination is no more than 300-miles, and conditions at the destination are known, if a course can be plotted which keeps land in sight and reachable, the weather forecast is favorable, and there aren't other obstacles to safely reach the destination, then it might be worth the risk.

However, just being able to evacuate safely on a boat isn't enough. The destination must be viable as a safe-haven, too. The reward must be worth the risk.

A larger boat with a cabin shares the attributes of a motorhome that is similar in size. More sustainable than an open watercraft such as a sports or ski boat, a craft with living quarters can be piloted to a remote location, anchored offshore, and then used as a safe-haven for a short-duration emergency situation.

Stockpiling a sufficient quantity of water and food can be problematic for a medium-size or small vessel. Nonetheless, a boat may still be a suitable for both emergency shelter and as a method of transport to reach a safe-haven retreat location that is on the coast.

Spearfishing will remain viable long after hunters have decimated the land-based animal population. Certain seaweeds and various other foods can be harvested from the ocean, and these can augment a supply of stored food.

On the sea, it's difficult to live for an extended period on even an ocean-going yacht, unless it has desalinization equipment designed to process salt water into drinking water. And, you are living in a sunny environment, and your boat is equipped with solar panels and a rack of deep cycle batteries.

If a vessel is going to be purchased for this safe-haven purpose, consider a motorsailer that is equipped with sails and a diesel motor. Though inefficient as both a sailboat and as a motorboat, the flexibility of being able to operate the boat using two power sources is an advantage. Having the ability to travel using the motor on a windless day, and by sail to conserve fuel, makes long-term operation possible. A motorsailer is not fast, but it is flexible.

Trailered Boats: Often left behind in an emergency situation, if you get out early, hauling a boat can provide three advantages over leaving it behind.

First, it can be used as a trailer to haul extra gear. Second, a boat with a cabin can be used for lodging. (If it has a kitchen, icebox, emergency radios, etc., so much the better.) Third, if you evacuate to a place where there is an expanse of water, having a boat provides another transportation option.

The downside is significant if you fail to leave early, as hauling a trailer in an evacuation traffic jam is fraught with problems. So, if you are considering pulling your boat on its trailer, it is essential to evacuate early, before others are even aware of the need to leave the area.

Airplanes

If you are a pilot and own your own airplane, evacuation by air may be a desirable choice, but there are several caveats.

First, you, or a member of your immediate family, needs to be a competent pilot of the aircraft which will be used. Having your own pilot is nice, but what happens if they don't show up to fly the plane? Someone else better be ready and able.

Second, you need to own the airplane. Leased planes, corporate aircraft, and timeshare-owned planes may be a problem. One of the other users of that aircraft may have the same idea. Or, an employee at the airport may decide to "borrow" your plane before you arrive.

Locks on airplane doors and ignitions are notoriously easy to defeat. Therefore, a backup plan isn't just desirable, it is required.

Third, unless you have a locked and secure storage room at the hanger where your airplane is kept, you will need to transport all your gear and passengers to the airport. Since planes have limited hauling capacity, you will need to tightly manage the passenger roster and stores, as it is easy to exceed the aircraft's limits, and therein create a dangerous situation. Since your passengers may not understand this risk, you will need to monitor loading and the actual weight of your passengers.

Fourth, the plane needs to be regularly maintained and kept fully fueled. And, your aircraft needs to be equipped with navigation aids, and you need to know how to use them—even if you are a VFR pilot. That extra equipment may become necessary.

Note: If your course takes you over an urban area affected by the emergency situation, your aircraft should remain as high as possible, and your cruising speed should be maintained at 100 knots or faster. If this isn't possible, chart a different course. During the Hurricane Katrina disaster, even relief helicopters were routinely shot at by miscreants on the ground.

Fifth, and perhaps most important, you need to live near the airport and have ready access to your aircraft. If you can't get to it in a few minutes, the window of opportunity may close as the airport may close, or aircraft may be grounded. Inclement weather, threats of terrorism, EMP and other electronics and communication problems, will quickly shut down an airport. Therefore, consider hangaring at a nearby private field, or live at an airpark. These locations may provide you with a distinct advantage.

Special-Needs Transportation

Alternate transportation for an elderly person, or an individual who has health problems or mobility issues, will present additional challenges. These must be fully resolved in advance. The same rule applies; you need at least two alternate forms of transportation.

Conventional wheelchairs are often not the answer. They are designed for smooth flat terrain and short distances. You will need to prepare other options from the previous pages, or recruit help from someone who can help you satisfy this need.

Other Problems/Solutions for Evacuation Transportation

Other obstacles to safe evacuation include reflectors, bright colors, and shiny finishes which draw attention to you. Control of interior dome lights of vehicles; ability to view the interior as needed, and to switch-off the interior lights to avoid detection or the unwanted illumination of the occupants.

The failure to maintain clear visibility for the driver or navigator when the vehicle is loaded with gear and supplies is a common problem that must be remedied. You need to be prepared to accomplish minor on-the-road repairs and have a basic toolkit designed for your vehicle and locale.

Regardless of the mode of transportation, you need to have tires that are appropriate for the terrain. For bikes and motorcycles, install puncture-resistant tires or tubes, and have a tire removal/installation and tube repair kit, and a method to inflate the tires after performing a repair. For cars and trucks, carry at least two cans of Fix-A-Flat aerosol tire inflator, so that you can get back on the road after a tire has been punctured by a nail. (The 12-oz can is for standard tires; 20-oz for large tires.)

> **#1 Reason for Equipment Failure:** Overheating; water cooled engines may need extra radiator coolant or radiator hose-repair tape to fix a leak.

> **#2 Reason for Equipment Failure:** Overloading; failure to take into account what you can reasonably carry, and the weight limitations and capacity of your vehicle.
>
> This includes transporting too many people, as well as carrying payload that exceeds the manufacturer's specifications. Or, loads that may be under the stated maximum load but using the vehicle in a way that overworks the engine, overheats it, or the suspension is overtaxed by off-road or other-than-intended use.

Whatever vehicle you choose, consider installing extra-bright headlights or off-road lights, and night vision. Be able to monitor an AM/FM/SW radio during your evacuation, and have 2-Way radios available for communication between you and your traveling companions, and those you intend to meet at your rendezvous location or your safe-haven.

Threats to Transportation #1: Theft and Vandalism

Theft is a common problem in the best of times, but during a period of shortages or anarchy, expect theft to escalate to an outlandish level. Not only will your supplies be vulnerable to theft and you to armed robbery, expect carjacking and vehicle theft to also become frequent occurrences—even in "good" neighborhoods.

If it can be avoided, don't leave anything unattended, including your transportation. If you must leave it, try to park it in a spot where you can observe it—and secure it using extra security measures.

Vehicle wheels should have lug-nut locks (get a recommendation from a tire store), and your fuel supply protected by a locking gas cap.

If you are hauling a bike or a trailer, using a roof rack, or anything else that can be removed or pilfered, plan now for a locking method. You need to not only lock items like bikes to the bike rack, but you also need to lock the rack itself to the vehicle. Both trailers and hitches need to be locked to the vehicle, as well.

In 'safe' environments, short term, it may be enough to lock theft-prone transportation by securing it to something immobile like a light pole, then feeding the chain or security cable through both wheels and the frame before it is padlocked. But in most circumstances, it is advisable to chain your car or truck to a solid object, as well.

Use a 3/8" or heavier case-hardened chain around a lamp post or other solid object, and then loop it through the vehicle's frame, or at least through a slotted wheel or a trailer hitch support. Lock the chain using a DISCUS-style (disc) padlock such as the ABUS 20/70, or a lock which provides similar security.

These measures alone will not prevent theft. The best we can hope for is to make theft difficult and time-consuming, so that the criminal will leave to find an easier target.

Vandalism is an act of malice that is often the result of pent-up frustration or anger. Since emotions often run high during periods of adversity, anger is often channeled into senseless acts of destruction. Therefore, don't be surprised if thieves who have been thwarted by your good security measures, retaliate by slashing tires or other acts of violence. These may be senseless acts or intended to deprive you of transportation or supplies you had the foresight to prepare.

Hide/Guard: If it becomes necessary to park your vehicle, whenever possible, hide and lock your vehicles and valuables in a place where they cannot be easily discovered. Use a hidden armed guard(s), especially if your transportation or supplies are irreplaceable. Unless it is absolutely necessary, don't even leave hidden and locked vehicles or valuables unattended, even if you think they are secure.

Threats to Transportation #2: Electromagnetic Pulse Weapons and Solar Flares

EMP Resistant Vehicles: If you are concerned with the threat posed by an electromagnetic (EMP) incident, whether it is initiated by the discharge of an EMP/RF device, a nuclear detonation, or a naturally occurring solar flare (CME), then you need an EMP-resistant motor vehicle.

In general, the solution is to obtain a pre-1968 carbureted (gas) car, or a pre-1972 truck, or a pre-1980 era diesel vehicle, or a surplus military field vehicle, or, a motorcycle which has a kick starter and a carburetor. (A motorcycle with an electric starter may be okay, as long as it also has a kick-starter.) The issue is if the vehicle's engine will still function without any electronics. Therefore, any vehicle under consideration must be evaluated according to this capability.

Whatever motor vehicle is chosen, it needs to have a pre-electronic electrical system and a carburetor rather than fuel injection. Though most motorcycles now utilize electronics, there are a few manufacturers who have continued to offer models which do not use sensitive microcircuitry. Often, these are the lower cost or "trail" models which are designed for durability and harsh use.

Why is this necessary? The concern is that microelectronics are susceptible to catastrophic failure when exposed to EMP and CME power pulses. These pulses don't generally harm people, but they are deadly for electronics. This concern is well accepted.

We know that modern vehicles contain an abundance of these highly-susceptible electronics, thus the concern. Even uncomplicated parts such as fuel injectors and ignition systems are now controlled by microcircuits. Therefore, these components may stop working, making the vehicle inoperable.

Unfortunately for us, this continues to be a much-debated topic within the scientific community, as well as among many verbose preppers who don't really know what they are talking about. This has caused a lot of confusion. Since top-tier scientists disagree, we need to take the musings and advice of laymen with a grain of salt.

Furthermore, since testing is impractical because for experiments to produce conclusive results, the detonation of a nuclear device is necessary. Since this is no longer done, we won't know which theory is correct until it happens.

In a Congressional hearing[9] on this topic, one expert witness had this to say about an EMP incident…

> *"when our field people were in here, I asked one of them how much of his capability would remain after an EMP laydown, and he told me, he told the committee, it is on the record, five percent. He would lose 95 percent of his capability with an EMP laydown."*

With this testimony, they were talking about critical infrastructure that is supposedly already shielded, and yet the projection was that only 5% of the systems would survive. Do you think it is reasonable to assume that our modern civilian vehicles will fare better?

Scientists agree that at some point we will be hit by an electromagnetic or RF pulse, or a similar pulse caused by a coronal mass ejection (CME, aka/solar flare). This has become a mainstream viewpoint.

Though NASA didn't report it at the time, apparently out of fear of panicking the public, in July 2012 we had a close call. The earth was almost hit by a CME the size of the Carrington Event of 1859. So, it can happen. We need to expect it, and prepare for it.

The experts seem to all agree that an EMP or CME will hit us again at some point. What they don't agree on is, "when?" But many scientists point to recent solar activity as evidence that it will be soon. Yet, an EMP device detonated in the United States or Europe by a rogue nation or terrorists might be even sooner.

---

[9] Hearing before the U.S. Military Research and Development Subcommittee on Armed Services [H.A.S.C. No. 106–31] "Electromagnetic Pulse Threats to U.S. Military and Civilian Infrastructure," House of Representatives, 106th Congress.
http://commdocs.house.gov/committees/security/has280010.000/has280010_0.htm#48

Personally, I am confident that an electromagnetic pulse poses a legitimate safety concern for all of us. Admiral James Woolsey, former director of the CIA sure thinks so, as does Dr. Peter Vincent Pry, head of the U.S. Government's Task Force on National and Homeland Security. It's a grave danger that is on our doorstep.

What no one can tell us with any certainty is the effect. An EMP or CME might only mean an extended period without power and economic disaster. Or, it could be a catastrophic event which plunges us into a new Stone Age—or, it might be something in between.

With any of these outcomes, including those proffered by the most optimistic experts, we can expect life as we know it, to change. If we are prepared for it, this will make a world of difference for us.

In my view, the old adage, *"Hope for the best, prepare for the worst,"* is particularly sage advice when it comes to these 'pulse' threats. If the naysayers who claim the damage will be minor,[10] and that only vehicles currently being operated when the pulse hits will be damaged, and that only 10% of the parked cars will not start afterward, that's great. Maybe you will be one of the lucky majority.

On the other hand, if the more conservative experts are correct, and our electronics and most modern cars and trucks stop working after an EMP, we'll need a plan. If we want to have the benefit of motorized transportation, then we had better have an EMP-resistant backup transportation plan.

This backup plan will either include an old vehicle or military truck. Or, a form of transportation that does not utilize any electronic components. Or, transportation that uses simple electrical components which can be stored in an EMP-resistant container, and then installed after an event to repair the vehicle.

* For more on this subject and instructions for building a simple but effective Faraday Cage to protect electronics from EMP pulses and Solar Flares (CME), see Appendix-C at the end of this book.

---

[10] Report of the Commission to Assess the Threat to the United States from Electromagnetic Pulse (EMP) Attack, Critical National Infrastructures, April 2008. *Note:* The EMP example used as the basis for this report was a low-yield device, so the conclusions are overly optimistic.

Transportation Summary
"We have a need for speed."

Even if we wanted to live off-grid, for my wife and I, it isn't practical to move to a wilderness redoubt in rural Montana. Our need to work also means we need jobs that are only available in a major urban area. At some point, maybe this will change, but for now, we need the city. Therefore, when disaster does strike, we need to be able to evacuate quickly and get to a safe place fast. Cities are ground zero for disaster-related problems.

To meet our 1-hour work-to-home-to-rural-area evacuation goal, we needed to select a different location for our home. So, we moved.

Though we need the city, a few years ago we moved our home to a location outside the city's suburban circle. We now live 25 miles away from our workplace in the city, so it's 40-minute commute to work, but the route is pleasant. The road is wide, lightly traveled, and travel does not require any freeway driving.

There is also another important feature of our new location. It is on the way from our workplace to our safe-haven retreat. This means that if we are in the city and decide we need to evacuate; we won't need to travel any unnecessary extra miles. We can go home, first, and then continue on to our safe-haven. If we aren't together when this happens, we can meet-up at home.

In our situation, we can now leave work, get home, load up, and be on the road and in a rural agricultural area, all in under an hour. Moreover, as a result of our pre-planning, the entire route to our safe-haven can be traveled without getting even close to a freeway or an official evacuation route. As a result, we should be able to avoid the hordes of panicked people and the problems of gridlocked traffic.

We have practiced our evacuation. We've done it more than once, so we know we can meet our 1-hour evacuation goal. We are confident that it's a goal we can reach. And yet, if we are somehow delayed, we should still be okay. Even if it takes twice as much time to get out of the city, we will still have evacuated from the area before most people begin the process of leaving town.

I'm not patting myself on the back here, nor am I trying to impress you. Rather, I've mentioned this personal information as a way to encourage you to, if necessary, make changes in your life.

Where my wife and I work, and where we live, are features of life that we were able to adapt. This is true for most people. Even if we can't alter these details immediately, they are aspects of life that we can change over time, if we plan for it and work to accomplish it.

For us, this was worth the effort. When the time comes, and we find ourselves facing a dire emergency, we have vastly improved the survivability of our family, particularly during those volatile first few hours. As it turned out, for us, this level of preparation wasn't a significant sacrifice, either. Quite the contrary.

Though commute time to work may be a bit longer than before, there are benefits. In addition to our ability to bug-out quickly, we now enjoy a healthier lifestyle, too.

We live in a tranquil vacation-like setting. Our neighbors are friendly and helpful, and in our downtime, we relax in an Eden-like setting. So, we aren't just prepared for a future emergency situation, we are also enjoying a healthier lifestyle, today.

As yet another side benefit, our "alternate transportation" methods are not only available for emergency use, they are now an enjoyable part of our new, more pleasant and healthier lifestyle.

This is something I encourage you to work towards. For us, it's been a welcome change. I suspect it might be for you, too.

This morning I was thinking about the time when Jesus walked the hills of Israel. As Jesus taught His followers, He warned them[11] to be ready to evacuate at a moment's notice. Because of that warning, when Jerusalem was about to be overrun in 70 A.D., the Christian population was prepared. They got out quickly.

In the writings of a well-known Jewish historian of that era, Josephus,[12] we learn that more than a million Israelis died in that siege. Most of the people living in Jerusalem were slaughtered. But apparently, none of their Christian neighbors were killed. Why? Because they were ready to evacuate.

The Christians listened to Jesus' warning. They were prepared. They got out early. And, they got out fast.

---

[11] Holy Bible; Mark 13:1-23, Luke 17:26-31.

[12] Flavius Josephus. The Wars of the Jews or History of the Destruction of Jerusalem." Book VI. Chapter 1.1

Chapter 7

Communication During Emergency Situations

We are a technology-driven society. We live in a world where we expect to be able to contact our family and friends without delay. Whether it be through texting, instant messaging, telephones, or other communication mechanisms, we expect to be able to communicate whenever we feel the need.

In an emergency situation, expect this to change. When this happens, expect the fear-factor to rise exponentially. When your spouse, family members, and friends are unable to reach each other, and help generally, panic may quickly follow.

This is the reality you should expect. Plan for it, and prepare your family and friends for this situation.

Your plan should assume that you will not be able to communicate with family members and friends. Period. If you can connect via telephone, that's great. However, if you are not able to connect, each person needs to know what to do, and how to bug-out, without additional communication.

Without a doubt, adaptability and resiliency during an emergency situation are greatly enhanced by communication. Therefore, develop alternative methods to communicate. This is important, but rarely is it adequately addressed.

If your mobile phone doesn't work, your brief Plan Summary document (included in each GO-Bag), and practice sessions, should include a reminder to try text messaging. Texting will often work even when voice calls do not. Next, think about what else you can do to establish communication.

If texting doesn't work and you have a smartphone or tablet device, you may be able to use it to send an email message via the Internet. In advance, make sure your devices are set-up for sending email messages via Wi-Fi (aka/WLAN). Even when the cellular phone system is down or has been shut off, you may be able to send messages by using the Internet.

Since your phone's battery won't last, your GO-Bag should include what you need to recharge your phone using a standard electrical connection and a battery-to-battery recharger. You might also consider including a cable to draw power from a laptop computer, a small solar panel, or a hand crank recharger. These can become invaluable accessories during an emergency situation.

If voice mail and texts go unanswered, and you don't have a 2-way radio, resort to the old-fashioned method of using paper messages left at prearranged locations.

For example, additional information on routing, or changes to the Plan, can be communicated by messages left at the point of departure and along the route. An individual, forced by circumstances to walk home from work rather than drive, should leave a message at a specific spot at their workplace (ex. top left desk drawer) or a prearranged site which is nearby. Yet another message(s) should be left along the prescribed route if it becomes necessary to deviate from the primary 'Plan-A' route.

Of course, the mechanism for how to leave messages needs to be determined in advance, too. A written reminder on how to communicate, along with communication materials, needs to be included in each GO-Bag.

Each GO-Bag also needs to contain a notepad (ideally with waterproof paper) and a pen with indelible ink. These simple items not only make it possible to record important information gleaned from a radio broadcast, but they also make it possible for you to leave a note at prearranged places and along your pre-planned route.

Also include a small roll of orange or brightly colored "flagging tape," like that used by construction workers, to mark the location where you leave a note. To avoid confusion, each GO-Bag for your family/group should have the same color tape.

Flagging Tape, also known as 'Survey Tape' or 'Contractor Ribbon,' is not adhesive. It is bright-color plastic ribbon, and it is commonly used on construction sites. Our use for it is location and trail marking—and messaging.

To call attention to the site of a message, use a 2-3 ft. length of bright-color 'flagging tape' to mark the location of the message. Simply tear a piece from the small roll in your GO-Bag, and tie this 'flag' to a tree branch adjacent to the roadway. Or, wrap it around a telephone pole. Either way, use enough of the plastic ribbon so that the tails move in the wind, to help draw attention to the flag.

This dangling 'flag' draws *private* attention to the message site. It serves as a confidential indicator that a note has been left at that location. In your brief Plan Summary (contained in each GO-Bag), there should be an explanation of this communication method, and instructions on where to place/find the associated note.

This communication method is a good example of when your Plan Summary needs to include specific details. Your brief Plan Summary, which is included in each GO-Bag, needs to remind each family and/or team member of this communication method. They need to be reminded how the process works, what to look for, and why the flagging tape is even included with their supplies. Don't assume that they will remember. The Plan Summary needs to remind them to look for messages, and how to leave messages.

Specifics need to be included; don't depend on memory.

For example, in the Plan Summary included in each GO-Bag, in the section that explains how to leave a message along a travel route, there might be a brief, simple and to the point, bullet-point instruction such as this:

> "Mark the message location by tying a 2-3 ft. piece of orange flagging tape to a tree branch or telephone pole. The placement of the flagging tape needs to be easily seen from the roadway. Put the note inside a plastic bag, or inside an old fast-food cup or something similar. Anchor it to the ground in the area under the flag, using a rock. If the message is of high importance, repeat this process a hundred feet further down the road."

Note: In the above example, one paragraph was ample to explain this communication method. Don't be wordy.

Expect a 'New Normal.'

Many of us have become so conditioned to our usual travel routes that we jump into our car and go without any conscious thought about how to get to our destination. Even when we need to drive to an unfamiliar location, most of us are conditioned to use a GPS device or a map app on our phone. However, in an emergency situation, our usual route may not be the best. What's more, it's dangerous to depend on these electronic devices. For a variety of reasons, they may not work.

Most of us are ill-prepared to operate without these electronic tools. Even if you can function without such paraphernalia, what about your family and friends, can they? Do they know how to read a paper map and use a compass?

If you expect to reconnect with family or friends in an emergency situation, each person needs to have several different paper maps, a compass, and these skills. They may be lost without them. Literally. (For more, see Chapter-5, Maps, Routes, and Navigation.)

We don't know who might be alone when disaster strikes. Everyone needs to know how to navigate using a map and compass. You need to make additional, special plans for your most vulnerable family members and friends.

The heart of the problem is that most of us have become wholly dependent on mobile phones and electronic devices. If we get lost, or we need help, we telephone a friend or family member—or 9-1-1. However, as you plan for an emergency situation, keep in mind that mobile phone systems are at best unreliable, and in a disaster, 9-1-1 help is often either unreachable or available.

During an emergency, your mobile phone, tablet device, GPS, and other electronic devices may not work for a variety of reasons. For example, a severe storm, earthquake, or power outage, can cause the mobile phone system to fail. Cellular towers are relatively intricate systems, and they are not resilient to damage. In addition to being overloaded by increased demand, there is a host of other reasons why your mobile phone may stop working.

You may not even know that cellular service is down. System problems can be invisible to the user.

For example, as a First Responder where I live, recently we were notified by county dispatchers that the fiber optic cable which provides phone service to most of our area was cut in a construction accident. Since the damage was not part of the cellular phone system, mobile phones appeared to work.

In this situation, when a person placed a call, their mobile phone would provide the standard ring tone, as if the phone was working. But it wasn't.

The cellular system thought it was sending its signal to the other phone, but the line itself was severed. It was giving a false indication of connection.

A situation like this can be additionally distressing since the user thinks their phone is working, so they start to worry about the other party, wondering "why?" they aren't answering. Unfortunately, they don't understand that the problem is with the phone system, not with the person they are trying to call.

In this example, both cellular phones and landlines were effected. Don't assume that your phone is working, just because you get a dial tone or because you hear it ringing.

For your emergency plan, don't rely on being able to use your mobile phone, GPS, or radio transmission repeaters.

If your cell phone or GPS is still operational during an emergency situation, or the map app on your phone still works, that's great. But if it doesn't, you will need to go "old school." You will need paper maps and a compass. And you, and every member of your family/group, will need to know how to use them.

Electronics

Mobile phones, map apps, and GPS devices

Don't expect your mobile phone to work in an emergency situation. Period. This will include map and compass apps on your smartphone. Though some applications do not require access to the Internet, most do. Either way, electronic devices are prone to damage. Use them if they work, but don't depend on them.

To test an app, switch your phone to "Airplane Mode" and see if the app still works. If it does, this is not a guarantee that it will work when the cellular system is down, but it is a first-step test method.

An additional heads-up reminder: Text messages and even email messages can sometimes be transmitted when the cellular circuits are overloaded with voice traffic. If you are unable to connect by phone, try texting.

Keep in mind that most cellular towers operate at near peak levels during rush-hour on an ordinary day. Therefore, expect the added traffic caused by a panicking public to quickly overwhelm phone systems, including 9-1-1 and emergency-service dispatchers.

As you develop your emergency plan, do not depend on being able to utilize mobile phones. Make sure that each member of your family/team understands that their mobile phone and other electronic devices may stop working. If they know this and understand their other communication options, they are less likely to panic.

If you consistently can't get through using your mobile phone (or another battery-operated communication device), consider turning it off to conserve power. You may have better success later, after others have exhausted the battery in their phones, thereby freeing-up the cellular network.

Note: In chaotic emergencies, particularly those which involve Homeland Security or the military, expect the government to shut-down the cellular phone system, or block its civilian use. This is a common practice in terrorist incidents, during periods of civil unrest, and also at other times of crisis when the mobile phone network is commandeered for security reasons, or to augment overtaxed First Responder radio channels.

Off-Grid Cell Phone *Texting*

Though you can sometimes use your cell phone to send a text message even when voice communication is impossible, texting is *not* a reliable communication method. In an emergency, texting may work, but it may not. Therefore, since you cannot depend on your cell phone working during an emergency situation, it should not be considered a primary communication tool. Notwithstanding, there is a "texting" alternative which is worth considering.

When you combine a *'goTenna'* (or similar add-on device) with your iPhone or Android smartphone, you can bypass the cellular network and its inherent unreliability. Essentially a 2-way radio that is designed to work with your smartphone, the *goTenna* uses your phone's Bluetooth connectivity, the goTenna app and the goTenna device itself, which is like a text-dedicated walkie-talkie. So even when you are off-grid, you can pair this device with your phone to send text messages.

How Does it work? You launch the app, compose a text message, press "Send," and your text message is immediately on its way, without any system delay. It is automatically transmitted using the goTenna's short-range (2-watt), text-dedicated MURS radio which broadcasts your message using a radio signal, rather than the cellular phone system or Internet. (151.820 – 154.600 MHz)

Think of it as a third option. Your smartphone is already designed to work using both the cellular phone network and Internet wi-fi. This just adds a third option, 2-way radio.

'goTenna' Positives

EASE OF USE: The *'goTenna'* is easy to use. Since even young children are often comfortable using smartphones, this add-on device for mobile phones gives both kids and adults alike, an alternative communication method. This is particularly useful during an emergency situation when cell phone towers are busy or inoperable, or when the user is in a no-coverage rural area. No license is required to use this device, nor is there an age requirement.

RANGE-BOOSTING CAPABILITY: Another advantage of the *goTenna* is that when multiple devices are in use, the radio signal can be automatically relayed by the other *goTenna* devices which are operating in the same geographic area. This provides added range. And, though the standard signal is encrypted to provide communication privacy, this feature can be bypassed, giving the user the ability to broadcast an emergency text message to all *goTennas* in the immediate area.

GPS AND MAPPING: The *goTenna* app can also be paired with your smartphone's GPS, a feature which adds yet another level of usefulness. With this 'location' feature enabled, the goTenna can be used to find a user who is lost. Or, you can use it to send your own location to another goTenna user.

OPTIONAL SUBSCRIPTION SERVICE: For those who have opted for the optional "goTenna *Plus*" service, which requires an annual paid subscription, the 'location' and 'mapping' functionality is expanded to include some additional useful enhancements such as:

1. Up to four topographic maps of regions of your choice, to help you with land navigation, and to make it easier to find another user.

2. It can be used to repeat-send the same message again-and-again over a 12-hour period, at a timing frequency of your choice. That way, if your initial message was not received, the device will keep resending it, so you don't need to stop and physically resend your message.

3. It can be used to chart your route, which makes it easy to retrace your steps, or you can send your routing information to another user.

4. The "plus" subscription lets you 'group chat' with up to six users, and it provides 'message received' confirmation.

SUMMARY: The primary advantage of the *'goTenna'* is that it is: a) simple to use, b) compact in size (5.8 x 1 x .5 in. / 147 x 25 x 13 cm), c) lightweight (1.8 oz. / 52 g), and d) you can learn how to use it in under five minutes.

'goTenna' Negatives

COST: Though less expensive than a GMRS radio with a built-in GPS, and cheaper than a single brand-name ham radio walkie-talkie, the goTenna is still relatively expensive. (Later in this chapter, you will find specifics on various 2-way radio options.)

The *"goTenna MESH"* is a cheaper version of the standard, 2-watt *"goTenna."* But in our view, it is a waste of money since it has half the power (1-watt) of the standard goTenna, which is already an underpowered device.

LIMITED FUNCTIONALITY: Though the features of the goTenna are robust, its usefulness is nevertheless limited since it can only be used for texting. Conversely, a GMRS or Ham radio can be used for both digital and voice communication, and they can be operated over greater distances—but advanced features do require more expertise.

PROFESSIONAL VERSIONS: The *"goTenna Professional"* devices use a different radio technology to extend the operating range of the unit, but they are substantially more expensive. This added cost diminishes their usefulness for the emergency communication needs of most people, which are better served by more robust 'ham' (aka/amateur) radios.

RANGE: The biggest downside of the *goTenna* is its limited range. In a downtown city environment, don't expect to communicate at a distance greater than ½ - 1 mile. If you are in a nearly flat, unobstructed rural environment (or if you get to a higher vantage point), you might be able to communicate with another *goTenna* user at a distance of 2 - 4 miles. Despite the fact that users have claimed successful communication at much greater distances, such success is highly unusual and cannot be expected.

Note: Both the sender and receiver need to have a goTenna and a smartphone, and have them switched "on." The goTenna will probably not work from inside a concrete, masonry, or steel structure, and it will have limited connectivity when used from inside a vehicle.

Short of hacking the device, there is no way to extend its range, other than to make sure it is not in contact with the human body when in use. For best reception and to achieve the greatest range, carry the goTenna on the outside, very top of a knapsack, or hold it by its strap over your head while transmitting.

DURABILITY: The goTenna is not waterproof, but it is water-resistant so it can be exposed to rain. The goTenna is reasonably durable, but it is not ruggedized to military specifications.

GPS & Mapping Features: The GPS and mapping features are dependent on the Global Positioning System (GPS) satellites, which can be damaged, turned off by the government, or intentionally misdirected when the U.S. Government has identified a threat which might utilize the GPS system to coordinate an attack. Therefore, even elaborate GPS devices cannot be relied upon as your only navigation tool.

Battery: The built-in Lithium-Ion battery of the goTenna has a useful life of only about 20-hours, but this can be extended by switching the device and your phone "off" when they are not needed. To further maximize the battery life of the goTenna and your smartphone, switch your phone to "airline" mode, followed by turning "on" the phone's GPS.

Like most mobile phones, the goTenna's battery can be recharged in about two hours. Unfortunately, the device cannot be repowered using disposable batteries, but a battery powered recharger can be used to recharge the unit partially.

Legal Issue: It is technically illegal to use the goTenna outside the U.S. However since these devices have such limited range and look innocuous, their use may not create a legal problem for the user.

Electronic Devices: Electronic communication devices like mobile phones are inherently unreliable and subject to damage, as well as exhausting their battery power, so a backup communication method is essential. Therefore you will need more than a goTenna, but this device may still be a viable backup communication tool that is worth considering. It is included here due to its ease of use by adults and teens alike, and because it is a lightweight add-on which can transform your phone into functioning texting device, even when the cellular network is inoperable. We have also included it here because we consider it to be a "kid friendly" device that phone-savvy children can quickly learn to use.

Communications: 2-Way Radios

Since communication is vital for adapting and adjusting your emergency plan to the circumstance, 2-way communication is a high priority. So, consider including a walkie-talkie in each GO-Bag. It may not be as useful as a functioning mobile phone, but it is better than having a dead phone and no other communication option.

Regardless of the claims made by the manufacturer, or those printed on the product's packaging, even the best walkie-talkie radios will only operate at relatively short distances. Line-of-sight is typically the maximum range. And, if there is an obstruction between you and the person you're trying to reach, such as a hill or building, it may not work even if the distance seems trivial.

Therefore, moving to a higher location can provide a substantial advantage. If there are no obstructions between you and the radio you are trying to connect with, you may be able to communicate with someone who is many miles from your location.

In real-world use, that's it. Don't expect more, and don't panic when you are unable to connect with someone who is supposed to be only a mile or two away from your location. If there are line-of-sight obstructions or radio-wave interference, the range of your 2-way radio may only be a few hundred feet – or less. (The same goes for goTenna texting.)

Just because your radio is able to receive a transmission, this does not mean that same person will be able to hear you when you transmit. Most radios are far more efficient at *receiving* a radio signal. Sending (*transmitting*) requires more power and a tuned (optimized) antenna. This means that even when you can hear another radio's signal clearly, they may not be able to hear you at all.

FRS, GMRS, MURS, and CB – 2-Way Walkie-Talkies

For GO-Bag use, probably the best choice in the "inexpensive" 2-way radio category, is to select a walkie-talkie designed to operate on the GMRS radio frequencies. These radios are readily available online and from large sporting goods stores. The substantial disparity in purchase price usually relates to brand-name reputation, the wattage (power) of the radio, durability, quality of the antenna, and the accessories bundled with it.

The packaging on these radios often includes grandiose marketing claims, such as "Operating Range of 20+ Miles." Though perhaps scientifically possible, these claims are pure marketing hype. Don't use this information to compare one radio to another.

If it isn't practical to actually test the radios you are considering, inspect them visually for the quality of the radio's case, button/knob use, and durability. Carefully inspect the antenna for cracks and other damage, and that the antenna connection is tight.

Then, compare the specifications of the radios you are considering. These details are sometimes listed in fine print on the packaging, or you may need to open the users manual and find the radio's technical specifications.

As you compare these details, check the wattage used for transmitting, and also battery life estimates. Radio brands with a reputation for quality include: Motorola, Midland, Uniden, Cobra, Backcountry Access, and Garmin.

Technically, GMRS radios require one family member to have an FCC license. However, a few years ago, the FCC recommended removal of the licensing requirement. Though not yet rescinded, this is reflected in their lack of enforcement. In any case, the lack of a radio operator's license is rarely enforced for genuine life-or-death emergency use of a 2-way radio.

Importantly, these GMRS radios are easy to use, but you should preset and lock the frequency on each of your walkie-talkies. In each GO-Bag, be sure to include the User Guide instruction booklet for the radio, along with extra batteries.

Note: Cheap, poor-quality FRS (Family Radio Service) walkie-talkies are commonly found in various types of stores, but they do not have the range or variety of channel options of a good GMRS (General Mobil Radio Service) radio. CB walkie-talkies are yet another 2-way radio option, but they are typically older technology radios which are larger, heavier, and drain batteries more quickly. As a result, for most people, CB walkie-talkies are less desirable for inclusion in a GO-Bag.

Ham Radio, aka/ Amateur Radio

Under the right conditions, 2-way radios designed to operate on 'amateur radio' frequencies, also known as 'ham radios,' can connect with another radio operator that is hundreds, or even thousands of miles away. This makes them the best 2-way emergency radio available to civilians.

However, in hilly terrain and unhelpful atmospheric conditions, a low-power amateur radio with a poor antenna will only achieve at line-of-sight operating distances. Therefore, using an amateur radio is not a guarantee that the operator will be able to communicate over long distances.

Retailers sell these radios in three configurations: *walkie-talkies* (hand-held), *mobile* (vehicle-based), and *base station* (fixed installation, as in a home or command center). We rate all three as the #1 choice for 2-way communication during an emergency situation.

We rate a shortwave radio as the #1 choice for news listening, but it must be digital and able to receive AM-FM-WB (weather band)-GMRS-CB frequencies-2 meter- and some HF frequencies. See Appendix-D.

Walkie-talkies and vehicle-mounted radios are the best choices for GO-Bag mobility, whereas base-station radios are the best choice for installation at home and at your safe-haven retreat location. In general terms, a properly located HF base station amateur radio can communicate at a much

> *Ham radio* and *amateur radio* are two terms used to describe the same type of 2-way radio.
>
> In contrast, the word "shortwave" is often misused to describe a radio that receives radio broadcasts from *amateur* radio operators as well as other frequencies that are beyond those used by AM-FM car radios. This is misleading. If you are looking for an emergency radio, first understand that most shortwave radios are only able to receive radio transmissions. They are not 2-way radios. They do not transmit (send).
>
> Also, not all radios sold as 'shortwave' are the same. Some only receive a few extra radio bands, while others can rceive transmissions from all the different radio types mentioned in this chapter. Therefore, before you buy a shortwave radio, use this chapter and Appendix-D to identify the frequencies you want to listen to, and then check to make sure these are included in the radio you purchase.

greater distance because they use more power (wattage) for transmitting, and they can be matched with a larger antenna. A mobile amateur radio designed for use in a vehicle is able to communicate at greater distances than a walkie-talkie, for the same reason. Nevertheless, for most people, a small, lightweight dual-band walkie-talkie amateur radio is best for inclusion in a GO-Bag.

While there is no restriction to listening to any of these frequencies on 'amateur' or 'shortwave' radios, transmitting (talking or sending data) does require the user to have a license. In the United States, these are issued by the Federal Communication Commission (www.fcc.gov).

The licensing levels for amateur/ham radio have been consolidated and now consist of three levels of licenses. The basic level is, *"Technician,"* followed by *"General,"* and the advanced license is *"Amateur Extra."* The more advanced the license, the greater the number of frequencies available for transmitting. Licensing is enforced, except for life-saving emergency use during a disaster.

For most of the frequencies used in walkie-talkies, the long-distance communication often talked about, is largely dependent on the use of 'repeaters.' Often mounted on the roof of a tall building or a high hill by an amateur radio club, these rebroadcast the radio signal from an elevated location. Unfortunately, these repeaters may not be functioning during an emergency situation, so use them if they are working, but don't count on them.

Another option for achieving greater transmission range is to use a high-power "mobile" ham radio (high wattage), but these require lots of power (often 100-200 watts), so they are usually powered by a vehicle engine or plugged into an electrical wall outlet.

Yet another factor which relates to the operational range is the frequency being used. The frequencies referred to as "HF" (high frequency) typically deliver the greatest communication distances. Still, even a small dual-band 5-watt amateur (ham) walkie-talkie will provide a vast improvement over the use of the GMRS, FRS, MURS, CB, SSB radios which are commonly used by civilians.

On the downside, amateur (ham) radios tend to be more complicated to operate. And, since their power and substantial operating range can create conflicts with commercial radio stations, in the U.S. and most countries, a competency test is required before the government will issue an operator's license. Because of this, for most people, amateur (ham) radios aren't a viable option. Yet, for those who are willing to spend time learning how to operate an amateur (ham) radio and have the money to buy the necessary equipment, this is the best 2-way communication option.

In addition to voice transmissions, ham radios can achieve even greater transmission distances by using Morse code, which can now be computer generated using free software. Or better yet, a licensee can use computer-aided HF Digital (PSK31, RTTY, JT65, JT9, etc.) to achieve impressive, long distance text-based communication.

* Note: Amateur (ham) radios are not necessarily expensive. For more information, review Appendix-D in this book, and visit the 'Resources' page on the author's website to download supplemental information for this book.

Antennas for 2-Way Radios

There is a lot of talk about 2-way radios and transmitting power, but equally important is the radio's antenna. If you connect a great radio to a low-quality antenna, the result is poor performance.

For example: When a large, well designed and properly installed antenna is attached to a 100+ watt HF amateur (ham) radio, the user can routinely talk to people on the other side of the world. However, when the same radio is attached to an inefficient antenna, the operating range may be reduced to a mile or two. Having a good antenna that is matched to your radio, is important.

Unfortunately, antennas capable of other-side-of-the-world communication are large and therefore not mobile. Nevertheless, a quality mobile antenna connected to a good radio, is still capable of communicating at far distances, even to distant countries, under the right weather and atmospheric conditions.

It is better to purchase a quality medium-priced amateur radio and a modestly priced antenna suited for that radio, then to spend a lot of money on the radio and buy a low-quality inexpensive antenna.

A quality antenna needn't be elaborate or expensive. A simple dipole antenna can be made in a few minutes from wire and a few other parts, and cost less than $50. When used with a walkie-talkie, this antenna can be strung between trees or buildings to vastly improve the operating range of even a low-power radio.

For more on amateur radios and antennas, visit the website for the National Association of Amateur Radio, www.ARRL.org.

FAQ Legal Info

In the United States, it is illegal to use a 2-way radio to send an encrypted message. However, increased privacy can be legally obtained through digital text communication which defeats listeners without specialized equipment. A similar outcome can be achieved by transmitting digital documents, such as Word, Excel, PDF files, or digital photographs or video images, but the transmission time is quite long.

Radio Accessories

Whichever radio you select for your GO-Bag, be sure to get an earphone that works with your brand of radio, a 12-v adapter to provide operating power from your vehicle, and lots of extra batteries. These radios do not use a lot of power when "on" in their listening mode, but the batteries are quickly drained by transmitting.

Two other accessories to consider for your 2-way radio is a sturdy nylon radio pouch, for both protection and carry convenience. Plus, an external car-top antenna with a magnetic mount. When this antenna is connected to your 2-way radio and placed at the center of the metal roof of a car, it can extend its operating range, especially if it is used inside a vehicle. (If your vehicle is a convertible or has a fiberglass top, place the antenna in the center of the trunk lid.)

Be sure to pre-set each radio to the same frequency, and use a Sharpie Permanent Marker pen to write the frequency on the case of the radio. Also, include your chosen radio frequency in the Plan Summary (Chapter-8) that you include with each Go-Bag.

In addition to pre-setting the radio frequency on each radio, establish a backup frequency to use in case you find that someone else is using your primary frequency. Print this information on the radio's case, too, and be sure to include it, along with the radio's User's Guide, in each GO-Bag.

AM/FM/WB Radios for Receiving News Broadcasts

(Commercial News and Government Weather Broadcasts)

These won't help you communicate with the other members of your group, but "news" is valuable when you are trying to get from Point-A to Point-B. News and weather reports can provide essential information on traffic problems, road closures, locations of rioting, and other factors which will help you circumvent problems and dangers. NOAA Weather channels continually broadcast essential information during a disaster.

A small, battery operated AM/FM/Weather radio that will fit comfortably into your GO-Bag is a valuable asset for updating your route selection and timely evacuation. It is also essential in an emergency situation if you need to find temporary medical facilities, community shelters, and other disaster services. If your trek to your safe-haven has stalled, and you are unable to communicate with friends and family, you will likely feel in desperate need of news. A small radio can help meet this requirement.

Having a portable radio equipped with the NOAA Weather band is essential if you live in the United States. Extra batteries are a must, too. Consider using an earphone (earbud) to avoid drawing attention to yourself. On many radios, this will also reduce power drain, thereby extending the life of a set of batteries.

Caution: As with all electronics, don't store the batteries in the unit as they can leak, rendering your equipment inoperable. Do store batteries with the equipment, so that the item can be quickly put into use. These batteries should be wrapped in several layers of plastic wrap, then cover the plastic-wrapped ends of the batteries with a layer of tape to keep them from coming into contact with something that may inadvertently drain their energy.

Operating Tip: Be sure that the antenna is tightly attached to the radio. If you are using a 2-way radio or walkie-talkie, a loose connection between the radio and the antenna can cause static, cutting in and out, and can even burn-out the radio.

This chapter provided a brief overview of radio options.
Additional information can be found in Appendix-D
of this book, and in the "Supplemental Info" document
available on the 'Resources' page of the
author's website: www.SIGSWANSTROM.com

Chapter 8

Prepare and Share a 2-3 Page "Plan Summary"

Everyone needs to know the plan. Establish a basic plan today and then expand on it over time. Talk about your plan with family and friends, and put an outline of the Plan in each GO-bag. Everyone needs to know the basic Plan.

Remember, too, that you or your other family members and friends may not be together when disaster strikes. If this is the situation, do they know what to do?

In emergency situations, particularly those which strike suddenly, various family members and friends will probably be somewhere else. You may be away from home, children may be at school or at a friend's house, your spouse may be at work or shopping, and various loved-ones may be out of town. Do they know what to do?

Everyone needs to know what to do. Improve your plan over time, but create a basic plan, now. Communicate the details to family and friends.

The solution is to develop an adaptable, flexible and resilient plan that is straightforward and easy to remember; a plan that is supported by a printed 'Plan Summary' which includes brief but specific reminders of the key details. A copy of this 2-3 page summary document should be kept in each person's GO-Bag.

Maps, routing details, addresses, notes and reference materials are all useless if not readily available when disaster strikes. Your brief, 2-3-page Plan Summary, along with maps marked with routes and related reference materials, needs to be easy to find and readily available, so keep a copy of these materials in each GO-Bag.

If you have a smartphone, store a PDF copy of the plan, maps, and reference materials in your phone, too, and in the phone of each family member. The screen may be small and hard to read, but this backup copy may nevertheless prove to be invaluable.

Vigilance without adequate preparation is like a baseball player stepping up to the plate without a bat. Don't leave important details to chance, or assume that the information will be remembered during a high-stress situation.

Just as a baseball player can't expect to score a run without coaching and practice, you and your team need to get ready, too. Pre-planning, recollection of the plan's details by everyone involved, and adaptability (contingency plans), are all essential components of every emergency plan.

Plan now. It will save lives later.

If you don't have a plan, start today by making a basic bullet-point plan or numbered list that can be expanded over time. If you do have a Plan, use this reminder as an opportunity to update it, and to remind each participant of the details.

When disaster strikes, most people will not stop to read a lengthy Plan document. This is a trait of human nature, so don't expect to change it. Yet, you can mitigate this problem by making sure they are familiar with the Plan. If they understand the Plan, then they are far more likely to use the Plan Summary to find the details they need.

What to include in a Personal Emergency-Plan

Don't delay. Take the time now to...

1. Investigate route options for getting to your gathering place, with departure points from the locations you and your family/friends frequent often. Identify at least four very different routes which will get everyone home or to your gathering spot, with departure locations starting at work sites, school, church, shopping, and other places frequented.

Google Maps, Google Earth, and similar online map resources can be helpful for this process, but don't limit your efforts to the high-traffic main-road type routes that most computers identify. Backroads provide necessary alternatives. If you live in a flood-prone area, you will need to use a flood map or topographic (land features) map to help with your route planning.

2. Next, repeat the same exercise but for traveling on foot, and/or by bicycle.

3. Using a highly-detailed paper map, identify your potential routes.

4. Drive or walk each route to verify the viability of each one. Include the distance between turns. (Mapping software can provide distances between turns and other useful route details for both driving and walking. Add this to your paper maps.)

5. Use this opportunity to make additional notations to your maps. Use a fine-tip waterproof pen (Sharpie) to indicate the locations of gas stations, convenience stores, hospitals and clinics, police and fire stations, sources of water, places to hide or sleep, possible rendezvous sites where you can comfortably wait for others, hazards and potential dangers, etc.

6. Mark your map with landmarks and other land features which will be helpful if street signs are missing. Since disasters can destroy signage and buildings, be sure to include structures and landmarks which will likely remain.

If accomplished at the same time as the practice-run you make using your routing options, you can also include photos of key landmarks. These might be helpful, especially if street signs are missing or areas are not easily recognized due to damage.

7. Now, transfer your route and notes to a new map. Then make a duplicate set for the GO-Bags of each of your family members and for each member of your group, plus each vehicle that will be used.

Paint each map with a clear waterproofing/durability-enhancer such as 'Map Seal' made by AquaSeal. After waiting several days to make sure each map is dry, fold and store each map set in a large waterproof plastic bag that is large enough to use the map without removing it from the plastic bag. Or, use a waterproof map case such as the clear vinyl 'Dry Doc' Map Case made by Seattle Sports. Each vehicle and each GO-Bag should have a complete set of these maps.

If your mobile phone can store photographs, create a photo backup of your maps, including sequential close-up pictures of any map section where additional details might be needed. Keep these on your phone as a backup in case they are ever needed.

8. By design, your plan needs to be adaptable, too. So don't just formulate a 'Plan-A,' but also a Plan-B, Plan-C, etc. Social upheaval, developing events or damage can make your primary 'Plan-A' strategy impossible. Therefore, your 'Plan Summary' needs to reflect contingency planning, too.

Anticipate potential problems, and build adaptability and resiliency into the structure of your plan. For example, even if you put a lot of effort and money into preparing a 'safe haven' retreat location, you still need to have a backup 'Plan-B' site, just in case something happens and your first-choice is no longer viable. There isn't space in a 'Plan Summary' to include a lot of detail about these contingency plans, but it does need to prioritize alternative routes, meetup locations, etc.

Print a 2-3 Page 'Plan Summary' for each GO-Bag

The printed 'Plan Summary' that is added to family member and friend's GO-Bags, should be emblazoned with the words, "READ THIS NOW." Follow that headline with concise, clearly printed essential details. Place this Plan Summary in a clear Hefty Slider plastic bag for protection.

Along with this Plan Summary, use another Hefty Slider bag to assemble your route maps, and yet another Hefty Slider bag to protect an inventory list of what is in the GO-Bag. These three plastic bags should be the first thing seen when the GO-Bag is opened.

Among other things, the Plan Summary needs to include a one-paragraph summary of the plan itself, and what is expected of them. It needs to explain why they should read this Plan Summary as soon as they can do it safely. It needs to explain that these are instructions on where to go, and how to get there.

As you prepare your Plan Summary, use bullet points and topic subheadings. Follow these with keyword sentences that highlight core details, and valuable reference information.

When possible, include location-specific information on your maps, or attached to them. Don't forget to include addresses and locations of family and trusted friends. If these are circled on your map, it will also serve as a reminder during a time of need.

In addition to the other route details, don't forget to include emergency shelter sites, plus elevated places where you can make observations or receive stronger radio signals, and also GPS coordinates for rendezvous sites, and compass bearings that will help you make confident and rapid progress as you follow your prearranged route.

On the routing and reference maps packaged with the Plan Summary, include reminders of other important details that they may have forgotten.

Make the overview route map the 'master map' and label it as such. You won't have space to add a lot of extra details on this map, but you can

> If you use a highlighter pen to mark your route, make sure it is discernible in low light conditions. Avoid adding notations to your map that obscure important details printed on the map.

use it to refer to other more-detailed maps that have useful details. To help with this, use a bold felt pen or printed label to number each map. This will assist the user to quickly discern which map you are referencing on the 'master map' or in your written instructions.

Don't expect the user to automatically switch back and forth between various maps as they may be highly stressed and distracted. They may not be thinking clearly. Therefore, use the master map to indicate when they should refer to one of the other maps or the Plan Summary, for additional details.

Include a few brief words of loving encouragement, too. The reader may be scared. Your words need to give them hope, the support they need to keep going, and the ability to regain focus.

In high-stress situations, the level of distraction can be very high. Don't expect family members and friends to remember details that are not included in your Plan Summary.

Practice will help cement these details in the user's mind. It will also assist them to become familiar with the Plan and the related evacuation-route maps.

The printed copy of the Plan Summary needs to be extremely brief and to the point, but it does need to include specifics when they are needed for clarity. Avoid the temptation to add unnecessary details. Brevity, with clarity, is your goal.

> Keep it short. Keep it simple.

Even children should have their own GO-Bag. They may not be able to understand everything, but if they are fortunate enough to have help from an adult, this will still be advantageous.

When presented with the need, after the initial shock, most kids are resilient. Don't underestimate them and their ability to use the supplies you included in their GO-Bag.

Whatever format you use to summarize the key points of your emergency plan, be sure to prominently remind the reader to look for flags and messages that have been left for them. Make it clear, too, that they only need to leave messages if they have been delayed, if they are encountering a particular danger, or other information which would be useful to those who are trying to find them.

At the very least, make it clear that if they need to deviate from the pre-planned route, they need to leave a message in a prominent location, explaining their revised plan. Remind them that a message needs to be left for those who may be looking for them, even if they are only transitioning from Route-A to Route-B.

Practice the Plan

Walk or drive each route and alternate route. Or, you can make it fun for family and friends by making it into a Geocaching-type game. Most geocaching clubs utilize electronic devices, but you can create your own, similar games using just a map, compass, and 'clues' based on permanent land features.

- - - - - - -

Geocaching is a game that is similar to a treasure hunt but uses tools such as a compass and a map (or GPS). Since GPS devices and the mapping software on your phone may not work during an emergency situation, don't use these items if you want your game to provide serious benefits.

Chapter 9

GO-Bag: Evacuation Kit (Bug-Out Bag) Overview

* Lists of gear and supplies, by category, are in Chapters 10-12, and also in Appendix-A at the back of this book.

What is a GO-Bag? It is a pre-packed provision and gear kit stored in a knapsack. A GO-Bag is the fundamental, core component of disaster and emergency preparations.

Whether you are forced to evacuate from your home due to a storm, or you have decided to flee the area due to civil unrest or some other disaster that is approaching, or you need to shelter-in-place when away from home, you need a pre-packed comprehensive GO-Bag (Get-Out Bag). Since it may be required at a moment's notice, this bag of supplies is usually kept in the trunk of your car. However, you might also have one at your home, your place of employment, or another handy place where it is always available to grab and hit the road. You need at least one GO-Bag for every member of your household, including children.

Sometimes referred to as a 'GOOD Bag' (Get-Out-Of-Dodge Bag), 'BOB' (Bug-Out Bag), or by other terms or acronyms, these all refer to the same item: A lightweight bag containing essential supplies that can be easily carried on foot if that becomes necessary.

A GO-Bag is not the same as a "Survival Kit" such as those which are stored on boats and aircraft. Nor is it the same as a "Patrol Pack," "Rapid Response Kit," or "Active Shooter" bag. These are specialized kits used by government agencies, military, police, or for security purposes. Though all of these different kits may be knapsacks containing some of the same supplies, they are not the same.

*The purpose of a pre-packed GO-Bag is to ensure that you have what you need to escape **from** danger, AND, to get **to** a safe place.* Whether you are heading to a neighborhood shelter to wait out a storm, or you are making a solitary journey to a distant safe-haven, a GO-Bag should contain everything you will need.

Whether your need is to escape from danger, wait-out turmoil, survive a catastrophic event, or evade chaotic changes, a GO-Bag is your lifeline. It will *not* contain everything you would like to have. But when combined with what you routinely carry in your pockets or purse, and what is included in your GO-Bag, you should have everything required for 98% of the emergency situations you will face.

When evacuation (bug-out) is necessary, at that point, it's too late to pack. Very likely, it is literally too late to shop for supplies, or even gather together what you need from the things you have on-hand.

Decisive speed-of-action can save your life. This is why it is vital to assemble, in advance, a lightweight, easily transported kit which is prepacked with well-selected provisions and gear.

If you try to accomplish this last minute, you will probably throw things into a bag and leave with only a few of the things you need. Or, if you take the time to do it right, and try to shop before you hit the road, the window of opportunity for a safe and painless evacuation will likely close before you are able to leave town. Being properly equipped in advance and ready to evacuate quickly, is often the difference between those who are victors rather than victims.

As with all disaster preparations, pre-planning is essential. This applies in particular to the need for a well-equipped GO-Bag. It is the 'first task' of emergency preparations.

The fiction story at the beginning of Book-1 in this series is a poignant reminder of how important it is to be prepared and ready to leave quickly. If you aren't ready to roll, you may expose yourself to all sorts of unnecessary dangers.

A GO-Bag that is pre-packed and ready to use is an essential component because it helps empower you. Not only does it equip you with the right gear, it arms you with pre-emptive forethought. With a personalized GO-Bag and the associated planning, you are ready to take action. You can "roll" in advance of the hordes of panicked people and predators who can ambush your safe escape.

When you live life "Ready to Roll," you can evade the 2nd disaster which often follows an emergency situation. But the goal isn't just to sidestep the confused, gridlock-causing masses, it is to avoid being trapped by circumstances so you can help others.

General GO-Bag Advice

Make your own GO-Bag. Even though ostensibly 'complete' GO-Bags are available in the marketplace, we have never seen one that is adequate. It is far better to assemble your own kit based on your operating environment and your personal needs.

Similarly, a plastic bin, suitcase, or duffle bag containing supplies, is *not* an adequate substitute for a GO-Bag knapsack. Why? It's because you need to be able to carry your supplies on your back. This is the most comfortable carry method when you need to convey supplies a distance, or for an extended period of time.

Since the contents of your GO-Bag may encompass all of the supplies you will have for several days, it needs to include the essentials for safety, shelter, navigation, and provisions. And, since mobility is also an important feature, your GO-Bag needs to be compact and reasonably lightweight, too.

You, and every family member and friend who might need to evacuate, needs to have a GO-Bag. Even a 5-yr old can carry some supplies.

If you plan to leave in a car, keep in mind, at some point you may still find yourself walking. Anticipate this situation and prepare for it with gear, footwear, and proper clothing. Store these additional supplies with your GO-Bag. Remember, at some point, you may be forced to leave almost everything behind and head out on foot, so your GO-Bag needs to be pre-packed with all the essentials.

A pre-packed GO-Bag may literally be a lifesaver, but weight and bulkiness is an enemy to moving quickly. So, your fully-loaded GO-Bag should ideally weigh less than 25-pounds (11.3 kg).

Bag #2: A second soft-sided bag of any type, which contains additional supplies, should be stored with your GO-Bag. This extra bag should hold durable, functional earth-tone clothes, boots or hiking shoes, and eight or more ½-liter (16 oz) bottles of water. Some may want to store a third bag in the trunk of their car. This bag might contain a sleeping bag, tent, car-camping supplies, more water, and additional food.

If you have had the foresight to haul all these supplies, don't sacrifice your safety to protect convenience items. At some point, you may need to leave everything other than your GO-Bag behind. Don't risk your life to hold onto things that only make your life more comfortable.

Or your car may run out of gas, get stuck, damaged in an accident, or trapped in gridlocked traffic. Will you stay with your vehicle just so keep your "stuff?" Will you try to carry your extra supplies, resulting in slow travel, the rapid onset of fatigue, and additional vulnerability to victimization?

Or, will you have the wisdom to leave unnecessary things behind, put your GO-Bag on your back, and head out on foot? If early on you changed into the clothes you stored in Bag #2 and emptied the water from that bag into the containers that are in your GO-Bag, then you are ready to transition to your backup Plan, and walk. You can do without the rest—if circumstances require it.

For most people, a knapsack-size GO-Bag is a better choice than a full-size backpack because the larger bag is heavy. And ungainly, if the situation develops where you need to have nimble speed. If your GO-Bag is large, you might be tempted or forced to leave it behind.

A GO-Bag is not for backpacking—it is exclusively for quick, lightweight, emergency evacuation. Its purpose is to provide you with the basic life-sustaining essentials required for 3-5 days on your own. It needs to be suitable for carrying while on-foot, perhaps for many miles. If you have the luxury of driving, the contents of your GO-Bag can be augmented by the extra supplies contained in Bag #3.

Opting for a large backpack, instead, will make it possible for you to carry additional supplies. That's true. A large GO-Bag *backpack* that also includes camping gear may be a great asset if you will be operating in the wilderness for an extended period. Or, if you are preparing for a particular type of emergency situation that requires specialized gear. But in an urban, suburban, or near-a-town rural location, the added size and weight manifests a distinct disadvantage.

If you are carrying a large backpack in the proximity of other fleeing people, this will signal that you are in possession of valuable gear. This makes you a target for robbery or theft. When ill-equipped people suddenly awaken to their plight, and they have a gun, knife, or are much stronger than you, then you will be a tempting target.

Even ordinarily good people who are feeling a sense of panic have been known to rob their fellow travelers. This urge is additionally strong among unprepared parents who have young children in tow, when they realize that they don't have the means to care for their hungry kids. This tendency for theft is an unsavory fact of life during emergency situations.

Further, if you are weighed down with gear in a "fight or flight" situation, you may not have the option to run away. You may be forced to fight to retain your personal life-sustaining supplies. So if it can be helped, you don't want to reduce your options. You don't want to be forced to fight.

Escape & Evade: Often the best defense. When we diminish our agility, we become an easier target for robbery and violence. By being quick, often we can by-pass new dangers which develop during an emergency situation. Taking unnecessary risks is foolish.

The purpose of a GO-Bag is to facilitate both emergency evacuation and self-sufficiency. To achieve this first objective, our best option is often to flee from circumstances which have the potential to become dangerous. In other words, *escape* from the threat. Or, it may be best to *evade* (avoid) the situation entirely. (Or, both.) This can sometimes be accomplished through the shrewd application of 'Situation Awareness' principles (See Chapter-18).

Sometimes a GO-Bag isn't enough. If our objective is sustained independence in a wilderness or wasteland, we will need the components of a GO-Bag plus additional supplies. If this is the situation you are planning for, most people will want to have the elements of a GO-Bag, but set-up in the same configuration as used by experienced backpackers who are engaged in wilderness trekking.

Conversely, if the situation you expect to encounter is not an evacuation or wilderness trekking, but rather community security, and you will be carrying a rifle, too, then you need to assemble a "Patrol Pack." Similar to a GO-Bag, a Patrol Pack is small-in-size, but the contents of the bag are geared for this very different purpose.

Don't be confused. While there is some crossover with the substance of all knapsack-based emergency kits, it is essential to assemble the bag you need for the purpose and needs you anticipate. If that objective is primarily getting out of town in an emergency situation and to a safe place, then it's probably a GO-Bag that you need.

Keep your GO-Bag, clothing/boot-bag, and extra supplies-bag (additional food, water, and specialty gear), together. Perhaps in a duffle bag, and store it in your car's trunk. If your vehicle is a truck, you may need to use multiple small bags so that you can fit them behind the truck's seat. If your vehicle is a hatchback car, and the contents will be visible through the windows, do what you can to conceal your supplies in innocuous containers that blend-in with your vehicle's interior.

If you are leaving your home and packing-up your vehicle for evacuation, fill it up, that's fine. But don't routinely keep your trunk filled with bug-out gear if you might need that space to haul something else.

But if you are going to carry extra gear regularly, use duffle bags or soft-sided luggage with wheels, as you can compress soft-sided bags. This makes it possible to take more than you can with plastic bins which squander your limited storage space.

Another aspect of the real-world is that you will periodically need to haul groceries and other things in your trunk. If it's filled with GO gear, you'll soon start leaving some of your gear behind because you need the space. Supplies left behind are not going to do you any good, so only use your vehicle to store that which you can routinely keep in it. And, don't ever be tempted to leave your GO-Bag behind because you need the trunk space. You might find that it's that day when you need it. Don't forget Murphey's Law.

Murphy's Law

"Murphy's Law" teaches us from experience. It reminds us that when we desperately need a tool, we won't be able to find it. It tells us that if we only have one bottle of water when we're desperately thirsty, we'll find that our one bottle has leaked and is now empty. It also coaches us to carry extra batteries, as a stored flashlight is invariably dead. Mr. Murphy has many laws.

Regarding this topic, Murphey's Law teaches us never to leave your GO-Bag behind, and never "borrow" food or other items from it when it's a non-emergency. Why? Because that will be the day when something will happen, and you will need what you don't have.

Murphey's Law is a tongue-in-cheek set of rules, but it also conveys wisdom. Don't be tempted to use, or remove essentials. Keep your GO-Bag in your vehicle, without fail.

And, don't pilfer the contents of your GO-Bag when you're hungry, thirsty, or in need of a flashlight, knife, or some other item that you have in your bag. Your GO-Bag needs to be kept intact, always. You don't know when you'll desperately need your GO-Bag and its full complement of water, food, and emergency supplies.

A GO-Bag, and emergency gear generally, should not be considered multi-purpose supplies. They should be reserved for emergency use, only.

If you are able to stay with your car, then extra supplies that you have stored in it, that are in addition to your GO-Bag, may prove to be a godsend. On the other hand, if you need to leave your car, your GO-Bag needs to be self-contained and complete. Remember, if you suddenly find that you need to flee on foot, you need to be able to grab a fully-stocked and intact GO-Bag without delay, and run.

GO-Bag Storage: Whether your GO-Bag is kept in the trunk of your car, or you store it at your place of employment, or you keep a GO-Bag at both locations, your GO-Bag(s) needs to be maintained and refreshed quarterly. One aspect of maintenance is to keep your bag clean and free from water, mold, insects, and other damage.

For this purpose, many people store their GO-Bag in a plastic trash sack. This may be a bad idea. Not only might it inadvertently get disposed of as, well, trash, because it's in a garbage bag, it might also be damaged by mold and bacteria which flourish when air can't circulate. For this reason, it may be better to keep your GO-Bag in a cloth duffle bag, or large paper sack such as those used for yard waste.

Whatever you use to protect your GO-Bag, consider sealing the protective cover in a manner which makes tampering evident. If someone has gotten into your your bag you want to know it. Even if you think it's just been looked at out of curiosity, use the inventory list you have in your bag to check the contents, to make sure that nothing is missing or inadvertently damaged. This tamper-protection is particularly useful if you have children, or if other people sometimes use your vehicle.

The A, B, C's of Evacuation

It may seem odd, but color matters for clothes and GO-Bags. The colors and appearance of your GO-Bag and emergency clothing should be subdued; ideally similar to the color of the terrain where you will be traveling. We recommend that you avoid camouflage clothing and military-looking gear as these attract attention.

In suburban and rural areas, earth-tone clothing is generally the best choice. Whereas if you live in a densely populated urban area, clothes which are gray in color may be your best option. This is because it blends well with street and building colors.

Whatever clothing color you choose, understand that subdued colors will help you blend in with the crowd. This is an important attribute, even more so if you find you need to hole up somewhere.

Old, faded tactical clothing and gear in OD Green (Olive Drab), Forrest Green, or Desert Tan, may be okay, too, as long as your overall appearance does not communicate a military-look.

Clothing which tends to create problems is anything that captures the attention of those who are around you. This includes clothing or knapsacks in bright colors or white, items with bling or light-reflecting appliques or surfaces, designer clothing or expensive shoes, and camouflage.

Military camouflage (camo) clothing is generally unhelpful, or worse. Bold camo patterns such as Woodland, Brushstroke, Tigerstripe, 6-Color Desert (aka/ Chocolate Chip), foreign military camo including Flectarn, or current- and recent-issue U.S., Eastern Bloc, or Chinese military camo uniform patterns, are the most problematic. These often increase unwanted and detrimental attention, which translates into a greater risk of victimization and harassment.

If wearing camo clothing appeals to you, consider one of the many patterns used for hunting. For combined urban and rural bug-out, use a hunting pattern such as Realtree, or one which matches the foliage in your area. In our experience, the camo patterns which resemble a faded Hawaiian floral design attract the least attention.

Perhaps the best camo option is to use the innocuous approach. This combines camo-pattern upper-body clothing, with durable, solid-color trousers. This way, it doesn't look like you are part of a military or police unit, nor a militiaman. But if you do need to hide, you still have the advantage of camo on your upper-body. To be clear, we do not recommend wearing camo clothing, but if this is what you want to do, be intentional about looking innocuous.

Being nondescript might involve wearing faded blue jeans, or well-used solid-color tactical pants in the same color-tone range as the camo pattern you select for your upper-body clothing. By using this approach, you can more safely take advantage of a modern but-not-as-popular camo pattern such as Kryptek, A-TACS, or some other pattern design which does not make you a threat to criminals.

Especially when you are alone, you don't want to be mistaken for a member of the military or a law enforcement officer. It's not unusual for these people to be targeted.

If you are operating in an area that is mostly desolate or wilderness, camouflage clothing which matches your environment may be appropriate. MultiCam and Scorpion W2 (OCP) may be universal, but they are not necessarily the best for your location.

Whichever camo pattern you choose, keep in mind that it is not a fashion statement. Your clothing selection should be based solely on function, durability, and how well it meets the need to blend in, and if necessary, hide. The color and pattern need to be conducive to disappearing into your environment.

The 'camo' and clothing problem: The issue with distinctive, upscale clothing is that it is designed to make you stand out. Oddly, the problem with camo clothing is exactly the same—if it doesn't do what it is intended to do, which is to make the wearer disappear.

In an urban or suburban setting, most camo clothing makes the wearer stand out more than a businessman wearing a D&G suit in a Thrift Store. Yet, the same suit worn on Wall Street isn't noteworthy. The issue of what to wear while evacuating is to wear clothing which helps you blend into the environment in which you are traveling. This is difficult since many people have spent their life trying to get noticed, but during a crisis, you want to become Jack Griffin (The Invisible Man).

The best camouflage is often a color and clothing-design which renders you unnoticed. Wear clothes, and carry gear, that lets you blend in, and behave so that you remain unnoticed. Be as invisible.

When you want to be noticed.

If your situation is the opposite, and you want to be spotted by family or friends who will be looking for you, solve this need by including a colorful hat with your GO-Bag supplies. A bright orange 'hunters' ball cap is an easy-to-find choice. You put it on if the need arises, and keep it hidden if you want to blend in.

Under normal circumstances, avoid bright-colors and attention-grabbing garb. Do what you can to be invisible to criminal predators and authorities alike. When in a crowd, blend in. When trudging down a road alone, look nondescript. If you are not trying to stand out so that you can be located, blend into your environment.

A warning to women...

In the aftermath of a natural disaster or during an emergency situation with a risk of lawlessness, it may be advisable to appear unattractive intentionally. During even a typical evacuation 'travel' scenario, be as plain as you can be; little-to-no makeup, hair tucked into a cap, no visible jewelry or bling, and wear clothing that is gender neutral and doesn't look expensive. Remove jewelry. Avoid eye contact when it isn't necessary.

Be alert, and let those around you see that you are alert. Don't be waylaid by anyone you don't know, including those who claim they are just looking for directions. If you are in a group, the leaders may choose to help someone who needs assistance. However, if you are alone and the aid isn't required to save a life, for women who are not burly, it is usually best to move on and let someone else help. This may seem harsh or rude, but it is the prudent approach. During an emergency situation your mantra needs to be *safety* and *speed*.

Operate in a constant state of heightened caution. Be vigilant. Don't live in fear, but absent divine guidance to the contrary, don't be quick to trust, either. It is often safer to travel with others, but only align yourself with those who are worthy of your trust.

Don't be 'conned' or 'guilted' into traveling with someone who may slow you down. Nor, a person who isn't 100% trustworthy. Avoid staying with an individual or a group that makes you feel edgy or unsettled.

Be hyper-vigilant. Trust your instincts. Don't sacrifice safety for comfort, companionship, extra food, or for a ride. If you aren't careful, you may find that you have traded one problem for a new one that is even more dangerous.

Barebones GO-Bags for children, elderly, and those with physical limitations

Each family member and individual who is physically able should carry their own GO-Bag. Even if they can only handle a small, ultralight GO-Bag, that's still a significant contribution.

Young children, elderly, and physically feeble individuals may not be able to carry everything they need, but they may be able to tote some drinking water, food, and essential items that are unique to their needs. This will include their prescription medicines, spare eyeglasses, toilet paper and sanitation items, and maybe some basic gear.

You may shudder at the thought of becoming separated from a child, elderly parent or another loved one. But if that does happen, or if you need to transfer them to the care of another person, you will want your loved one to have their personal items and other essential supplies which they may urgently need.

Most children, as well as elderly or infirm people, can carry an ultra-lightweight knapsack containing their bare essentials. When loaded, these barebones bags can still weigh less than 6 pounds (2.7 kg)—and yet these supplies can save their life.

Barebones GO-Bag Example: Ultra lightweight knapsack: 6.5 oz.; one plastic pill bottle with pills, 4-oz.; spare eyeglasses, 1-oz.; one ziplock baggie of personal hygiene items, approx. 6-oz.; mini survival kit, 9-oz.; three 16-oz bottles of water, 3.1 lbs.; four meal replacement bars (1,000 Calories), 10-oz. Total weight: 5-1/4 pounds (2.4 kg).

GO-Bags for Pets

What about your pets? Will you abandon them in a disaster? If you have the choice, it's inhumane to leave them behind to fend for themselves. You can't expect a neighbor to help, and even if a vet or kennel will accept them, which is highly unlikely, that probably isn't a reliable solution. Further, most FEMA emergency shelters and some other shelters will not allow you to bring your pet in with you. Therefore, you need to solve this problem in advance.

If you plan to bug-out with your pet, you'll, of course, need to bring food for them, too. Keep a leash in your GO-Bag, and pack dog food in Hefty Slider plastic bags. (Dry food is much lighter weight than canned food.) If your pet is hungry enough, they will eat dry dog food even if they ordinarily turn their nose up at it. If necessary, feed it to them by hand to encourage them to eat.

Store the bag of dry food in a Tupperware container. Remove the bag of food, and the Tupperware container becomes a water dish. If you have three days of food for yourself in your GO-Bag, have at least two days of pet food for your animal. Use filtered water for them, too, and don't let them drink from puddles, lakes or rivers. If they get sick as a result of consuming tainted water, your troubles have multiplied.

Replace pet food every 3-months; more often if it has been exposed to high temperatures or moisture. Pack pet food in Ziploc-style clear plastic freezer bags, or better yet, Mylar bags or a container which will protect the contents from insects and pests. If you don't want to bother with heat-sealing a Mylar bag of dog food quarterly, purchase Mylar bags with a Ziploc-style closure. The best dog food container for a GO-Bag is probably a 5-mil or thicker odor-proof ShieldPro Ziploc-style aluminum foil Mylar bag, because it is lightweight as well as resealable.

Seasonal Clothing and the Special Needs of a Specific Location, or for Adverse Weather Conditions

In addition to your GO-Bag, as mentioned earlier in this chapter, you need to have a clothing/boot bag containing items that are seasonally appropriate; warm/cold weather clothing, rain/sun/heat protection, and boots and socks suitable to anticipated conditions.

Your clothing and boots must be durable, functional, allow freedom of movement and be unobtrusive. When an emergency situation is upon you, change into this clothing as soon as you can do so safely.

Having multiple changes of clothing is overrated. What you need are the right clothes for the situation. Change into your situation-appropriate clothing early, and leave the impractical items behind. More about clothing will be covered later.

If space allows, you can keep additional clothing in your vehicle. That's great, but don't worry about taking extra clothing with you if you are fleeing on foot—it's likely weight you can't afford to carry.

The point we're making here is that your extra pants, shirts, sweaters and jackets, should be in a second bag, not in your GO-Bag. The items in your clothing bag should be changed seasonally. Select contents to match the time of year, weather, and the terrain where you will be traveling. For a list of clothing, see Chapter-12.

Personalize the Contents of Your GO-Bag

As you consider the lists that are in Chapters 10-12 and Appendix-A, understand that you can't include all these items in your GO-Bag. There won't be enough space in your knapsack, and it will become a heavy burden to carry if you include too much gear. However, if you have several people in your family or bug-out group, many of these items can be added to your "shared" supplies by dividing up these lists, so that a small portion is allocated to each group member.

Individually, everyone should periodically review their list of supplies, adding and subtracting from their GO-Bag as experience, needs, financial ability, and operating environment, changes.

Packaging & Packing: Remove unnecessary packaging from all items, and compress clothing and gear in Hefty Slider-style plastic bags or re-sealable vacuum-sealed bags. To help stay organized while you're on the go, use the appropriate size of clear plastic bag that is needed for each category of gear. For example, all fire-starting items should be together in one clear plastic bag, another bag for sanitation (soap, toilet paper, etc.), another for electronics and related supplies, and yet another for food items, etc.

These smaller, clear plastic bags should be stored inside a lightweight white or light-colored, bigger plastic bag, like a kitchen garbage sack. This larger, more durable plastic bag will protect your GO-Bag contents from rain and dirt, and it will also enable you to easily remove the contents as you sort, or search for an item.

Think *Multipurpose:* As you select your gear, think 'multipurpose.' For example, in an emergency situation when your resources are limited, an ordinary trash bag can be used for many different purposes...

A large, white kitchen trash bag can be utilized as a ground cloth, or a tablecloth to keep food clean during food prep or while eating. Or, to keep your posterior dry when sitting on damp ground, or to keep your supplies off the wet ground while searching for something in your knapsack. Plus, it can be used to keep small items from getting lost in ground clutter when changing batteries, or when filtering water, or for sorting gear at night, or when you want to reorganize your Hefty Slider gear bags. Or, you can use it to layout the contents of your medical kit or help keep a person's injury clean during treatment. In a pinch, you can cut head and arm holes in it, transforming it into a raincoat, or a shirt that can be worn to increase body warmth. When you need shelter, the sides can be cut to convert the bag into a plastic tarp, which can be combined with a tree branch and some Paracord, to build a screen to protect you from the wind, rain, or the sun. If left intact, it can be utilized as a carry-bag to haul things you have scavenged along the way. And, when attached to a signpost, it can serve as an attention-getting signal flag.

One item. Multiple uses.

A small, lightweight, inexpensive item such as this can be a solution for dozens of problems you might face. There isn't space in a GO-bag for a lot of specialty gear (tent, sleeping bag, etc.), but there is room for a multi-purpose trash bag that weighs less than one ounce.

As you select items for your GO-Bag, keep this "multipurpose" concept in mind. This is also an important consideration when you need to choose between two similar-purpose products.

A Frequent GO-Bag Mistake

GO-Bags are typically assembled to support the needs of one person. If more than one person often travels in the same vehicle, additional GO-Bags are necessary to outfit each individual. If you routinely travel with young children that are old enough to carry a small knapsack, they should carry some of their own emergency supplies. If it can be avoided, one person should not try to haul supplies for multiple people. A parent's bag may be larger and heavier than those worn by small children, but if possible, everyone needs to haul some water, food, and gear.

Go-Bags: What to Include

What should be contained in a GO-Bag is a much-debated topic. Unfortunately, these disputes rarely start with the fundamental question. This is, "What is your anticipated use?" That is the foundational starting point.

The next questions are, "What are the environmental factors (dangers, risks, and obstacles) that you are likely to encounter?" "What are your physical limitations (if any) and how can you overcome what needs to be overcome?" and "Where do you need to go to reach safety, and how are you going to get there?"

Your answers to these four questions will dictate the number of days you will likely need to use your GO-Bag, what your GO-Bag must contain and what can be stockpiled or scavenged or along the way, and what you will need if it becomes necessary for you to walk to safety.

If you are assembling your GO-Bag for one particular purpose, such as evacuation to a nearby community shelter due to a storm or wildfire, then this will primarily orient your GO-Bag toward comfort and convenience in that setting. You will want to have a toiletries bag, snacks, reading materials, a book light, maybe even a sleep sack (ex: Sea to Summit's 'CoolMax Adaptor Traveler's' sleep sack). For this type of evacuation, you may not be concerned with having a water filter and fire-starting gear.

Notwithstanding, this kind of evacuation bag will not be adequate if you encounter an emergency situation which you need to handle on your own, without the help of a community shelter. So, since you'll be assembling a GO-Bag anyway, you might as well build it to accommodate various types of disaster.

The first rule of disaster planning is to prepare for self-reliance—without aid from the community, the federal government, the Red Cross, or anyone else. If they are there to help, that's great. But be prepared to handle the situation alone, without the luxury of using supplies furnished by others.

Are you assembling a GO-Bag to care for your needs if you are stranded away from home by a storm? Or, are you assembling your GO-Bag to make sure you have the emergency supplies you will need to walk from work to home after a natural disaster—or a man-made disaster? Or, do you want your GO-Bag to contain essential provisions for a 5-days trek, because you may be forced to walk a long distance to join your family or friends at a prearranged safe-haven retreat location?

The 'needs' of being alone and needing to be self-sufficient, will be very different from the 'inconvenience' you will experience at a community storm shelter. With this in mind, plan for the greatest need, not just the expected inconveniences. *Hope for the best. Prepare for the worst.*

As you prepare, keep reality in mind. *Your* reality.

If your place of employment or school is many miles from home, your GO-Bag supplies will need to be very different. Plan for this.

In the United States, a significant number of people commute more than 60 miles to reach their place of employment. What is your situation? How long would it take to walk home from work? What will you need to do it safely?

If it is a long distance, maybe you should make arrangements now, to go to a friend's house who lives along your route home? And, since you may choose to walk home, ask that friend if you can store a box of supplies in their garage.

What are the emergency situations you will likely face? Is it a winter storm, hurricane, flooding, earthquake, power grid failure, or social unrest. Or, might it be all of these? Focus your provisioning on the most likely, first, but don't forget to prepare for the unexpected.

If required, a properly provisioned yet lightweight GO-Bag will help you shelter-in-place for up to 5-days, and it will also help you get back home or to a prearranged rendezvous location, so you can meet-up with your family or friends. In addition, it will have what you need for walking to a distant safe-haven 'retreat' location.

Don't limit your preparations to one type of emergency. And, don't limit your ability to move quickly.

Be prepared, and, ready to *roll*—even if you will not be able to roll in a vehicle and find that you need to walk.

GO-Bag, *PLUS* Emergency-Supplies Kits

As you develop your lists of emergency supplies to purchase, remember that you need to prepare a GO-Bag plus three other kits of emergency supplies:

1) Personal GO-Bag which you can carry for an extended distance if circumstances force you to evacuate on foot. (One 'GO-Bag' should be prepared for each individual. Non-essentials can be shared, but each bag needs to contain the core essentials.)

Note: The following kits are in addition to your GO-Bag.

2) Home and work emergency supplies (for yourself and your co-workers);

3) Vehicle-transported supplies;

3b) Bike Pannier Kit (mountain bike or motorcycle-carried supplies (optional);

4) KOP Kit (Keep-On-Person) or EDC (Every-Day-Carry) [Chapter 11]

This is a wallet-sized pouch that is always carried with you, no matter what you are doing. It contains a small handful of essential items which are often of vital importance in an assortment of emergency situations.

Selecting the best knapsack /backpack to use for your GO-Bag

There are some decisions that you need to make before you buy a knapsack or backpack to use for your GO-Bag. Don't be in such a hurry to buy a bag, that you bypass the following selection criteria.

> Since you may be forced to walk a long distance or in adverse conditions, your GO-Bag must be reasonably lightweight and comfortable to carry.

> **Terminology**
>
> The terms *'knapsack'* and *'rucksack'* are interchangeable. Militaries, and serious backpackers often use *'rucksack'* to describe a sturdy sack with shoulder straps that does not have a frame. Whereas the terms 'pack' or 'backpack' are used for a larger bag that is supported by an internal or external frame. Regardless of nomenclature, all of these are carried on the back by two shoulder straps. Most GO-Bags utilize a knapsack/rucksack to hold gear.

Pick a knapsack that matches the bulk and shape of your contents. Keep in mind, if you fail to get a large enough backpack, you will add gear until it's full and then be forced to leave other essential items behind. Or, if your backpack is too large, most people will add nonessentials to fill the available space. This adds weight and bulk that will reduce your mobility.

Even if you don't succumb to the temptation to fill the bag, it's still far from ideal. The contents of a partially filled bag will shift and can flop around, especially if you find that you need to run. And, when walking on uneven paths or climbing, a shifting or poorly balanced load can throw you off balance, resulting in a perilous fall.

Specifications: The selection of your knapsack is a strategic decision. Unless finances require it, don't choose your bag based on what you find in your garage or thrift store. Get a bag that matches your needs; one that also has wide, padded shoulder straps and a waist belt to keep the bag tight against your back. Unless money isn't an issue, it's better to buy a medium-priced knapsack rather than an expensive one. Spend the money you save on buying better quality gear. A quality bag is a valuable asset, but it is the contents that may save your life.

Assemble your contents *before* you buy a knapsack: To better understand the size of the bag you will need, purchase and bring together the items you intend to include in your GO-Bag. Put all of this into a pillowcase to help identify the size knapsack you will need. However, before you select a bag to purchase, weigh your pillowcase filled with gear, to see how much weight you will be carrying around. (Don't forget to include water.) You may find that it's too heavy, prompting you to remove some of the items to reduce the weight. Once you have reached the optimal weight which matches your body size and physical strength, then shop for your knapsack.

Chapter 10

GO-Bag Contents: Food and Water
(The Top-2 Most Essential GO-Bag Supplies)

GO-Bag Food

Plan for an *absolute minimum* of 1,800 Calories of food per day in warm weather, and twice that if you will be operating in cold weather. Research conducted by the U.S. military concludes that a warrior needs 4,200 Calories per day, and the nutritional breakdown should be 13 percent protein, 36 percent fat, and 51 percent carbohydrates. It is to our advantage to keep this Calorie and nutritional information in mind as we select our GO-Bag food.

By design, an urban GO-Bag is smaller and lighter in weight than a military rucksack or a pack used for backpacking, so many tradeoffs will be required as you select your supplies. To pull together a GO-Bag that has a total weight of only 18-22 pounds, you will need to leave out a lot of things that it would be useful to have.

Due to this weight and size limitation, our first decision is how many days of food we will plan to carry. Even three days of food, at the absolute minimum level of 1,800 Calories per day, represents a lot of bulk and weight.

We need to keep in mind, too, that variety is necessary. If you include meal replacement bars or sports bars, use bars made by different companies and a selection of different flavors. Taste your food choices in advance to ensure they are palatable to *you*.

On the following pages are two examples of what might be included in a one-day food supply. If you use one of these examples, don't forget to multiply it by the number of days of food you are planning to include in your GO-bag.

To help you better understand the quantity of food you will need to satisfy a minimum Calorie intake, variety, plus space and weight requirements, here are 2 examples, each with a different Calorie count.

Example #1 - 2,130 Calories/Day

1   MRE Dinner *Entrée* = 11 oz. of weight in your knapsack, including an MRE flameless heater / 160-560 Calories (varies by meal); approx. 31 cu in of space required for each entrée (.5 dm3).

3   CLIF Energy Bars (or equivalent), each approx. 2.4 oz. / 270 Calories. [3 x = 7.2 oz. of weight in your knapsack / 810 Calories combined]; approx. 4 cu in ea./x3=12 cu in (.065 dm3 / .195 dm3).

½   Lifeboat Ration, 4 oz./600 Calories; 7 cu in (.15 dm3).

2,130 Calories Combined Total (3,000-4,200 Calories *per day* is considered optimal for high-stress periods involving moderate levels of activity. Conversely, 1,800 Calories are a *minimal at-rest* amount.)

31 oz. (.88 kg) – Including packaging, the weight of the above 1-day supply of GO-Bag food is just under 2 pounds (not including water).

71 cu. (1.2 dm3) – If tightly packed, this is the minimum amount of space that will be needed for this 1-day supply of GO-bag food.

To put this in context, if your goal is to consume at least 1,800 Calories daily, you need to eat a nutritionally balanced combination of compact, lightweight foods. This 2,130-Calorie example is what we consider to be the minimum 1-day GO-Bag food supply. Note: Our examples include one MRE entrée per day, *not the entire MRE meal.* Since these entrées vary in Calorie count, we used the average of 360-Calories here, but we recommend selecting the higher-Calorie entrées. Though an MRE entrée may only represent a modest 32.7 Calories-per-ounce vs. 97.5 Calories-per-ounce of a high-Calorie CLIF Energy Bar, we include it because a hot meal that is near-normal tasting, eaten at the end of the day, can provide a needed psychological boost.

A combination of foods such as used in the above 2,130-Calorie example should be considered the <u>minimum</u> per-day quantity for one person.

Tightly packed, this modest 1-day food supply will require approximately 71 cubic inches (1.2 dm^3) of space in your GO-Bag, and about 2 lbs. (0.9 kg) of weight that you will need to carry. Remember, this is just for a 1-day supply of food—at a Calorie level that most people will not find adequate for curbing their hunger.

Example #1 (continued) - 2,130 Calories/Day
Space and weight required for 1-7 Days of these GO-Bag Foods

1 – Day Food Supply = 71 cu in of space in your GO-Bag, and 31-ounces of weight to carry (1.2 dm3 / 0.88 kg)
2 – Days = 142 cu in / 3.9 lbs.   (2.3 dm3 / 1.8 kg)
3 – Days = 213 cu in / 5.8 lbs.   (3.5 dm3 / 2.6 kg)
4 – Days = 284 cu. in / 7.8 lbs. (4.7 dm3 / 3.5 kg)
5 – Days = 355 cu in / 9.7 lbs.   (5.8 dm3 / 4.4 kg)
6 – Days = 426 cu. in / 11.6 lbs. (7.0 dm3 / 5.3 kg)
7 – Days = 497 cu in / 13.6 lbs. (8.1 dm3 / 6.2 kg)

Example #2 - 3,810 Calories/Day

To attain this higher Calorie count, we added an additional 4-sports/meal replacement/energy bars, plus a full 1-day lifeboat ration, for a total per-day quantity of: 1 MRE entrée (with heater), 7 bars, and 1 (complete 1-day, 1,200 Calorie) lifeboat ration. This represents a total of 3.2 lbs. (1.5kg) of weight to be carried, and approximately 101 cu in (1,655cm^3) of space, just for a *one-day* supply of food. Note: The below amounts are approximate. Due to variations between brands, flavors, and packaging, these products will differ slightly in weight, space, and Calorie count. Foil packaging generally provides longer shelf life.

Adding only a little more than an extra pound (20 oz.) of carry-weight for each day's food supply may seem like a modest increase, but when combined with water and additional gear, this added weight can be significant. Therefore, before deciding on your food supply, factor in your circumstances, anticipated operating environment, and the level of strenuous activity you expect.

1 – Day Food Supply of 3,810 Calories = 101 cu in / 3.2 lbs.
2 – Day = 202 cu in / 6.4 lbs.   (3.3 dm3 / 2.9 kg)
3 – Day = 303 cu in / 9.6 lbs.   (5.0 dm3 / 4.3 kg)
4 – Day = 404 cu. in / 12.8 lbs. (6.6 dm3 / 5.8 kg)
5 – Day = 505 cu in / 16 lbs.   (8.3 dm3 / 7.2 kg)
6 – Day = 606 cu. in / 19.2 lbs. (9.9 dm3 / 8.7 kg)
7 – Day = 707 cu in / 22.4 lbs.   (11.6 dm3 / 10.1 kg)

The Top-4 GO-Bag Foods: A Summary of the Best Options

1. Military MRE meal entrées with their water-activated heaters.

On average, each MRE (Meal, Ready-to-Eat) has 1,250 nutritional Calories, as well as 1/3 of the U.S. Department of Defense's Recommended Daily Allowance of vitamins and minerals. A full day's worth of meals consists of three MRE packages (envelopes), but the actual Calorie count varies between entrées.

An 'MRE' is a complete, self-contained meal for an individual. It is packaged in a durable plastic bag/pouch and designed for field use. However, for your GO-Bag, we recommend that you purchase only the entrée and heater portions, or remove these two items from the MRE meal package. You will save a lot of space and weight by using only these two parts of the meal; the foil packet which contains the MRE *entrée* and the water-activated heating envelope which transforms the entrée into a piping hot meal.

Due to the space requirement, the full MRE meal is not a good choice for a GO-Bag. Soldiers have learned the same lesson. Those who are operating on foot, rarely carry the entire meal. It just isn't practical. But they do carry the entrée, plus the crackers and a few other easy-to-carry favorite parts.

The MRE entrée is a lot heavier than a freeze-dried meal such as those used for backpacking, but the simplicity is hard to beat. Without a cook pot or cook stove, you can enjoy a hot, almost normal-tasting meal in 5-minutes. This is an excellent way to boost your spirits and nutritiously curb your hunger, especially before sleeping. For most people, a simple-to-prepare hot meal will help alleviate stress and help provide comfort and normalcy during a chaotic situation.

Oddly, MRE *entrées* vary widely in Calorie count (160-560 Calories), so choose high-Calorie meal entrées for your GO-Bag. The carry-weight is the same. Higher-Calorie entrées include: Beans with Potatoes (560 Calories), Lentils and Vegetables (560), Bean Salad (440), Chicken Pesto Pasta (360), Spaghetti with Meat Sauce (330), Lentil Stew with Ham (320), Sloppy Joe BBQ Beef (310), Pasta Marinara (300), Beef Ravioli (300), Meatballs with Marinara (290), and Pork Rib (290). Vegetarian and special-diet entrées are also available.

If water is in short supply, activate the MRE *"Flameless Ration Heater"* using any source of water, including urine. One MRE entrée, plus the water-activated heater, weighs approximately 11 oz. (.3kg) and requires approximately 31 cu in (508cm3) of space in your bag.

For more about MREs, see Chapter-15 and Appendix-B.

MCW/LRP (Meal, Cold Weather / Long Range Patrol): Similar to MREs, special-operations military units sometimes use these specialized meals which have a higher Calorie count and are lighter in weight. MCW/LRP have replaced RCW and LRP meals. The current MCW/LRP meals are packaged in pocket-sized components which resist freezing. Each meal contains 1,540 Calories (15% protein, 35% fat, and 50% carbohydrate), and requires 34-ounces (1kg) of water to rehydrate. Packaging is white or tan.

LRP (Long Range Patrol): These freeze-dried meals, which are still available through some outlets are increasingly hard to find. If you want a lighter-weight balanced-nutrition alternative to MREs, buy backpacking food such as the meals made by Mountain House. Unfortunately, to prepare these meals, you will need a method to heat water. Each freeze-dried meal uses about 1-1/2 cups of *pure*, boiling hot water; some brands use a retort pouch, others require a cook-pot.

FSR (First Strike Rations): Developed for spec-ops troops and soldiers who are engaged in high-intensity sustained battle, these pocketable eat-on-the-run meals are compact and lightweight. An FSR package contains sufficient nourishment for a 24-hour period and is half the weight and size of three complete MRE meal packages. Nutritionally, it contains 2,850 Calories vs. the 3,800 Calories contained in 3 full MRE meals. Due to inherent nutritional shortcomings, these rations should not be used for more than three days. Notwithstanding, some military manuals still specify an unhealthy maximum of two weeks. FSRs are difficult to find on the civilian market, and most people will find them less satisfying than our recommendation contained in Example #2. The shelf life is 3-years, just like MREs. These cost the government 50% more than MREs, so expect a price differential in the retail marketplace. Watch for fraudulent products.

2. Meal-Replacement Bars, Energy Bars, Fruit & Nut Bars, Nutrition Bars, and Protein Bars. (Include several of each type.)

Before selection, first, check the contents and nutritional information for the product. Unlike the requirements of daily life, you will probably want to select food bars which provide high-Calorie content and fats, as the quantity of food you will be consuming will be significantly reduced. Also, at least some variety is desirable. Keep in mind the nutritional balance recommended in the first paragraph of this chapter.

> *In your GO-Bag, also include* medicine for upset stomach, constipation and diarrhea. Stress, combined with a radical change in diet—such as eating these foods exclusively, can cause not just discomfort, but health issues which make you vulnerable to other problems. Keep these medicines handy.

Shelf life on packaging: Select bars which contain at least 3+ grams of protein, 15+ grams of sugar, 3+ grams of fiber, plus some healthy fats and carbohydrates. A variety of flavors is a good decision, but make sure that each bar contains at least 150 Calories and some fiber. Selecting several brands will minimize digestive problems. Unlike our goals for normal healthy eating, in a bug-out (evacuation) emergency, we want to increase our intake of Calories because we need energy.

Top brands to consider: CLIF, rated by many independent sources as the best meal replacement bar. LUNA, high in protein. Kashi ROLL, high in protein. Marathon by Snickers, high in both protein and carbs. Odwalla bars and Kind bars, high sugar content and they taste good. Fruits of Life contain probiotics, a feature which may be advantageous to maintaining health and warding off illness, plus the fruit flavor bars can be a welcome departure from the candy-like taste of many bars. Pure bars are 100% organic, and the manufacturer uses minimal processing). PowerBar is perhaps the most sticky bar of all the major brands, so they may increase the risk of damage to teeth that have fillings or crowns. OATMEGA bars are high in protein and carbohydrates, and also high in Omega 3. Zing bars, often the top rated in polls as having the best flavor, also have bars which are gluten-free, dairy-free, and soy-free. Fruition bars are high in carbs. CLIF Mojo, expressly designed for the palate and needs of older children are nevertheless suitable for adults, too, while the Z Bar products may be a good choice for younger children.

Opinions vary widely on which bars taste best and which has a pleasing texture, so we recommend doing your own taste test before you purchase a quantity of any brand of bar. Frankly, most of these are not tasty when eaten under normal circumstances so you may want to sample them at a time when you are hungry. If you are selecting food for other family members or friends, involve them in your taste test.

3. Lifeboat Survival-Kit Ration Bars
aka/ aviation survival-kit bars

* We recommend these 2 brands of survival-kit ration cubes/bars:

Recommended Brand: MAINSTAY
Manufacturer's Website: www.SurvivorInd.com
Flavor: Mild Lemon
Product Options:

- Mainstay 1200 Ration Bar - contains three 400-Calorie meal replacement bars, 2.7 oz./ 80 g.

- Mainstay 2400 Ration Package - contains six 400-Calorie meal replacement bars (same as above, but a larger quantity of individually wrapped bars); 16 oz. / 473 grams (Lower cost per meal but same product), space requirement: 6 x 3.5 x 1.25 inches. These are also available in a 3,600-Calorie package.

Recommended Brand: DATREX
Manufacturer's Website: www.Datrex.com
Flavor: Coconut
Product Options:

- DATREX DX1000F Aviation Ration Bar - contains four 250-Calorie meal replacement bars, 6.4 oz. / 190 g.

- DATREX DX2401F Ration – White Brick - contains twelve 200-Calorie meal replacement bars, 17 oz./482 g, 3.5 x 2.5 x 2.5 inches. This product is also available in a 3,600-Calorie package.

Brand Selection: For most people, the choice between these two products is based on flavor or the number of Calories in each individual bar. If the taste is the main issue for you and you don't want to try both brands, select the product which has the flavor you find most appealing (lemon or coconut). Most people are satisfied with either brand, but you might as well choose a preferred flavor since nutritional differences between the two brands are insignificant.

When Purchasing: When ordering these products on the Internet, be sure to read the product description carefully. Some vendors associate the wrong photo with the product being sold, and the quantity is often different from that which is illustrated. Also, it is not unusual for one vendor to offer twice the amount for nearly the same price as a single item sold by a different retailer.

If you consider purchasing lifeboat rations manufactured by a different company, be sure the product is "U.S. Coast Guard Approved," as this certification is the primary indicator of product quality, nutritional benefit in an emergency situation, and documented shelf life.

> *Though a 1-day "lifeboat ration" or "aviation survival kit ration" may be enough to keep a person alive for a long time, it is not adequate for maintaining the health, mobility, and the physical and mental performance of an active person. Therefore, in our opinion, these rations should only be used as a supplement to others foods to help reduce space and weight while increasing your Caloric and nutritional intake, and also, for on-the-run consumption.*

When comparing these products as sold by various vendors online, it is best to compare the total Calorie count for the item and quantity they are selling. Some product packages contain 1-meal (400-Calories), 1-day of meals (1,200 Calories), while others contain food sufficient for 3-days (3,600 Calories), so the number of pieces is not a useful factor for comparison. Since the product photos often inaccurately depict the product being sold, pay close attention to the product description.

Note: When evaluated based solely on weight and space required, lifeboat rations are an extremely efficient condensed form of vitamins, nutrients, and high in energy-producing Calories. The taste is acceptable, but it does become an uninteresting meal after a few bites.

Most importantly, though the U.S. Coast Guard has determined that the intake of 1,200 Calories per-day is sufficient to maintain life while floating in a lifeboat, these rations should not be considered adequate nutritionally for long-term sustenance nor for an active person engaged in physical exertion associated with evacuation. So, even when the label indicates that a package contains a 1-day supply of food, if that is all you eat during the day, expect your stomach to communicate a very different opinion.

Food Shelf life: Except for lifeboat and aviation survival-kit rations, most of these foods have a shelf life of 12-36 months. Therefore, check the expiration date and set a replacement schedule. Thankfully, if stored correctly, most of these foods can be safely eaten many months or even years after that date. The nutritional value may diminish, but the food is often still safe to eat if the container is undamaged and not swollen.

4. D-I-Y "Mylar Packaging" of Emergency Food.

This is a do-it-yourself (D-I-Y) method for creating your own meals-*almost*-ready-to-eat. But, this option does require boiling water, so it is best for long-duration GO-Bags. For GO-Bags carrying 3 days of food, most people will prefer a combination of the first three options found in the previous pages of this chapter.

In use, these D-I-Y meals are similar to the backpacking meals made by Mountain House and other vendors, but with one important difference: They are inexpensive.

Mylar bags and oxygen-absorber packets are often used by do-it-yourselfers to package large quantities of food for long-term food storage. This method is a low-cost and healthy way to meet long-term food storage needs or special dietary requirements. Importantly for this GO-Bag food topic, this same, simple technique can also be used to create single-serving meals.

Directions: This process is typically accomplished by putting rice or pasta into a heavy-duty Mylar envelope. Then add some freeze-dried vegetables purchased in bulk #10 cans from a company such as Numanna, Thrive, Wise Food, Augason Farms, or Mountain House.[13] In addition to these food products, add dry seasoning or dry sauce-mix for flavor. Just before sealing the bag, add an oxygen-absorber packet to remove the oxygen from the air that is trapped inside the Mylar bag.

The use of the oxygen absorber packet and the Mylar bag which is far more impervious to air leakage than even extra heavy-duty plastic is what makes it possible for this D-I-Y food storage method to provide a long shelf life. As long as you didn't include meat, or foods with fats or oils in the bag, this dry food concoction can often be eatable and nutritious 20-30 years after you packaged it. (Be sure to remove the oxygen-absorbing packet before preparing the food.)

---

[13] If a freeze-dried food company does not offer their products in #10 cans as well foil pouches, I would not consider them a serious contender in the long-term food storage marketplace. Note: 5-gallon plastic buckets of freeze dried food often contain foil pouches, so don't automatically reject these manufacturers before checking on how their food is stored inside the bucket. Mountain House is the biggest and they do make quality products, but they are not necessarily the best.

The last step in this D-I-Y method is to seal the Mylar bag, a task that must be done with some precision to make sure that air can't leak into the sealed bag. This can be accomplished using a hot iron (clothing iron) placed for a few seconds on top of the bag's opening. If you do this with a metal surface underneath the bag, it will reflect the heat back into the bag and improve the seal.

Though it adds a little weight, when a small can of tuna, beef, or chicken is packed with (not in) the sealed Mylar bag after preparing it, the result is a tastier meal. When the meat from the can is added to the Mylar envelope a few minutes before eating the food, it can provide an almost home-cooked meal experience.

Note: Do not include meat, fish, nuts, or anything containing fat inside the Mylar bag before sealing it. Fats and oils will cause the food in the bag to spoil at a much faster rate. Even dehydrated meats will reduce the shelf life of your D-I-Y food package to less than 5-years.

To eliminate the need for a pot for cooking the meal, use a larger size Mylar bag. If the appropriate-size Mylar bag is used, and the do-it-yourselfer has left enough space in the bag to accommodate the boiling water needed to cook the food, a quick and easy meal can be created in the same bag. If this is what you choose to do, roll the top of the Mylar bag before sealing it, to remove as much air as possible, then flatten it for sealing. And, use an extra (or larger) oxygen-absorbing packet to compensate for the increased volume of the bag.

Before making a quantity of these cook-in-bag meals, be sure to test your method by preparing a meal in the bag. Use extra caution to avoid burning yourself. When the bag is filled with boiling water, it will be very unstable unless you used a flat-bottom Mylar bag.

Take the time to develop and taste-test your recipes for these Mylar-bag meals. And don't forget to add to your gear a small backpacking stove, and pot, to heat the water. The Mylar bag is metalized, but it cannot withstand being placed directly on a stove or in a fire.

In most situations, you won't want to use a campfire to boil the water as it will disclose your location. The wind carrying the smell of a great-tasting meal will be enough of a problem!

Larger Quantity / Longer-Term Supplies of Food: If you anticipate a longer-duration bug-out situation, or you have the need for extended shelf life, use a gallon-size Mylar bags to package rice and beans, add the appropriate size/quantity of oxygen absorbers, and then seal the bag as described on the prior page. These self-packaged bags of staples are inexpensive and yet they can deliver a 20+ year shelf life, plus many days of food in each bag. Yet, even though much of the world subsists on rice and beans, eaten alone, it will not be savory. But it can provide protein and carbs that are dietary essentials.

If you add a $1/8^{th}$ pound of bulk-purchased freeze-dried vegetables per pound of rice and beans, and several small envelopes of spices, many days of healthy eating can be accommodated for you and your family (or group) in a very lightweight, compact package.

If you further augment this food supply with separately packaged freeze-dried, dehydrated (or even canned) meat or fish, or foraged food, you can carry several weeks of meager but healthy sustenance in one backpack.

Freeze dried meats are lightweight and yet can deliver near-normal taste. Dehydrated meats are not as nutritious as freeze-dried, but they are lightweight, and the taste is generally acceptable. Canned meats provide good taste but are heavy due to the water and other liquids contained in the can. Yet, the purchase price for canned meat is far lower than freeze-dried and dehydrated meat. Some brands of canned meats are much better than others in reducing the amount of unneeded liquid, taste, and unhelpful chemicals. If you opt for canned meat, utilize small single-serving cans or foil pouches.

Note: All meats and fish, including those which are freeze-dried, have a much shorter shelf life than dry rice and dry bean staples. Professionally packaged meats designed for long-term food storage will generally only last 3-5 years.

For this reason, do not add meat, butter, eggs, flour, or any food containing oil or fat to your bags of Mylar-packaged foods. By not including these items, you can replace only your freeze-dried and dehydrated meats, or canned meats and other fat or oil-containing foods, on a regular schedule rather than needing to replace your entire food supply.

Salt, Pepper, and Spices: When D-I-Y packaging in Mylar bags is used for packaging, as previously described, salt and unground peppercorns will last for decades. Whereas most other spices will become less flavorful, but most will remain safe to eat even after a decade of dry, uncontaminated storage. When possible, use unground spices for your long-term food storage. Don't grind your spices until you are ready to use them.

Regardless of whether you store unground or ground spices, after opening, smell the spice and inspect it to make sure the odor and appearance is appropriate to that spice. Then taste a small sample to verify the flavor before using it in your food.

For more on do-it-yourself Mylar packaging, visit the "Resources" page of the author's website: www.SIGSWANSTROM.com.

Related supplies you *may* want to add to your GO-Bag

- Metal Cup with large handle (Suitable for boiling water)

- Spork – Titanium or stainless steel 'spork' (spoon/fork combo utensil), or metal silverware designed for backpacking. For long-term use, avoid cooking with aluminum utensils and aluminum pots due to health concerns.

- Metal Spoon, with 8+-inch handle for cooking over a fire

- Knife – 4-inch blade or larger

- Disposable Utensils - plastic knife, fork, spoon (Plastic utensils are popular, but we only include them here as "extra" utensils, not as primary cooking and eating tools because of their lack of durability.)

- Magnesium Fire-Starting Tool

- Butane Lighter (fire starting) – BIC or major brand (3)

- Storm Matches, sealed in a watertight container

- Waxed Tinder – Zippo Waxed Tinder Sticks, or equivalent

- Can and Bottle Opener Even if your GO-Bag does not include canned food, still pack a small can and bottle opener with your gear, just in case you need it. Opening a can or bottle with a knife or another object can be dangerous, whereas a small can opener, like the U.S. military P-38, and P-51 (easier to use). Also useful is a mini can opener, which is included with many keychain multitools. These devices can weigh less than 1-ounce and yet be a lifesaver if you are able to scavenge canned food or bottled beverages.

- Soap - A sliver of antibacterial bar soap provides the best weight-to-purpose benefit. Hand soap can be used to wash dishes, as well as wounds, cuts, and the body. Store the bar in a plastic sandwich bag.

- Backpacking Stove & Fuel - Needed if your GO-Bag food is either backpacking meals such as those made by Mountain House, or if you are using the do-it-yourself Mylar Bag food-storage method described on the prior pages. Multifuel stoves made specifically for lightweight backpacking, are best.

For additional details on products, links to manufacturer's websites, and other periodically updated information, visit the author's website. On the "Resources" page, look for "Supplemental Information" for this book.
www.SigSwanstrom.com

GO-Bag Water

As you decide what to include in your GO-Bag, first consider the space and weight requirements of your water supply. For reference, a 1-gallon supply of water requires at least 231 cu in (3.8 dm3) of storage space in your bag, and will weigh 8.34 lbs. (3.8 kg).

Note: The totals listed here do not include the space requirements of the water container you have chosen. Nor do they reflect the amount of space wasted by round bottles, or the weight of the containers themselves.

Recommendations

Minimalist GO-Bag
3-days of Food (Example #1 - 2,130 Calories/day), plus a 1-day supply of water. Requires 444 cu in space in your GO-Bag, and weighs 14.1 lbs.[12]

Standard GO-Bag
3-days of Food (Example #2 - 3,810 Calories/day), plus a 1-day supply of water. Requires 534 cu in space in your GO-Bag, and weighs 17.9 lbs.[12]

Fully Independent and Self-Sufficient GO-Bag
3-days of Food (Example #2 - 3,810 Calories/day), plus a 3-day supply of water. Together, these require 996 cu in space in your GO-Bag, and weighs 34.6 lbs.[12]

Space / Weight Summary

The **"Minimalist"** GO-Bag is for those who want to assemble the lightest, smallest GO-Bag possible. Summarized in the text box on the left, this *'minimalist'* Go-Bag is just barely adequate. It contains a subsistence-level amount of food. So it will not boost your energy much, but it will give you adequate nutrition for a few days. Designed for use in locations where water can be found along your evacuation route, this example only includes a 1-day supply of water, so your water supply would need to be replenished along the way. Of course, water found en route will likely need to be purified, so you will also need to pack purification supplies.

A lightweight, compact purification method is Chlorine Dioxide. It is found in 'Katadynn Micropur Purification Tablets' which are popular with backpackers. Purification methods are discussed later in this chapter.[14]

---

[14] The space required and weights listed do not include the GO-Bag knapsack itself, nor does it include the space/weight for water purification and other supplies.

With this example, it is assumed that you will *not* be engaged in a strenuous physical activity, or need extra Calories to fight exposure to cold weather. With the 'Minimalist' option you may feel hungry, but you won't starve.

The **"Standard"** (prior page) represents the typical amount of food and water contained in a typical GO-Bag. The example used here includes a 3-day supply of food that is nutritiously, and calorically similar to the standards set by the U.S. Department of Defense for a soldier engaged in field exercises or combat (The DoD standard calls for 4,200 Calories vs. the 3,810 Calories used in our example). This food supply plus a 1-day supply of water will require approximately 444 cu in (7.3 dm3) of space in your GO-Bag and will weigh close to 14 lbs. This is just for food and water, it does not include other essential gear.

Keep in mind that you may need to carry your GO-Bag on your back if you find that you need to evacuate on foot. This limits the amount of other gear you will be able to carry, at least if you plan to keep your GO-Bag weight under 25-pounds.

It's important to bear in mind, too, that just as with the 'Minimalist,' this example only includes a 1-day supply of water. If you select a solution such as this, you must be confident that you will be able to find additional water as you travel along your evacuation route. And, you will need to have a water purification method along, too, as it is advisable to purify any water you are not 100% confident that it is pure. As with all essential gear, it is best to have two water purification methods, in case one fails.

The **"Fully Independent and Self-Sufficient GO-Bag"** example is designed for those who want to be able to operate independently for 3-days. This might be walking your evacuation route, or being engaged in some other physical activity in moderate weather, where you want to be wholly self-reliant and not need to find sources of water to augment what they are carrying in their bag. This extra water adds an additional 16.7 lbs, so it nearly doubles the weight, but this is necessary if it might be difficult to find water en route and purify it. The total weight of this option is almost 36 lbs (16 kg), and this only represents food and water. It does not include any other gear, or the weight of water containers, nor the knapsack itself. Therefore, this option is not a viable solution for most people.

Food & Water Minimums: Many experts agree that the combination of 3-days of food and a 1-day supply of water is the absolute minimum for a GO-Bag designed to support the needs of 1-person. However, this does assume that you will have access to water en route and that you can purify it before using it, so the lighter weight does bring with it an inherent risk that you must evaluate.

If you suspect that you may not be able to find additional water as you travel along your evacuation route, you need to use the third example or something similar. Or, you might devise your own strategy which is a hybrid using elements of the other examples.

If you elect to carry a 3-day (or more) supply of water, you may opt for a diet of lifeboat rations to save weight and space. Food is optional; water is not.

A 3-day supply of food (3,810 Calories/day), plus 3-days of water, will require more than 900 cubic inches (14.7 dm3) of space in your GO-Bag. And, this supply of food and water will weigh a whopping 31 pounds (14 kg). This is a lot of weight to carry in an evacuation scenario.

Nonetheless, this might be necessary for the situation you think you might encounter, so it may be unavoidable. If this is the situation you are planning to confront, consider leaving almost everything else behind and exclusively use lifeboat rations for your food. It's either that or resign yourself to carrying a too-heavy and too-large GO-Bag.

But if your goal is a 16-22-pound (7-10 kg) GO-Bag, which is optimal, consider packing a 3-day supply of food (2,130 Calories/day) and a 1-day supply of water. Unfortunately, even with this nominal amount of food and water, and a lightweight water purification filter (which is necessary), you will only be able to carry a few pounds of other supplies.

As you can see, this creates a dilemma. Even if you opt for carrying a 22-pound or slightly heavier GO-Bag, you will need to be extremely selective in what gear you include.

Amount of Water Needed

To maintain health, on average, adults need to consume 1-gallon (128 oz./3.8-liters) per day of pure drinking water. If the temperature is high, or if your daily activities include trekking or physical exertion, you will need to consume additional water. If your physical activity causes you to sweat, you will need to drink even more. Yet, in addition to physical stamina and health, water is necessary for proper brain function, too. If you are operating in an emergency situation you will need every bit of brain function you can muster, so don't skimp on water.

Pets: If you might have an animal companion with you, don't forget to include the water and food that they will need. Food is not critical for a day or two, but just like humans, animals need ample water. Observe your pet's water consumption and plan accordingly.

Water Purification

Clean looking water is often not pure. Yet, pure water is essential for drinking, cooking, oral hygiene, and for medical needs.

Don't be fooled. Even clean looking, cool, clear mountain streams often contain giardia, crypto, and other illness-causing microorganisms. Water runoff from roofs, farmland, and manufacturing plants may also contain dangerous, hidden chemicals.

Warning: Some contaminants, such as manufacturing waste products and pesticides, are not removed by standard water purification methods. So, be attentive to your water source and potential problems.

Don't take unnecessary risks. Don't let urgency or fatigue distract you from using safe, pure water for drinking, food preparation, hygiene, and your medical needs. If you are not 100% sure that the water is pure, purify it.

During a bug-out situation, it's best to purify all water before drinking it. Waterborne viruses and bacteria can not only make you sick, but they can also immobilize you or create a deadly health problem if medical care is unavailable.

After storms, floods, and certain other emergencies, even tap water and well water may not be safe. If you are not 100% satisfied that the water is pure, purify it.

Top-2 Water Purification Methods for your GO-Bag

These methods are easy, reliable, and straightforward. Since redundancy is necessary, we recommend having, and using, two purification methods since maintaining operational health is so important.

Recommendation

To purify water, follow this 3-step process.

1. If the water is not already clear and clean looking, pre-filter it.

2. Boil the water, or use a water filter rated at '1-micron *absolute.*'

3. Add Chlorine Dioxide tablets or use a UV device like a SteriPEN. If neither of these are available, use household bleach or one of the other treatment methods described here and in Chapter 14.

Whenever possible, use more than one water purification method.

Step-1: Pre-filter the Water

Cloudy, colored, or dirty-looking water should be pre-filtered. This step does not purify the water, but it will remove some of the contaminents. As a result, your filter will last longer, your chemical treatment methods will be more effective, and, it will help the water taste better. (Later in this chapter you'll find instructions on how to make an inexpensive pre-filter.)

Step-2: Filter the Water

Products sold as "water filters" are very different from "water purification filters." And, not all water purification filters provide the same level of protection. You need a system which will kill 99.99% of pathogenic bacteria. Your water filter should remove *protozoa, bacteria,* and *viruses.* To accomplish this, you need a filter that is rated "1-micron *absolute.*"

When you are shopping for a water purification filter, be sure you are comparing apples-to-apples. Also, there are high-quality filters which have not been subjected to costly independent verification. Nevertheless, the industry standard is NSF 53 or NSF 58, so this and "cyst removal" are worth looking for on the packaging.

Note: Bad tasting water is not necessarily contaminated water. If you have purified the water and it still has an unpleasant taste, and you don't have another water option and you have no reason to suspect that it's laced with fertilizer or industrial chemicals, use a sports drink powder to mask the flavor.

Step-3: Use a Chemical or UV Light to Purify the Water

There are various water treatment tablets available for water purification, but they are not all equally effective. You need a product that will kill 99.99% of the bacteria in the water, but you also want a product which will kill viruses. Most water filters do not provide this level of purification, nor do most purification tablets. Boiling is ideal, but often impractical in an emergency situation, especially if you are engaged in evacuation. If you select a method or product other than the below recommendations, be sure it offers the same level of effectiveness as these recommendations:

Recommended Chemical: Chlorine Dioxide (Tablets)

'Katadyn Micropur Purification Tablets' (www.Katadyn.com) is one of the few truly effective products. Its active ingredient is chlorine dioxide, which will kill most protozoa and viruses in 15-minutes, giardia in 30-minutes, and cryptosporidium within 4-hours. This product is easy to use, and the tablets are packaged in small, individually wrapped foil packets.

Recommended UV Light Method: SteriPEN (Uses batteries)

Follow the manufacturer's directions for the product selected. Most are simply dipped into the water contained in a canteen or water bottle, turned on, and then the water is gently stirred with the tip of the device for 90-seconds.

Redundancy: For adaptability and additional redundancy, many people include all three of these purification methods in their GO-Bag; a water purification filter, chlorine dioxide tablets, and a UV treatment device. This may sound excessive, but since maintaining health is so critical, this is worth considering.

Caution: Most water purification methods, including these, are not 100% effective. This is why it is so important to use two top-rated methods back-to-back. This same redundancy is also recommended by the CDC (Centers for Disease Control) as essential for obtaining reliably safe drinking water during an emergency situation. For more on purification, see Chapter-14.

Whichever method you use, pre-filter the water before you purify it.

The pre-filter concept is to use an additional filtration method to remove debris and larger particles from the water before the water reaches the filter. This will significantly extend the life of the filter. Pre-filters can be purchased, but they can also be easily made.

To make a simple pre-filter: Use a new white sock and a fine-mesh nylon stocking. Cut the foot portion (i.e., the closed-end tube at the foot section of the sock) to separate it from the ankle section. Do the same with the foot portion of a fine-mesh nylon stocking. Place the cotton sock inside the nylon-stocking foot, to form a double layer pre-filter. (The advantage of using a white sock is that it will be more obvious when your pre-filter is dirty and needs to be washed.) If possible, use new, unworn socks for this purpose as even laundered previously worn socks can contain contaminants.

Insert your water purification filter's water-intake tube into the opening of the pre-filter (sock-foot that is inside the nylon sock-foot), and hold it in place with two rubber bands.

Whenever possible, let the debris in the water settle before you use your pre-filter. A lot of dirt, plant matter, and even industrial chemicals will settle to the bottom, or rise to the top, if the water is allowed to remain still. So, if practical, suck water from several inches below the water's surface, but above the debris on the bottom.

We recommend that you always use your pre-filter, even when the water looks clear.

When finished, squeeze the water from your double-sock pre-filter, and store it in an unsealed plastic bag so it can air dry. Or, if you are operating in a clean environment, hang it on the outside of your knapsack. You don't want to seal your pre-filter in a plastic bag as mildew will develop if air is unable to flow around it.

Warning: Pure water isn't your only concern. Electrolyte imbalance and dehydration are serious health risks during emergency situations.

Electrolyte imbalance and dehydration are a common, and major, potential health problem. These conditions routinely surface in post-disaster environments, and also when you are engaged in outdoor activities in warm or hot weather, and anytime you are involved in long walks, running, or strenuous physical activity.

Give additional attention to this potential health risk if:
- The ambient temperature is high,
- If you feel cold or hot,
- If you are engaged in any prolonged physical activity,
- If you are exposed to direct sunlight for more than an hour and the temperature is above 80 degrees,
- If you are ill and running a fever, or
- If you are sweating profusely for any reason.

Any of these circumstances can cause dehydration and/or an electrolyte imbalance.

Under these conditions, drinking more water may not solve this health problem. The consumption of alcoholic beverages, including beer and wine, will further exacerbate this health hazard.

I'm not a medical professional, but I do have experience with these problems in the field. *I am including this commentary since my experiences with these problems may be of interest to you. In any case, my message is, "This is not a theoretical risk. I have repeatedly encountered these problems in real-world emergency situations."*

Personally, I have concluded that the consumption of an adequate amount of water is a good start for solving this potential health problem, but it is not enough. Absent professional medical care and testing, I've found a simple method that helps me monitor dehydration and electrolyte imbalance. It's simple: I keep track of urination.

I have found that if I am urinating every hour or two, and the color of my urine is nearly clear, then I am probably adequately hydrated. However, if my urine is dark in color, I need to start drinking more water.

Electrolyte Replenishment: If I am walking or working in the sun, and the temperature is higher than 80-degrees, or if I encounter any of the other bulleted points listed on the prior page, I add to my water a packet of a sports drink powder that is formulated for electrolyte replenishment. (Gatorade may be better than nothing, but it is not what I choose if I have better options available to me.)

I select my sports drink powder based on its ability to replace the electrolytes needed by the human body. When shopping, the first thing I do is check that the product has at least 80 mg of potassium. I also buy sports bars which contain real coconut or banana, and the same 80+ mg of potassium. Both work, but for me, using sports drink powder seems to be a quicker solution.

What do I look for in a sports drink or food bar? As I select these products, first, I check the label and verify that the product contains *at least* 80 mg of potassium, as well as the minerals calcium, magnesium, and sodium (salt). If it contains phosphate, chloride, and an assortment of vitamins, that is even better.

Next, whether by drinking water to which I have added a sports drink powder or eating a sports bar, in both low and high-temperature conditions, I am deliberate about consuming potassium.

I've found that I need at least 160-200 mg of extra potassium when the temperature is below freezing or greater than 95 degrees. Or, at any temperature if I am sweating heavily from exertion.

If I am engaging in a strenuous activity in an environment where the temperature is 95+ degrees, or when I am exposed to high-stress, I increase this amount, but generally not more than an extra 400 mg of potassium in a 24-hour period.

Personally, I never consume more than two servings of a sports drink or sports bars in a three-hour period. You can overdose on electrolytes. So, I have also learned that I shouldn't go crazy and consume unnecessary quantities as this can cause other problems.

Warning Signs: If I notice unusual weakness or fatigue, cramps or muscle spasms, irregular heartbeat, loss of appetite, lethargy, moodiness, or mental confusion, these are all indicators of electrolyte imbalance, so I take corrective measures. Very often, these indicators are first noticed by a traveling companion since mental impairment reduces our ability to self-diagnose this problem. Therefore, we need to observe each other, looking for signs of this deficiency.

For those who anticipate prolonged strenuous activity in a low or high-temperature environment, such as in an arctic or desert region, I urge you to get professional medical advice in advance.

Dehydration and electrolyte imbalance are not minor concerns. In field operations with which I have been involved, we have had to airlift more operators by helicopter for the health emergency of electrolyte imbalance than all other medical problems (which were not battle related), combined.

> **Dehydration** is when your body doesn't have as much water as it needs. Extreme dehydration will cause an **electrolyte imbalance**; a chemistry change which brings serious health problems that can result in death. *More water will overcome dehydration, but it will not correct an electrolyte imbalance.*

Fortunately, we had team medics on the ground, medivac helicopters nearby, and hospitals a short flight away. It is unlikely that you will have these resources. So, I encourage you to take preventative action by intentionally consuming electrolyte replacement drinks, bars, or capsules. And, monitoring how much of it you consume.

These health problems can also hamper judgment at a time when you need to be at peak performance, and they can even cause death. If you are alone, take extra care.

Fortunately, these serious health problems can often be wholly avoided by just eating fruits and vegetables, even in dehydrated form. And by drinking water to which you have added electrolyte-replacement powder, or sports bars which contain the needed minerals and vitamins. My GO-Bag contains food bars which contain fruit and vegetables, plus sports bars and a sports drink powder that contain the needed electrolyte-replacement minerals and vitamins.

These are not trivial additions to your bag of supplies. Yet, if you are confident that your bug-out situation will not involve physical exertion, hot weather or high stress, you may not need to be as concerned with this potential health risk.

Another plus is that many sports drink powders also include an assortment of other vitamins, minerals, and flavoring. Therefore, these same drink supplements can be used to improve your diet *AND* help mask the flavor of bad-tasting water.

Of course, other vitamins, sugars and flavoring are trivial when compared to the need for adding those nutrients which restore electrolytes. Still, these can be noteworthy additional benefits.

For me, it's my electrolyte balance that is my #1 concern when I am operating in adverse conditions in the field. It's more important than eating to curb my hunger. Electrolytes aid essential bodily functions such as regulating your heartbeat, they facilitate the work of your muscles, your ability to walk, and mental acuity, so I encourage you to consider this topic when you outfit your GO-Bag.

Water Containers

Your GO-Bag should contain at least two hard-plastic wide-mouth 32-ounce water bottles which will fit into your GO-Bag, or into a pouch on the outside of your GO-Bag knapsack.

Favorite water bottle brands include Nalgene 'Wide Mouth' and Camelbak 'eddy' or 'Chute,' which are made from durable BPA-free Eastman Tritan copolyester (plastic), and Kleen Kanteeen 'Wide Mouth Stainless' which is steel. Don't waste space and weight with insulated bottles for your GO-Bag. It is unlikely that you will have access to hot or cold beverages. Selecting clear plastic bottles means that you have the advantage of being able to inspect the contents.

To save space, put damage-prone supplies, such as energy bars, inside these empty bottles—but don't pack them tight. You need to be able to empty them quickly so that you can fill the bottles with water. Store your bottles inside your GO-Bag, at the top of your bag's interior so they can be quickly retrieved and filled with pure fresh water before you bug-out.

In addition to these plastic bottles, a 3-liter (100-oz.) water bladder weighs just under 7-pounds when filled with water, so it is a compact and weight-efficient method for transporting water. Equipped with the integrated drinking tube, these are a desirable addition to a GO-Bag.

For young children, you might need to outfit *their* GO-Bag with a smaller water bladder. A 2-liter (70 oz) bladder filled with water still weighs 4.5 lbs (2 kg), so this might be the maximum they can carry.

Yet, even a child's GO-Bag needs to contain water plus food and a few other necessary supplies. Remember, you don't need to fill a water bladder completely, so you can reduce the weight in a child's bag if necessary. The bladder itself weighs only 7-ounces (170 gm), which is almost the same as one 32-oz Nalgene bottle. Yes, a plastic bottle is more durable, but a water bladder is lightweight, and the convenience it provides will encourage more water consumption.

Many knapsacks have a large pocket designed for these bladders that are built into the interior of the bag. But even if your pack has a special pocket for a water bladder, to avoid puncture, place soft objects next to the bladder or insert a piece of corrugated cardboard between the bladder and the bag's contents. Be intentional about keeping sharp objects away from the bladder's soft, vulnerable sides.

Knapsacks designed for these bladders usually have a slot for the attached drinking tube, too, and a way to secure it to the shoulder strap of the bag. This makes it easy to drink water even while on the move. There is no need to stop to fetch a canteen from your pack, and the drinking tube prevents spilling. If you don't opt to include a water bladder in your GO-Bag, you will need to include additional water-transport containers.

Each GO-Bag needs to be capable of transporting a minimum of 1-gallon (3.8 Liters) of pure water.

Use a *designated additional* water bottle, collapsible bucket, or a bucket made from a 1-gallon milk jug, for gathering water that has not yet been purified.

Water-Bladder Caution: Only purchase a water bladder from a manufacturer who is known for making quality products. Others can have weak seams and not survive prolonged storage.

When empty, do not fold a bladder tightly as this will weaken the plastic. Only put pure drinking water into a water bladder. Since the bladder itself is more porous it can be difficult to sanitize. Bladders are also prone to retaining flavors and odors, so only use a bladder for pure water. Even sports drink powder can impart a lasting flavor to the plastic of some bladders.

> To make a milk-jug bucket/water-scoop to gather water, use a jug that has flat sides. Carefully cut the top off the jug but leave the carry handle in place. When not in use, keep this makeshift bucket inside your GO-Bag and keep breakables in it, to enhance protection.

Water storage: Maintain a supply of drinking water with your GO-Bag, but not inside it. When your GO-Bag is needed, then empty the bottled water into your water bladder and reusable plastic water bottles. By utilizing this method, you can conveniently replace your stored water bottles every three months. This makes it easy to maintain a fresh supply of emergency drinking water for your GO-Bag.

Recommendation for teens and adults: At a minimum, your GO-Bag should help you comfortably transport at least 1-gallon of water. This task can be easily accommodated by using two 32-oz plastic wide-mouth water bottles such as those made by Nalgene, and one 100-ounce (3-liter) water bladder with drinking tube assembly, such as the mil-spec bladders made by Camelbak. You only need to purchase the reservoir and drinking tube assembly, unless you plan on using the related 'pack' to contain your GO-Bag supplies.

When these two bottles and this one bladder are filled with water, the user can carry 1.3 gallons (4.8 Liters) of water. One-gallon is the minimum amount recommended, but a little more provides a safety margin.

Having three separate containers for pure water is also a hedge against one larger container that might become damaged and unusable. The military adage which reminds us of the importance of redundancy, "Two is one, and one is none" (Chapter-14), is worth remembering as you assemble your GO-Bag.

Recommendation for children: Use durable plastic drinking bottles with a lid that limits water loss if the container is dropped. Since bladders are prone to puncture, they may not be the best choice for young children. Since the amount of water needed varies by age/size/absorption rate/activity, you need to consider your needs.

Plan for comfortable hands-free carry: GO-Bags for adults and teens need to be capable of hands-free transport of *at least* 1-gallon (128 oz. / approx. 4-Liters) of water per person. It is not enough to have the containers. You also need to be able to comfortably carry all your gear and your filled water containers, *inside* your GO-Bag or in the outside pockets of your bag.

GO-Bag exterior: Nothing, except perhaps a jacket or water pre-filter, should be attached to the outside of your GO-Bag. The bag, and what you are carrying, should be a compact package. Nothing should dangle from the bag, flop around, jostle, make noise, or off-balance your bag when you are walking or running.

Canteens: Water bottles and canteens which have a carry strap, and are designed to be slung over one shoulder, are not ideal. Why? If you need to run, they will bounce. If you are walking through brush, the strap can snag on branches. If you are climbing or engaged in an activity which requires balance, a flopping Go-Bag or canteen can make you lose your balance, possibly resulting in a hazardous fall.

Only carry water *inside* your GO-Bag: Due to the hazards inherent to an off-balance bag, whether you use a water bladder or plastic water bottles, your water should be transported inside your knapsack, in a secure pouch attached to it, or in pocket built into the exterior of your bag.

Comfortable, safe carry: Since water is very heavy, it is a distinct advantage to use a knapsack or backpack that has padded straps for each shoulder, and a waist belt and chest strap. This style of bag will provide the most comfortable, secure, safest, and most practical way to carry your water, food, and gear.

Summary

These water and food recommendations are for a GO-Bag designed to meet the needs of one individual person. If there is a possibility that these supplies will need to be shared with another person(s) or a pet, plan accordingly by adding extra supplies, especially additional water. Or, better yet, by preparing an additional GO-Bag(s). Even young children can usually carry at least some of their supplies.

An adequate supply of water, plus the ability to purify water obtained from local sources, is the most critical component of a GO-Bag. If you are preparing multiple GO-Bags for adults, each should contain water, food, water purification supplies, and other essentials.

If there is any possibility that you will be alone, and will not have access to other GO-Bags, then it is necessary for your bag to contain more than one method of water purification.

For additional details on products, links to manufacturer's websites, and other information which is periodically updated, download the "Supplemental Information" which can be found on the 'Resources' page of the author's website:
www.SigSwanstrom.com

Chapter 11

Go-Bag Contents: Supplies & Gear

This chapter includes tips, advice, and lists of supplies, to help make sure you start with essentials and then add what is necessary to match your own personal situation. If you build your GO-Bag based on these instructions, you will be better prepared than those who spend a thousand dollars on a pre-built GO-Bag. Your bag will be far better than any commercially available pre-assembled "complete" bag that we have ever seen in the marketplace—and it'll be *hundreds of dollars* cheaper!

Designed for emergency use, "GO-Bag" is an acronym for "Get Out" bag. The concept is simple. It is an easily carried collection of essential emergency supplies which you may need when forced to evacuate, or if you need to shelter-in-place away from home.

A GO-Bag is the same as a GOOD-Bag (as in Get-Out-of-Dodge bag), Bug-Out Bag (military term), Emergency Kit, or Evacuation Kit. Different names, but they all refer to a single bag which contains an assortment of essential supplies, assembled to help you through the early days of a disaster or emergency situation. Though a GO-Bag shares some of the same contents as a Patrol Pack (military/police) or Survival Kit (marine/aviation), the purpose of a GO-Bag kit is different.

Your GO-Bag *'Bag'*

As explained in more detail in Chapter-9, use either a well-made knapsack or a medium-size or small internal frame backpack to hold your emergency provisions and gear. If it has an internal pocket for a 100-oz (3 Liter) water bladder, buy a bladder to fit it, but store the bladder empty until it is needed.

Your knapsack or backpack needs to be constructed of waterproof materials and designed to be carried on your back using two padded shoulder straps. A waist belt and chest strap are helpful to keep the bag from shifting during times when balance is vital, and to prevent the bag from bouncing if you need to run. If finances are tight, go to a second-hand store and buy an old school-bag knapsack.

The decision on whether to use a knapsack or a larger backpack should be based on your needs and abilities. Factors such as your physical fitness, the terrain you are likely to traverse, the duration of your travel, the possibility of criminal victimization and your need to run or evade, and the space limitations of where you will store your GO-Bag, are considerations that should influence your decision. Notwithstanding, for most people, a knapsack will be the best choice.

For most reasonably-fit and healthy people, the weight of a fully-packed GO-Bag (weight of bag plus contents) will ideally be fairly close to 15% of their body weight. Extremely fit people wearing good boots can carry more, but since a bug-out may require high mobility, unnecessary weight should be avoided.

Overweight, elderly, and unhealthy adults will already struggle in a 'bug-out' evacuation situation, so they should avoid carrying more than 15 pounds (7 Kg). Good footwear will help, but those who struggle with walking should not carry much extra weight.

In an emergency situation, always keep core essentials with you in your pockets, or in the pockets of a vest or fanny pack which is worn constantly. Wear your KOP (Keep-on-Person) Kit[15] supplies even while taking a nap at a campsite, or when stopping to rest during your evacuation. Be alert and ready to roll. You don't know when circumstances might force you to instantly flee.

If you are just starting this preparation process, assembling the following lists of supplies may seem like a daunting task. So, start by purchasing a knapsack and the most vital supplies first, and then add to your emergency provisions as finances allow.

But don't wait. Get started today.

When preparing to face an emergency situation...

---

[15] Details on what to include in your KOP Kit (Keep-on-Person Kit) is addressed later in this chapter; see Section-XI.

Priority #1: If this is all new to you, putting together a GO-Bag is your first priority. With this task, you will stockpile drinking water and food, develop a basic emergency medical kit, prepare for physical security, and shelter (protection from cold, rain, sun, etc.). These are your "Right Now" Essentials, so concentrate on acquiring these supplies first. But don't neglect the "Planning" section (Chapters 1-7), as it will help you work smart, not just be busy. For all of us, these tasks are never done. We do the best we can at the beginning, and as we learn, we need to further refine our preparations. If you work on "Planning" at the same time as your "Right Now" Essentials, you will avoid wasting time and money. You will be PREPARED and Ready to Roll, much sooner.

Reminder: GO-Bags are typically assembled to support the needs of one person. If more than one person often travels in the same vehicle, additional GO-Bags should be stored in it. If you use several different vehicles, you need a GO-Bag for each.

Each person needs a GO-bag. If you routinely travel with young children that are old enough to carry a small knapsack, they should carry some of their own emergency supplies. If it can be avoided, one person should not try to carry supplies for multiple people. Everyone needs to do their part to the best of their ability.

You may find it helpful to photocopy the following list of supplies. After adding a check mark ☑ to each item that you have included in your GO-Bag, and your own list of additional items (if any), put your 'GO-Bag Contents' list inside your bag, on top of your supplies.

We recommend that you staple these pages together, and put them inside a clear 1-gallon Hefty Slider plastic bag. Your 3-page Plan Summary (Chapter-8), maps (Chapter-5), and this list of supplies should be the first things that are seen when the bag is opened. This will be an immense help when an emergency situation strikes.

By using this simple method, the user of the bag is reminded: 1) "What to do," 2) "Where to go," and 3) the "List of Supplies" reminds them of their resources. It may seem odd, but in high-stress situations it's not unusual for people to carry a bag of supplies but never take inventory of its contents.

GO-Bag Contents: List of Supplies
Lists by Topic / Category

I. GO-Bag Food and Water

Before use, water is stored *with* the bag but *not inside* the bag. If possible, drinking water needs to be poured into the water containers that are in the bag, before evacuating. See Chapter-10 for details.

II. GO-Bag Emergency Shelter
- [ ] **SOL Emergency Bivvy** (AdventureMedicalKits.com) or similar, or a
  - [ ] Plastic Tube Tent, or 2 large heavy-duty trash bags; and a
  - [ ] Thermal Blanket

III. GO-Bag Medical / Dental Supplies
- [ ] **Trauma Kit**
- [ ] **Medicines Kit**
- [ ] **Main Medical Kit**

   For specifics on these three medical kits, see Chapter-19.

- [ ] **Dental Kit,** including repair kit for crowns, and care for broken teeth with exposed roots. For details on this kit, see Chapter-20.

IV. GO-Bag Communications Gear

   For details on communication, see Chapter-7 and Appendix-D
- [ ] **Radio Receiver** AM/FM/NOAA Weather channels
- [ ] **Walkie Talkies** – 2-Way Radio (See Chapter-7 on radios)
- [ ] **Extra Batteries** – Store in plastic, not metal. Keep the positive (+) ends protected with plastic or a nonconductive material.
- [ ] **Ballpoint Pen** (Write-anywhere *"Space"* pen)
- [ ] **Indelible Marker Pen** – Black Ink (*Sharpie*)
- [ ] **Notepad** (Ideally, waterproof paper, *Rite-in-the-Rain Outdoor Journal*)
- [ ] **Flagging Tape** (aka/ 'Survey Tape' or 'Contractor Ribbon;' this is bright-color plastic ribbon.) A small roll is included in your GO-Bag to mark important locations, caches of supplies, routes for others to follow, and to communicate where to find messages. Include instructions in your Plan Summary. (*For more on this topic, see Chapter-7 in this book.)* Group should use same color.

V. Signaling Items

- [ ] **Signal Mirror** – Small, plastic or lightweight metal
- [ ] **Whistle** on Lanyard
- [ ] **Chemical Light** *(Cyalume Light Stick);* not dependent on batteries and safe in flammable environments, these chemical lights can be hung from a branch, or even used under water. Yellow and green light-sticks are the best colors for communication purposes.

VI. GO-Bag Navigation (Keep these items together.)
For details, see Chapter 5: Maps, Routes, and Navigation.

- [ ] **Maps: Local** Street Map (Put maps in *Hefty Slider* plastic bag.)
- [ ] **Maps: High-detail** topographic, such as the 7.5-minute, 1:24,000 quadrangle available from USGS.gov.
- [ ] **Compass** (for specifications, see Chapter-5)
- [ ] **Map Aid** - Universal Transverse Mercator or Military Protractor (GTA 5-2-12) [optional item, but recommended]

VII. Flashlights and Emergency Lighting
For details, see Chapter-21.

- [ ] **LED Flashlight and/or Krypton-bulb Flashlight**
  If you are concerned with threats such as solar storms and EMP situations, include a conventional flashlight which uses a Krypton bulb rather than a LED, and make sure it does not utilize any electronic circuitry. Hint: If the flashlight has high-low settings, or can be switched to flash-mode, it has circuitry which may be damaged by an EMP. Note: Alkaline batteries will likely be unaffected, but high-tech batteries and chargers may cease to work after being subjected to an EMP or solar flare. For more on these threats, see Chapter-1 and Appendix-C. And, for more on flashlights, see Chapter-21.
- [ ] **LED Headlamp**, adjustable brightness to extend battery life.
- [ ] **Micro Flashlight** (attach to zipper-pull on knapsack)
- [ ] **Lithium-Ion Batteries**, 2-sets for each electronic device (If possible, select flashlights and electronic devices which use the same type battery (i.e. AA or AAA batteries). Optional: Small solar panel and charger (substitute Lithium-Ion rechargeable batteries).

- [ ] **ChemLights** (2) – white or yellow. Nonflammable chemical powered disposable lights (*Cyalume Light Sticks*)

VIII. Hygiene

- [ ] **Soap** – A sliver of antibacterial bar soap, such as Dial or Dr. Bronner's peppermint or tea tree soap, in a plastic bag. Or, a small 2 oz plastic bottle of the same soap that is in your first aid kit, Chlorohexidine Gluconate 4%. These soaps can be used for washing hands, bathing, cleaning cooking utensils, water purification equipment, etc. Ideally, you will have a mild, regular bar soap, *and* Chlorohexidine Gluconate soap in your medical kit.
- [ ] **Toilet Paper** – small quantity, or Cotton Buds Toilet Tissue pkg
- [ ] **Hand Sanitizer** – 1-oz
- [ ] **Hand Lotion** – 1 oz (travel size)
- [ ] **Chapstick**
- [ ] **Toothbrush & Paste** – Small, travel size
- [ ] **Towel** – Small microfiber or quick-dry towel
- [ ] **Toenail Clippers** – lightweight model
- [ ] **Tweezers & Sewing Needle** – Sliver removal, etc.
- [ ] **Sports Socks**, or hiking sox. (Always wear dry socks to help prevent blisters.)
- [ ] **Underwear**, style which extends below crotch, to reduce leg chafing
- [ ] **Sports Bra** (women) (optional)
- [ ] **Feminine Urinary Director**, *Freshette* or *GO Girl* (optional)
- [ ] **Menstruation / sanitary products** (optional)
- [ ] **Razor** (optional)
- [ ] **Comb** (optional)
- [ ] **Plastic Bowl** (optional) – If you used a *Rubbermaid Lock-its* container or equivalent for inexpensive waterproof storage of electronics, it can double as a wash basin. Your signal mirror (Section-V) can double as a mirror for shaving, as well.

- [ ] _____
- [ ] _____

IX. Miscellaneous - *Essential Items*

- ☐ **Maps & Routing Plan** – Also in Section-VI (Details in Chapter-5)
- ☐ **Plan Summary** - Evacuation details; explained in Chapter-8.
- ☐ **Contents List** - Keep this list which itemizes the contents of your GO-Bag, as the first thing seen when the bag is opened. Instructions on how to use various items, such as radios, should be packaged with the product. Cut-down packaging to save space.
  * The above items should be kept in large, clear, *Hefty Slider* plastic bags to reduce wear and avoid water damage.
- ☐ **Pocket Knife**, Stainless Steel – Victorinox 'Swiss Army' pocket-knife, *'Explorer'* model or equivalent.
- ☐ **Scarf or Shemagh** - Multipurpose face protection, plus bandage, towel, sweatband, etc.) – 1) Color: earth tone; 2) Large Handkerchief, cotton, bright color, can also be used for signaling.
- ☐ **Work Gloves** – Leather, heavy duty.
- ☐ **550 Paracord or 750 Paracord** (or Para-Max cord]–100 ft (30m). Military-grade braided nylon cord, Paracord 550 has a break strength of 550 lbs; 750 Paracord has a break strength of 750, and Para-Max 1,200 lbs. If your body weight is 125+ lbs. (86 kg), we recommend using 750 Paracord or Para-Max in case you need to use it for descending. (For important details, see the 'Primer on Rope and Paracord' section, found later in this chapter.)
- ☐ **Duct Tape** – 10 ft. roll.
- ☐ **Aluminum Foil** –2 sq ft (0.2 m^2) Many uses such as distillation of water, direct heat or shield food when cooking, reflect light/fire.
- ☐ **Super Glue** (several small tubes; useful for repairs, and also to seal cuts and wounds).
- ☐ **Insect Protection, Head-net**
- ☐ **Insect Repellent** – 90+% DEET (liquid, not aerosol) - Sawyer *'Jungle Juice'* 2 oz, pump spray, or equivalent.
- ☐ **Sunglasses** which double as eye protection. The glasses need to be imprinted with Z87+ which indicates compliance with ANSI Z87.1 federal safety standards, or better yet, find glasses which comply with the U.S. military standard, MIL-PRF-31013.
- ☐ **Firestarter** - 2 cigarette lighters, plus flint/magnesium fire starter.
- ☐ **Spare Prescription Eyeglasses and Reading Glasses** (if used)

- ☐ **Compact Binoculars** - 10-20 magnification power, w/neck strap
- ☐ **Cash** – Since credit cards and debit cards cannot be used without electricity, it is prudent to keep some paper money and coins in your GO-Bag. Small denomination bills are best since vendors may not have the ability to make change. The quantity of physical cash needed will vary according to your circumstances and your financial ability. Regardless, everyone should have some paper money and a few coins in case you find a working (mechanical) vending machine or pay phone. Use a money belt for valuables.

   Paper money in denominations of $5 and $10 should be your largest denomination bills unless you want to be able to make a major purchase, such as a vehicle or to buy a ride. For routine transactions, gold, silver, and other precious metals will probably be of little-to-no value during the first weeks after the onset of a disaster. Keep in mind, too, that barter transactions may be more viable when trying to purchase something from an individual, as they will tend to undervalue your precious metals.
- ☐ **Firearm(s), Ammo, Pepper Spray.** See Chapters 16-17.
- ☐ **Data Storage Device(s)** – Scan and store copies of critical and important documents, including your driver's license, passport, vehicle and medical insurance cards, medicine prescriptions, bank records, and relevant ownership documents, deeds and titles. These personal records must be encrypted. Store them on a USB drive or micro SD card. PDF reference documents should not be encrypted. (See Chapter 23 for instructions and document list.)
- ☐ **Photocopy of Identification and Reference Docs** – Photocopy your driver's license, passport, vehicle and medical insurance cards, and business access cards, and keep this paper copy in your GO-Bag. Include anything for which you might need a paper backup, but not those items which would breach your personal security. Protect paper in a Hefty Slider plastic bag or waterproof container.
- ☐ **Holy Bible**–New Testament with Psalms & Proverbs, to provide comfort; valuable even for non-Christians. Pick an actual translation, not a paraphrase. Popular translations include the *King James Version* translated into English during the time of Shakespeare, *The Living Translation* translated into conversational English, and the *New American Standard Version* known for its phrase-by-phrase accuracy. See page-515 for examples of each. Store your Bible in a waterproof pouch or in a *Hefty Slider* plastic bag.

X. Miscellaneous – *Optional Items*

These will not all fit in your GO-Bag, so only add those items which seem essential for you and your situation. The others might be included in your car-kit, and in your at-home kit.

- ☐ **Mobile Phone Chargers (3)**, battery powered, plus car charger, and plug-in charger. (optional)
- ☐ **Collapsible Limb-Cutting Saw** (optional), 7-in stainless steel blade. As used for gardening, but the use here is to cut limbs for firewood and boughs to make a shelter. Extra blade to cut metal.
- ☐ **Machete – 15-inch blade** (optional) – check local laws
- ☐ **Pry Bar – 15-inch** (optional)
- ☐ **Fence-Wire Cutters or Bolt-Cutters** (optional)
- ☐ **Spare Keys** (optional) – Spare keys and fobs to all vehicles you may want to use. Plus, keys to places you may need to access, such as a storage shed, a friend's house, etc.
- ☐ **Mechanical Wrist Watch or Pocket Watch** (optional). If your goal is to be prepared for an EMP or CME (solar flare) event in addition to other emergencies, you may want to include an old-style watch. Choose a watch that is powered by winding a spring rather than a battery. Modern watches which use a battery or microcircuits may stop functioning after an EMP or CME, yet knowing the time may be more important than you might think. For example, if you have established wait-times, a contact schedule, need to take a person's pulse, etc. Choosing a model with a second hand may be useful for various needs.
- ☐ **Aerial Flare** (optional). Disposable, small, marine signal product.
- ☐ **Laser Flare** (optional)
- ☐ **Underwear & Socks** (optional) If underwear or socks become wet it will cause chaffing, which can distract from dangers and make travel more laborious. Wet socks will cause foot blisters.
- ☐ **Candle** (ex. UCO 9-hr lantern candle or 4-hr tealight candle)
- ☐ _____
- ☐ _____
- ☐ _____

XI. Pocket Kit, also known as a KOP Kit (Keep-On-Person) or EDC (Every-Day-Carry) supplies. Details follow this list.

- [ ] Pocketknife. Ex. Victorinox brand, Swiss Army 'Explorer' model pocketknife, or quality multi-tool with knife;
- [ ] Small cigarette lighter or fire starter;
- [ ] Paper filter mask, or a cotton handkerchief (large enough to use as a face mask);
- [ ] P-51 can opener (small, military can opener);
- [ ] Chlorine dioxide water purification tablets (Katadyn Micropur, or equivalent), 4+ foil-packaged tablets. See Chapter-10 and 14.
- [ ] Collapsible bottle, or to save space, a non-lubricated condom (2) or large balloon to transport water. (Condom packaging is more durable than an unpackaged balloon.) Include a plastic straw (cut to 3-6") and a wire twist-tie as used on a loaf of bread. Use the plastic straw for drinking, and the twist-tie to seal condom after filling it with water. A standard condom will hold more than 18-oz (.5 L) of water, but to avoid damage don't overly stress it. Practice with the brand you choose. To increase durability, insert the condom or balloon into a sock before filling it. For purification, use ½ Katadyn chlorine dioxide tablet for 16-oz of water.
- [ ] Compact whistle (to signal for help when you can no longer yell);
- [ ] Small liquid-filled compass (such as designed for a watchband);
- [ ] Signal mirror, small, plastic or metal;
- [ ] Flagging tape. (See section-IV in this chapter.)
- [ ] AA or AAA flashlight - small penlight or 1-battery flashlight;
- [ ] Spare battery(s) for flashlight.

Optional KOP Kit Items. Include in your KOP Kit if space allows. For airline travel, put the knife in your checked luggage, but include all of the above and below items in your carry-on bag (as laws allow).

- [ ] Paracord, 550 or 750, length: 12^+ ft (or what will fit into your kit);
- [ ] Wire, flexible, baling wire, 1-2 feet, and a large paperclip;
- [ ] Pepper spray. (For specifics, see Chapter-17.)
- [ ] Sewing needle (Such as used to sew upholstery. Paracord can be stripped and used as thread to make a makeshift bag, jacket, etc.);
- [ ] Micro SD data storage card, wrapped in Cling Wrap (Chapter-23)

- ☐ Plastic garbage sack (Cut holes for head and arms to make a raincoat, cut sides to make a tarp for shelter, or use it to haul water, scavenged food, or other items. Use Paracord to tie the bag shut, and to make a carry handle or shoulder strap for carrying);
- ☐ Space pen (will write in any position) and a small notebook;
- ☐ Cash Money (Phone/vending machine coins and paper money in case credit cards and electronic payment methods are inoperable).

This above list of essential KOP Kit items only requires a small amount of storage space, equal to that of a wallet, yet this little collection can make a huge difference.

Example: During the World Trade Center attack of September 11, 2001, occupants used small KOP Kit items to save lives. Pocket knives and a can opener were used to cut escape holes in sheetrock when doors were blocked by fire or debris. Wet handkerchiefs were used to help filter smoke to aid breathing. A thin rope/cord was used to help lower people when a stairway collapsed. Flashlights were used to navigate interior hallways and stairs. And, when a trapped person lost their voice after prolonged yelling, they used a whistle to get the attention of firefighters. Simple little items such as these, saved lives. Our KOP Kit list is slightly broader, because it is designed to be useful in a wide range of disaster-related situations.

How to Carry your KOP Kit? Cloth passport pouches and metal wallets are favorite containers for these supplies, but some people prefer carrying a few items in a small tin such as an Altoid or Sucrets box, with others on a keychain, and still others, like a pocket knife, loose in a pocket or purse. It doesn't matter how these things are carried, but that they are kept close at hand.

Better-than-nothing 'Micro' KOP Kit? At least carry a small pocket knife, cigarette lighter, compass, a compact whistle, P-51 can opener, 6 water purification tablets, 2 non-lubricated condoms to use as canteens, a large handkerchief or a folded N95 face mask, and a micro LED flashlight. (For descriptions, see previous page.)

Paracord Survival-Bracelet: Depending on the knots used to make the bracelet, these can condense 1 to 1.5 feet of paracord into each 1-inch of bracelet length. (i.e. An 8-in bracelet contains 8-14 ft of paracord). These can utilize a fire-starter buckle plus a watchband compass, and conceal such things as fire tinder; P-38 can opener; ceramic knife; micro SD card; fishing line & hooks; signal mirror; large, curved sewing needle; mini glow stick; and, a Nano flashlight. Both pre-made and D-I-Y bracelet instructions can be found online.

IX. GO-Bag Cooking Equipment

Only for use in extended-duration GO-Bags. The addition of these supplies is to accommodate scenarios such as extended treks in a wilderness area or long road trips. These items are ***not*** needed in an ordinary GO-Bag as they add weight and bulk. See Appendix-A for additional details and supplies for extended-duration GO-Bags.

- [ ] Extra food; *
- [ ] "MSR DragonFly" multi-fuel stove (or equivalent), plus an extra full-bottle of fuel, plus a repair kit for the stove;
- [ ] Pot with lid and heat exchanger (store stove inside);
- [ ] MSR (or equivalent) windscreen and heat reflector for cooking;
- [ ] Insulated mug with lid and handle (Size: 16+ oz.);
- [ ] Stainless steel spoon, plus sturdy plastic or metal spork (fork/spoon combination);
- [ ] Dish/pot scraper, brush, and small bottle of backpacker's soap;
- [ ] Dish soap.

* For long-duration bug-out situations, include several pounds of rice sealed in Mylar bags with oxygen absorbers to extend its shelf life. For more on this topic, see Chapter-15 and Appendix-A.

What to Expect with a Loaded Go-Bag

Not including water, my personal GO-Bag and the contents listed on the previously described Sections II to VIII (excluding firearm), plus the recommended 3-day supply of food (see Chapter-10), weighs 21 pounds (9 kg). But once I add the minimum recommended amount of water (1-gallon / 3.8 liters), my bag-weight jumps to nearly 30 pounds (13.6 kg). This is the upper-maximum recommended weight for a GO-Bag. So, don't be quick to add additional items.

Your GO-Bag may need to be lighter if it will be used in an urban environment. Or, if it will be used in an area where danger(s) might force you to move quickly, or where you may need to climb or traverse difficult terrain. In these situations, a lighter bag may be essential.

Personal Recommendations: The knapsack itself (the bag) should *not* be bright in color, and *should not* have reflectors or reflective tape which might attract attention at night. If you want reflectors, use add-on devices which can be removed. (Chapter-11)

A GO-Bag should be compact. When worn, it should fit the body snugly, and have nothing attached to the outside of the bag which will bounce or flop around.

It should have a strap for each shoulder as this distributes the weight, and a waist belt and chest strap to keep it tight to the body, so it doesn't bounce around if circumstances require you to run. (A swinging bag can also cause you to lose your balance.)

Pack your bag compactly, but not so tightly that it takes effort to repack after removing something. Use clear plastic freezer bags to pack your supplies by category, so it is easy to find things.

For additional details on products, links to manufacturer's websites, and information which is periodically updated, download the "Supplemental Information" document available on the Resources page of the author's website: www.SigSwanstrom.com

Primer on Rope and Paracord

Ordinary hardware-store rope or cord will not safely hold the weight of a person. Yet, in an emergency, a rope that you have in your garage that you purchased from a neighborhood store, might be your only option. Nevertheless, keep in mind that a strong-looking rope is not necessarily strong. Keep in mind, too, that a rope's "break strength" rating is not the same as a "safe load" or "working load." With most ropes, a safe load is only 10% of the break-strength that is listed on the product label.

In reality, military-grade 550 Paracord, which is only 5/32-inch (4 mm) in diameter, is stronger than many of the heavy-duty-looking ropes you will find in a hardware store. This is why it is included in our recommendation for inclusion in a GO-Bag. Even though 550 Paracord is rated at 550-pounds break strength (250 kg), it cannot be used to support more than 55-pounds safely. This acknowledged, in an emergency, you may be forced embrace risks that you otherwise wouldn't take.

> ### 200-lb Person Example
>
> Since 550 Paracord has a rated working-load strength of 55-lbs, a 200-lb person will need four segments of cord to make a decent (55 x 4 = 220-lbs working load). So, the math tells us that a bundle of four cords can support the weight of one 200-lb person. Yet, there are other factors involved. This makeshift rope is not the same as using a mountain climbing or rescue rope. But, as this truism reminds us, *desperate times require desperate measures*.
>
> So, in an emergency, it might be a *reasonable risk* to descend using four segments of Paracord, but it would be *high-risk* to only use two. Either way, avoid jerking and unnecessary stress on your makeshift rope. Lower your GO-Bag and extra weight rather than wear it while descending.

If you need to support more weight with a rope/cord than it is rated to hold, apply the 'parachute principle.' Just as a parachute uses multiple strands of Paracord to support its human cargo, a rope can be doubled (or tripled, or quadrupled, etc.) to increase the amount of load it can safely support. This is not ideal, but we're talking here about emergency use.

For example, if you find that you need to exit a burning building through a window, a 200-pound person should use at least four strands of 550 Paracord bundled together. Applying this 'parachute principle,' a 100-foot length of 550 Paracord would need to be doubled at least twice to form a 'safe' rope that is 25-feet in length.

Personally, if my choice is to stay and burn in a building or use Paracord to descend from a window, I will use as little as two strands of Paracord. I'm going to accept the rope-load danger if there isn't another escape option. But, I'm going to do it gingerly, because jerking the rope will stress it and greatly reduce its loadbearing capability.

This is why I carry 750 Paracord rather than standard 550 Paracord. It gives me almost 50% more useful load than the traditional parachute cord, it is only 1mm larger in diameter, and yet it is still lightweight so I can carry 100-feet (30.5 m) of it in my GO-Bag.

Recommendation: Carry 100-feet of Paracord in your GO-Bag. If your body weight is under 125-pounds, 550 Paracord may be adequate, but 750 Paracord is a safer choice.

550 Paracord: Purchase cord manufactured to comply with U.S. military specifications MIL-C 5040H, for **Type-3** (Type III) paracord. Ideally select Paracord made by a supplier to the U.S. military for use in making parachutes. To comply with these manufacturing standards the paracord must be 100% nylon, and have at least 7-strands inside it's woven outer layer. It should be made from continuous strands of nylon, not spliced. (By the way, these strands can be separated to make sewing thread, fishing line, animal snares, and for many other uses.)

750 Paracord: Also known as **Type-4** (Type IV) paracord, has 11-core strands and should be made by a U.S. manufacturer who guarantees the same high standards as above. It will be labeled as Type-4 and guaranteed to conform to U.S. Military specification MIL-C-5040, Revision H.

General Packing Recommendations for GO-Bags

* Use *Hefty Slider* or *Ziploc Slider*, or equivalent, high-quality plastic bags with a zip-closure to organize your supplies by category. This will also help mitigate the possibility of losing small items, and will provide some protection from water and dust. When appropriate, include the portion of the packaging that includes instructions, or printed instructions on use, how to add batteries, etc. Add cardboard or paper padding if appropriate. If needed, this paper padding can also be used for fire starting.

* Do not pack your Go-Bag so compactly that it will be difficult to repack in a hurry. Select your knapsack after you have gathered your supplies, so you can confirm the fit. Decisions on what to include should be based on need, then weight, not on what fits into your bag.

* Do not store flashlights or electronics with batteries installed. Keep a ChemLight (Cyalume Light Stick) with your flashlight, and store your flashlight batteries, and batteries for each piece of electronic equipment, with that item. Other spares can be stored elsewhere in your GO-Bag, but at least one set of batteries should be stored with each piece of battery-operated equipment.

If an emergency situation occurs at night and a flashlight isn't readily available, illumination from a ChemLight will make it possible for you to install the batteries.

*** **WARNING:** *If you store a gun, pepper spray, knife(s), prescription medicines, matches/lighter, water purification chemicals, or other potentially dangerous items with your GO-Bag (or emergency supplies), make sure that children and unauthorized people cannot gain access to it.*

* Add to your calendar a recurring schedule of dates to replace your supplies of water, food, to recharge rechargeable batteries, and maintenance of other items susceptible to quality or safety degradation. Check your GO-Bag and emergency supplies at least quarterly. Never use items from your GO-Bag for non-emergency purposes.

The big GO-Bag debate, "What to Include?"

What should be included in a GO-Bag is a much-debated topic. Unfortunately, these disputes rarely start with the key question. The starting point must be, "What is your anticipated use?" And, "What are the environmental factors you will encounter?" Your answers will dictate the size of your GO-Bag, as well as what it should contain.

If you are assembling your GO-Bag for one specific purpose, such as evacuation to a nearby community shelter due to a storm or wildfire, then this will orient your GO-Bag toward comfort and convenience. You will want to have a toiletries bag, snacks, reading materials, a book light, maybe even a sleep sack (ex: Sea to Summit's *'CoolMax Adaptor Traveler'* sleep sack). However, you may not be concerned with having a water filter and fire-starting gear.

Are you are assembling a GO-Bag in case you are stranded away from home? Or, to make sure you have the emergency supplies you will need to walk from work to home?

If your place of employment or school is many miles from home, your GO-Bag supplies will be very different. A significant number of Americans travel more than 60 miles to get to work. What is your situation? How long would it take to walk home? What will you need to do it safely? If it is a long distance, maybe you should make arrangements with a friend who lives closer. Maybe they will let you store some supplies at their place. For more on this topic, read Chapter-9.

What is the emergency situation that you are preparing to face? Focus your provisioning on that situation, but don't forget to also prepare for the unexpected.

This book was designed to help you prepare for a both a natural disaster and other emergency situations. Its primary focus is to help you flee from where you are, to reach a more distant location that is a lace of safety; a safe-haven.

A properly provisioned GO-Bag will help you do five things:

1. Escape from a building or dangerous place,
2. Shelter-in-place for 3-5 days,
3. Get to your home or rendezvous location,
4. Travel to a more distant safe-haven 'retreat' location, and
5. Equip you to find a missing family member or friend.

When you consider what it will take for *you* to accomplish this, we need to drill down deeper, to consider the conditions and situations we might face. For example, a person in reasonable health can walk ten miles in a few hours. If disaster strikes at the end of your workday, how long would it take you to walk home? Will it be dark? What hazards will you face along the way? How can you prepare for them?

In your situation, should you design your GO-Bag to help you survive two days cooped up in your office, three days walking home, or what you need for a 5-hour hike to a friend's house where you will hang-out until the emergency is over? Or, might your GO-Bag be needed to facilitate a long trek to a place of safety that might be more than a hundred miles distant?

Do you expect to use your GO-Bag in an urban environment, or will it be used to get from one rural location to another? Will you be riding a bike along city streets or back roads? Or, will you be trailblazing on foot through a wilderness area? The supplies you carry in your GO-Bag should be selected to match your needs in these very different environments. Remember too, it needs to meet your needs for expected problems *and* the unexpected.

Your answers to questions such as these will guide your decisions on what to include in your GO-Bag. Use the lists of supplies and gear found earlier in this chapter, to stimulate your thinking, and then add or subtract as is appropriate for you and your situation.

What to choose? A big, heavy GO-Bag with lots of supplies and gear? Or, a small, lightweight bag that keeps you agile, that you can carry a greater distance? As Chapter-10 made clear, if you need more than a 3-day supply of food and a 1-day supply of water, you won't be able to carry much else—unless you utilize a larger backpack that will be heavy. But if you will be operating in an urban environment, a decision to utilize a GO-Bag that weighs more than 25 pounds may be a serious mistake. So, what do you do?

Whether traveling on foot, by public transportation or in a private vehicle, in an urban area the ability to move quickly is essential for safety. In the days following a natural disaster, becoming a victim of assault, rape, or robbery can become a greater threat than coping with the aftermath of the disaster itself. Don't be a victim. Proper planning can help you avoid severe problems.

Keep this fundamental precept in mind: If there is *any possibility* that you will be bugging-out on foot in a large city or suburban area, you need to utilize a small or medium-size knapsack to contain your GO-Bag supplies. If you will be traveling in a rural or wilderness area for many days, and not traversing cities, then a backpacking pack may be your best choice—*but only if you are physically fit*.

Maintaining a low profile may not be as important if there isn't any threat of criminal victimization. However, as the fiction story at the beginning of Book-1 in this series reminds us, even rural areas that are ordinarily safe can become dangerous. Criminals and gangs may control an entire geographic region when the police are overwhelmed by an emergency situation.

> *Don't pack your GO-Bag with what you will want to make your life more comfortable. Pack it with what you will actually need for coping with the various emergency situations that you might encounter.*

Design your GO-Bag for versatility. Make sure it contains all the essentials, but don't confuse what will make you comfortable, with what you may really need.

If you can get water along the way, carry a water purifier rather than extra gallons of water. If the food in your GO-Bag may need to last for 5-days, pack concentrated nutritious food like Lifeboat Rations rather than the better-tasting MRE entrees.

Your primary objective should be to prepare for situations you will likely encounter. Unfortunately, it isn't practical to thoroughly prepare for every eventuality that we might encounter. So, we need to do is prepare the best we can for the likely problems, and then, prepare at a minimal-level for the unlikely.

Chapter 12

Clothing and Footwear for Evacuation

The items included in this chapter are in addition to that which is contained in your GO-Bag. Select from the following list those things which are appropriate to your situation, environment, weather, and terrain. Then add to it those additional items which you might need, and adapt it to the season of the year. Update it seasonally. Store this emergency clothing bag, with your GO-Bag.

You don't need to haul around winter clothes in the summer, nor summer clothes in the dead of winter, but it is better to have unneeded garments than to have inadequate clothing if you encounter a 'surprise' weather event. If you find yourself on foot, select what you need from your emergency clothing bag and leave the rest behind. This extra bag is to give you options at your time of need.

These clothing items should be stored 'with' your GO-Bag— but NOT 'in' your GO-Bag. This is a bag of *optional* gear.

Keep this extra clothing in a second knapsack, duffle bag, or a small travel bag with handles. The bag type is irrelevant. What's important is that it be stored with your GO-Bag. Always.

Store a supply of factory-sealed water bottles in the same bag as your emergency clothing. When you switch clothing to match a change in season, use this opportunity to replace your water, too. Discard the old water bottles. Over a few months' time, especially if your gear is stored in a vehicle, your bottled water will have been exposed to hot and cold temperatures which may leach chemicals from the plastic bottles. These water bottles may not be old, but they may nevertheless contain water that is stale or even unhealthy. So, discard these bottles, and put a new supply of bottled water in your clothing bag.

When a disaster is upon you, and it's time to change into your emergency clothing, use that opportunity to fill the water containers in your GO-Bag, too. This can be quickly accomplished since your supply of bottled water is right there in your clothing bag.

Change Your Clothes ASAP

When an emergency situation arises, change into your boots (or walking shoes) and emergency clothing, as soon as possible. If it is impractical to change your clothes, at least change your shoes as soon as it is safe if your current footwear is unsuitable

If circumstances make it imprudent to change your clothes, or you are in an unsafe area, get to safety first. If your environment is dangerous, put your GO-Bag on your back, grab your clothing bag, and run to safety. Then, when danger is no longer looming, and it's reasonable to do so, change into your emergency clothing.

Your GO-Bag itself should *not* contain clothing. The only exception is a hat, medical gloves and durable work gloves, and one pair of extra socks and underwear, and a large bandana.

When you evacuate, change into durable, innocuous-looking clothing from your Emergency Clothing Bag. Then, if other clothing is essential, add it to your GO-Bag. Or, attach it to your GO-Bag with straps. If you are on foot, leave the rest behind.

If you have a purse, briefcase, or computer bag with you, transfer important items to your GO-Bag and leave the rest behind. Ideally, your hands will be totally empty as you may need them for other activities. Don't carry extra bags if it can be avoided. It's far better to add a pouch to your GO-Bag than to succumb to carrying a purse or handbag in your hand.

Emergency Clothing Bag – Recommended Contents

Stored with your GO-Bag, your Emergency Clothing Bag should only contain clothes to change into before evacuating, and essential seasonal clothing. Other extra clothes should only be taken along if you will be traveling by vehicle. If you find yourself on foot, non-essential extra clothes should be left behind or discarded. Select clothing that is innocuous in appearance; does not look expensive, colors that are not bright, and will not attract attention.

- ☐ Hiking Boots; made from a waterproof but breathable material, with boot tops which extend above the ankle to provide lateral support and ankle protection. 2nd Choice: sturdy walking shoes.
- ☐ Moisture-wicking sock liners (first-layer), 3-pair (wear 1-pair);
- ☐ Backpacking socks, padded foot, 3-pair (wear 1-pair);
- ☐ Undershorts (3-pr). Ideally, a style which extends 3+ inches below the crotch, such as boxer-briefs or sports-shorts, to reduce the thigh chafing problem that plagues many hikers.
- ☐ Women: A comfortable sports bra.
- ☐ Ripstop BDU pants, 2 pair (wear 1-pair);
- ☐ Heavy-duty belt with strong buckle;
- ☐ Shirt (long sleeve, roll-up sleeve style (wear);
- ☐ 2 Polyester t-shirts; one with long-sleeves (wear 1);
- ☐ Polar fleece long-sleeve pullover (1).
- ☐ Poncho - Gore-Tex or military surplus GI-issue for use in rain, to use as a makeshift shelter, or to hide unattended gear;
- ☐ Gore-Tex rain pants or snake-proof waterproof gaiters;
- ☐ Gore-Tex lightweight waterproof shell (top). In cold climates, a waterproof insulated parka with high collar and hood, drawstring waist, in a style that is long enough to cover your buttocks and protect your posterior when sitting;
- ☐ Gloves: Waterproof, warm ski gloves for cold weather environments. (Durable work gloves and surgical or latex gloves, should already be included in your GO-Bag.)
- ☐ Hat: Cold/cool climates - wool watch cap (stocking cap). Warm climates: Sweat-wicking brimmed cap such as a 'boonie.'
- ☐ Polyester long underwear (1 pair – Cold climates);
- ☐ Long-underwear shirt (1 – Cold climates).

* As wonderful as it would be to have all of these things with you when evacuating, it is only practical to bring extra clothing and other items along if you will be traveling by vehicle. If you find yourself traveling on foot, unnecessary clothing and supplies will reduce your mobility and speed. And, the added weight and bulk will increase fatigue at a time when you need stamina.

Storing Your GO-Bag and Emergency Clothing Bag

For most people, their GO-Bag should be kept in the vehicle they routinely use. However, every vehicle you use should also have a GO-Bag in it—a GO-Bag that is appropriate for you, and additional GO-Bags for everyone who might travel in that vehicle. And, an Emergency Clothing Bag to meet the needs of these individuals, as well.

If you can't have a fully equipped GO-Bag for each family member in each vehicle, then at least have a GO-Bag for the regular user of that vehicle. Plus, add several generic GO-Bags that would be useful for anyone who might be in that vehicle.

If you can't afford to add fully-stocked GO-Bags for every family member, in each vehicle, at least include a few generic, lightweight GO-Bags. Every individual transported in that vehicle should have a bag of supplies.

If cost is an obstacle, purchase a used school knapsack at a second-hand shop. These may not be ideal but they are better than nothing. Add into these 'extra' or 'backup' GO-Bags whatever you can afford to include. Just by adding a half dozen liter bottles of water, a few cans of food (and a can opener), and a handful of other essentials, you will be equipping them to handle an emergency situation better than most of your neighbors. Something is better than nothing.

While it is true that your GO-Bag and Emergency Clothing Bag can be moved from vehicle-to-vehicle, most people will eventually become lax or forget to make the transition. This can be an egregious mistake if it happens at the wrong time; yet, the effects of this error can be minimized if each vehicle is GO-Bag equipped.

A GO-Bag can be useful to someone other than it's intended user, but clothing is not similarly flexible. Therefore, each vehicle needs to contain attire suitable to those who ride in that vehicle.

Off-road Vehicles & Trucks: Even infrequently used vehicles should be equipped with generic GO-Bags for the driver and passengers. And, an Emergency Clothing Bag with apparel that is suitable for each family member. Plus, it should be equipped with other emergency supplies for rural and wilderness use. Even used gear and clothing is better than being totally unprepared.

Chapter 13

Emergency Kits: Vehicle-based and Home Supplies

Our recommendation for emergency supplies is to follow a three-part implementation process. First, create a complete 3-day+ GO-Bag for each member of your household, next, augment these with additional supplies stored in each vehicle, and lastly, a 2-week supply of food, water, and other supplies, stored at your home. Provisioning your safe-haven retreat location is included in Book-4 of this series.

If you are an employer or supervisor, you will want to add another category, which is to stockpile at least 3-days of emergency food, water, and related supplies at your place of business. In addition to food and water, this needs also to include accommodating the need for lighting, heat/cooling, medical, and sanitation if utilities fail.

As an employer, it is better to err on the side of caution and send your employees home in advance of a crisis. Nevertheless, you have a moral obligation to care for the needs of your employees if it becomes necessary for them to shelter in place.

If cost restrictions make it impractical to immediately assemble a GO-Bag (evacuation bag) for each member of your household, start by making bags for those family members who work or attend a school that is more than 3-miles (5 km) from home.

If public transportation is used, store the GO-Bag at work. If the location is a school and storage of a GO-Bag is unrealistic, at least store a few essential supplies and a knapsack in the student's school locker.

Food & Water

Of the two, pure water is more important than food. You can live as long as 4-weeks on almost no food, but your body and brain will start to suffer after just one day without pure water.

Your at-home water and food supplies should be sufficient to last for 14-days, plus you need to be able to purify additional water if needed. The water purification gear contained in each GO-Bag should suffice to fill this need, but having extra on hand is still advisable.

Prepare for extra people. You may end up with extra children, neighbors, or friends so you will need additional supplies. Some equipment can be shared, but water, food, sanitation, shelter, and related supplies must reflect per-person usage.

For most people, it would be impossible to carry a 14-day supply of food in a backpack, but it may be possible to store this quantity of food in the trunk of your car. Unfortunately, even a 7-day supply of military meals would be too much to carry in a GO-Bag knapsack along with your other gear. (See the chapters 10, 14, and 15.)

So, for food supplies stored at-home and in your vehicle, be sure to include quantities of dry goods such as pasta and instant rice. This will make it possible for you to create a more lightweight and compact food supply for transport in your vehicle, if this becomes necessary.

One of the advantages of stockpiling military MRE meals and the water-activated heater made for them, is that the heater does not require the use of pure water. Notwithstanding, care must be taken to keep the opening edge of the foil food pouch, uncontaminated.

Freeze-dried prepared food, such as those made by "Mountain House" are the lightest weight and most easily packed. And since you only need to add pure hot water to prepare these freeze-dried meals, it's convenient if you have access to hot water. Though not very palatable, these foods can be eaten after rehydrating with cold water. Rehydration is necessary, and these foods should not be eaten without adding the required amount of *pure* water.

Freeze-dry backpacking meals are not as quick and easy as an MRE entrée heated by using the disposable MRE heater, but it is still a practical and straightforward way to prepare an actual meal during an emergency situation. Again, if you have access to pure water and your kitchen is operational, traditional food preparation is desirable.

However, since most people do not maintain more than a few days of fresh food and water at their home, stockpiling cases of MREs or extra canned goods may be an easy way to maintain a 2-week supply of food. If you are using canned products for this purpose, be sure to put a date on the lid of the can when it is purchased, and then rotate these supplies to keep them fresh.

On backpacking meals and most other prepared foods, when the product label indicates "Serves 2," it is generally only adequate for feeding one modestly active person.

Energy bars (PowerBars), meal-replacement bars, and lifeboat survival rations (available at marine-supply stores and online) can supplement these MRE or freeze-dried meals in a pinch, so they are a great addition to your at-home food larder.

If it wasn't necessary to use your GO-Bag to get home, there is a temptation to consume the contents at home. Yet, since you may still need your GO-Bag to evacuate from your home to your safe-haven or another, safer location, it is often best to leave your GO-Bag intact. See Chapters 10, 15, and Appendix-A, for more on food.

Low cost, lightweight foods to have in your vehicle
(The below items are in addition to the food in your GO-Bag.)

- ☐ Peanuts or trail mix (dried fruits, nuts, and seeds), must be in foil packaging or shelf life is too short.
- ☐ Meal Replacement Bars, Energy Bars (12+), and Beef Jerky (4+ packages), and similar quick-use sources of nutrition. If not already packaged in foil, repackage in Mylar with oxygen absorbers. (See chapter on Mylar food packaging.)
- ☐ Electrolyte-Replacement Sports Drink Powder. (Important to offset physical exertion. See Chapters 10 and 14 for details.)
- ☐ 1-gal Hefty Slider bag of oatmeal, and a 1-gal bag of rice. (For long-term storage, seal food in Mylar bags with O_2 absorbers.)
- ☐ Raw honey, cinnamon, salt & pepper, plus a small bottle of Tabasco sauce or another strong seasoning to help make any food more palatable.
- ☐ Pre-packaged water bottles, 12-16 ounce or 1-liter bottles

At-Home Emergency Supplies

Be prepared with a propane camp stove and propane lantern. Stockpile a least two dozen disposable 1-pound propane cylinders, or one full 5-gallon (20-pound) propane tank along with the adapters needed to connect the tank with your camp stove and lighting. (Keep in mind that you may be without electricity or natural gas, so your kitchen stove and conventional cooking methods may not be functioning). Since camp stoves, lanterns and portable heaters produce carbon dioxide gas, only use them with adequate ventilation.

For more on cooking, lighting, and fuel, see Chapters 15, 21, 22, and Appendix-A.

Remember, redundancy is essential.

As the old military adage reminds us, "Two is one, and one is none." Keep this in mind. Things break or don't work when they are needed, so having "extra" is always a good idea, particularly with essential gear. Also, since lightweight gear is usually selected for GO-Bags, you may want to choose more heavy-duty gear for your at-home and vehicle-based emergency kits.

The following list of supplies is in addition to your GO-Bag. This list intentionally duplicates some of the items which should also be included in your evacuation kit and GO-Bag.

To get you started, a partial list of Emergency Supplies

☐ First Aid Kit (see Chapters 19-20 for details).

☐ Extra Water and Food (Chapters 10, 14, 15, and Appendix A-B)).

☐ Road flares (Also useful for starting fires, but don't use for cooking).

☐ Jumper cables for emergency vehicle starting.

☐ Portable battery-operated AM/FM/WB/SW radio, ideally one which is equipped with both a hand crank and solar panel for emergency power. The radio you select should also have the capacity to recharge your cell phone. (Be sure to purchase the adapter to connect the radio's battery charger to your brand/model of mobile phone.) You should also have a 110/220v power adapter for your portable radio. If your emergency kit is for use in the United States, purchase a radio that is capable of also receiving NOAA emergency weather broadcasts (WB). (Details in Chapter-7 and Appendix-D.)

☐ An empty fuel container (Better yet, a filled container if it can be safely stored and carried.) Even a 2-gallon container of fuel may be enough to get you to a service station, but a 5-gallon fuel container is even better. (For details, see Chapter-22.) Note: If you think you are going to run out of gas, add your emergency fuel supply to your vehicle's tank at a safe location, before you run out of gas. It can be difficult to restart a vehicle that has stopped because it ran out of fuel.

☐ Tool, natural gas and water shut-off wrench (home kit)

☐ Extra electrical fuses for your vehicles (and for your home, too, if it uses them).

☐ Duct Tape

☐ Bailing Wire (fence wire to repair cut fences)

☐ Tarp

☐ Rope

☐ Vehicle tow strap (optional)

☐ 550 Paracord, 100-ft (30m). Or the stronger, 750 Paracord or Para-Max. (see Chapter-11 for details)

☐ Compact Vehicle Repair Tool Kit (basic set of tools)

☐ Multitool such as the Leatherman Wave, or similar multi-tool containing knife/screwdriver/pliers/wire cutter, etc.

☐ Knife sharpener (pocket-size).

☐ Small shovel or spade

☐ Backpacking saw (blades for wood and metal), or a limb-saw such as those used for gardening.

☐ Pry bar, 25+ inches in length.

☐ Extra topographic maps of bug-out location and route alternatives, laminated or sealed in slide-lock plastic bags.

☐ Heavy duty Dacron sail-maker's thread and needles, or upholstery needles and thread.

- [ ] Insect repellent – 95+% DEET. (Liquid or pump plastic-bottle, not aerosol.) Store it in slide-lock bag with a patch of absorbent cloth to absorb leakage.
- [ ] SPF 50 sun-block and Chapstick.
- [ ] Polarized sunglasses, also rated as eye protection. (Chapter-11)
- [ ] Safety glasses (Z87 rating)
- [ ] Extra toiletries
- [ ] Field guide to edible plants (region-specific).
- [ ] Photocopy of ID (driver's license / passport / medication prescriptions).
- [ ] Cash, plus items to barter/trade. (Needed if power grid is out.)
- [ ] P-51 can opener, military-style, non-mechanical, pocket size.
- [ ] Victorinox 'Swiss Army' Knife - Explorer model pocket knife, or similar multi-tool with a can opener, screwdriver, etc.
- [ ] Knife, 4+-inch stainless steel blade, with sheath. [Check your local laws to determine legal blade length.]
- [ ] Laser Rescue Flare (or a laser pointer).
- [ ] Flashlight [at least 2] (Details in Chapter-21)
- [ ] LED Headlamp (For details, see Chapter-21.)
- [ ] Extra Batteries for each battery-operated light and device; ideally Lithium rechargeable batteries, and a solar battery charger.
- [ ] Gun Oil or, fine multipurpose oil (1-oz).
- [ ] Gun cleaning kit, small, multi-caliber (if you have a gun)
- [ ] Super Glue (6-tubes, store in Hefty Slider bag in refrigerator, replace annually).
- [ ] Sharpie (black ink)
- [ ] "Rite in the Rain Outdoor Journal" and Fisher Space pen
- [ ] Compass (For recommendations, see Chapter-5.)
- [ ] Plastic Whistle, with lanyard.

- ☐ Trash Bags (5) 3-mil, 42-55 gal. construction-grade plastic garbage bags, useful for: shelter, making a makeshift raincoat, to hide or protect gear, for water collection, and many other uses.
- ☐ Lightweight Mesh Bag (food foraging and carry).
- ☐ Bible, New Testament w/ Psalms & Proverbs, small-size.

  Note: Even atheists, agnostics, and non-religious people often find the Bible to be a source of comfort and wisdom during difficult times.

Hunting, Fishing, and Foraging Supplies

For information on firearms and ammunition, see Chapters 16-17.

- ☐ Selection of fishhooks, lures, flies, bobbers, line-weights, and a spool of monofilament fishing line or leader.
- ☐ Small-mesh fishing net, 3 x 9 feet; 1-inch mesh.
- ☐ Animal Snares (if you are willing to learn how to use them).
- ☐ Wrist-Rocket slingshot (or, 5' surgical tubing to make a slingshot, and for siphoning fuel, water, etc.).
- ☐ Binoculars, small, lightweight, 8 x 25 or higher magnification).

Storage Containers

There is a tendency to use plastic bins for the storage of these at-home and vehicle-based supplies. This is acceptable, but it is a less versatile option. It is far better to store these items in duffle bags as these provide a more compact form of storage.

If you find that you need to transport your gear, the ease of carry and more compact nature of duffle bags will accommodate your need to transport more gear and supplies. And, these soft-sided bags can be emptied and refilled if you need to travel on foot. This transportable storage method is particularly valuable if, when disaster strikes, you find that you have more people than GO-Bags. Most duffle bags can be carried on the back like a knapsack, or slung over a shoulder.

If you favor the orderly appearance of stacks of plastic bins, still consider using duffle bags, just store the loaded bags inside the bins.

Best Protection: To protect your supplies from rodents, insects, water, and other damage, store your duffle bags, knapsacks, and any foods not already packaged in metal cans, in steel drums. Some of these have lid-clamps that can be secured with a padlock.

Plastic drums are great for water storage, and may be fine for gear storage, but they do not provide adequate protection for food. Regardless of the type of container you select, when storing food, use a new drum or barrel, or one that previously contained a food product and has not been contaminated. If you are not sure what it previously contained, don't use it for food as chemicals can leach through food packaging and contaminate your stored food.

An alternative to the use of steel drums, is to use new galvanized-steel garbage cans. Be sure to properly label these containers to avoid confusion. Other options include metal footlockers, military surplus medical bins, or other transportable steel containers.

If your steel drums or other large steel containers will ever need to be moved, set them on a roller base before filling them. Both a 55-gallon drum and a 35-gallon galvanized garbage can will likely be too heavy to move after they have been filled.

Plastic bins and plastic buckets, including hard-plastic gamma lid containers such as those sold for storing long-term food supplies, do not adequately protect food. Rodents can gnaw through even heavy-duty plastic containers. Despite what many self-proclaimed 'experts' and food companies say, this is a serious potential problem that is easily eliminated by using steel containers for food storage.

Environmental Protection: Your supplies will last longer if stored in a low humidity environment, and at a temperature between 40-70 degrees. So, if possible, keep all your supplies inside a climate-controlled house, garage, or storage facility that is under your direct control. Keep your stored items in a place where they will also be protected from tampering and theft.

Locations which are ordinarily safe may be targeted during an emergency situation. When ordinary people start to look for supplies, unattended storage locations are easy targets for theft. These storage places can be compromised without warning.

Chapter 14

Water Purification Methods, Finding Water, and Safe Water Storage Options

In a disaster or emergency situation, even when things seem relatively normal for you personally, your source of drinking water may have become contaminated. Therefore, it is essential to know how to purify water before drinking it, before using it to brush your teeth or wash your face, before using it to rehydrate dehydrated food, or cooking food such as spaghetti or rice that requires the use of water.

Reminder: Contaminated water may not look dirty. In fact, it may look crystal clear and still be dangerously contaminated. Even water from previously reliable sources such as the faucet in your home, or a well on private property, can become contaminated after a disaster.

After an earthquake, major storm, flood or another geo-disaster, even if you still have running tap water it may not be safe to drink. This is also true of well water. (After hurricane Harvey, the wells in an entire region were tainted.) Contamination may be the result of damaged sewer pipes or water treatment plants, nearby chemical and fertilizer storage tanks that are leaking, or water storage cisterns and aquifers that have been inundated by contaminated water. Even bottled water which has been exposed to flood water, or stored for a long time, or exposed to high temperature or frozen, may look normal but have become contaminated.

When in doubt, purify. If you aren't sure it's pure, don't risk it.

Even pristine-looking mountain water, river water, and crystal-clear lake water usually contain *giardia*, a protozoan that can make you violently ill. Don't let convenience and a false sense of security lull you into risky behavior.

This chapter will provide you with what you need to know to purify your water quickly and inexpensively, even if you don't have purification equipment.

First, it is essential to understand that most water filters do not purify water, they only clean it. And clean water isn't enough. It must be purified because even clean-looking water may be contaminated with illness-causing bacteria, viruses, chemicals, toxins, or other pollutants.

To maintain health, you need *clean* water that is also *pure* water. Having a supply of pure water on hand should be part of your preparations for an emergency situation, but the need to clean and purify water is often still a necessity.

An expensive purification system isn't necessary. You can make your water 99.9% safe by following this simple 2-step process:

STEP-1: **First, clean your water.**
STEP-2: **Then, purify your water.**

If your water is already clean looking and clear, start with Step-2.

STEP-1: Clean Your Water

If your source of water is cloudy, off-color, dirty, or might be contaminated with dirt, garden or roadway runoff, or effluent (sewage, factory waste, animal excretions, etc.), you need to do what you can to clean it before you attempt to purify it.

Even if you have a household water filter such as a Brita, Pur, ZeroWater, or Clear2O (best of these four), *these are not adequate for the task of purifying your water*. But they are helpful for cleaning water prior to purification.

Notwithstanding, since water filters are quickly clogged, water which is dirty or colored should be pre-filtered using one of the following methods. It may be beneficial to use a household-type water filter for an additional level of cleaning or for improving the taste of the water, but the water-cleaning process should be used first so that your household-type water filter will have a longer useful life.

Clean Your Water Containers Before Use

If your canteen, water bottle, or container for storing drinking water might be contaminated, wash it before you use it.

Soap: The use of soapy water is the easiest method to clean a water container. If you opt for this technique, use antibacterial soap if it is available, but any soap will work. Rinse with pure water. If pure water is not available for rinsing, use clean water and place it in direct sunlight until it is completely dry.

Cleaning Technique: For cleaning the container and its component parts, use either a clean cloth, ideally with a rough weave, or a clean soft-bristle brush to scrub the interior and then the exterior. For the lid and opening, carefully scrub the inside and outside surfaces, especially the threads, as well as the seal or seal-area of the cap. If the container has a strap, pouch or handle, clean that and any other related parts, too. If it is used with drinking tubes and flow valves, wash those using the same techniques. For drinking tubes, repeatedly flow soapy water through it, and leave both ends open to dry.

If pure water is not available, use the cleanest water you can find. The use of soap will make cleaning with non-pure water safer than using an unwashed container. If the water used for cleaning is not pure water, dry the container, lid, and other parts in direct sunlight. Sunshine can help further purify these items.

Dry the container inside and out with clean, absorbent cloth. If you are not able to dry it before use, wash it with fresh soapy water a second time. If you will be using a funnel or some other object to transfer water from your boiling pot (or treatment container) to your drinking water container, be sure to wash it.

Household Bleach: A bleach solution can also be used to clean your water containers. Ideally, clean and then soak the container in the bleach solution for a minimum of 5-minutes. A diluted bleach solution can be made using 1-part bleach to 10-parts of clean water. Even filling the container with a weak solution of 1-part bleach to 100-parts water will still kill many types of bacteria. But if your mixture does not smell like bleach, increase the amount of bleach used in the solution. If you cannot smell the distinctive bleach odor, there may not be enough residual chlorine in the water.

Alcohol or Hydrogen Peroxide: If bleach is not available, alcohol or hydrogen peroxide can be used to wash your container, but these should not be diluted.

Boiling Water: If the container can be boiled for 12-minutes, this is a very effective method to purify it. However, pouring boiling water over a container, or into it, is not adequate. For this boiling method to work, the container and related parts must be continually covered by water that is maintained at a rolling boil. Most bacteria and viruses will be killed if the container and component parts are boiled for 1-minute for each thousand feet of elevation, but it takes 12-minutes to kill all harmful contaminants. Since both metal and plastic containers can be damaged by even this reduced exposure to boiling water, this method is often not practical.

How to Make a Pre-Filter for Cleaning Water

It is easier to purify water that is cloudy if it has been pre-filtered, plus, it can make the water taste better. There are various products and ways to pre-filter water, but the following do-it-yourself (DIY) technique is perhaps the simplest and least expensive:

How to transfer and pre-filter water from a tank, stream or pond, to a first-stage water container: Use a water scoop, jug, or bucket to gather water from a source such as a pond or rainwater collection barrel. Then, pour this water through a pre-filter to remove particulates and debris, before it enters your first-stage water storage container.

To make a simple, inexpensive but effective pre-filter, insert the foot portion of a new nylon stocking into the inside of a new, white, athletic sock. Then, hold this double-sock pre-filter over the opening of a clean water container, and pour the water into the opening of the sock so that the water is filtered before entering the water storage container. Rinse this pre-filter regularly. Wash this pre-filter with soap and water between sessions or when the socks start to look dirty.

How to pre-filter water before it enters a suction-type water purification filter: To avoid premature clogging of your purification system, use a pre-filter.

This DIY technique is similar to the above method, but in this application, the nylon stocking becomes the outer layer. The mesh of the nylon stocking will strain large particulates while the fabric of the athletic sock will screen out smaller ones.

Cut a new nylon stocking just above the ankle, to remove the foot portion. Then, place the foot of a new, clean, white athletic sock inside the foot portion of the nylon stocking. Insert the suction-tube of the water purification filter into the inside of the double sock, loosely, and secure it to the tube with a rubber band.

By using this double-sock pre-filter method, large dirt particles and debris will be trapped, preventing them from entering the water purification filter. This will significantly extend the life of your water purification system. Clean the double-sock pre-filter when it starts to look dirty, and allow it to air dry, preferably in the sun.

If you don't have access to a NEW fine mesh nylon stocking and a NEW athletic sock, use a combination of several layers of clean cloth or clothing items to obtain similar results. (If using the sock method, it is preferable to use new socks as even freshly laundered socks can contain foot bacteria.

Other pre-filter methods: Use a paper coffee filter, paper facemask, or cotton bandana to achieve similar results.

Pre-filtering fine-point technique: Reposition your pre-filter periodically so that the water is always flowing through clean fabric. Keep the sock/fabric filter from touching the cleaned water. And, make sure dirty water does not overflow your sock/fabric pre-filter, as this will foul the water that was previously filtered. If necessary, repeat this process until the water looks reasonably clean and clear. A water purification filter can easily last 10x longer if it is only used to filter clear water, rather than water which contains debris.

Indoor water source: A dishpan, children's play pool, or bathtub can be used to store water temporarily. This will give sediment time to settle before you draw water from it for purification.

Outdoor water sources: If your water source is a pool, pond or puddle, the surface water is usually cleaner, but the surface of a stagnant water source may contain oil or insect larvae, so inspect the source before proceeding, and then use your best judgment.

If possible, draw water from 2-inches below the surface of any pool, lake, or water source, but well above the sediment layer that has settled to the bottom. This technique will help you avoid both the contaminants floating on the surface as well as the dirt and heavy particulates that have sunk to the bottom.

If you are using either a water purification filter, pre-filter, siphon hose, or even a water bucket to gather water, use your hand to gently brush away the top surface of the water at the place where you will draw water. This won't eliminate surface contamination problems, but it can reduce the quantity of oil, larva, insect and surface debris.

Use of a Syphon Hose: A self-priming clear plastic hose, such as the "Super Syphon" or "Jiggler Pump," is a lightweight, useful tool for siphoning water from an elevated source such as a rain barrel, water tank or tarp puddle. However, do not use this hose for water if it has previously been used with gasoline, diesel fuel, or a chemical.

STEP-2: Purify Your Water

The best purification method is often thought to be boiling water, but there are other effective ways to accomplish this same task. Thankfully, several do not require fire, nor the time it takes to purify by boiling. This includes using relatively low-cost but high-quality water purification system which filters to 1-micron *absolute*. Or, the use of sodium chloride tablets such as Katadyn Micropur. Other water purification methods are generally less practical or less effective, but are included here in case they are your only option.

Warning: The popular bleach or iodine treatment methods will *not* consistently kill *cryptosporidium* (aka/ *crypto*), a common microscopic parasite that causes diarrhea. Boiling the water, or a filter designed for this level of purification (1-micron *absolute*), or sodium chloride, is required to neutralize this purification problem.

Medical Use of Water: *For medical use and other times when purity needs to be confirmed, use two water purification methods back-to-back. The best combination is first to boil the water, and then after it has cooled, add the proper dose of sodium chloride. If you don't have access to sodium chloride, use chlorine bleach that does not have any additives such as fragrance or fabric softeners.*

Waterborne Illnesses: No one wants to get sick, but even so, most of us are somewhat cavalier about prevention. This needs to change. Deterrence is a high priority during an emergency when your safety depends on your ability to problem-solve and operate at your peak level of performance.

In addition to a sickness being ill-timed when you are already dealing with the difficulties of an emergency, even a minor illness can be life-threatening. For example, diarrhea might ordinarily be an uncomfortable nuisance, but during a crisis it can lead to debilitating immobility, dehydration, and even death. At times such as these, simple preventative measures such as hand washing, water purification, and routine sanitation, rise to the level of critical functions.

Evaluation of Popular Water Purification Methods

Pure water is vitally important. Before drinking any water, brushing teeth, or using water for food preparation or a medical purpose, be sure that it is not just clean, but also pure. *If you are not sure that it's pure, purify it.*

Option "A" – Boiling Water

Unfortunately, the instructions contained in many disaster preparedness books and materials, including some produced by Red Cross and FEMA, which suggest boiling for 6-12 minutes, are out-of-date. Current scientific research has demonstrated that prolonged boiling is not necessary. This is a welcomed revision since the fuel it takes to boil water is often at a premium during an emergency situation.

However, as altitude increases so does the required boiling time. This is because water boils at a lower temperature at higher elevations, and continuous high heat is needed for water purification.

> **Recommendation**
>
> To purify water, follow this 3-step process.
>
> 1. If the water is not already clear and clean looking, pre-filter it.
>
> 2. Boil the water, or use a water filter rated at '1-micron *absolute.*'
>
> 3. Add chlorine dioxide tablets or use a UV device like a SteriPEN. If neither of these are available, use household bleach or one of the other treatment methods described here and in Chapter 10.
>
> *Whenever possible, use more than one water purification method.*

Revised Boiling Times:[16] At sea level, bring the water to a rolling boil for 1-minute. For each 1,000 feet of elevation above sea level, increase the boiling time by 1-minute. (ex. If your altitude is 5,000-feet (1,524m), maintain a rolling boil for 5-minutes.)

When boiling water, use a kettle or put a lid on your pot. This will help keep the heat in and make the water come to a boil faster—and

---

[16] Research conducted by the U.S. Centers for Disease Control (CDC) indicates that 1-minute of rolling boil is adequate for those who are operating at an elevation of less than 6,562-feet (2,000m), and 3-minutes of rolling boil is sufficient for higher altitudes. Other research suggests a graduated method as cited above.

you will use less fuel in the process. If you don't have a kettle or a lid for your pot, use another pot or pan as a lid, or aluminum foil.

Exercise caution with this process. Hot lids, your heat source, the pot used for boiling, steam, or the boiling water itself, can all cause serious injury if not properly handled.

During an emergency situation, it is essential to exercise additional caution even with mundane tasks such as boiling water. It may be difficult or impossible to obtain medical care, so even a minor burn or slight injury can magnify your problems.

Caution: After boiling, leave the lid in place and let the purified water cool sufficiently before drinking. If you are pouring it into a plastic container, the water should be at drinking temperature before transferring the water. Once filled, immediately cap the container to prevent airborne contaminants from drifting into it.

> Reverse osmosis is an excellent water purification method but it is not addressed here since these systems are not portable.

Purify it. Cap it. If not using it, keep your water container capped. Unlike city tap water which contains residual chlorine, boiled water only remains pure until a contaminant touches it. If you plan to store boiled water for more than a few days, treat it with chlorine or bleach. (Instructions later in this chapter.)

Take steps necessary to avoid contaminating the water and its container when you drink from it, and also when you transfer purified water between containers. If contamination occurs, restart the purification process.

Note: Since this method requires a stove and fuel, scarcity of fuel and the need for fire may make this method impractical or undesirable. Thankfully, you do have other options...

Option "B" – Water Purification Filters

This is a convenient method, but proper product selection is critical since many filters are inadequate to the task. Also, manufacturer's instructions need to be closely followed for the use, care, cleaning, and maintenance of the filter.

Select a filter system that has a pore size of '1-micron *absolute*' or smaller. This will remove microbes 1-micron or greater in diameter, such as the nasty protozoa cryptosporidium and giardia which pose serious health problems.

Clarifying a common point of confusion: There are several types of water purification filters— "*absolute* 1-micron" filters and "*nominal* 1-micron" filters. Unfortunately, not all filters that are supposed to remove objects that are 1-micron or larger, are the same. The *absolute* filters will be more consistent in removing cryptosporidium than will a *nominal* filter (sometimes simply labeled a "1-micron" water purification filter.) During field use, some nominal 1-micron filters allowed 20-30% of 1-micron particles (like cryptosporidium) to pass through.

NSF Testing: NSF-International (NSF) does independent testing on filters to determine if they remove cryptosporidium. To discover whether a water filter has been 'certified' as being able to remove cryptosporidium, look for the NSF trademark plus the words "cyst reduction" or "cyst removal" on the product's packaging. You can also contact the NSF in the U.S. by phoning 800-673-8010, or by visiting their website: www.nsf.org/certified/DWTU/

At their website, enter the model number of the unit you are researching to see if it is on their certified list. Or, you can look under the section entitled "Reduction claims for drinking water treatment units – Health Effects" and check the box in front of the words "Cyst Reduction." This will display a list of filters tested for their ability to remove cryptosporidium. (Or, visit my website for a recommendation in the supplemental document for this book.)

Many high-quality water purification devices have not been tested by NSF. Since this laboratory testing protocol is expensive and voluntary, some filters that work against cryptosporidium have not been NSF-certified. If you choose to use a product that has not been subjected to this independent test, select a product that at least claims to eliminate cryptosporidium. Filters which may live up to this claim include reverse osmosis systems and filters which have an absolute pore size of 1-micron *absolute* or smaller.

Water Filter Shelf life: All water filters need to be correctly maintained, and some need to have the filter element dried or the unit air dried before it is sealed in plastic. Read the instructions.

Option "C" – UV Water Purification Electronic Devices

Advanced filtration systems capable of filtering water at the 1-micron level are a great alternative to the chemical purification methods described later in this chapter. But another, more unique non-chemical water purification method is to use a water purification device which produces ultraviolet (UV-C) light, such as the SteriPEN.

> **Redundancy + Simplicity**
>
> Since all electronic and battery-operated devices can break or fail, and since a supply of water treatment chemicals can be used up, every GO-Bag and Emergency Supply Kit needs a mechanical backup method for water purification. This device needs to be simple and durable. And, it needs to be able to be field stripped, cleaned, and restored to a fully operational state by an inexperienced user.

The SteriPEN can purify 32-ounces of water in just 90 seconds. But like all electronic devices, it is subject to damage, and it needs a battery to operate. Therefore, for many, it is an excellent choice due to the convenience and high-level of water purification it offers, but it needs to be accompanied with a backup method in case it fails.

Purification filters are far more expensive than chemical methods ($70-500), but these units are a better choice for long-term use. Notwithstanding, even if you have a high-quality purifying filter, chemical purification methods should still be available to use as a second treatment for water which is suspected of being highly contaminated. And also, as a back-up to filters which can clog, and for mechanical water purification filters which can break.

The highest degree of safety for *long-term* use is provided by using a combination of a high-quality mechanical water purification filter PLUS an ultraviolet purifier. For example, a Katadyn Pocket Water filter *plus* either a SteriPEN Defender designed for use by the military (or a SteriPEN Adventurer Opti Water Purifier with Solar Charger).

When shopping for these products, be sure it is capable of removing or destroying protozoa, bacteria, and viruses. All three. And remember, electronics including UV devices, will fail if subjected to a significant electromagnetic pulse (EMP) or solar flare (CME), so it is necessary to have a backup purification method.

Option "D" – Using Chlorine or Iodine to Purify Water

Chlorine Dioxide Tablets: Retailers who cater to serious backpackers, sell *chlorine dioxide* tablets packed individually in foil packets. The most popular brand is Katadyn Micropur MP1. Chlorine dioxide is the best and simplest, chemical water purification method for inclusion in a GO-Bag. It is also the only chemical treatment method certified by the EPA, and it is recommended by the CDC.

Dose: Use 1-tablet to treat 1-quart / 1-liter of water.

Treatment Time: 30-minutes for eliminating bacteria, viruses, and giardia, but 4-hours to defeat crypto.

Iodine Tablets: Unfortunately, the backpacking community has not entirely caught up with the above new standard, so the most popular brand of chemical purification tablets is still "Potable Aqua." With this product, each iodine tablet contains 20mg of tetraglycine hydroperiodide, which releases *titratable iodine* into the water.

Dose: Use 1-tablet to treat 16-oz (.5 Liter) of water.

Treatment time: 30-minutes for bacteria, viruses, and giardia. *This method is ineffective against crypto.* Also, it should not be used by pregnant women, those with thyroid problems, or if allergic to iodine.

The companion product, "PA Plus," is needed to remove the unpleasant iodine taste. (Or, use a sports drink or flavoring to mask the taste.) Unfortunately, though it does work against many protozoa, bacteria, and viruses, it is *not* effective against cryptosporidium.

Regrettably, "Potable Aqua" has now released a chlorine dioxide product using the same product name. This is causing confusion in the marketplace.

Both chlorine dioxide and iodine tablets are compact and easy to use, albeit more expensive and inadequate for long-term use. However, for inclusion in a GO-Bag or KOP-Kit (Chapter-11), nothing is easier than these tablets. Yet, the 4-hour wait before being able to drink the water is a major downside. Many people shake or stir the water to speed dissolving the tablet, but it is still necessary to wait the required 4-hours to drink the water. Just because the tablet has dissolved, does not mean that the purification process is complete.

Liquid Household Bleach

> Household bleach is not nearly as effective as chlorine dioxide. Its advantage is that it is a low-cost, readily available option.

Though not nearly as effective as chlorine dioxide, liquid household bleach (sodium hypochlorite) as used for laundering clothes, is a simple and often available water purifying method.

Liquid bleach is also far less expensive than chlorine dioxide tablets. Even though it is not 100% effective, at less than $ 0.01 per quart of treated water and ready in only 30-minutes, it is one of the most cost-effective and fastest water purification methods. Expensive brands do not offer any extra benefits.

Type of Household Bleach to Use for Water Purification: If you opt to use "regular" household bleach for water purification, do not use scented bleach (lemon, lavender, etc.), nor "color-safe" bleach or bleaches which contain additional cleaners. It is essential to avoid using bleach which contains any additives. Only unadulterated bleach should be used to purify drinking water.

Check the Ingredients: A bottle of liquid household bleach typically contains: water, sodium hypochlorite, sodium chloride, sodium carbonate, sodium chlorate, sodium hydroxide, and sodium polyacrylate. If the front of the label indicates "regular" or "concentrated" bleach and does not tout other features such as scents, color boosting, or added cleaning capabilities, it's probably okay.

"How-To" Use Household Bleach to Purify Water: If the water is not clear or nearly clear, filter it. Add the dose of bleach to the container and then add water. Stir the water (or cap and shake a not-quite-full bottle of water) to mix the bleach into the water thoroughly. Then, let it sit for 30 minutes before drinking.

After the waiting period, the odor of chlorine should be detectable when you sniff the water. If not, add a second dose (same quantity of bleach as previously used), and wait for another 30-minutes. If the water still does not smell like chlorine, discard the treated water, and try again with a fresh bottle of bleach.

If the fresh bottle of bleach still fails to produce a slight chlorine smell even after a double dose, then the water is either too contaminated for this simple purification method, your container was not adequately cleaned, or your bleach is old or degraded.

If this is your situation, first smell your bleach bottle. If it does not have a pungent bleach smell, it is too old or degraded to be useful. But if the bleach seems okay, then try using a new source of water, and repeat the purification process.

Household Bleach Shelf life: Buy your bleach from a store that turns-over its inventory quickly, as this will improve freshness of the product. Small convenience stores may have old bleach on their shelves, and most brands do not use an easily decipherable manufacturing date, so it is hard to determine product freshness by checking the product's label.

An unopened bottle of household bleach should have a shelf life of 4-12 months. Old household bleach does not become more dangerous, it only diminishes in strength. If your bottle of bleach still has a strong chlorine smell then it's probably suitable. However, if your bleach is old, you will need to add more of it to achieve the faint chlorine smell that is an indicator of residual chlorine in the water.

To maintain maximum shelf life of your bleach, keep it tightly capped when you're not pouring it, and store the bottle in a cool, dark place. Exposing the bottle to sunlight, even through a window, will reduce its effectiveness. If you leave your bleach bottle uncapped, or in the sunlight for even a few minutes, it will significantly degrade the chlorine-level in the bleach. Without the chlorine, the bleach will not purify the water. (It won't be as useful for your clothes, either.)

Shelf life Comparison: Unopened containers of chlorine dioxide and Potable Aqua iodine have a shelf life of 4-years if stored in a cool, dry place, and if the package/bottle has not been opened. Conversely, an unopened bottle of bleach under the same conditions has a shelf life of only 6-12 months. A glass eyedropper bottle which has been completely filled with fresh bleach can have a shelf life of 1-year if stored in the same conditions, whereas a plastic eyedropper bottle will generally only provide a 6-month shelf life.

Safety Considerations for Bleach: Carefully read the manufacturer's safety and usage information which is on the bleach bottle label. Bleach is <u>not</u> safe to drink except in the extremely diluted quantities as specified in this chapter. Keep bleach and other chemicals away from children and unauthorized users. Read the product label.

Liquid Bleach for Use in a GO-Bag: Use a 2-oz glass bottle which has a glass eyedropper, and fill it with regular household bleach. A bottle made from dark-colored or opaque glass is best as even a small amount of sunlight will degrade the bleach. Be sure to label the bottle, seal it tightly, and then double-bag it in two Zip-Lock baggies, with a piece of paper towel to absorb liquid if the bottle leaks. Old bleach can still be used to purify water, but the amount of bleach needed will increase as the bleach ages.

Properly dosed water will have a slight chlorine smell. If the odor is strong to the point of being somewhat offensive, it probably contains too much chlorine. In this situation, either add more water or leave the cap off the container for an hour or two to expose the water to air, so that the chlorine can dissipate naturally.

Note on Eyedroppers: Unfortunately, not all eyedroppers produce the same size drop of liquid, so you will need to test your dropper and compensate accordingly: 76-drops should equal 1-teaspoon. If your eyedropper requires more or less drops to fill the measuring spoon, adjust the quantities indicated in the following chart.

Shelf life of Bleach Stored in a GO-Bag: If you keep bleach in a dropper bottle in your GO-Bag, be sure to fill the bottle completely, including the eyedropper itself, as exposure to air will degrade the bleach. This, and protecting the bottle from exposure to sunlight, will prolong shelf life.

Unfortunately, even when fresh chlorine bleach is stored correctly in a GO-Bag, it will have a maximum shelf life of only 6-months due to temperature fluctuation. So, if this is the method you select, mark your calendar with a reminder of when you need to replace your bleach. Maintaining a replacement schedule is too important to leave to chance.

Concentrated Bleach: *"Concentrated"* bleach" is usually 8.25 % strength rather than the 5.25-6% of regular bleach. Check the label to verify the amount of concentration. If you intend to use this to purify water, adjust the dose amount to compensate for the higher concentration. For example, when using an 8.25% concentrated bleach, use 6-drops for each 1-gallon of water, rather than the 8-drops needed when using regular (5.25-6%) household bleach. Therefore, a 5-gallon container of clear water will require 30-drops of *concentrated* liquid household bleach.

Water Purification Using Liquid Household Bleach

If the water is slightly cloudy, off-color, or cold, double these quantities. If it is dirty, pre-filter it repeatedly until it is only slightly cloudy.

1-Quart (32 oz.) or 1-liter – Use 2-drops of household bleach

100 oz. (3 liters) Water Bladder aka / Water Reservoir – 7-drops
Note: Do not use a water bladder for long-term water storage.

1-Gallon – 8-drops of household bleach

2-1/2 Gallon (10-liter) – "Military Water Canister" (MWC)
20 drops (1/4+ teaspoon). Scepter Military is the manufacturer of the U.S. military's MWC (www.Scepter.com).

3-1/2 Gallon "Waterbrick" – 28 drops.
Filled weight for transport = 31.8 pounds (14.4 kg)
Manufacturer: Waterbrick Intl - www.Waterbrick.org

5-Gallon (20-liter) "Military Water Canister" (MWC)
40 drops (1/2+ teaspoon). Scepter Military is the manufacturer of the U.S. military's MWC (www.Scepter.com).

15-Gallon (60-liter) Food Grade Barrel – 120 drops (1-1/2 tsp.)

30-Gallon (120 liters) Food Grade Barrel – 240 drops (3 tsp.)

55-Gallon (220 liters) Food Grade Barrel – 440 drops (6 tsp.)

Conversion of Drops to Larger Measuring Units

- 10 drops = 1/8 teaspoon (tsp.)
- 19 drops = 1/4 tsp.
- 38 drops = 1/2 tsp.
- 76 drops = 1 tsp.
- 228 drops = 1 Tablespoon (tbsp.)
- 456 drops = 2 Tbsp. (1-fluid ounce)

Source: www.Clorox.com and www.EPA.gov

* For convenience, it is okay to use a bit more—but not less.

Using Swimming-Pool Chlorine to Purify Drinking Water:

Calcium hypochlorite is commonly used in swimming pools. It has a longer shelf life than liquid bleach or liquid chlorine, and it is far more compact and lightweight to stockpile. If stored in a dry (non-humid), cool, and dark place, calcium hypochlorite, aka "Dry Chlorine" can retain most of its potency for nearly 10-years.

Dry or granular chlorine is readily available from swimming pool supply stores, but since the strength varies by manufacturer, extra care must be used to determine the proper dose. Also, since many pool products have additional additives, it is critically important that the right product is selected for the purification of drinking water.

Directions: Using either dry or granular calcium hypochlorite, make a chlorine-concentrate solution. Do this in a ventilated place wearing rubber or medical gloves and eye protection. If using standard high-test granular calcium hypochlorite (HTH), add ½ heaping teaspoon (1/8 oz) of the chemical to the container. Then, 1-gallon of water and stir gently until the particles have completely dissolved. To disinfect clear water, add 1-part of this solution to 100-parts of water.

For a 100-oz water bladder, this equates to 1-oz of solution to a nearly-full bladder of water; for 1-gallon of water, add 1-1/4 ounces of the solution. For 5-gallons, add 8.5 teaspoons of the HTH solution. The water will be ready to drink in 30-minutes. If the smell of chlorine is too strong, let the container sit for 30-60 minutes and then smell it again. (Exposure to air will dissipate the chlorine.) Again, this method is not nearly as effective as chlorine dioxide tablets.

Option "E" – Tincture of Iodine (First-Aid Kit Iodine)

Tincture of Iodine (2% solution) is a water purification method that has been used for many years. Do-It-Yourself enthusiasts often make their own inexpensive crystalline iodine solution. But just like chlorine bleach, iodine is not effective against cryptosporidium, and it also has an unpleasant taste. Chlorine bleach is slightly more efficient than iodine, but neither is adequate for reliably eradicating cryptosporidium. Use 5-drops to purify 1-quart/liter of clear water.

Caution: Water disinfected with iodine should NOT be consumed by pregnant women, people with thyroid problems, or those with a known hypersensitivity to iodine. Iodine treated water should not be used continuously for more than a few weeks.

Note: The type of iodine used for water purification tablets is <u>not</u> the same as the iodine used for protection against radiation sickness. Caution: Do not consume chlorine or Iodine Water Purification Tablets like a pill. For safe use, they must be adequately diluted in water.

Option "F" – Hydrogen Peroxide to Purify Water

Similar in effect to chlorine or household bleach, peroxide has a somewhat similar ability to purify water. However, since peroxide degrades very quickly, especially if the container has previously been opened, its primary benefit is that it might be available in an emergency situation when other purification methods are not.

Since the strength of peroxide declines quickly even if the container is unopened, it is impossible to provide reliable dosing information without test equipment. Therefore, if hydrogen peroxide is all you have, the best option may be to dose the water with double the amount of the recommended quantity of bleach. Shake the container, or stir the water with a sanitized object, and then wait 30-minutes. Do not use peroxide and liquid household bleach together.

If there is a slight odor of peroxide to the water, it is probably safer to drink than untreated water. If there is no peroxide odor in the water, repeat the process. After the additional 30-minute wait, if there is still no peroxide odor to the water, the treatment may not have provided a substantial purification effect. However, the treated water will likely still be safer to drink than untreated water.

DO NOT drink undiluted hydrogen peroxide even if it is odorless.

Option "G" – Stabilized Liquid Oxygen (Activated Oxygen)

The chemicals chlorine and iodine both create health problems if used for an extended period of time, whereas stabilized liquid oxygen has no such undesirable side effects. An additional benefit is that stabilized liquid oxygen does not adversely affect the taste of the water as do most chemical treatments.

Dosage: Use the manufacturer's recommended dosage. If not available, purification dosage is typically 10-40 drops of stabilized liquid oxygen for 16-ounces of clear water, shake or stir and then cap the container. Let it stand for 5-minutes before consuming. For purification powders, such as Katadyn Micropur and Micropur Tank Clean, use one gram of powder to treat 1-liter of water, let it dissolve thoroughly and then wait for at least 5-minutes before drinking.

For short-term water storage, treat 1-gallon of already-chlorinated water by adding 10 drops of liquid stabilized oxygen. For tap water which is to be stored long-term, add 20 drops. For 55-gallon drums, use 55 ml or 1,100 drops. Store stored water in a cool location, away from direct sunlight. Keep your bottle of liquid stabilized oxygen tightly capped and away from heat and sunlight.

The use of liquid stabilized oxygen for water purification is a lesser-known treatment method. It can be hard to find locally, except perhaps in health food, vitamin, or homeopathic retail stores, so it may be more expedient to shop for it online. Commonly found brand names of liquid stabilized oxygen are: Aerox, Aerobic Stabilized Oxygen (formerly Aerobic 07), Aerobic Life, Aquagen, Dynamo 2, Dexterity Health, Genesis 1000, and Katadyn Micropur.

Option "H" – Wine to Purify Water

My winemaker friend Don will especially appreciate this method, but for the rest of us, this technique is not as farfetched as it may sound. Since ancient Bible times, water was often insufficiently pure to drink untreated. By mixing 1-part red wine to 3-parts water, a limited level of purification was achieved. In modern laboratory tests, various bacteria were killed using this method.

In these laboratory tests, red wine ranked 3 to 4 times more effective than alcoholic beverages such as tequila. It is believed that wine is more effective due to the phenol compounds in the red wine, which are enhanced by the charred wood used in some wine-aging casks. This factor is additionally noteworthy as phenol compounds may be related to the sulfur drugs historically used as antibiotics. (Source: Dr. Trichopolou, British Medical Journal, discussing the Greek Villager's Diet.) Unfortunately, this method will probably not kill giardia and cryptosporidium, so view this treatment as a last-resort method which may be better than no treatment at all.

Option "I" – Salt Water Desalinization, or Water Purification Using a Distillation Method.

Do not drink saltwater. If seawater or saltwater is your only source of water, the salt must be removed *and* the water purified, before drinking it. *Water purification filters do not remove salt.*

If you don't have desalinization or distillation equipment designed for this purpose, this task can be accomplished using sunlight or by boiling the salt water and reclaiming the steam vapor. The method described below for distilling water requires a fuel source, but it will produce more drinking water than the sunlight methods. Unfortunately, neither will produce a lot of pure water in return for the effort expended, but they are far better choice than drinking salt water.

Using Salt-free Water: This same process can be used for the purification of regular water, too, as distillation produces pure water and leaves most chemicals and contaminants behind.

If you will be using this method repeatedly, be sure to clean the container used for boiling the water, before using it again. This will get rid of the contaminants that were left behind in the prior session.

Distillation by Condensation: Once the water reaches a rolling boil, capture the steam coming off the water. As the steam cools, it will return to liquid water; water that is pure and suitable for drinking.

How To: To accomplish this task, use an oversize lid or aluminum foil dome over the boiling pot to capture the steam. The steam that is trapped by the lid (or foil) will cool and condense, and transition back into liquid water. Design the water recovery system to flow the distilled water into a clean container. This is now pure water.

To be effective, your do-it-yourself desalinization apparatus needs to collect the pure water as it drips from the lid or foil dome. Without contaminating this purified water or burning yourself, direct this runoff into a clean container for collection. This collected water is pure, distilled water, and ready to drink as soon as it has sufficiently cooled. However, it will only maintain its purity if the collection container is clean, and your hands are clean.

The condensation and collection method is the most challenging part of this do-it-yourself project. Often the simplest way to accomplish this steam capture, condensation, and collection process is to extend the lid over the side of the pot, and use aluminum foil to direct the dripping water. Additional foil can be used to form a trough to channel the flow of the condensed water, directing it into a second container which serves as temporary storage.

Even expensive water purification filters *will* *not* remove salt and some hazardous chemicals from the water. Salt, and many chemical contaminants, can only be removed from the water by converting it into steam, and then back again into liquid water. This process leaves the salt and chemical residues behind.

Desalinization: Drinking water can also be produced by using specialized desalinization equipment. Small desalinization units are popular with those who operate pleasure boats in ocean waters, so they are available from maritime stores. Navy ships, and some maritime communities use large desalinization plants, but units designed for the pleasure boat market are adequate for extended use by a family, if maintained properly.

Health Note: Health professionals do not agree on the merits or disadvantages of the long-term use of distilled water for drinking. Some claim that since the distilling process removes all minerals from the water, it is not safe for long-term use. Whereas others assert that these same minerals are in food, too, so this problem is amply offset by the vitamins and minerals in the foods we eat. Since unadulterated rainwater is distilled water, and people around the world use rainwater for drinking, this seems to support the second viewpoint.

Option "J" – Moringa Seeds to Purify Water

In the Middle East since before the time of Jesus, crushed seeds from the Moringa Oleifera tree have been used to clarify cloudy water. Modern research suggests that it can also be used to purify water as the proteins in these crushed seeds can kill some of the common waterborne microbial contaminants. Plus, the crushed seeds can accelerate the settling of other impurities.

Known as the "miracle tree" because of its many nutritional, medicinal, and other uses, the Moringa tree is unfortunately rare in the United States and Western Europe. We only mention it here in case you are fortunate enough to have access to one of these hearty trees, or in case you'd like to plant them at your safe-haven retreat location.

Research has shown that the seeds harvested from a mature Moringa Oleifera are the most effective for purification. Next, are seeds collected from mature trees during the dry season. Seeds from immature trees can be used for purification and clarification, it's just that they are not as effective.

Process: After harvesting, the seeds are crushed and then added to the water, and allowed to settle. There is not yet scientific consensus on the wait-time before the water is safer to drink. However, researchers do agree that the water should be transferred to a safe container within hours as the purification process does not continue during storage. Adding purified sand to the water can further accelerate the clarification and purification process. Some research suggests that this Moringa-sand mixture can be reused.

This water purification process would be difficult to accomplish during evacuation, but is viable when bivouacked. Either way, this is a purification process of last resort because it does not neutralize all contaminants. Yet, it does seem to be far better than not using any purification method. If you have access to a Moringa tree, this topic is worthy of additional research. And if you are preparing a safe-haven retreat location, see if they will grow at your location as the seeds, leaves, sap, and other parts of the tree have many practical uses.

Commonly Found Waterborne Health Risks

Cryptosporidium, aka "Crypto."

Cryptosporidium is a microscopic parasite that causes the diarrheal disease cryptosporidiosis. Both the parasite and the disease are commonly known as "crypto."

There are many types of cryptosporidium that infect humans and animals. In all of them, the parasite is protected by an outer shell that allows it to survive outside the body for long periods of time, and they are all resistant to chlorine and iodine disinfection methods.

While this parasite can be spread in several different ways, drinking water and recreational water are the most common method of transmission. Cryptosporidium is one of the most frequent causes of waterborne disease among humans in the United States.

Reverse osmosis water treatment and water purification filters which are labeled as providing "absolute 1-micron" filtration are the best consumer-level GO-Bag methods for minimizing the risk of Cryptosporidium contamination.

Other Waterborne Health Hazards

Radiation or radioactive material, heavy metals, farm chemicals, pesticides, oils and petroleum products, and manufacturing waste can be serious health problems. A water source which is downstream from any of these sources is automatically suspect.

If your water source is contaminated with radiation or heavy metals, you will not be able to clean it using these purification methods. However, if there are no other sources of water available to you, these processes will still be helpful. Also, if the water has been undisturbed for several days, some of the contaminants will have settled to the bottom. (Some contaminants are heavy and will settle to the bottom, while others will float to the surface. You want to avoid both.)

If pollutants are suspected but you don't have another option for water, then follow these steps. 1. Carefully remove and discard the top surface of the water, while using care to avoid agitating the bottom where other contaminants may have settled. 2. Purify the remaining water, but avoiding murky water and water at the bottom.

Often Forgotten Sources of Water

Sources of reasonably clean water within a home or business are the water heater, ice in the refrigerator, swimming pools, toilet tanks, fish tanks, and water pipes (if you have turned off the water at the point where it enters the building). Water recovered from a source such as a toilet or fish tank should always be purified before drinking.

Pipe Water: Once the water has been turned off, go to the highest water faucet (top floor, or to the *highest* faucet in the building), and open it. Next, put a clean container under the *lowest* water faucet in the building (basement, or the lowest faucet), and open it. This 2-step process will eliminate the natural vacuum that is in the pipes. Any water in the system will immediately start draining into the container, so be ready to turn off that faucet to avoid wasting water.

Toilet Tanks store water but are unreliable regarding water quality. Nevertheless, it may be a source of water that can be used as long as you have access to purification supplies.

Bottled & Canned Drinks such as soft drinks, carbonated beverages, sports drinks, canned fruit juice, and other canned foods containing water, are viable alternatives if pure water is unavailable. However, alcohol consumption should be avoided as it is counterproductive to hydration. Beer and coffee are better, but since they stimulate urination, drinking them can result in net water loss. Sports drink products such as Gatorade are good but may upset the body's electrolyte balance if consumed in quantity. For some people, these sports drinks cause stomach upset or vomiting if consumed on an empty stomach. As to wine, it is better to use it to help purify water than to drink it undiluted. Drinking straight alcohol is detrimental.

Human Urine may not sound like a pleasant source of drinking water, but it is nevertheless a better alternative than dehydration. The urine of a healthy person is 95% water, but the other 5% is waste products, and urine is not sterile as urban myths suggest. It contains some bacteria, but that isn't necessarily a reason to avoid drinking it in an emergency situation. If you (or the donor) are healthy, and you don't have another source of pure water, it may be a reasonable risk to drink urine for 3-5 days. But first, clean your hands and the discharge area to avoid the transfer of undesirable microorganisms. Again, it's better than being dehydrated. The salt it contains may even be beneficial.

Shelf life Summary
Drinking Water and Purification Products

Shelf life of Purified Drinking Water

Water which has been chlorinated per the instructions in this chapter will usually have a shelf life of 1-year as long as it is stored in a dark place or in a container that is impervious to light.

Recycled milk jugs with twist-off caps that have been adequately cleaned will work for water storage, but they should be replaced every 6-months due to the type of plastic used in these bottles. Whereas water stored in quality water containers, such as the MWC (military water container) or Waterbrick which are designed for water storage and transport, should be inspected every 6-12 months but the water needn't be replaced.

At the time of inspection, if the stored water has retained a chlorine smell, it is probably fine, but it will likely taste flat. Thankfully, this taste-problem can be easily remedied. Before drinking, slosh the water back and forth between two containers to reintroduce oxygen into the water. This should solve the problem.

Even when using high-quality water containers, the water should be re-treated annually with the specified number of drops of bleach, as this will help maintain purity. However, a more prudent decision is to replace the water each year, and still add a few drops of bleach to each container before it is capped. This will increase the amount of residual chlorine in the water; a step which is an additional hedge against contamination. At the very least, even re-chlorinated water should be replaced every two years.

Shelf life and Useful Life of Purification Filter Systems

The useful life of filters depends on the brand selected, the clarity of the water filtered, and the number of gallons of water which have been run through the system. The purchase price is not a reliable measurement of filter quality.

If water is pre-filtered until it is clear, before running it through the purification system, most pump-style and gravity-filter purification filters will last for several years of modest use. In all cases, be sure to read the fine print on the package as it should include the number of gallons the filter is rated to process, before it needs to be cleaned, or disposed of and replaced. If the product's packaging does not disclose this information, choose a different water purification filter system.

The useful life of a purification filter varies widely by manufacturer and filter model. For example, the "LifeStraw" is only rated as capable of filtering particles that are larger than .2-microns and is only capable of processing a skimpy 264 gallons (1,000L) of water. Conversely, the "Sawyer Mini," which also weighs 2 oz, is capable of filtering at the desirable .01-micron *absolute* level and yet it is able to purify 100,000 gallons of water. Oddly, the price of the LifeStraw is only a few dollars less than the Sawyer Mini.

Also, some systems have filter membranes which can be cleaned and reused, while others require replacement of the filter, and still others are actually disposable because they can't be serviced. So, although you may not need a cleanable filter for inclusion in a GO-Bag, this attribute is significant if you want to be able to use your water purification system long-term.

"Pump" and "gravity" filter systems made by MSR, Katadyn, Sawyer, and Platypus, and a few others, have models that have filters which can be cleaned and are still rated as 0.1-micron *absolute* filters, which are also suitable for long-term use. In addition, they have easy-to-use and cost-effective models which can meet the water purification needs of a small group.

These larger units are compact, but unfortunately, probably still too large to be included in a GO-Bag. Nevertheless, they should be considered for use at home or at your safe-haven retreat location.

Shelf life of Household Bleach and Iodine

When stored at room temperature, bleach in an unopened jug has a shelf life of 1-year. Chlorine and iodine tablets have a shelf life of 4-years if unopened, 3-6 months if even briefly opened.

Product Expiration Dates: Unfortunately, chlorine and iodine tablets are not required to have an expiration date, so these products should be purchased from the manufacturer or a trusted retailer which turns over its inventory quickly. Some manufacturers, such as Potable Aqua, print a code on the bottle which they use to track the manufacturing date and lot number. You can use it to decipher the age of the product. For example, Potable Aqua code: 9 17 33

The date code is generally a five or six-digit number. The first digit(s) represent the month of manufacture. The next two numbers represent a two-digit year, and the last digits represent a batch number for that month and year. With the code example used in the prior paragraph, the product was manufactured during the 9th month of the year 2017, and was the 33rd batch of product made that year.

When needed, inspect the tablets before use. Gray or dark brown tablets are probably undamaged. But if they are light green or yellow, they may have become degraded or even ineffective. If you have no other method for purification, use 2-4x the standard dosage. If the treated water has an unusually strong odor after the tablets dissolve, discard the water and try again using fewer tablets.

How-to Store Bottled Water

Unopened bottled water products can often be safely stored for years, provided the bottles are kept in the proper environment, and the plastic material of the bottle is BPA-free. When in doubt, discard or treat bottled water which is more than 6-months old.

Water is also available in aluminum cans and foil pouches, but since these products cannot be inspected before purchase or use, there is little opportunity to evaluate the contents. For water stored in these containers, it is essential that it is obtained from a reputable source. If the container does not have a "bottled on" date or "use by" date, the water should be purified before use.

Canned water distributed by a government agency or a reputable relief organization, which is contained in a soda or beer cans, is typically safe. During a disaster, soft drink manufacturers such as Coca-Cola and brewers such as Budweiser, are often called upon to provide safe drinking water.

Always store bottled water away from chemicals such as cleaning compounds, paints, and gasoline. And, keep the plastic bottles on pallets or shelves, and off of concrete or other types of flooring which might leach chemicals into the bottles. Don't store bottled water in a garage, storage shed, or another location which will expose the water to temperature extremes. Don't store bottled water in direct sunlight for more than a day or two.

Bottles which have been exposed to very high or low temperatures (freezing) will likely lose their structural integrity and may leak or become contaminated. If you suspect any of your stored bottled water has become contaminated (smells funny, has a plastic taste, shows signs of algae growth, fogging, leaking, particulate matter floating in the water, etc.), discard or boil it before using it.

Many experts tout Fuji bottled water as the best, but regardless of whether it deserves this high distinction, the square-ish shape of the Fuji bottles makes storage and transport easier, as the bottles pack more compactly. A less expensive option includes brands such as Dasani bottled water, a company which uses plastic bottles which are much stronger than the budget brands. The added bottle strength is significant for emergency use and transport. The 24-bottle packages of Dasani are also wrapped in heavy-duty plastic wrap, a factor which makes transport and handling easier, as the packages are less likely to break open and dump the bottles.

For a complete list of NSF Certified bottled water brands, visit: http://www.nsf.org/certified/consumer/listings_results.asp

How to Prepare Drinking Water for Storage

Pure water is susceptible to bacteria growth and contamination. Just because it was pure when you put it into your storage container, does not mean that it will still be pure a few months later. The most straightforward method for maintaining its purity is to add a tiny quantity of liquid household bleach. When water purification is boosted by the residual chlorine which was introduced into the water by the bleach, it will continue to fight contamination.

Use the ratios listed on the following page. Add the bleach first, using a clean, uncontaminated medicine eyedropper, measuring spoon, or measuring cup. Then add pure water and fill the container (canteen, bottle, barrel, etc.) almost full. If using a hose to fill the container, make sure it is food grade, such as those sold for use with recreational vehicles.

How-to Prepare Barrels for Water Storage

Be sure that the water you are treating is drinking-quality water to begin with. To treat water for storage in a large container such as a stackable 3.5 gallon "Waterbrick" which can be hand carried, or a larger container such as a 50-55-gallon plastic drum or a 275-gallon IBC Tote, use liquid household bleach that contains 5.25 percent sodium hypochlorite (chlorine). Do not use bleach that is labeled as containing soaps, brighteners, color enhancers, or scents.

1. Prepare a Container: First, make sure the container is food grade. These will have a small triangle embossed on the container, and the number 1, 2, 4, or 5 will be imprinted in the center of the triangle. Except in an emergency when there isn't another option, do not use a container that is not food grade. Next, even if the container is new, clean it with soapy water, and then rinse it with pure water.

Container Types: Plastic barrels are the most popular, but large plastic water storage tanks and concrete "ring" tanks may be a better choice for safe-haven retreat locations. (With both plastic and concrete tanks, be sure you have repair materials on hand.)

Do not use a wood barrel such as a whiskey or wine barrel; the wood grain and cracks between staves can trap bacteria. Avoid using metal barrels, too. Steel barrels can rust, which will taint your water. Some "new" steel barrels have a bonded vinyl liner on the inside. These provide a significant improvement over using an untreated steel barrel. Again, any water-storage container needs to be labeled as food grade. Used aluminum barrels often contained chemicals, making them unsuitable for this purpose, but new food-grade aluminum barrels are an excellent choice but expensive.

2. Purify the Container: After cleaning, the container must be purified before you fill it with the water you plan to store. Your plastic food grade container should look and smell clean. Place it in a shady place such as in a well-ventilated garage. Do not expose your water barrel to direct sunlight.

For the container-purification-process, add 5-cups of liquid household bleach to the barrel. For other size containers, use the ratio: 1-cup liquid household bleach to 10-gallons of water.

Next, fill the barrel with pure tap water, seal the lid, and let the barrel sit for at least 24-hours. At the end of this time, use a siphon hose or other method to drain the container.

Let the barrel air dry. While it is drying, protect the interior from airborne contamination by laying a clean towel or fabric over the top.

Note: Do not use a "used" barrel or container that has ever been used for the storage of anything other than a non-acidic non-leaching food, or food or drinking-beverage ingredient.

How-to Prepare Rainwater Recovery Tanks

For chlorinating water collect in rain tanks, first-time chlorination is often accomplished by adding as little as 7-grams of dry chlorine (1/4 ounce by weight), or, 40ml (1.35 ounces) liquid pool Chlorine for 1000 liters (264 gallons) of untreated tap water. Mix thoroughly if possible, or at least agitate the water to aid the mixing process. Let the water stand for at least 24-hours before drinking.

To maintain safe levels of chlorination in tanks: In a 1,000-liter (264 gallon) tank, each week add 1-gram of dry (.035 ounce by weight) or 4ml (.135 ounces) of liquid pool chlorine. Stir. Let the water stand for two hours after treatment, before drinking. Keep the tank out of even indirect sunlight, and sealed tightly.

Caution: Proper dosage differs depending on the form and strength of the chlorine being used. *Sodium* hypochlorite is the liquid form of pool chlorine and is typically in a concentration of 12.5%. *Calcium* hypochlorite is the solid form of pool chlorine and is typically a 65% concentration. Household bleach is *sodium* hypochlorite and its concentration is generally 5.25 - 6%. Check the product label for details on the concentration. Adjust your mixture according to the concentration of chlorine being used.

How-to Clean Water Containers

Accomplish this process outdoors if possible, but in the shade, out of direct sunlight. Keep your bleach and water out of the sun.

When possible, add the liquid household bleach to the container first, then add the water. If you are unable to use a food-grade hose and quickly flowing water from a faucet, stir the water and bleach mixture. Then cap the container.

Allow the bleach/water container to stand for 30 minutes, then remove the cap and smell the water. The odor of chlorine should be obvious after this 30-minute waiting period.

If the water does not smell like chlorine, repeat the dose, and let the container stand for another 15-30 minutes. If it still does not have a chlorine odor, cautiously smell the bleach in your bleach bottle. Do this by sniffing as you approach the open bottle of bleach, ideally from the side, so you can stop breathing the chemical as soon as the strong odor of chlorine is detected. If you do not detect a pungent chlorine odor, your bleach has likely become ineffective.

Once you have verified that your water has a noticeable chlorine bleach smell, replace the cap on the container. Attach a label to the container describing the contents and the date of preparation. Water stored in metal containers should not be treated in advance of filling for storage since chlorine is corrosive to most metals.

How-to Disinfect Surfaces and Objects

Use ½ cup regular liquid household bleach to 1-gallon water. This disinfecting solution is cited by the EPA as effective. These instructions are based on the use of Clorox Regular-Bleach, with efficacy for medical and other critical disinfection uses. In critical circumstances, mix a fresh solution daily.

Directions: For general household use, such as sanitizing kitchen counters and cleaning silverware, use 2 tablespoons diluted in 4 cups water. If fresh bleach is used and the mixture kept out of sunlight, it should be effective for 2-3 days. When cleaning an area that may be conducive to the spread of bacteria (i.e., after cutting raw meat, etc.), use fresh solution.

Chemical and Bio Warfare Agents: This mixture is highly caustic and requires protective measures, but it is what U.S. biological warfare facilities use to clean contaminated equipment. Mix 50% sodium hypochlorite and 50% water. (Not 50% household bleach as it is only 5.25-8.25% sodium hypochlorite.) To minimize risk, carefully add the chemical to the water (not the water to the chemical as this will produce chlorine gas.

Chapter Footnotes

U.S. Centers for Disease Control (CDC)
Source: http://www.cdc.gov /travel/page/water-treatment.htm
Source: http://wwwnc.cdc.gov/travel/page/water-treatment.htm
Source: http://www.cdc.gov/healthywater/drinking/travel/emergency_disinfection.html

U.S. Federal Emergency Management Agency (FEMA)
Source: http://www.ready.gov/managing-water
Source: http://www.fema.gov/pte/foodwtr.htm

U.S. Environmental Protection Agency (EPA)
Source: http://water.epa.gov/drink/emerprep/emergencydisinfection.cfm

King County Public Health Department, Washington State
Source: http://www.kingcounty.gov/healthservices/health/preparedness/disaster/SafeWater.aspx
Source:http://www.doh.wa.gov/Emergencies/EmergencyPreparednessandResponse/Factsheets/WaterPurification.aspx

Chapter 15

Emergency Larder: Evaluation of Food Choices

(GO-Bag food is addressed in Chapter-10)

The Internet is full of advice and marketing hype on food for emergencies and long-term food storage, but what is actually the best? What is the most affordable? What will last the longest? Which provides the best nutrition? Knowing the answer to these questions is vital. To help you make informed decisions, this chapter provides a summary of our choices and the merits and disadvantages of each.

Each food option has its merits and disadvantages. Canned goods and foil packaged foods such as those available in your local grocery store, as well as retort-pouch foods like military "Meals, Ready-to-Eat" (MRE), freeze-dried foods, dehydrated backpacking food, lifeboat rations, meal-replacement bars, and home-canning, all have a place in a properly stocked emergency food larder.

Nevertheless, only a few of the following food types are suitable for inclusion in your GO-Bag (Chapter-10). Some of the others work if you are evacuating by vehicle, while still others are ideal for inclusion in an emergency food larder at home, work, and at your "safe-haven" retreat location. Food requirements change with the scenario.

This primer on food choices is designed to help you select the best types of food to meet your needs. This includes food to have packaged and ready for immediate evacuation on foot, in a vehicle, for sheltering-in-place, for stockpiling both short-term and long-term supplies at a rendezvous point and at your safe-haven retreat location, and for charitable distribution.

Since each person's situation is different, this chapter focuses on the pros and cons of each category of food so that you can make informed choices. The topics of how to store these foods, do-it-yourself packaging, water, and what food should be included in your GO-Bag, are topics which are expanded upon in Chapters 10, 13, 14, and Appendix A and B.

Getting Started

The simplest way to begin is to increase the quantity of canned food and dried foods (beans, rice, pasta, wheat, etc.) that you maintain in your pantry at home, making a deliberate effort to store a nutritional variety of food. For those who live on a tight budget, purchase a few extra cans of food each week until you have enough to sustain your family for at least two weeks.

Step-1: Start with a 2-Week Supply: Increasing your quantity of canned goods and foil-packaged grocery store food is your first step in emergency food preparation. You need a minimum of two weeks of canned goods and water stored in your pantry. And, you need a way to cook it, without using grid electricity or natural gas.

Where to shop: If you can afford it, go to a big-box store like Costco or Sam's Club, or a restaurant supply store, and purchase canned meats and other staples by the case. It is far less expensive, the food fresher and often better quality than low-cost grocery-store brands. Plus, the food bundles are more compact for storage and transport, the shrink-wrap packaging and boxes make them stackable and provide another layer of securely.

What to buy: If you don't have lots of money and can't afford to buy a supply of freeze-dried meals or MREs that need to be replaced every three years, purchase the types of foods that you routinely eat and convert them for long-term food storage. Not only is this more cost-efficient, it is to your advantage to keep your meals as 'normal' as possible during an emergency situation. This is especially important for children who might be finicky eaters.

Give particular attention to stockpiling foods which provide both variety and a balanced diet. This will typically include canned foods such as meat and beans, vegetables and fruit, as well as dry goods such as pasta and rice. Foods which contain lots of water, like soup, are inefficient if you need to maximize limited storage space.

Don't forget to include additional foods such as sugar, salt, and flour, as well as the condiments and spices you will need to make your food tasty. There is a tendency to not eat enough during a high-stress, busy, emergency situation. Palatable easy-to-prepare meals will help, particularly with children.

Supplies Needed for Preparing Meals: Keep in mind that fresh food such as milk, butter, eggs, and bread, will likely be unavailable to you in an emergency. Therefore, it makes no sense to stockpile a food such as breakfast cereal unless you are prepared to eat it with water rather than milk. Similarly, prepackaged foods which require fresh or frozen ingredients to complete the recipe, are useless. Since you will be without refrigeration, food products which spoil without refrigeration should be avoided.

Expiration Dates: For those food cans and packages without an apparent "expiration" or "use before" date, use a permanent marker pen, such as a Sharpie, to print the purchase date on the lid/package. Rotate these items so that nothing gets old. Check dates periodically and donate aging food to a food bank before it gets close to the expiration date, so nothing is wasted. Keep in mind, too, that many foods can be safely eaten many years after their expiration date.

Infants: Even breastfeeding mothers should stockpile baby formula. It might be needed as stress can dry-up the flow of a mother's milk. If you find that you don't need the baby formula, donate it to a food bank before the expiration date.

Pet Food: If you have pets, be sure to store food for them, too. Contrary to conventional wisdom, most dry dog food (kibble) has a shelf life of only 6 months, whereas cans of dog food can last 2 years. Select pet foods that tolerate extended storage, and serve it to your animals now, so they are conditioned to eating it.

Cooking: In addition to stockpiling food, don't forget that you will need a liquid fuel or propane camp stove, along with sufficient fuel. In an emergency, you may not have electrical power or natural gas. So, acquire a camp stove and learn how to use it. Store extra fuel in a safe place with your stove. (For details, see Chapter-22.)

Caution: Camp stoves need adequate ventilation. This is needed to avoid carbon monoxide poisoning.

Food Storage Containers: As you expand your inventory of stored food, purchase airtight, insect and rodent-proof food containers for dry foods, and add other types of food (freeze-dried, dehydrated, retort packaged, vacuum packed, etc.) to this larder, to create your long shelf life emergency food supply.

Many canned goods only have a shelf life of a year or two, but dry beans, rice, grains, and a few other staples will last more than 30-years if properly stored. Note: Mylar bags and even heavy-duty 5-gallon plastic food pails with omega lids, are not rodent- proof.

Store your food in steel containers. Mylar bags are great for re-packaging bulk foods into more use-friendly sizes, and for extending the shelf life of foods such as rice, beans and other dry goods. But, since they aren't rodent-proof, we recommend storing Mylar bags and other packaged food items, in a steel drum or new galvanized trash can (sealed and well labeled, to avoid accidental disposal).

Oddly, if using 1-gallon Mylar bags for your food storage (recommended), a 55-gallon steel barrel will often hold as much as 2-1/2x more than a standard galvanized trash can (35-gallons). Either way, don't forget to put the container on a wheeled dolly, or make other provisions for moving it if the need arises.

Indispensable information on storing meat, and all foods containing fats, oils, nuts, or natural vegetable acids.

Meat and fish: None of the food storage technologies available to the general public are adequate for reliable long-term (20+ years) storage of meat or fish. None.

Even lean meat contains enough fat to cause the food to go rancid after a few years. This includes foods which claim to be suitable for long-term storage such as retort and foil packed meats and fish, metal cans and glass jars; anything containing meat, fish, oil, or fat. This also includes pre-packaged meals which include freeze-dried meat, pemmican and native recipes touted as being able to last forever, and dehydrated meat such as beef jerky—even salted meat. Don't be fooled by the hype. All of these methods are prone to spoilage. Even properly-packaged "survival" meat will start to spoil in 5-years.

Meat substitutes: This is why meat substitutes such as tofu and textured vegetable protein have become so popular for long-term food storage. If you want the taste of meat, these are your best alternative for long-term storage.

Shelf life: As with everything, there are exceptions, but 5-years is typically the maximum for safe storage of any food item which contains real meat or fish. If you want to include meat in your emergency food larder, rotate it regularly to keep your supply fresh.

Ordinary canned meat such as found in your local grocery store, will typically begin to spoil when it has been in the can for more than 2-3 years. Therefore, if you are buying canned goods, particularly beef, chicken, pork or chicken, be sure to purchase it from a store that frequently turns over its inventory. The food on the shelf of a small grocery store may have already been sitting on the shelf for more than a year, so keep this in mind when you shop for your emergency supplies.

Add the purchase date to your cans and food packages: Since date codes are sometimes difficult to decipher, mark the purchase date on the can/package using a black-ink permanent marker such as a Sharpie.

We need fat in our diet: It's a surprise to many, but to remain healthy our diet needs to include fats. Rotation of our supply of foods which contain meats and oils is the easiest way to meet this need. Either way, check the labels. Fat is essential for health, but products which contain fat have a shorter shelf life.

Extending shelf life: Regardless of the type of food or packaging, food stored in a cool, dry location will typically extend the product's shelf life. Food stored in metal cans or foil pouches, Mylar bags, or glass jars, will last far longer than foods packaged in plastic, including vacuum-packed plastic bags and omega buckets.

Culprits that reduce shelf life: Heat, freezing temperatures, temperature fluctuations, moisture, high humidity, exposure to sharp objects or rough handling, dented cans or damaged packaging, are factors which typically reduce the shelf life of stored food products. Failing to avoid any of these factors can reduce shelf life of your food by 75%.

Eating past-date canned food: If your choice is starvation or eating old canned goods, personally I'd take the chance and cautiously evaluate each container and eat what appears to be safe.

While doing research for this book, I learned from one of the largest food banks in the United States, that they have tested old canned foods. Their research results indicate that it is not unusual for properly stored foods that are as much as 50-years old, to be safe.

They do not intend to publish this information. This is because storage conditions and proper inspection of the cans, is so critical to safety. Plus, liability and the concern that the general public will not exercise sound judgment, are why they won't publish this information. Nevertheless, for us, this is useful to keep in mind.

This lines-up with my own personal experience. During a field operation that lasted far longer than expected, my team and I ran out of MREs. So, we needed to scavenge for food. Fortunately, one of our contacts had access to a long-neglected military storage bunker. In a cool dark corner, we found boxes of old U.S. military C-Rations. We were hungry, so we gave them a try. Even though these foods were canned at the end of World War II, they tasted fine. We found everything but the crackers to be edible. Even though they were manufactured long before some of us were born, no one became ill.

Be willing to operate outside your comfort zone: During an emergency situation, we are often forced to do things we are uncomfortable with doing. This doesn't mean that we should engage in risky behavior, but it does mean that it might be necessary for us to do things we wouldn't ordinarily do. This includes eating food we don't like to eat.

Once during a major disaster, our security team was sent into the field, supplied with cases of fresh MREs. But by some administrative REMF mistake, each case of food contained the same meal. Exactly the same.

We had plenty of food; enough for three meals a day – but we were eating the same meal for breakfast, lunch, and dinner. We weren't going hungry, and we didn't get sick, but we did get sick of eating beef stroganoff.

Fortunately, we were able to scavenge some fresh food from a hotel's kitchen. Unfortunately, it was a vegetable that I have detested my entire life—cauliflower. What I discovered was that absent other options, within a few days I was actually enjoying it because it added variety.

To this day, I periodically eat cauliflower. It's still not a favorite food, but it's amazing how opinions can change when we are hungry or no longer spoiled by the luxury of having many food options.

Children: Regrettably, though this is often the reaction of adults, it does not always happen with children. Young people, especially toddlers, can remain finicky and may literally starve themselves to death rather than eat food they don't like. The old adage, "they will eat when they get hungry enough," is not true. Keep this in mind with your food planning.

Use discernment. When there is no other option than old cans of meat, fish, and acidic vegetables, be willing to operate outside your comfort zone. But don't just eat, eat after you have evaluated your options and measured the risk.

Inspect each can before you eat from it. If a past-date can or foil pouch is intact and shows no evidence of swelling, the food it contains may still be safe to eat and savory, but before you enjoy your meal, conduct a test.

The Risk of Food Spoilage:
How-to test old cans of food before eating the contents.

Step 1: Before opening, inspect the can for bulging, damage, and rust that may have penetrated the can. (Surface rust is okay.) If it has a paper or plastic label, remove it so you can inspect the entire can.

Step 2: If the container is intact, add a small amount of pure water to the top of the can's lid and tilt it toward the place where the can opener will penetrate it. Position the can opener so that it penetrates the metal can under the water that is trapped by the rim. Then, as you puncture the lid, watch and listen.

If the water does not bubble, and you did not hear a "hiss" indicating that pressure was released, the food may be safe to eat. Rotting food often emits gasses which build-up pressure in the can, so the lack of a telltale hiss is an encouraging indicator. (This technique only works on canned goods or foil pouches. It is not applicable to food which is in home-canned glass jars.)

Step 3: After removing the lid from the can (or opening the foil package), inspect it visually, and then smell it. If the food looks and smells normal, pour it out onto a plate or clean plastic bag, and examine it and give it the sniff-test, again.

Step 4: If it looks and smells like it should, then take a small bite. If you discover that it looks, smells, *and* tastes normal, the food may be safe to eat. But, if there is even a hint of an odd odor or foul taste, don't eat it.

When in doubt but still determined to eat, consume a small amount. Before eating the rest of the food, wait 2-4 hours to make sure you don't feel queasy or ill. It can take as long as 24-hours for the effects of food poisoning to develop, but it's unlikely anyone is going to wait that long to proceed. So be aware of the risk.

Don't eat more than one questionable container of food at a time. After eating one can of food, wait several hours before indulging in another. If the food does turn out to be unsafe and it does make you ill, limiting your intake may help moderate the impact of food poisoning.

In such unenviable circumstances such as these, eating is a danger, but if starvation is the alternative it may be worth the risk. It's a judgment call.

Don't make the decision using your stomach. Use your head.

This is a decision made even more difficult because one can of food may be safe, while another can that looks identical may contain unhealthy bacteria or dangerous toxins. Therefore, evaluate each container individually before eating the food.

Food poisoning can cause a mild and inconvenient problem such as a bout of diarrhea or upset stomach, but it can also develop into a severe health risk. Even getting mildly ill during an emergency situation can be dangerous as it reduces your mobility and mental acuity. Don't take unnecessary risks.

Added Risk - Acidic Vegetables, Fruits and Foods: Even relatively bland foods such as spaghetti or tomato soup contain acid. Alkaline foods, such as lemons and grapefruit, can also be a problem. These foods tend to have a much shorter shelf life because they can interact with the metal of the can itself. As a result, products which contain tomatoes, the prime offender, tend to have a much shorter shelf life. Therefore, don't include them in your emergency food larder unless you rotate these items frequently.

Fortunately, the new canning methods which utilize a chemical liner bonded to the inside of the metal can, will extend the shelf life. Nonetheless, a manufacturing error or dent which exposes the food to the metal of the can may still result in acid etching and contamination.

Unlined and improperly lined cans will, over time, be damaged from the inside out by certain foods. As a result, the exterior of the can may look fine, but the food inside it may still be spoiled and unsafe to eat. So, an intact, normal-looking, un-swollen can, is not a guarantee that the food is safe to eat.

Nonetheless, if you have not eaten for several days, don't automatically reject old cans of food just because they are old, discolored, or the label is damaged or missing. Just use reasonable caution, these safety tips, and common sense. Evaluate the food containers and the food contained in them, before you eat it.

Note on BPA and food: Many companies which can food, coat the inside metal of the can with "Bisphenol A" (BPA). They do this to help the food remain fresh, longer. Tests conducted by the U.S. Food and Drug Administration (FDA) find this material safe for use in canned foods, but there is evidence which suggests that it may be unhealthy. Regardless of your position on this controversy, BPA lined cans do extend the shelf life of the can's contents. It is for this reason that nearly ¾ of U.S. food companies use this material to line the inside of their metal food cans. If you want to avoid BPA, you will need to research which companies and products don't use this type of liner. But, you may be escaping from one danger only to land on another; reduced shelf life.

Evaluating Popular Emergency Foods and Long-Term Food Storage Options

Grocery-Store Canned Foods and Foil-Packed Foods

Pros: These foods are inexpensive in comparison to MREs and freeze-dried food, and quality canned good tend to taste better. And, since many of us routinely eat grocery-store canned food, this makes it possible to keep your diet as normal as possible during an emergency situation. This makes it a simple task to keep your stored food fresh, too. (If you make it a practice to eat the oldest items first). Canned foods are often higher in Calories; this is a benefit as during an emergency situation you may need extra energy.

Cons: Canned foods which contain acidic ingredients, such as soup or chili which include tomatoes, will usually have a shorter shelf life because the acid interacts with the metal of the can. Though glass jars are not durable like metal cans, they are better for storing acidic foods—as long as they are stored upright and the contents are not in contact with the metal lid. Also, prepared foods such as soup, contain a lot of water making the weight/nutrition benefit very low. Similarly, prepared foods which include a gravy or sauce, are also heavy if you find it necessary to transport them.

At the very least, test the various brands of canned vegetables and fruit, and select those products which do not contain unnecessary liquid that you will discard. If you include canned food in your GO-Bag or vehicle-based evacuation supplies, this added water-weight quickly becomes significant.

U.S. Military MREs, aka "Meals, Ready-to-Eat"

Designed originally for the armed forces of the U.S. military, "Meal, Ready-to-Eat" food, more commonly referred to as MREs, are now available in the civilian market. These quick and easy meals meet the need for a short-term emergency food supply, and the 24+ menus offer great variety and entrée choices that meet the needs of meat lovers, vegetarians, and those with some food allergies.

However, MREs are bulky, and it is a surprise to many that they have a very limited "official" shelf life. Nevertheless, there are many advantages provided by including MREs in your emergency food larder. Especially worth noting is that a hot, nutritious meal can be ready in five minutes if the water-activated disposable heater is used to prepare the meal.

HDR (Humanitarian Dailey Rations) are similar to MREs in the appearance of the package, but that is where the similarity ends. These meals are packaged in a salmon-color plastic pouch, and are designed to meet the survival needs of people who are modestly malnourished and inactive, living in a refugee camp. This nutritional goal is very different from that of an MRE which is designed for warriors who are operating in a war zone.

HDRs contain no meat products or animal by-products, and meals are regionally spiced and grain oriented, such as bean salad, barley stew, rice with tomatoes, beans with potatoes, or pasta with tomato sauce. Each package contains two meals which together total at least 2,200 calories; 10-13% protein, 27-30% fat, and not less than 60% carbohydrates.

MRE Pros: The U.S. military has undertaken extensive research to develop the optimal food for combat troops operating in the field. Civilian versions of these pre-packaged meals are available from the same manufacturers that make these meals for the government, but care must be exercised to make sure you are purchasing a meal that is equivalent to the MREs made for the U.S. Government. Terms of military contracts prohibit manufacturers from selling the exact same item to the general public, but most produce a variation that is reasonably comparable.

Each U.S. military MRE contains approximately 1,200 Calories of food which has been fortified with vitamins and other nutrients. White envelope MREs are designed for cold weather and to provide more Calories.

Each MRE is a complete meal, including condiments, dessert, powdered drink, and even a hand wipe and bit of toilet paper. MRE meals do not include water.

Since these meals are already hydrated and precooked, they can be eaten directly from the package without any food preparation. However, disposable flameless-heaters which are water activated (sometimes sold separately), are designed to heat the entrée in 5-minutes, thereby providing a quick, hot meal.

With more than two dozen menu selections, including vegetarian, MREs have become popular for emergency food storage. MREs or similar are what the U.S. government generally distributes to disaster victims, both in the U.S. and abroad.

Companies which produce MREs for the U.S. Government are: Sopakco (Sure-Pak 12), Ameriqual (APack), and Wornick (Eversafe). These companies are not allowed to sell the actual military MREs to civilians, so they produce a civilian version that is similar. If you find military MREs in the marketplace they may have been stolen or discarded as past the shelf life date.

Cons: The full MRE meal packet is bulky and heavier than dehydrated or freeze-dried backpacking food, but since these meals don't require any food preparation, they remain popular. Soldiers and civilians seeking to reduce weight and bulk, often separate the entrée and flameless heater from the other contents of the heavy plastic envelope, and carry only the items from the meal which they like. This practice defeats the balanced nutrition provided by consuming the entire meal, but the convenience often overrules this negative. Since this practice has become so commonplace, the entrée and heater portions of the MRE meal can now be purchased separately.

When consuming the entrée-only for multiple days, or the complete MRE meal for more than two weeks, constipation is likely. Therefore, a MRE diet needs to be augmented with high-fiber food supplements such as high-fiber meal-replacement food bars.

Though MRE meals are incredibly convenient and reasonably tasty, they are expensive. When purchased in a case of 12-meals, the cost is typically $7.50 per meal (for true military-specification MREs). Be cautious as the marketplace is full of counterfeit MREs. Even the three "authorized" manufacturers of military MREs, produce lower-quality or abbreviated meals, so look at the specifications before you make your purchase.

MRE meals may be safe to eat for 20-years, but shelf life is only listed as 3-years because nutritional values tend to decline after this period. In the civilian market, many of the MREs are past the shelf life date. For more on MREs and expiration date codes, see Chapter-10 and Appendix-B.

Military meals produced by other governments, ostensibly the same as MREs, are reportedly not the same. We have not tested MRE-like products manufactured in a country other than the USA.

Freeze-Dried Food

Freeze-dried foods are available in single-serving meals which are recommended for GO-Bags containing food for 5+ days (Appendix-A), as well as in bulk #10 cans and 5-gallon pails. It's relatively expensive per serving but does deliver tasty meals that rival fresh food.

Approximately the same size as a 3-lb can of coffee, a #10 can of freeze-dried food provides economies of scale, and a quantity of food that can generally be used before the contents of the open can begins to spoil. The purchase of #10 cans is the recommended quantity for family-size meals, and for packing pre-prepared do-it-yourself (DIY) meals in heavy-duty Mylar bags.

If left unopened, cases of #10 cans of freeze-dried foods are ideal for most long-term food storage needs. The 5-gallon bucket (pail) quantity is only useful for large families or groups, or for do-it-yourself packing parties where it is divided and distributed among several families for Mylar-bag storage, because an open container is susceptible to spoilage. The long shelf life only applies to an unopened can.

Pros: Using a process originally designed by NASA for the Apollo space missions, freeze-dried food is made by sublimating fresh food in a three-stage process; flash freezing, heat evaporation under vacuum, and then packed with nitrogen to displace any air that remains. These foods are incredibly lightweight and do not require refrigeration or any special handling.

Once reconstituted with water and cooked, these foods retain much of the fresh taste, color, and aroma of frozen food. With nearly 98% of the water removed before packaging, the weight of the food is reduced by 90% compared to fresh food. Since quality manufacturers vacuum pack their foods in Mylar bags, foil packets, or specially designed cans, the flavors, textures, and nutritional values are retained and standard recipes can be used for meal preparation.

Quality manufacturers such a 'Mountain House' boast a shelf life of 7-years for their backpacking meals, and 25-years for food which the factory packs in #10 cans. For these reasons, freeze-dried food has long been a favorite of wilderness backpackers, so manufacturers routinely pack their foods both in bulk quantities and in pouches of almost-ready-to-eat complete meals. These meals are considerably more expensive than the bulk food, but they are convenient and therefore ideal for long-duration GO-Bags (see Appendix-A).

Eggs and even ice cream can be freeze-dried, so this process offers a great deal of food variety. Five-gallon buckets lined with Mylar bags filled with freeze-dried food are also available. The freeze-drying process, the use of lined #10 cans, coupled with the oxygen removal / nitrogen flushing process, also helps retain the nutritional value of the food better than any other process. So, selecting food packed in #10 cans is the best option unless you're making meals for a large group.

Cons: Food packages labeled as "Serves 2" are generally only sufficient for one person. Pound-for-pound, freeze-dried prepackaged meals are typically the most expensive emergency food. Since re-hydration and cooking is required, pure water and a stove (and time), are needed for food preparation. Individual meals can often be prepared by pouring hot water into the foil packaging, but bulk foods need cookware.

Unfortunately, once the package is opened the storage life drops quickly, so #10 cans are often a better choice even for families. Just as with MREs, freeze-dried foods have a reduced shelf life if exposed to temperature fluctuations and high ambient temperatures. The foil pouches used for backpacking meals are often not sufficiently durable, so when transporting in a Go-Bag, protect the foil package by inserting it into a Hefty Slider freezer bag or similar plastic bag. Unlike MREs which utilize a disposable heater, freeze-dried foods require a cook stove and pot for preparation.

Despite the claims of manufacturers, due to the fat and oils in meat and fish, even when freeze-dried, these foods start to break down and begin to spoil after about five years. For this reason, it is best to purchase products which contain meat-flavored tofu or vegetable protein so that the long shelf life can be maintained.

Dehydrated Food

Dehydrated foods differ from freeze-dried in that the moisture is removed by standard drying processes which utilize heat and evaporation. Because of this, dehydrated foods are often far less expensive than freeze-dried.

Many foods can be dehydrated at home using simple methods and relatively inexpensive equipment. Unfortunately, dehydrated foods do not retain the natural food flavors nearly as well as commercial freeze-drying techniques. Nevertheless, the best of both worlds can be obtained by adding a small amount of freeze-dried food, such as a vegetable, to a much larger quantity of dehydrated food or dry food such as rice and beans. Using this technique, low-cost foods can be used to develop tasty meals.

Pros: Less costly than freeze-dried food, and sometimes even cheaper than fresh food, dehydrated foods are a cost-efficient alternative to freeze dried. Commercial dehydration works better on some foods than others, so experimentation is advised before you purchase any food item in quantity. Dehydrated mashed potatoes (flakes and powder), puddings, peanut butter, pancake and bread mix, and vegetables and fruits designed to be added to a meal as a supplement, are the most popular dehydrated foods. Though not as nutricious as fresh or freeze-dried food, dehydrated foods still maintain decent taste and adequate nutrition.

Cons: Though less expensive, even professionally produced dehydrated foods have less than half the shelf life than freeze-dried foods. Only meticulous amateurs and professional manufacturers can produce dehydrated foods which have a stable, long shelf life. Homemade dehydrated foods such as apples, bananas, and apricots, rarely have a shelf life longer than two years.

Even with professionally dehydrated foods, over time, the nutritional value declines, textures change, and taste diminishes. For those dehydrated foods requiring reconstitution with water before eating, some do not fully rehydrate, which makes the food less palatable. However, dehydrated foods such as potato flakes can be used to make delicious mashed potatoes after many years if properly packaged, or repackaged into Mylar bags with oxygen absorbers. Before purchasing any of these foods in quantity, do your own taste test as both quality and taste vary widely between manufacturers.

Even after repackaging these foods in Mylar bags with oxygen absorbers, dehydrated foods such as vegetables should be replaced every 8-10 years.

As with most food, meal preparation using dehydrated food requires the use of a stove and cook pot. Some freeze-dried foods can be eaten cold after adding tepid water to rehydrate the food, but most dehydrated foods require hot water to reconstitute the food.

Dry Food Staples, aka "Staple Foods"
Rice, dry beans, pasta, potato flakes, wheat berries, flour, dry food-grade corn, sugar, salt, etc.

When bought in bulk at a restaurant supply store, long-lasting dry foods can be repackaged at home using Mylar bags. This do-it-yourself method is easy, but it does require the addition of oxygen absorbing packets before sealing. These absorbers, combined with the metalized "Mylar" pouch, is what makes this method viable for long-term food storage (20+ years).

For more on the do-it-yourself Mylar-bag method, download the free instructional PDF on Mylar packaging of food and gear. It is available on the "Resources" page of the author's website: www.SIGSWANSTROM.com.

Note: We do not recommend the use of plastic, including 5-gallon food-grade buckets, as they do not provide adequate protection against rodents.

Storing "dry food staples" represents the most economical way to prepare a long-term food supply and a simple do-it-yourself method for making your own GO-Bag foods. However, these foods alone do not provide adequate nutrition, plus they are uninteresting to eat.

As you include these staples in your food larder, we also recommend that you add recipes which feature these specific foods, and that you stockpile the ingredients needed to make these meals. Other food products such as freeze-dried vegetables which can be used to change flavors and textures, as well as spices, condiments, sauces, and gravy mixes should also be included in your emergency food larder.

An easy and excellent addition to these dry staples is freeze-dried vegetables, fruits, meats, soy products, eggs, and condiments. These can be purchased in large #10 cans from various "survival foods" vendors. Keep them sealed until needed. Sauces made from fresh foods and dehydrated condiments can also be used to transform a meal consisting of dry-food staples into a savory feast.

For those willing to tackle a simple do-it-yourself project, heavy-duty Mylar bags can be used to prepare your own backpacking-style prepared meals for GO-Bags. These can also be used for long-term food storage stockpiles of quick-to-prepare meals.

For these GO-Bag and quick-to-prepare meals, use a Mylar bag that is large enough also to hold the boiling water that will be needed to hydrate the food. This eliminates the need for cleaning a cook pot. Note: With this method, since the Mylar bag is larger than the single-meal quantity of dry food staples it contains, you will need to use extra oxygen absorbing packets. Remember to remove these packets before you prepare your food.

Pros: When considered by weight and space, dry food staples provide a lot of food per dollar spent, and they require little space for storage. When stored in airtight, food-quality, insect-proof and rodent-proof containers such as heavy-duty Mylar bags, most dry foods naturally have a long shelf life. However, this can be extended by inserting oxygen absorbing packets into the bag before it is heat-sealed. Stored using this simple oxygen-removal technique, and in the proper containers, many dry staple foods can be safely stored for 20-30 years or more.

Cons: Since these dry staple foods require water to hydrate and cook, you must increase your water supply accordingly. Having sufficient water for drinking is more important than using water for food preparation. Yet, consuming dry foods, including cereal, without first hydrating them, can cause serious health problems.

Once water has been added to dry food, it must be eaten soon, as it will spoil quickly without refrigeration. Therefore, only prepare the quantity of food you intend to consume at that meal.

Many dry staple foods do not need to be cooked before eating, but they are generally unpalatable if they have not been heated. So, cooking equipment should be considered essential.

Since most people will only eat dry staple foods after adding a sauce (spaghetti sauce, etc.), gravy, spices, or combining the food stable with other foods to make the meal more interesting, supplemental foods are necessary. Alone, these foods do not constitute the ingredients required to produce a complete meal.

Also, some dry foods such as Raman-Noodle "meal" packets, will quell hunger but they do not have enough nutritional value to constitute a healthy meal. Flavorings may make food tasty, but do not add nutrition. So, as you assemble recipes which use these dry foods, also check the nutritional value of the meal you plan to prepare.

Don't forget that meal preparation requires a functioning stove, fuel for it, cook pots, plus utensils and measuring cups/spoons, plates, etc. A basic cook stove such as one of the Coleman multi-fuel "Guide Series" camp stoves, is not food but it should nevertheless be stored with your emergency food larder.

Retort-Packaged Milk Products

Pros: For milk which more closely resembles fresh milk in taste, ultrahigh-temperature pasteurized milk stored in retort packaging, is the answer. Non-fat cow milk stores better than low-fat milk, but rice and soy milk have a longer shelf life. Since many grocery stores do not stock these items, they must be purchased from a vendor such as Walton Feed (WaltonFeed.com) or from Ready Made Resources (www.ReadyMadeResources.com).

Cons: Though the taste of these milk products is better than powdered milk, the taste is nowhere close to its fresh counterpart, so many people will not want to use these products routinely. For most consumers, these milk products will work in recipes, and maybe on cereal, but may not be desirable for drinking. Unfortunately, the shelf life is only 6-months, but it can be extended if unopened and refrigerated.

Note: Dehydrated milk, also known as dry milk or powdered milk, also has a short shelf life. However, retort-packaged (liquid) milk tastes better and is easier to use in cooking. Yet, the dry version is lighter in weight and more compact.

Home-Canned Food ("Glass Jar Meals" / "Ball Jar" Canning)

Home canned goods can be nutritious, less expensive to stockpile, and they are an essential component for on-going and long-term food storage when you have access to fresh vegetables and other foods. Even meat can be canned in glass jars.

However, since the shelf life varies due to the equipment used and the skill of the canner, this topic cannot be addressed briefly. What is relevant to the scope of this book is that it can be risky to depend on food stored in glass if there is any chance that the food supply will need to be moved from one location to another.

Pros: Home canning provides the same ease-of-use benefits as grocery store metal-can foods, but home-canned food can be far more nutritious and still low cost. Unlike the prepared foods purchased from a grocery store, you can be confident in the contents of your home canned foods. Also, when you grow and store your own food, you can avoid unhealthy GMOs, chemical pesticides, growth hormones, dioxins, MSG, and other substances found in commercially produced foods.

If you use vegetables grown from heirloom seeds and free-range meats, your home-canned food can be fresher, more nutritious, and far more healthy than what you can buy in a grocery store. This method makes it possible to store individual foods, and also to create complete meals-in-a-jar spiced to your taste, and storing them without refrigeration.

If the food you 'can' is grown from true heirloom seeds, and canned without unhealthy additives, it can be the healthiest do-it-yourself method for ongoing food storage; additionally so, since the jars can be reused.

More types of food can be stored safely in glass than in a metal can or Mylar bag. Glass is generally the safest canning medium. It is also one that makes it possible to inspect the food before opening it.

Cons: Food cleaning and preparation is time consuming, and sanitation and proper canning methods must be strictly monitored to ensure safety and stability. Home canning is generally accomplished using glass jars, so the food supply is more susceptible to breakage. Proper storage is essential. Transportation of food canned in glass jars is problematic.

When opened, glass jars should emit a distinct sound indicating a release of the vacuum seal. If the glass jar opens silently, the food may be spoiled. Extra lids are needed for repeated re-canning, but this added cost is minimal. Meals may require a stove and pot.

Lifeboat Rations (aka/ Aviation Rations, Survival Rations)

Lifeboat rations are not suitable for long-term use as a supply of food, but they are a valuable addition to your GO-Bag or for storage in a vehicle. Be sure to select a brand that is labeled as "U.S. Coast Guard Approved," and make sure the foil packaging is intact. Even a pinhole in the foil can reduce the product's shelf life, or provide an entry point for insects or contamination.

Pros: Lightweight and inexpensive, these are the most compact of all the emergency foods. Despite the low cost, these food-bar rations are an amazingly complete nutritionally-rich on-the-go meal.

Unlike most sports bars and meal replacement bars, these rations do not increase thirst. They are also more durable than sports bars and meal replacement bars, and they have a much longer shelf life. For many years, these rations have been a Coast Guard-required component in the survival kit packed into the lifeboats of large ships.

These compressed food bricks are vacuum packed in durable foil, which gives an unopened ration a 5-year shelf life. Unlike other emergency foods, these rations retain most of their nutritional value even after exposure to temperature extremes.

The most popular and palatable brands are: "Mainstay" and "Datrex." The manufacturer of Mainstay Rations claims a formulation that is also designed for more active, land-based survival needs.

A 9-meal packet of Mainstay is inexpensive, requires only the space of a paperback novel, and weighs a modest 24-ounces. Each pre-measured meal cube offers 400 Calories of nutrition. Rations are available in 400-Calorie, 1,200, 2,400, and 3,600-Calorie packets. This can make purchasing a challenge as the buyer must be careful to secure the desired size packet.

Whichever brand you purchase, make sure it is fresh and that it has been approved for use by the U.S. Coast Guard. (Coast Guard approval is like a Good Housekeeping seal-of-approval for this type of food ration). At least one packet of these rations is a prudent addition to every GO-Bag as they can eaten when you're on the move, or when other provisions have been exhausted. For more, see Chapter-10. No stove or heating is required for these food cubes.

Cons: The taste and texture is acceptable but unappealing, and these bars (or cubes) are not stomach filling, but they do provide short-term emergency sustenance better than energy bars or meal replacement bars. However, since they lack fiber, they can cause constipation if not eaten with other foods. Though the taste is acceptable, these meal cubes will not make you look forward to your next meal, so you may need to discipline yourself to eat because you must. If given any other option, these rations are not suitable for long-term use. True, they have kept many inactive sailors alive after more than a month floating in a lifeboat on the sea, but these rations lack many essential micronutrients and fiber which are needed for an active life and robust health.

Tasty Food is a Necessity

Meal preparation needs to involve more than a quest for balanced meals and nutrition. It also needs to include solutions for making meals more tasty, refreshing, and enjoyable.

This may seem unimportant and out of place in this guidebook, but it is actually a necessary inclusion. In high stress or challenging times, it is almost essential to be able to make mealtime enjoyable. Well chosen *simple* recipes which introduce variety through the use of available spices, condiments, sauces, gravies, and other flavor-enhancing and variety-producing foodstuffs, can be a godsend.

Food, particularly uninteresting dry goods such as rice and beans, as well as repetitive foods such as a fresh garden vegetable that is currently available in abundance, need to be transformed into nutritious, balanced, *enjoyable* meals. This need must be incorporated into your planning.

This is particularly true for Americans and others who enjoy a plethora of food options; a blessing which makes unappealing foods, or the repetitive consumption of the same food, a factor which can lead to skipping meals or undereating. This, in turn, results in diminished energy, melancholy, depression, and eventually despondency.

A warm, savory meal is not only beneficial for health and restoring energy, but it is also helpful for maintaining emotional well-being, reinvigorating the psyche, and restoring hope. This can often be accomplished by sitting down and calmly enjoying a tasty meal.

Ideally, you will utilize various spices for flavor, and a small quantity of bulk-purchased freeze-dried vegetables and/or meat to your larder, too, as these foods will provide added nutrition.

Understanding Long-Term Food Storage Needs

When planning for a food supply designed to provide food for more than 2-4 weeks, additional planning and a variety of foods are required to meet nutritional needs.

Further, whole grains such as wheat, corn, and oats will require a hand-crank grain mill, but it is these whole-grain foods that last the longest. Remember too, that having baking soda and yeast are helpful as they are used for baking.

Salt has many uses in addition to adding flavor to food. This includes using it to preserve foods as well as for many medical purposes, plus it can be used to attract game animals. It is also a useful commodity for barter. Therefore, a large quantity of salt should be included in a larder containing long-term food supplies.

> For a day or two, not eating nutritionally balanced food may not be a big deal. However, after three days we need to be diligent about eating balanced meals. Research conducted by the U.S. military indicates that an active person needs to consume 3,750 Calories per day (more if working outdoors in cold weather), and these Calories should be 13% protein, 51% carbohydrates, and 36% fat.

Honey, cinnamon, turmeric, and certain spices add flavor to food, and they also provide medicinal benefits. Certain other spices, like cayenne pepper, can be used for other purposes such as encouraging animals to stay out of your vegetable garden.

Note: *Fats and oils are essential to health. In a protracted emergency situation, each adult will need approximately 96-pounds of fat or fatty oils per year. This equates to about 17-gallons per person, yet most freeze-dried, dehydrated, and long-term food storage, contain almost no fats or oil. You need to make provisions for this need. And, you need to rotate these supplies often, to avoid spoilage, because fats and oils have a short shelf life.*

Long-term food storage requires extra planning, as does gardening. These subjects are outside the scope of this book. For these topics, refer to Book-4 in this series.

You *do* need to plan for longer-term food storage, but these supplies should be stockpiled at a safe-haven retreat location—not at an urban or suburban dwelling. At your metro-area home, it is usually adequate to store 2-weeks of food for you and your family, plus extra for needy friends and neighbors.

Why? Because if your neighbors are without food for an extended period, it is unlikely that you will be able to live safely in that environment. When hungry, ordinarily "good" people will become criminals, stealing food and other supplies. Recent events have shown this again and again. So, it isn't necessary to have a long-term food supply at your home.

You can't feed an entire community, or even a neighborhood for months or even weeks. Therefore, if the emergency situation might become protracted, it is essential to get out of town early. This why your long-term emergency food larder needs to be maintained at your safe-haven retreat location—not at your home.

Various plants and fruits, such as the Moringa tree, are low maintenance yet provide many health and independent living benefits. The leaves of a Moringa tree provide complex nutrients, and the tree can also supply you with therapeutic oils, and even cooking and lubrication oils. The seeds can even help with water purification. Trees and plants such as this can be planted at your safe-haven retreat. (Chapter-14)

Comfort Foods: Coffee, tea, sugar, and chocolate syrup are not essential, but nevertheless important. Don't forget to include foods and "treats" like hard candy which have a long shelf life.

Everyone has a different idea as to what constitutes a comfort food, so this can't be adequately addressed here except to affirm that the inclusion of these foods is worthwhile as they can help normalize life during difficult times.

Food Related Products: Aluminum foil has scores of uses, as do Mylar bags and canning jars. Even if you aren't into canning, a supply of Ball jars with extra lids, is a good investment.

Gardens: Since you don't know how long a widescale emergency will last, plant a vegetable garden at your home and at your retreat location. This will give you fresh, nutritious food today, and it will help you gain skills that may be essential in the future.

Be prepared with the heirloom seeds and gardening supplies you will need to plant a garden to augment your food supply. The website: TexasReady.net contains a wealth of useful information. You will need sprout seeds (short-term), and heirloom seeds (long-term), gardening equipment and supplies, and a few reference books.

Summary of long-term food storage considerations

Due to the lower cost, most families will want to store nearly all bulk grains, legumes, peanut butter, honey, and other bulk foods in dehydrated form. These foods should *not* be stored in plastic buckets. Even food-grade buckets are not rodent-proof. Therefore, store food in steel containers with tight-fitting lids. Plastic containers, no matter how substantial they appear to be, are not rodent safe.

It is generally better to store these food supplies in Mylar bags, which in turn, should be stored in steel drums, or at least steel trash cans. Before these bags are heat-sealed, they need to be flushed with nitrogen, or an oxygen absorbing packet needs to be added before the container is sealed.

This is best accomplished by a reputable supplier who specializes in vacuum packed food for long-term storage. However, for those who are more budget minded, do-it-yourself methods, using food-grade Mylar bags, are easy to accomplish. For instruction on this do-it-yourself topic, visit the "Resources" page on the author's website.

To make basic foods such as rice and beans more palatable, store a smaller quantity of freeze-dried vegetables, fruits, and meats, and also spices with your staples. Use these as supplementary foods to make your meals more interesting and nutritious. Review recipes, and purchase cookbooks designed for these foods to help you select supplemental foods and spices to include in your larder.

Reference materials such as cookbooks should be stored with your food, after protecting them in either plastic freezer bag (minimal protection) or in Mylar bags with desiccant (better protection).

Desiccant packets can be purchased online or at supply stores which serve the medical community, gun stores, large sporting goods stores, or at electronics supply outlets. Remember to label each package of food with a description of the food the bag contains, date, and the weight and volume (ex. 4-cups) of the food. Cover the label with packing tape or some other method to ensure it remains legible. You'll probably find that it's easier to label the bag before you fill it.

Food Planning Summary: Step-by-Step

First, prepare food for your GO-Bag (Chapter-10) as well as 2+ weeks of independent living at home during an emergency situation. Then, plan for evacuation from your home and workplace to your safe-haven retreat location. This is the scope of this book—but it is only the beginning of your emergency preparations.

Next, you need to make the necessary preparations for you, your family and friends, to live on your own, without assistance, for 6-12 months at a rural safe-haven retreat location. This may sound ridiculous, daunting, or an impossible task to accomplish, but it is a necessary component for those who are serious about long-term preparations.

The U.S. Government has made far more elaborate preparations for their senior employees, so it's probably prudent for us to prepare as well. The government's preparations for their top employees includes highly-secure safe-haven facilities and food for several years.[17]

Don't let the scope of this task impede your implementation. Like any big project, it needs to be implemented one-step at a time. Fortunately, with this need, the completion of each step provides another layer of protection. Each milestone represents a material improvement in your ability to overcome adversity.

So, once your GO-Bag and 2+ week at-home emergency supplies are stockpiled, move forward with long-term preparations. As this relates to food, first secure a one-month supply, then two, then three, and pretty soon you will reach the six-month mark. At that point, it will be a a straightforward task to make the jump to a one-year+ supply of food. Oddly, what seems like a big undertaking now, isn't nearly as hard as taking that first step toward getting ready.

It is a road less traveled that requires effort and commitment. Yet, you are embarking on a journey that is worth the effort.

If you live in an urban or suburban area, and you want to prepare for an emergency situation which may last for more than a few weeks, you will need a rural safe-haven retreat location (Chapter-4).

If you already live in a rural community where locals are reasonably self-sufficient, you may be able to stay at home longer, but you still need to be prepared for a move to a more distant, more

---

[17] Details are provided in "Prepared: Ready to Roll – Book 1 – Why Responsible People are Preparing," by SIG Swanstrom.

isolated, safe-haven. This second location is always necessary. Though your need is a bit different, you too, need site options.

Unless trapped by circumstances, it is unlikely that city dwellers and suburbanites will be able to stay in their home for more than a couple weeks after a major disaster. The reality is that even if you have water and food for a long encampment, your neighbors don't. Either willingly or by theft, your food will become their food. It will be taken from you through guilt, threat, or force. This is an unpleasant reality that must be faced. This is yet another reason why it is necessary to prepare a safe-haven at a more isolated location.

If you don't think you'll ever need these longer-term preparations, that's fine. But don't neglect the necessary preparations for a minimum of 2^+ weeks of independent living, with no outside assistance. To depending on government assistance, or receiving help from other sources, is dangerous.

If you do get help, great. However, don't expect help to arrive. Be self-reliant. Or more accurately, prepare with family and friends, and only rely on each other for assistance. You do your part; they do theirs. Together you can become a self-reliant team.

As to food storage, each type of emergency food listed in this chapter has its place in your emergency food larder. Some of these foods, such as canned foods purchased from a grocery store, are easy to use in everyday life. So, these are an excellent choice for the first level of at-home or retreat food storage.

If you can't afford to buy everything you need on your next trip to the grocery store, buy two cans of food for each family member each time you go to the store. By using this labor-free and painless preparation process, your stockpile of food can be increased to a minimal level in a few months. Start with your next trip to the store.

For long-term food storage, it's hard to beat the great taste of freeze-dried food. Unfortunately, it is expensive, so use Mylar bags to store gallon-size bags of dry staples (beans, rice, etc.). This will save you a lot of money in your day-to-day budget as well, since these items can be used in everyday life, too. It may save you from some unplanned trips to the store, as well—but don't neglect replacement.

Fortunately, it's easy. For both daily life and emergencies, it makes sense to have a combination of these on hand anyway.

When you have your 2^+ weeks of food stockpiled, skip your next trip to the store and spend a weekend eating only emergency foods.

This will help you select which foods and flavors work best for you and your family. Then, on your next trip to the store, expand and enhance your emergency food larder with the additional supplies.

Preparation is an attainable goal. You get there one step at a time. First, assemble a GO-Bag for you and each member of your household. Next, pull together your 2-week emergency food supply. Then, go back to the beginning of this book and start implementing the step-by-step plan outlined for you. In the process, don't be intimidated by the distance you need to travel to reach your preparation goal. Learn to enjoy the journey, and celebrate milestone accomplishments along the way. Your one-step-at-a-time diligence will bring you to the goal.

Chapter 16

Gun Selection and Ammunition Choices for Emergency Situations

A gun is the great equalizer. Granted, some detest the idea of using a firearm, but regardless of your political view or the legal restrictions you live under, it is desirable to have a handgun, rifle or shotgun during an emergency situation. If you can own a gun, you need one—and you need to know how to use it.

On the other hand, if you have a whole gun safe full of firearms, what will you grab if you need to run right now? If you can only bring one or two guns with you, are those ready and stored with the proper ammunition, magazines (clips) and the gun gear you'll need?

When the police are overwhelmed during a disastrous event, at that point, gangs, violent criminals, and crazed, desperate people, often prey on others. You need to be armed.

This is lamentable, but it is true, so you need to plan for this eventuality. Often downplayed by the news media to avoid panic, skyrocketing violence is commonplace during a major disaster. Unfortunately, if you are caught in such a situation, you won't be able to downplay the effect. So, you need to be ready for it.

Bottom-line: If you aren't prepared to defend yourself, you may become a victim of violence, and your careful preparations and stores of food and water may be stolen or vandalized. Even if you welcome these people into your home with loving kindness, and even if you demonstrate admirable generosity, you and your loved ones may still be brutalized or killed. Does this sound illogical to you? It is, but this is what often happens, so you need to be vigilant.

Yes, hiding is often a better choice than resorting to the use of deadly force, but at some point, that may not be enough. Despite your best efforts, at some point, you may be confronted by a situation which will result in serious harm to you or your family if you fail to respond with decisive counter-force. Whether your attacker is wielding a gun or a baseball bat, or a kitchen knife or wasp spray, a gun is the only equalizer to a threat of grievous bodily injury or death. Being a black belt in karate is useless if your attacker is 20-ft away and has his AK-47 pointed at you.

Whether you resist the idea of gun use or not, read my book, "God, Guns, and Guts of Firearm Defense: The Bible View." If after reading it you still resist gun use, or, you live in a place where that option isn't available to you, you still need to solve the "self-defense" problem. You need a solution. To ignore the problem isn't a responsible response. If you are not going to have a gun for defense, jump to the next chapter.

--- --- ---

There is a great deal of debate among gun experts as to what type of firearm is best. If you take the time to seek recommendations from friends, salesman, bloggers, YouTube videos, firearms instructors and police officers, your effort will produce more confusion.

The truth is, no single weapon is the best choice for all emergency situations. With this reality in mind, this chapter will help you identify what gun(s) is best for you and your circumstance.

Situations and conditions vary, as does the use of firearms for self-defense vs. hunting, or the combination of the two. There is no universal solution, so, in this chapter, I will provide you with the pros and cons of each type of weapon. This, and your financial and legal restrictions is the place to start.

History Lesson: Even a cursory study of the past and the history of major disasters, makes it clear that the police and other First Responders may be unavailable when needed. Expect this problem and prepare for it.

Self-reliance for defense is as important as being prepared to meet your water, food, and medical needs. Actually, more so. Those who are ill-prepared for defense can expect to fall victim to those who are willing to use violence to get what they want. Therefore, having a plan for security is an essential component of any emergency plan.

Of course, having a gun does not make you ready to defend yourself. Gun ownership is only the beginning. The need for training and regular practice with your specific gun(s) cannot be overemphasized.

License-to-Carry and Gun Laws

Whatever firearm(s) you choose, it's important to understand that a License to Carry (LTC) or a Concealed Handgun License (CHL) is necessary throughout most of the United States and most other countries. There are federal, state, and local laws which regulate firearm ownership and use. Ignorance of the law is not a defense to avoid arrest and prosecution.

Even if you do not want to carry a firearm routinely, you may want to have a gun with you during an emergency situation. So, get a license to carry a concealed handgun now if you have that option. Prepare for this possible need, in advance.

During a community-wide emergency, laws regarding firearm possession and carry are not treated the same as other violations of the law. For example, during a natural disaster, you may not be hassled for making an emergency transmission on a shortwave radio even though you don't have a license, but you may experience an aggressive arrest for violating a firearm law. During a disaster or emergency situation, expect strident enforcement of firearm laws, at least initially.

If you own a firearm suitable for defense, don't neglect training and regular practice. Knowing how to hunt, or being a sharpshooter on a gun range, is not the same as being trained for firearm self-defense.

Remember, owning a gun does not prepare you for self-defense. Importantly, if you aren't adequately trained and mentally prepared to use a weapon, it may be taken from you and used against you.

Rarely do criminals buy guns from a sporting goods stores or gun shows. Typically, they get them from dealers in stolen goods who acquire them from burglars and car thieves. These weapons were taken from good people just like you and me. Therefore, safe storage of firearms is not only necessary to protect children, but also to keep guns out of the hands of criminals.

Handgun
Pros and Cons

Handgun Benefits:

a) With concealed carry, criminals don't know that you are armed, which gives you the advantage of surprise and the option of restraint;

b) Can be concealed, so you won't be making others nervous;

c) Semi-automatic pistols typically hold more ammunition and can be reloaded quickly, whereas revolvers provide the benefit of being easy to clean and mechanically simple to operate. A revolver can even be fired from inside a purse, bag or large pocket, whereas a semi-auto pistol will usually jam in similar circumstances;

d) When compared to rifles and shotguns, handguns are relatively lightweight (12 to 42-oz) and small. Not only are they more concealable, but they can also be stored in a small locked gun-box secured inside the trunk of your car, ready to be inserted into your GO-Bag before heading out.

Handgun Disadvantages:

a) Far less accurate than a rifle;

b) Limited to short-range use, typically 20-ft for those with modest training, 75-100 ft for those who are well trained;

c) Only minimal stopping power: Unlike what you may have seen on television or in the movies, most handguns do not have immediate "knock-down" stopping power.

A handgun caliber smaller than 9mm or 38 Special is *not* adequate for self-defense. While it is true that even a tiny bullet can cause death, they lack the power to 'stop' a violent attack. There are those who will argue with me on this statement, but I've experienced this first-hand as a police officer on the streets of the Los Angeles area, as well as in urban war, robbery, and kidnappings in Central America.

d) Revolver handguns vs. pistol-style: A revolver is slow to reload, does not hold as much ammunition, and is more difficult to conceal than a modern pistol-style handgun. Whereas the downside of a semi-automatic pistol is that it requires higher quality manufacturing, better lubrication, and more thorough cleaning.

Tactical Shotgun
Pros and Cons

Also referred to as a home-defense shotgun, self-defense shotgun, riot gun, and police shotgun. All of these labels refer to the same type of firearm, a *tactical* shotgun. Tactical shotguns are different from shotguns made for target shooting or hunting purposes.

Sporting shotguns are generally longer in length and not as maneuverable, especially in confined spaces such as inside a home. Even when they are the same caliber (gauge) and chambered with the same ammunition, they are far less useful for self-defense purposes.

Shotgun Benefits:

a) Intimidating in appearance;

b) Additional intimidation created by the sound of racking (cocking) a pump-action (slide-action) shotgun;

b) Require less accuracy when shooting;

c) Devastating knock-down power (when loaded with 00-Buck shotgun shells and used at relatively close range);

d) When loaded with OO-Buck shells (ammunition), each time the gun is fired, as many as 15-pellets (.33 inches in size, nearly the same diameter as a 9mm bullet) are discharged from the gun;

e) When loaded with "buckshot" or "shotshell" ammunition, shotgun pellets are less likely to penetrate the interior walls of a home than most handgun bullets. Ex. 12 ga. 00-Buck or #4 Buckshot pellets vs. a standard 9mm FMJ pistol bullet. (The 9mm bullet can penetrate three or more interior sheetrock walls.)

f) Different types of shotgun ammunition (shells) can be loaded to meet an assortment of very different needs. There are specialty shells designed for self-defense from human attackers, while others are more suitable for defense against wild packs of dogs or other wild animals. Still others, are intended for bear and hunting large animals, and yet others for birds and small game animals. There are even less-lethal specialty ammunitions such as tear-gas and pepper-gas, aerial distress flares for signaling, and nets designed for capturing small drones. Shotgun ammunition, particularly in 12-gauge (caliber), offers more variety in type and purpose than any other kind of gun.

Shotgun Disadvantages:

a) Size is the #1 drawback, and it is a major one. Even a pistol-grip-only tactical shotgun is not concealable unless it's slung under a billowy overcoat or duster. At almost 29-inches (73cm), the Mossberg 500 JIC II is among the smallest shotguns that can be purchased without an ATF "tax stamp" license. The take-down models of the JIC II will fit into a large GO-Bag knapsack or can be attached to it using a pouch. But, a shotgun which has a shoulder stock can be shot far more accurately. Unfortunately, a shotgun such as the Remington 870 Tactical has an overall length of 38-1/2 inches (98cm). It can't be easily disassembled into two pieces as can the JIC. Yet, either can be a powerful asset at home or when transported in a vehicle, but they are too large to be carried conveniently and unobtrusively when on foot.

b) Shotguns have a reputation for having harsh recoil (kick). In reality, though the recoil is more pronounced than with a tactical rifle like an AR15, the recoil is actually manageable once the shooter has been trained to use the proper technique. In our firearm self-defense classes for families, we routinely have 12-yr old 90-pound girls become expert marksmen with 12-ga tactical shotguns. Yet, the fear-factor persists among those who have not been properly trained.

c) Even when equipped with a magazine extension tube, most tactical shotguns still only hold 6 or 7 shells (6-7 shots). That's a negative.

d) Most shotguns are slow to reload, and

e) Ammunition (shells) is heavy and cumbersome, so you can't carry nearly as much extra ammunition as you can with a tactical rifle;

f) Shotguns designed for sporting purposes are difficult to use indoors as their longer barrel makes them ungainly. When the purpose is self-defense, use a "tactical" or "home defense" shotgun with an 18-20-inch barrel. Even then, a shotgun is difficult to use in a confined space such as in the hallway of a home.

g) Effective range of a tactical shotgun is medium distance; far less than a rifle but greater than a handgun. (With most shotgun self-defense ammunition, this distance is less than 100-feet. However, a tactical shotgun equipped with good sights and loaded with lead slugs or sabot slugs can be highly effective at 300-ft. (100m);

h) These guns are heavy, typically 8 - 12 pounds when fully loaded. Ammunition is also large and heavy. Therefore, the gun + ammo represents a large and weighty bundle; a problem if you're on foot.

A primer on shotgun actions (operating mechanisms): A shotgun can be a "tactical shotgun" even though it is operated using a manual "pump" (slide) mechanism to prepare the gun to fire, or it can have an auto-loading "semi-automatic" mechanism. Either way, for a shotgun to qualify as a tactical shotgun, it needs to have a shorter barrel and hold more shells (ammunition) than a standard model designed for a sporting purpose.

Rather than use a detachable box magazine or "clip" to hold ammunition, most tactical shotguns use a tubular magazine. This looks like a second barrel, but this similar-looking tube contains the gun's ammunition (shells).

A *pump-action* shotgun, such as a Remington 870 or Mossberg, is half the price of a *semi-automatic* Benelli M2. Well-funded police SWAT teams tend to use the Benelli because it can be fired faster and more accurately, but for mounting in police cars, police department's tend to purchase a lower-cost model such as the Remington 870 or Mossberg 590. It is worth noting that when an M2 is ordered with the optional ComforTech stock, it reduces the gun's recoil significantly. This is one of the reasons why even an untrained layman can fire an M2 more quickly and accurately.

Medium-distance self-defense: For home protection, and for medium-range self-defense needs, a tactical shotgun with an 18-20-inch barrel, loaded with 00-Buck shotgun shells or #4 Buck, provides the best protection and most effective stopping power for most self-defense situations.

At distances of 20-100 feet, due to the spread of the lead pellets when the gun is discharged, it is easier to hit an armed assailant with a tactical shotgun than with a handgun or rifle. At 20-feet, the impact area of a 9mm pistol or rifle bullet is smaller than ½-inch, so it is easy to miss the target. Whereas a tactical shotgun, loaded with 00-Buck ammunition and fired at the same distance, will produce a circular shot pattern the size of a salad plate. This provides a definite advantage, especially during stressful circumstances when fear and adrenalin make you shaky.

Legal Issue: In the United States, a shotgun with a barrel length less than 18-inches requires a special federal license. Technically a "tax stamp," these are issued by the *Bureau of Alcohol, Tobacco, Firearms and Explosives* (www.ATF.gov).

A shotgun barrel which is longer than 20-inches will produce a too-tight pattern of pellets, making it less useful for many self-defense applications. Police and home-defense shotguns have a barrel length of 18-20 inches. For self-defense use, it is best to purchase a gun designed and built by the manufacturer to be a tactical shotgun. It's usually a bad idea to adapt a shotgun made for a sporting purpose. Rarely does it save money, and it often creates legal problems.

A shotgun only qualifies as a serious "tactical shotgun" if it is 12-gauge, has a barrel that is 20-inches or less in length, and has an ammunition magazine which can hold at least 5 shells (5 + 1 in the chamber). Though some hold as many as 8-shells in their magazine tube, 6-7 is more common.

Self-Defense Tactical Rifles
Pros and Cons
aka/ Assault Rifles, Black Rifles, AR Rifles, Combat Rifles, etc.

Though a hunting or target rifle can be used for self-defense, this is not optimal. If you are serious about self-defense for an emergency situation, you need a semiautomatic tactical rifle such as an AR15.

Tactical Rifle Benefits:

a) Greater range and solid stopping power at much longer distances (0-200+ yards when using standard iron sights);

b) Superior accuracy at even greater distances if equipped with a quality scope;

c) Combat-style or "assault rifles" are fast to reload and durable;

d) Ominous appearance can intimidate potential assailants.

Tactical Rifle Disadvantages:

a) The size of the gun makes it difficult to conceal.

b) Heavy to carry. Standard assault rifles are 9-12 lbs., so they are heavy if carried for a long distance. A shoulder strap is a necessary option even if you opt for a lightweight model (4-7 lbs.).

b) If disassembled and stored in a backpack, the time it takes to reassemble the gun before it can be used may present a severe disadvantage. (Depending on the model of the rifle, this can be 3-seconds to 3-minutes.)

d) Rifle ammunition is lighter than that of a shotgun, but it is still heavy, and spare magazines (clips) are bulky. Ammo not in magazines is usually stored in steel, military ammo cans; a good choice, but this makes it even more cumbersome. So, pack extra cartridges into 'stripper clips' and use military bandoliers, loaded in the ammo can, ready to be swung onto a shoulder if it's necessary to travel on foot.

Additional Disadvantages of Sporting Rifles:

a) Cannot be concealed, even in a knapsack;

b) Sporting rifles hold fewer cartridges (bullets) and the reloading process is time-consuming, making a tactical rifle (assault rifle) a far better choice for self-defense.

Special Purpose Guns

'Special Purpose' guns come in many forms, some for unique and limited self-defense purposes, while others are designed for highly specific hunting or survival use. These firearms may work well for the narrow purpose for which they were intended, but they have limited value for general self-defense purposes. Nevertheless, one of these guns may aptly meet your needs. For example:

North American Arms (NAA) "Black Widow" and other micro-guns are incredibly small, but though the .22 Magnum cartridge this gun uses is tiny, it can still be deadly. Though it's punch has little 'stopping power,' carrying a small gun is always better than no gun.

This small, lightweight (9 oz) wallet-size gun is a 5-shot revolver. It is a valid choice when circumstances make it impossible to carry a larger gun. If this is your choice, consider loading it with high-velocity cartridges that have hollow-point bullets.

These little guns are sometimes carried by police officers who are operating in undercover assignments, as well as by uniformed police officers who want to have a tiny but reliable backup gun.

Yet another use is defense against poisonous snakes. Loaded with .22 Magnum 'snake-shot' cartridges, some rural sheriff deputies and some civilians unobtrusively carry this gun in their pants pocket, just in case they encounter a dangerous snake. If they need to put down an injured animal, they reload with .22 Magnum hollow-point cartridges. The smaller bullet accomplishes the task with less trama (and less drama) than using a standard self-defense handgun.

Smith & Wesson "Governor" and Taurus "The Judge," are large revolver-style handguns, considered 'combo guns' because they are chambered for both handgun and shotgun ammunition. In this case, .45 handgun ammunition as well as .410 shotgun shells.

As to handgun ammunition, the Smith & Wesson (S&W) "Governor" will shoot both .45 LC revolver ammo as well as .45 ACP pistol cartridges, whereas Taurus's "The Judge" can only use the LC revolver cartridge. However, both will shoot the same assortment of .410 shotgun shells. The Governor holds 6 rounds of ammunition, the Judge only 5, but the Governor is more expensive to purchase and is not available in as many configurations as the Taurus. Weight is similar; approximately 2-pounds. We consider these handguns to be multipurpose firearms.

The classic .45 LC cartridge is usually manufactured as a low-power cartridge suitable for old guns. Though harder to find, modern high-power LC cartridges with hollow-point self-defense bullets are also available. The Smith & Wesson variant of this handgun can be loaded with the .45 ACP cartridge, a more widely used caliber that has many different permutations for self-defense.

The .410 shotgun shell, which also fits into both guns, is unfairly maligned because it is small. Though less than half the size of a 12-gauge shotgun shell, it is still respectable, particularly for use in "survival" guns. Importantly, similar to larger shotgun shells, it can contain different sizes of lead shot (B-Bs) as well as lead slugs which are functionally similar to a single, heavyweight bullet.

While only useful at close range, these handguns can nevertheless be used for multiple purposes. When loaded with the proper ammunition, they are useful for self-defense, for protection against snakes, for killing nearby large animals, and for hunting small game animals and birds at close range. This versatility and the shell's lighter weight makes it possible to carry various types of shells; each designed for a different survival, hunting, and self-defense purpose.

These multipurpose firearms are *compromise* guns. As with many compromises in life, these handguns are not the best choice for any single purpose. Though they can be used for any of the mentioned uses, they aren't the "best option" for any of them.

Self-Defense Use: When loaded with a .45 LC/ACP or .410 slugs, the effective range of these revolvers is nearly the same as other handguns with the same length barrel. On the downside, they hold less than half as much ammunition as a modern self-defense pistol.

When loaded with a shotgun shell such as 000-Buckshot or a specialty cartridge such as the Winchester PDX-1, the operational self-defense distance is reduced to about 25-feet. However, the stopping power is impressive.

Hunting Use: When these guns are loaded with birdshot or snake shot, the effective range is only 10-12 feet. Nevertheless, this may be enough for these purposes.

Note: In normal times, most self-defense shootings occur at distances of less than 7-yards (m). However, since the circumstances of a disaster or emergency situation can be much different, this statistic is far less relevant. So, consider your likely scenarios before choosing what gun is best for you.

Again, these 'special purpose' firearms are *compromise* guns. Depending on the environment and need, it may be a reasonable choice if you will only have access to one firearm *and* you want it to be less visible, or more comfortable to carry, than a rifle or shotgun.

Typical Uses: For most people, this gun is too large and heavy for concealed carry purposes, yet some do carry it concealed. For those who are engaged in an outdoor task such as working on a ranch or farm, and want a firearm that is simple to operate, this gun is valued because it can be openly carried in a holster worn behind the hip or in the kidney area, where it is out of the way. It is also popular with backpackers, and for use in knapsack-size survival kits.

Rifle Version: The "Circuit Judge" is a simple-to-use short rifle (carbine with a 18-1/2" barrel, 35.6" overall length, 5.5 lbs) of "The Judge" handgun, but made under contract by Rossi. In addition to the .45 LC handgun and .410 shotgun shells, this rifle (and Taurus's Raging Judge handgun) can also fire the impressive .454 Casull handgun cartridge which is more powerful than a .44 Magnum.

Ironically, the Circuit Judge is not only popular with those in rural settings, such as ATV and horseback riders, but also with some urban judges who keep this gun under their bench (courtroom desk).

Guns for Survival Kits & Off-Grid Living: Semiautomatic rifles such as the Ruger "10/22 Takedown" which is collapsible, and the Henry "AR-7 Survival Rifle" which stores the barrel and action inside its floatation plastic stock, are only available in .22 LR caliber. Yet, they are highly versatile firearms.

Another option is single-shot guns. These are less expensive, and over/under versions which are single-shot but use two barrels (often two different calibers), are both ultra-reliable and also versatile. Still, this choice is only viable for those who are willing to expend the effort necessary for becoming proficient with their gun. A single-shot rifle takes time to reload, so second shots are rarely an option.

For survival use, these combination guns are typically chambered in calibers designed to meet two very different needs. This might include a small-game cartridge like the .22 LR, plus a more powerful rifle cartridge, or a .410 or 20-gauge shotgun barrel.

The Ultimate Long-Term Survival Gun: Though they can be hard to find, a rifle/shotgun combination gun chambered in both .22 LR + 20-gauge shotgun is perhaps the most versatile survival gun. However, these require more skill since it is nearly impossible to reload in time to take a second shot at the same target. Still, for many, these represent the ultimate survival gun. Notwithstanding, since most people are unwilling to take the time needed to learn how to be quick and accurate with these over/under survival guns, they are not what we recommend to most people. Instead, we focus on the .22 LR rifle because it is a better option for those who aren't gun enthusiasts.

The People's Choice Survival Gun: For those who find themselves in a long duration survival situation, a reliable gun chambered for the small, lightweight .22 LR cartridge may be the best choice. These are easy to use, and stainless-steel versions are more durable and easy to maintain. Single-shot rifles are the most reliable, followed by bolt-action models, but most people will nevertheless opt for a semi-automatic rifle. For 50 years, the Ruger 10/22 has been the best-selling semi-automatic .22-caliber rifle.

Ruger 10/22 '*Takedown*' vs. Henry U.S. Survival '*AR-7*' Rifle: These are the two most popular rifles in this category. Both are .22 caliber rifles which can be quickly assembled or disassembled into the gun's two main components.

Within a few seconds, either of these rifles can be quickly transformed into a functioning semi-automatic rifle. This added feature makes them not only easy to store compactly but also easy to transport unobtrusively, as they can be carried in a bag that doesn't look like a rifle case.

This "takedown" or "collapsible" feature makes it simple to carry a rifle inside a GO-Bag, knapsack, or backpack, or in a pouch unobtrusively attached to the frame of a bicycle or motorcycle. Or, these guns can be kept in a satchel-size survival kit that is stored in a small airplane or boat.

Safe and secure storage is still necessary, of course. Even when disassembled, as with all firearms, these rifles still need to be kept out of the hands of children and unauthorized users. Thankfully, standard trigger locks and small lock-boxes can be used even though these guns are a non-standard size when compactly stored.

Though the .22 LR caliber is the most popular in the world, and well suited for hunting rabbits and squirrels, in a survival situation a well-placed shot can kill a small deer or a wild pig. And, the lightweight and small-in-size aspect of the .22 LR cartridge facilitates the carry of a lot of ammunition in a small amount of space. I've found that I can comfortably carry 100-rounds of .22 LR ammunition in a front pocket of my jeans.

If you don't have another option, a .22 LR rifle, such as these, can be used for self-defense. Yet, it is far from being a first-choice weapon for this purpose. The .22 LR cartridge is certainly not adequate for self-defense—unless you don't have another option.

Humans and wild animals shot by a single .22 LR bullet can certainly die. These guns are dangerous. But that death may occur the following day, long after the threat has passed.

If you are considering one of these as a multipurpose gun which, in a desperate situation might also be used for self-defense, keep in mind that a single shot from a .22 LR gun will rarely stop the actions of a violent criminal. If you find it necessary to use a .22 for self-defense, my advice is to shoot and keep shooting until there is no longer a threat. You may even need to reload, so maintain quick access to extra magazines (clips).

When choosing between survival guns that are readily available, the *Takedown* is my one-gun backpack-size gun of choice for a survival kit—when self-defense isn't a primary concern. And, when I won't be operating in an environment where I might encounter dangerous animals. In my experience, the Ruger 10/22 Takedown in stainless steel, is the best choice of the two as I've found it to be more reliable and less prone to damage than the *AR-7* rifle.

Lightweight, Less-Concealable Self-Defense Rifle Options: If your need is for a self-defense rifle that is also lightweight and collapsible, then an AR-15 may be your best choice. However, if defense against violent humans and dangerous animals is not a concern, nor is the hunting of medium-large game, then a long barreled .22 LR pistol or revolver, or a collapsible .22-caliber rifle may be your best choice. A relatively inexpensive, small-caliber gun such as a .22, can literally be a lifesaver. .22LR ammunition is typically available everywhere, plus you can carry a lot of it, and practice is less expensive. These three attributes have far-reaching implications.

Semiautomatic Pistols vs. Revolver-style Handguns: Most people should select a high-capacity semi-automatic pistol, but these are not the best choice for everyone. If you have very little strength in your hands or physical disability which makes it difficult to load and cock a pistol, then consider a revolver. If you have the strength necessary to hold the gun on target and the dexterity to pull the trigger, you can load and fire a revolver.

Or, a revolver might be a good choice if you intend to carry your gun in a purse or pocket. If you select a revolver model that is hammerless (actually a shrouded hammer), then, unlike a pistol, your revolver can be fired from inside your purse or pocket. If you try the same thing with a semi-auto pistol, it will likely cause a jamming lock-up that prevents the gun from firing another shot.

Another reason for selecting a revolver over a pistol is that they require less maintenance. If you know you won't maintain the gun, get a revolver.

If none of these limitations apply to you, then seriously consider a high-capacity 9mm pistol. There are good reasons why this is the most popular self-defense caliber being sold today.

Women: As you select a gun for possible self-defense use during an emergency situation, avoid stereotype decisions. For example, women have a natural tendency to purchase small subcompact pistols. This is a common mistake made by those who lack experience.

Match the gun to your carry method: It is best to pick the largest handgun that can be accommodated by your intended carry method. This is more important than having a "ladies gun' which is ultra-concealable when you aren't going to carry it routinely. Remember, the larger the gun, the easier it is to control and shoot accurately.

Of critical importance is to select a handgun that fits your hand. Avoid preconceived notions of what is best. Handle different guns.

For example, when my son was buying a gun for his wife, he assumed that since she is petite, they would buy her a thin 'subcompact' pistol that uses a single-stack magazine (clip). This style holds less ammunition than one with a double-stack magazine, but the grip is considerably thinner, so he assumed it would fit her hand better. However, as they shopped, it became apparent that a 'compact' (middle size) pistol with a double-stack magazine (which fortuitously holds more ammunition), fit her hand better. The moral of the story? Don't assume.

Selecting the Best Gun Caliber for *You,* and Ammunition Selection for Self-Defense Use

Handguns: 9mm and .38 Special are an excellent choice for individuals who are new to guns, as well as for those who are only willing to spend a minimal amount of time training.

Noteworthy for new gun owners, these handgun calibers have less recoil than larger ones, but they still deliver reasonable stopping power. For self-defense use, we recommend against using a gun that uses a cartridge smaller than 9mm/.38 Special. Still, even a little NAA-22LR mini-revolver can be better than no gun at all.

In the United States, most self-defense handguns carried by police officers are in one these four calibers: 9mm (aka 9mm Luger), .357 Sig, .40 ACP, and .45 ACP.

No longer in routine use by police departments, which have now almost universally switched from revolvers to semiautomatic pistols, the .38 Special and .357 Magnum cartridges are still an acceptable self-defense option. A .38 Special can deliver ballistics and stopping-power that are almost equal to that of a 9mm pistol.

The U.S. military primarily uses 9mm pistols, a caliber that has less stopping power than the previous standard which was .45 ACP. Since high-capacity 9mm pistols hold more ammunition than the previous military sidearm (1911/.45 ACP), and they are easier to shoot accurately, this switch may have been a solid decision. In any case, the more modest recoil of the 9mm vs. .45, the reduced number of training hours needed to achieve the same level of accuracy, combined with the ability to carry more ammunition in a similar size pistol, are the key benefits.

Pistol-size and Caliber Selection: There is not a direct correlation between pistol size and caliber size. For example, a 9mm pistol, the gun itself, can be very small or very large. The 9mm cartridge (caliber) is often used in pocket-sized handguns (usually referred to as "sub-compact" pistols), as well as medium-size handguns (known as "compact" pistols), as well as large guns (often called "full-size" or "standard" pistols). There are even rifles, or more accurately carbines, chambered for pistol cartridges. Since the 1800's, these have been popular with cowboys who carried both a handgun and a carbine, and used the same caliber for both due to simple logistics—they only needed to maintain a supply of ammunition in one caliber.

It's a no-brainer that the smaller the pistol, the easier it is to conceal it on your body, or in a purse or pocket. Notwithstanding, many people make the mistake of buying a subcompact pistol when they don't have a need for a pocket-size gun.

Unfortunately, the smaller the gun, the more perceived recoil (kick) it produces. As a result, these little guns are not only harder to hold securely in your hand; they also make it harder to shoot accurately. And when time on the range is unpleasant, this often results in less practice.

Whereas a larger pistol, which uses the same caliber as the small gun, not only produces less perceived recoil when it's fired, but it is easier to shoot accurately, as well. Plus, they are more fun to shoot.

For those seeking a compromise between a concealable size, the capacity to hold more ammunition, and the inherent ability to shoot the gun accurately, the best choice is often a medium-size ('compact') pistol.

That fact acknowledged, in handgun-competition sports and in militaries worldwide, and among women and men who have small hands, most seem to do fine even with a full-size handgun. Concealability is generally the main issue, not that the gun is too large to shoot.

Purchasing Ammunition

Don't make your ammunition selection based on what is available in your local store. This decision is too important. And, don't be influenced by advertising hype, price, salesmen, or friends, either. Make your choice based on articles from reliable sources or genuinely knowledgeable advisors. Buy your ammo online or from a large gun or sporting goods store so that you can get exactly what you want. Since self-defense ammo is expensive, look for practice ammo made by the same company that makes your self-defense ammo. The point-of-impact for the bullet changes with brands, so you'll need to experiment, selecting practice ammo that has a similar point-of-impact.

Selecting Handgun Ammunition

Your selection of ammo is just as important as choosing the right gun. After doing your research or checking recommendations found on the Resources page of TXRFA.com, purchase several of the top brands and test each to see how they function in your gun. It's not unusual for one brand to run flawlessly while another will cause malfunctions. Once you find a brand that works well, don't switch to another absent a good reason.

Self-defense handgun ammunition should have hollow-point bullets. Or, a hollow-point that is filled with a plastic-like substance designed to limit fouling and help it expand on impact. The bullet's ability to grow in size is a crucial factor.

A hollow-point bullet is designed to expand when it hits something semi-hard like a human body or animal. This means the bullet's energy is converted to 'stopping power.' If this power is adequate and the point of impact is well chosen, it will stop the violent actions of the attacker. However, if that energy is not dissipated, it can create a problem. If it is allowed to retain its power, it may pass through the intended target and continue on its flight. As a result, it can still harm, or even kill an innocent bystander.

Traditional full metal jacket (FMJ) bullets such as used in practice ammunition and for military weapons, will often pass through a human or animal without releasing its energy. This is yet another reason why it is so important to carry hollow-point or self-defense ammunition when you are carrying a gun for protection.

If opting for a 9mm pistol, be aware that standard (FMJ) ammunition as well as many 9mm hollow-point bullets (JHP), produce excessive penetration due to the bullet's size, characteristics, and the high-velocity nature of this cartridge. Therefore, when carrying a 9mm pistol, it is additionally important to select a brand of ammunition that will expand fully upon impact.

With your preparations for an emergency situation, you also need a holster and at least 200-rounds (shots) of ammunition for each gun. Store your extra ammunition in a watertight box such as a steel military ammo can (box). In some regions, it must be a locked box.

Selecting Shotgun Ammunition

The popular 12-gauge shotgun, is the gold-standard (gauge/caliber) for self-defense shotguns. If concerned about recoil, use 2-3/4" shells—but don't buy low-recoil ammunition. Also, a gun that is in a smaller gauge, such as 16 or 20-gauge, is not optimal. Nevertheless, these still deliver more stopping power than most handguns.

Our tests revealed that low-recoil shotgun shells had a minimal effect on recoil reduction, but regardless of brand, they consistently produced unpredictable point-of-impact results. The pellet spread was unstable, and the pattern created, even when using identical shells taken from the same box, were often not uniform. If recoil is a concern, solve this problem by learning how to hold the shotgun properly. In our family classes, 12-year-olds do fine with standard 2-3/4" shells in a 12-gauge shotgun.

If recoil is a lesser concern for you, increase your firepower by carrying 3" Magnum 00-Buck (Double-Ought Buck) in your shotgun. Ammunition (shell) capacity for shotguns with an extended magazine is typically 6-7 shells, and this generally remains the same regardless of whether you use 2-3/4-inch or 3-inch shells. Yet, the slightly larger 3-inch shells hold more pellets. This can translate into a potent advantage.

A shotgun is large-in-size, and the ammunition (shells) are heavy, but it is an extremely versatile weapon. For hunting small game, load your gun with birdshot; for large game, use lead slugs. For long range accuracy (rifle-like), use sabot slugs. A 12-gauge shotgun can even be used to launch tear gas, as well as "rescue flares" for marine signaling and search and rescue operations.

Selecting Rifle Ammunition and Choosing a Caliber

5.56 NATO (or .223) and 7.62 NATO (.308) are the standard cartridges for military, police and civilian self-defense use because they are effective in many different situations and environments. There are other calibers which have more stopping power, but the 5.56 NATO and 7.62 NATO cartridges have the additional benefit of being widely available, so we rate these as our Top Choice for rifle calibers.

If you are rich or you enjoy reloading ammunition, you might want to select a different caliber. However for most people, 5.56mm or 7.62mm are the best choice.

These two calibers are the most popular, too. As a result, manufacturing over-runs and sales are common, plus they are available in military surplus as well as re-manufacturing outlets. Therefore, these calibers are usually the least expensive. This makes practice more affordable, yet another advantage.

An empty rifle is nearly useless, so a commonly-found caliber is an important attribute. Someday you may need more ammunition. This is additionally important since your time of maximum need is likely to be when availability is a problem.

Which caliber to choose? 5.56mm or 7.62mm?

The 5.56 cartridge is lighter in weight than the 7.62, making it possible to carry more ammunition. That is one of the reasons the U.S. military adopted it. Whereas the 7.62 cartridge provides superior stopping power, a benefit which becomes even more pronounced when shooting longer distances, or in a location where the field of fire is thick with brush or trees, or when it's necessary to shoot through barriers such as vehicles or wood structures.

Two shooters with equal skill will find that the individual armed with a 7.62mm rifle has a distinct tactical advantage. This is true in all but close-range encounters.

Yet, the purchase price of an AR rifle and ammo, spare magazines, ammo pouches, gear, parts, and repairs if you ever need them, is less costly than for a 7.62mm rifle. Plus, the 5.56mm ammo is much lighter to carry, and for many, an AR rifle is easier to shoot.

For most people, an AR rifle in 5.56mm caliber, equipped with a holographic sight such as an Aimpoint, will be a better choice than any 7.62mm rifle. It will be cheaper, too.

Nevertheless, the 7.62mm cartridge does provide substantially more stopping power. It is worth considering for those who can handle the added weight and cost.

The AR-10 is a 7.62mm version of the popular AR-15/M-16/A4 rifles. Another choice is the U.S.-made PTR-91, a civilian rifle licensed and tooled by Heckler & Koch, which is similar to their HK-91 and the G3 battle rifles. These rifles are in use by the British SAS, many European police and military units, and by militaries throughout the world. Yet another topnotch option is the FN SCAR, my personal favorite. The 7.62mm carbine version of this gun is popular among SEALs and other American spec-ops forces.

Not only does an equal-quality 7.62mm NATO rifle have greater effective range, but the flight path of its 7.62mm bullet is also less likely to be deflected by branches and other obstructions. Plus, it will often do a better job penetrating wood fences and vehicles.

For shooters who are older in age or less agile, the larger 7.62mm NATO tactical rifles provide an additional advantage since most attackers, such as street gangs, will be armed with stolen AR-15/M-4 rifles or AK-47/AK-74/AK-12 assault rifles, all of which are less effective at longer distances. It is these longer distances where the 7.62mm NATO really shines.

A small group of attackers armed with AR15 or AK rifles can be overwhelmed by a single, concealed and skilled marksman, who is armed with a scope-equipped 7.62 NATO semiautomatic rifle. But the dramatic disparity between the two forces is best observed when the distance between the two is greater than 100 yards.

Experts consider 100-yards (m) to be the optimal range for an AR or AK rifle. Yes, these rifles can be shot accurately at much greater distances, especially the 5.56 ARs, but both start to lose a lot of stopping power after 100-yards. For most AK rifles, their reliability is excellent, but accuracy often becomes abysmal beyond 100-yards.

Though both the 7.62 NATO rifle and its ammunition are substantially heavier than a 5.56mm rifle plus the same quantity of ammo, this can be overcome. How? A shooter who is well hidden and semi-stationary, minimizes the weight disadvantage while maximizing the advantage of better stopping power at a greater distance.

Still, the lighter-in-weight 5.56mm (AR) and 7.62x39 (AK and SKS) cartridge combined with the lightweight rifles that shoot these calibers, is an advantage, particularly for those who are traveling on foot. After the first mile, carrying a rifle and ammo becomes work.

Plus, the civilian versions of the popular AR-15/M-4 rifles, and the Russian/Chinese AK and SKS rifles which are popular with drug cartels and street gangs, have less recoil than the 7.62mm NATO rifle. Therefore, an AR or AK rifle may be a fine choice for those without shooting experience, and those who don't train regularly.

Ammunition selection is just as important as gun selection: Though the Full Metal Jacket (FMJ) bullets used by militaries are less likely to jam a rifle, and FMJ ammo is cheaper for target practice, we recommend soft-nose bullets for self-defense use. Soft-nose bullets are less likely to pass through your assailant; a condition which creates more risk to innocent bystanders. Also, a soft-nose bullet usually improves stopping-power for incapacitating an assailant.

Though 'self-defense' bullets are available in most rifle calibers, the soft-nosed bullets commonly used for hunting are easy to find and less expensive. Either can be a solid choice for self-defense.

Note: A semiautomatic rifle is less likely to jam when it is loaded with cartridges which have a soft-nose bullet rather than a hollow-point bullet. Hollow-point bullets are the best choice for self-defense handguns, but they are not necessarily required for self-defense rifles.

If your rifle works flawlessly when shooting both soft-nose and hollow-point bullets, then you have a choice. But most semi-auto rifles are more reliable when they are fed soft-nose or FMJ ammo.

Just as with all ammunition carried for self-defense use, be sure to test-fire that specific ammo in your gun. Fire a minimum of 100-rounds (shots) of that ammunition from your own gun, just to make sure it works flawlessly. If it doesn't, either try again using ammunition made by a different manufacturer, or have a gunsmith solve the problem. Don't use any ammo that does not work perfectly.

Your gun needs to work flawlessly all of the time. Don't be satisfied that it works most of the time—that can be a deadly mistake.

Note: The 7.62mm cartridge is also a popular choice for hunting larger game animals. Most hunters feel the 5.56mm cartridge is a poor choice for hunting animals larger than a wild pig or small dear. The 5.56mm is illegal to use for hunting in some locales—perhaps not a problem in a survival situation, but it does speak to its suitability for hunting larger animals.

Overview and Specific Recommendations

Whichever gun(s) you pick, training and practice are essential. But the decision as to which firearm is best for you, depends on the threats you will encounter, your physical strength, dexterity, and your commitment to train. Still, there are hundreds of makes and models to choose from, so this section focuses on specific recommendations to help you start your search.

A 9mm pistol with high-capacity (holds lots of ammunition in the gun) is the best choice for most people who are looking for close-range self-defense (2-50 feet). If you are willing to spend more time training, then a gun with greater stopping power, such as .40, .45, or 10mm might be a good choice. However, for most people, a 9mm pistol with a high capacity magazine, offers the best compromise between stopping power, manageable recoil, and convenient carry.

A holster designed to fit your specific model of gun is also necessary. Kydex, a form of plastic, is a durable material for holsters. It provides the best protection for a handgun, additionally so in inclement weather. Leather holsters tend to be more comfortable, and they are quieter when removing your gun from the holster; occasionally a distinct strategic advantage. However, since leather can retain moisture, it may not be the best choice for wet or humid areas.

Gun Brands & Models

Specific Handgun Recommendations

Gunmakers known for their stellar reliability and accuracy include: SIG Sauer, HK (Heckler Koch), and FN (Fabrique Nationale). These three brands are often the #1 choice of well-funded police departments and spec-ops soldiers.

Budget-conscious police departments use workhorse reliable guns, primarily those made by Glock. Popular pistols models include: G17 Gen4, G19 Gen 4, and G42. Other quality handguns include those made by Colt, Kimber, Ruger (both pistols and double-action revolvers), Smith & Wesson (for double-action revolvers), and Springfield Armory XD(M). Baretta pistols were used by the U.S. military for 32-years, but these have been replaced by the SIG P320 pistol. Considered to be "modular," the P320 is a 9mm pistol that can be configured in various grip and frame sizes.

Before you decide which handgun to buy, handle several guns made by different manufacturers. Compare the fit of the grip to your hand and your ability to operate the action and pull the trigger.

Make sure you don't need to alter your grip on the gun to operate the mechanism. Though a new firearm will have a stiffer operating mechanism than that of a similar gun that has fired 200-500 shots, you still need to make sure that you have sufficient hand strength and dexterity to operate the gun's slide (cocking mechanism). This is a learned skill, but some initial ability is nevertheless necessary.

If the gun has a 'safety,' be sure you can activate it without altering the way you hold the gun. (This is a rare feature on modern handguns since the best safety is to keep your finger off the trigger.)

> A self-defense gun shouldn't work well most of the time. It needs to work *flawlessly* all the time.

As a rule of thumb, I buy 'new' when it comes to selecting a gun for self-defense. You don't want to be buying someone else's problem. Remember, your life may literally depend on your firearm working correctly under adverse conditions.

Action type for handgun: For the novice, a double-action-only (DAO) gun is considered the safest choice for both a semi-auto pistol and revolver. With a DAO handgun, the trigger pull is stiffer, but the user is also less likely to shoot the gun accidentally. In all cases, keep your finger off the trigger until you are ready to shoot. This is the #1 most frequent safety problem we experience in our beginner-to-intermediate firearm training classes.

Specific Tactical Shotgun Recommendations

Most police departments equip their police cars with Remington 870 pump shotguns or the lower cost Mossberg 500 or 590. The Marine Corps uses the Mossberg 590. Police SWAT teams and U.S. military spec-ops units favor the Benelli M4 semi-automatic shotgun, but the M2 with a ComforTech stock is better for most civilian use as it absorbs a significant amount of recoil.

The Remington and Mossberg pump-action shotguns are less than half the cost of the Benelli semi-automatic shotguns, and yet adequate for most needs. There are many other brands which are also viable, but it is noteworthy that 90% of all police departments use either the Remington or Mossberg.

Also worth mentioning is that when I was a police officer, on several occasions the distinctive "racking" sound of my pump-action shotgun was enough to convince an assailant to surrender. I am 100% convinced that I didn't need to shoot several criminals because of the distinctive sound of my Remington 870. A tactical shotgun is an intimidating weapon.

If you have the money, the M2 and M4 Benelli tactical shotguns are impressive firearms. Unfortunately, semi-automatic shotguns are inherently unreliable, but the Benelli is an entirely different weapon system. In my experience, the Benelli shotguns are stunningly fast, accurate, and they produce less recoil than the Remington, Mossberg and other pump-action shotguns.

The Benelli model "M4" is imported, so different laws apply. If you want to carry the maximum number of shells in the gun, a new magazine tube and three other major parts need to be replaced. This drives up the cost by more than $500 above the purchase price. This additional expense isn't an issue with the Benelli M2 which is made in the U.S, so if you're a civilian, the "M2" may be a better choice.

Legal Warning: In the United States, a civilian-owned shotgun or rifle must have an 18-inch or longer barrel, unless the owner has a license to own a Short-Barrel-Rifle, technically, a SBR 'tax stamp' issued by ATF.gov.

For most people, this restriction isn't a problem because an 18-inch barrel is optimal, anyway. A rifle with a barrel much shorter than 16-inches produces less power and has a reduced effective range. (Since the barrel is shorter, the bullet has exited the gun before the gunpowder has finish burning.) As a result, the muzzle energy and the bullet's velocity are reduced, diminishing stopping power.

On the other hand, a shotgun with a short barrel can be extremely effective at distances of less than 30-ft. For this reason, some people are tempted to cut-short the barrel of a hunting shotgun and use it for self-defense. This is creates a legal problem, especially if the barrel is shorter than 18-inches. Notwithstanding, the 18-20"of a standard tactical shotgun is a good compromise for short and medium shooting distances.

Optimal Rifle-Barrel Length: As to rifles, contrary to popular opinion, an AR, AK, or SKS rifle equipped with a barrel longer than 18-inches does not provide a significant ballistic advantage.

The same is true with 5.56 and 7.62mm rifles.[18] Long barrels on 5.56mm rifles can create bullet drag, as well as make the gun more

---

[18] Calculations for "stopping power" of a bullet are VERY complex, so this is an over-simplification of a complicated issue, but to help illustrate my point: When comparing two AR-15 rifles, one with a 16" barrel, the other with one that is 26"—an entire foot of additional barrel length, there is an average increase of only 24 feet-per-second for each additional inch of barrel length. (However, an AR with a 12-14" barrel will lose 70-80 fps for each inch shorter than 16 inches.) The results are similar with 7.62 NATO rifles. These guns only add 22 fps for each inch of increased barrel length between 16-26 inches. So, "optimal" barrel length often has more to do with improving convenience-of-carry and ease-of-use, than it does with increasing stopping power.

cumbersome to carry in areas with undergrowth, so the optimal barrel length for a 5.56mm AR or M4 style rifle is 16-20 inches. Contrary to popular opinion, the same is true for a 7.62 NATO rifle.

From a self-defense standpoint, all of these guns are capable of stopping an attacker at distances of 0-100 yards (100m). However, the 7.72mm NATO cartridge provides a distinct stopping-power advantage at greater distances.

Necessary Accessories

Magazines (clips): You need a *minimum* of seven magazines for each gun. Tip: You may want to store rifle and shotgun magazines half full to reduce spring fatigue. For pistol magazines, rotate them full-to-empty. Keep two mags empty and the others full, ready for use. Rotate your pistol magazines monthly or at least quarterly, so the springs can rest. When it comes to magazines, don't skimp on quality. Factory mags for handguns are better than most after-market brands, but there are superior after-market rifle magazines such as MAGPUL.

Magazine Pouches: These are needed for carrying extra ammunition for all your handguns, rifles, and shotguns. For rifles, I personally favor chest rigs like the ones made by London Bridge (www.lbtinc.com) or the less expensive models manufactured by BDS Tactical (www.BDSTacticalGear.com). These can be worn with a GO-Bag, whereas many popular ammo rigs and vests are incompatible with wearing a knapsack (or patrol pack) plus ammo pouches.

Those who carry their rifle magazines on a belt will quickly develop sore hips unless the belt is supported by tactical suspenders. If extra shotgun shells are carried in a bandoleer which uses elastic loops to hold the shells, the elastic will soon fatigue if shells are stored in the loops. To counteract this problem, either store the bandoleer empty, or alternate the use of the loops: one empty, the next holding a shell, the next empty, etc. To mitigate this problem which is inherent to elastic, periodically rotate which loops are filled and which are empty. Also, shot-shell bandoleers and pouches should be of a style which minimizes bouncing if you are forced to run.

Holsters: A holster is needed for each handgun. Popular choices for law enforcement officers include pancake-style for belt carry (Kydex or leather), IWB (Inside-Waist-Band; select Kydex to resist perspiration), and shoulder holsters for those who are usually seated.

Rifle/Shotgun Slings: A 2-point sling is necessary for each rifle and shotgun. Connection points should be secure and not rattle, nor mar the gun. Nylon straps are generally more functional than leather. Padding at the shoulder can be advantageous. Simplicity is rugged duribility are paramount. Brands to consider include Vtac and TAB, or find something similar that is well constructed.

AR Rifles: Consider adding quick-disconnect pins so that the gun can be rapidly assembled and disassembled, and stored in two pieces in an unobtrusive knapsack rather than a gun case.

Cleaning Kit: In addition to your regular gun cleaning supplies, keep a small gun cleaning kit that can efficiently clean all of your guns. Store it, and a small tube of extra lubricant and patches, on your chest rig or in your GO-Bag. The compact Otis Deluxe Rifle/Pistol Cleaning System (and similar) is lightweight and can form the basis for what is needed for gun cleaning while in the field.

Commentary & Tips

Barrel Length for Rifles: The optimal barrel length for peak performance of an AR, AK, or SKS field rifle is 16-18 inches. Why? It's because military ammo is designed to have a near-complete gunpowder burn at this length. For 7.62mm NATO, it is $18\text{-}20^+$ inches.

Rifle Stocks: Rifles with collapsible stocks are generally less comfortable to shoot, more challenging to shoot accurately, and often produce more perceived recoil. However, a collapsed stock may allow a rifle to fit into in a knapsack, so this may be a significant benefit. Regardless, telescoping rifle stocks were conceived to accommodate the thickness of body armor, not concealability. Yet, this same feature may be useful to fit the rifle to smaller adults or children, too.

Rifle Accessories: Those who are "into" guns tend to over-accessorize them. Firearms for emergency-use need to be kept simple; easy to carry and instinctive to operate. Avoid complexity.

It may be useful to have a weapons light, bipod, forend grip, green laser, and a night-vision scope, but it's usually better to keep these items in your knapsack rather than mounted on your rifle. A heavy gun slows target acquisition, plus it increases carry fatigue.

Carry Method: Rifles, shotguns, and handguns should feel reasonably lightweight when they are being carried, so use a carry method that works for you. Be ready for long distance foot travel, and handsfree carry. A sling is essential for both rifles and shotguns.

Rifles and shotguns (and holsters) need to be snag-free in case you find yourself hiking through trees and brush. All guns need to be carried silently (no metal-against-metal sounds) and be glare-free. If you utilize a camo gun wrap such as McNett Camo Form, be sure it doesn't interfere with the operation of the firearm and sights.

Red Dot Sights: "Red dot" type scopes do not provide magnification, but they do make target acquisition faster. Whether you are new to guns or a seasoned combat soldier, a sight which uses a colored dot to show where the bullet will impact can be a valuable accessory.

Quality red dot sights like Aimpoint and Trijicon are battle proven for both function and durability. EOTech and MSE are also popular. If you use a battery-operated red dot scope, use gun-wrap to attach a spare set of Lithium-ion batteries to the scope. Use the same technique for a weapons light or flashlight.

Scopes: *If you have a scope mounted on your rifle, make sure your gun also has iron sights.* Your iron sights need to be sighted-in, too, in case your scope becomes damaged and must be removed.

Rifle scopes and night sights need to be durable. Unfortunately, many 'bargain' scopes will not stand up to the rigors of repeated recoil, and their accuracy starts to drift shortly after the warranty expires. If you want to mount a scope on your rifle, select a name-brand scope and buy it from a dealer who will stand behind the purchase.

Scope "rings" are used to mount the scope to a rifle. Sometimes the rings (or mount) come with a scope, other times they need to be purchased separately. If you've never mounted a scope, it's not a difficult task, but it's still worth getting experienced help.

Be ready to operate while lying flat on the ground: Confirm that your loaded gun, ammo pouches, and gear are conducive to using your firearm from a prone position. And, with gloved hands.

Keep your gear accessible: Have your GO-Bag and gun nearby. Store them with extra ammo and your loaded chest rig. Everything needs to be kept together, so you are ready to roll. If you store your magazines only partially filled to preserve the life of the springs, top them off at the first sign of trouble.

Chapter 17

Tear Gas and Pepper Spray as a Self-Defense Option

For those who are prohibited from having a gun, or who can't countenance using a firearm to defend themselves against violence, purchasing a tear gas or pepper spray device is an alternative that is worth considering. (If it is legal in your locale.)

Unfortunately, most major disasters are followed by a dramatic increase in the number and severity of violent crimes. Therefore, self-defense is an important aspect of all disaster preparation.

If a gun is not an option for you, consider obtaining a pepper spray device to use as a tool for self-defense. Pepper spray, like that which is used by many police departments, is similar to, but more effective than traditional tear gas (both CN and CS tear gas).

Though pepper spray is not legal for civilian use everywhere, it is legal in many places. In most regions, you don't need a license or special training, either.

Frankly, pepper spray isn't nearly as useful as having a self-defense gun. Yet, it is far better than most other alternatives.

For those who do have a gun, it is still a worthwhile less-lethal self-defense option that is worth having nearby. You may not want to carry pepper spray and a gun, as this may be cumbersome and impractical, but it can still be advantageous to keep a can of pepper spray in your home, car, and GO-Bag.

It's a simple and inexpensive solution. A can of pepper spray that costs about the same as a meal at a fast-food restaurant, can save your life or keep you from being seriously injured or violently abused.

What is Pepper Spray?

What is commonly referred to as "pepper spray" is a small handheld aerosol device which dispenses a liquid or gel formulation of the chemical Oleoresin Capsicum (OC). The OC chemical compound is derived from natural spicy-hot chili pepper fruit, thus the nickname, *pepper* spray.

When used against a normal, reasonably healthy assailant, Oleoresin Capsicum, aka *pepper spray*, is non-lethal and non-injurious. It is a chemical agent designed for use in self-defense situations where physical violence is imminent.

When sprayed into the eyes of an attacker, pepper spray can have a debilitating effect for 15-45-minutes. It does not cause permanent injury or physical damage to a healthy adult, nor does it require medical attention for them to recover fully. The effect simply wears off, or the chemical can be washed off to obtain relief.

When used on a human attacker, pepper spray is designed to produce a burning sensation to the skin, coughing, and copious tearing and swelling of the skin around the eyes. This response is designed to limit the aggressor's ability to see his or her intended victim, making it possible for the victim to escape. Also, since these effects often take the fight out of a violent attacker, the aggressor is motivated to disengage from the attack and often flees the area.

On the downside, pepper spray works somewhat like an allergic reaction, so effects vary. Unfortunately, results are inconsistent, but since it is somewhat debilitating 85% of the time, it's still worth having. It's certainly a lot better than being defenseless.

Just as some people can better tolerate spicy foods, the reaction to pepper spray can be very different from one person to the next. If you opt for pepper spray, keep in mind that results can vary greatly, causing some people to be completely debilitated, whereas others will not be affected at all.

Assailants who are hopped-up on drugs, intoxicated with alcohol, or mentally ill, tend to have little or no reaction to pepper spray. Nevertheless, pepper spray is still worth having, particularly if a firearm isn't an option.

3 things to look for when purchasing pepper spray

1. Select a product that shoots a stream of pepper spray at least 10-12 feet in distance.

2. The contents of the device should include **10%** Oleoresin Capsicum (aka / "OC," or "OC spray"), as this is the optimal strength for use against humans. This formula-strength is what police officers usually carry, and it is the same strength as that which is used for riot control.

A more accurate measurement of effectiveness is Scoville Heat Units (SKU), but this data is only found on the label of pepper spray dispensers which are marketed to law enforcement agencies. If this is the measurement you encounter, then 150,000 SKU should be considered the minimum level of potency.

The most accurate measurement of pepper spray effectiveness is "High-Performance Liquid Chromatography" (HPLC), but unfortunately, this method is rarely included with product advertising, except for devices aimed at the police market. If you do find this measurement, select a product that has an HPLC Capsaicinoid rating of 0.7% or higher.

3. The dispensing container needs to hold enough of the liquid to make it possible to deliver a minimum of seven 1-second bursts of OC spray.

A formula of 10% Oleoresin Capsicum (OC) is optimal for people, and it can be useful against aggressive dogs, too, whereas 50% OC compounds are formulated for large mammals such as bear. Note: Any formulation which contains less than 10% Oleoresin Capsicum is not adequate for self-defense use.

Pepper spray is a useful product, but it is not perfect. It doesn't always work as advertised. Nevertheless, it is perhaps the best non-lethal choice for most civilians.

There is some confusion between "pepper spray" and the terms, "Mace" and "tear-gas." Mace is a brand name for a company that sells self-defense products, and teargas is a different chemical (usually labeled as **CN** tear-gas or **CS** tear-gas). Adding to this confusion, some pepper spray dispensers also contain CN or CS tear-gas. (Of the two types of tear-gas, CS is more powerful.) The reason that tear-gas is occasionally included in a pepper spray formulation is that some people don't react to pepper spray, but they may react to tear-gas. However, most experts agree that tear-gas is not necessary since OC is more universally effective than any of the traditional tear-gas formulations.

Available in various types of dispensers, ranging from devices which fit onto a key ring, to those built into a cell phone case (usually inadequate), to different shapes and sizes of small canisters, there is a multitude of sizes and formulations of pepper spray.

Most devices utilize a water-like liquid or oil as a carrier for the Oleoresin Capsicum, but the gel is becoming increasingly popular as it sticks to the face and skin. When comparing products, the distance the spray or stream is projected is one of the most useful characteristics for use when comparing products. The greater the distance, the more useful the product.

How to Use Pepper Spray

Pepper spray is designed to be shot directly into the eyes of your assailant at a distance of at least 3-feet, but not further than the maximum range listed on the dispenser's label. If you are inside this effective range zone, be sure to aim for the eyes.

Don't stop delivering bursts of the spray until the assailant's eyes are entirely doused, or the attacker has run away. If an assailant has swollen-shut eyes, they will not be able to chase you, and they will not be able to continue with their acts of violent aggression. This stalling-action is the objective of pepper spray. Do not use it for lesser purposes.

Once struck in the face with pepper spray, it usually takes 2-5 seconds for the assailant to react. Nevertheless, don't wait to see if it's working. Keep delivering bursts of the spray into their eyes until the threat has stopped entirely. Or, just keep spraying an uninterrupted stream of pepper spray into your assailant's eyes until they cease their aggression *and* are entirely debilitated.

An assailant who is wearing eyeglasses, sunglasses, or a hat which protects the face, may take longer to react as these can interfere with the quantity of OC chemical that reaches the assailant's eyes. So, keep spraying until the aggression has completely stopped.

Some pepper-spray formulas include a dye which marks your assailant, making it easier for the police to identify them. Clearly a useful addition, but it's not an essential feature. More important is to select a device that is easy to carry, easy to use, and shoots its stream a significant distance.

Ergonomics of the Container: Unlike a lot of spray bottles which need to be looked at to determine which direction it sprays, a quality pepper-spray dispenser will be tactile. This is necessary since you need to be able to quickly grab the device and instantly point it in the proper direction, just by feel.

Side Effects of Pepper Spray or Tear-Gas Use

If you ever use pepper spray or tear-gas, expect to get some on yourself, especially if the wind is blowing toward you.

When you get hit by even a little mist of OC spray or tear-gas, it can make you cough uncontrollably. And, it can cause you to feel like you are having a heart attack, so keep in mind that it's harmless for those who are reasonably healthy. Remind yourself that you'll be okay, *and you can still run or fight if the circumstance demands it.*

OC spray, as well as tear gas, will not incapacitate you unless you get enough in your eyes to make them swell shut. Even then, you can usually see enough to get out of the area. So even if you are affected, don't delay, get out of the danger zone as soon as possible. This response is additionally essential as you may be further exposed to more OC, as the gas vapors will linger in the area.

After using pepper spray, don't touch your face with your hands, and don't rub your eyes with a finger, as this can introduce OC residue into your eyes or skin. Any sweaty portion of skin, like your neck and underarms, will be particularly susceptible to a burning sensation.

When convenient, remove and wash your clothing as they will likely have become contaminated. When possible, wash your hands with soap and water after using pepper spray, and again after removing your clothing.

* Be sure to read the cautions and usage directions on the label of the device you purchase. Absent other instructions, the following treatment is considered to be universal.

Treatment: Pepper Spray or Tear-Gas Exposure

If you become exposed to OC or tear-gas, the best treatment is to force yourself to breathe normally and flush your skin with cool, fresh water from a drinking fountain, garden hose, or spigot. You can use regular soap to remove the pepper spray from the skin, but *do not* use regular soap on your face, at least not initially. Just use plenty of fresh water, and repeatedly blink as this will produce a squeegee-like effect that will gently push the chemical out of your eyes.

If you have access to baby shampoo, combine it with the water to speed the recovery process for your eyes and face. You can use this mixture to splash on your face or put the baby shampoo and water mixture into a clean spray bottle that is capable of gently misting your face. To make the blinking process more efficient, use the gentle spray from the bottle to mist your face to augment natural tears.

Facing into a gentle breeze will also drive the chemical vapors away from your eyes. It can also increase tears.

Do not use other types of soaps around your eyes as it can introduce additional burning and irritation to the eyes, whereas baby shampoo does not irritate eyes and its detergent action can help remove the oily OC compound.

Baby shampoo, "yes." Other shampoos and soaps, "no."

Either way, the irritation will pass in 15-45 minutes, so the discomfort is only temporary. Breathe normally, and force yourself to relax as this will help the discomfort pass more quickly.

Implementation of a 'Pepper Spray Defense Plan'

Keeping additional devices in the door pocket of your car, and your pocket or purse, may also be a good idea, but for most people, it's best to use the same device. You don't want to become confused on how to operate it during a high-stress emergency situation.

Since pepper spray is a weapon, it is necessary to keep these devices out of the hands of children and unauthorized individuals. If kids do get into it, they'll probably only make that mistake once as it's genuinely unpleasant to be exposed to the chemical, but it is nevertheless your responsibility to secure these weapons.

It's a good idea to replace your pepper spray dispenser every four years. Once you purchase a pepper spray unit, test it using two quick

1-second bursts shot at a head-high target that is 10-feet distant from you. This step needs to be undertaken so that you know how your unit works.

Kimber Pepper Spray Devices: Don't use your device for practice if it is a Kimber pepper spray device that looks like a gun. These require the user to break-out a plastic "safety" before it can be used, and after removal, it is easy to discharge the spray inadvertently.

If you intend to purchase a Kimber pepper spray device, to avoid a potential risk, buy a colorful model so that it is evident that the device is not a regular handgun.

Important Legal Considerations

As odd as it may seem, pepper spray is not legal everywhere, so be sure that you understand your local laws before you possess or use pepper spray.

In most jurisdictions where pepper spray is legal, you still must be an adult to possess a pepper spray or tear gas self-defense tool.

If you ever use pepper spray—even if your assailant runs away and no harm came to you, call the police immediately. You must report the incident immediately, and express to the 9-1-1 dispatcher that you were in either in fear for your life, serious bodily injury, or other grievous harm. Reporting the incident to the police is necessary as criminals have been known to report the incident themselves— falsely claiming that they were the victim of an assault! To minimize the possibility of this and other unnecessary legal problems, be the first to report the incident to the police.

Wasp Spray Caution: Some people advocate using 'wasp spray' as a weapon, claiming that it is more effective than pepper spray. This tactic is ill-advised as it may cause blindness or life-threatening injuries. It may also result in criminal prosecution and substantial civil liabilities for anyone who intentionally uses it as a weapon. A court may conclude that using wasp spray as a weapon, is tantamount to the use of a chemical warfare device.

Where to Purchase

It's probably best to purchase pepper spray devices online, as the selection and price is better than what you will find at a sporting goods store. Moreover, often the models found in a local store will contain less than the optimal 10% of the **O**leoresin **C**apsicum chemical, so read the label carefully. It is *very* important to select a pepper spray device that contains **10%** OC.

Remember, you will need to select a device which contains more of the liquid if you want to be able to protect yourself (or others) from multiple attackers, or for use in more than one altercation. Needing it more than once may be likely in the aftermath of a disaster, particularly if you are traveling in a post-disaster environment. Therefore, we recommend selecting a product which contains a minimum of 1.8 oz of OC liquid.

For additional details on products, links to manufacturer's websites, and other details which are periodically updated to keep them current, visit the author's website. On the "Resources" page, look for "Supplemental Information" for this book.

www.SigSwanstrom.com

Chapter 18

"Prepared" vs. "Prepared and Ready to Roll"

What is the difference between being "prepared" for an emergency situation, and being "prepared and ready" for it?

It is essential for us to understand the difference. Moreover, real *readiness* requires a change in the way we live our life.

Don't misunderstand. Readiness is not a preoccupation with disaster, but it does include intentional living. In addition to improved safety, the benefits of readiness also include an increased capacity to live a fruitful and vibrant life.

To take the first step of readiness, we must adjust the focus of our life. To accomplish this, we become intentional about expanding our observation skills, increasing relevant knowledge and discernment, improving our problem-solving skills, and enlivening our mental, spiritual, emotional, and relational life. The initial step to reach this goal is straightforward. As a byproduct, we increase our *situational awareness*.

Here is an example: Researchers who know a lot about EMPs and other grid-down risks, tell us to expect Wild West-like effects. But what does this really mean?

They aren't suggesting that we will soon be riding horses, or living the life of a cowboy on the range. So, what are they telling us?

As we dig into this, we learn that their message is that we should expect economic changes, such as reverting back to the days when people used cash money and barter, and when people communicated with each other by writing on paper and through face-to-face conversations. In other words, they tell us that we will no longer be able to depend on electric and electronic technologies for communication.

Yet, while these low-tech conditions are features of the historic Old West days of the United States, there is more to it than this simple analogy. We need to understand what it means to be thrown into a new era that is akin to the *'Wild'* West.

To better understand this expected change, in the next few pages I'll relate a story which clarifies what the term "W*ild* West" really means. Hopefully, it will bring added understanding to the difference between being *'prepared'* and *'prepared and ready'* to roll (ready to act).

The concept of "readiness" is timeless, so this Wild West story is relevant for us today. Importantly, it is also useful as an example of what we can expect when evil people have the opportunity to run amuck.

The setting for this story is the era of America's Indian Wars. Specifically, the battle which transitioned the United States from its many years of having what they referred to as an Indian *problem* of conflict, to that of an actual *war*.

The war started on a rural family farm in Texas. It was in the spring of 1836.

Three years earlier, looking for a better life, an enterprising Christian family moved from Illinois to Texas. This extended family pooled their resources and acquired land in the wilderness area northeast of what is now Waco, Texas.

Led by their father, Daniel Parker, adult sons Silas, James and Benjamin, and relatives Sam and Robert Frost, L.D. Nixon, and L.T.M. Plummer, moved their families to Texas. Their objective was to escape the dead-end jobs in Illinois, and start a new more promising life in Texas.

The property they acquired had an abundance of wild game, and the nearby Navasota River was teeming with fish. Their acreage included fertile prairie land which was suitable for growing food, forests of trees for harvesting building materials, lush meadows, and an artesian spring of cool water. It was an idyllic setting.

It was perfect, except for one thing. There was a safety hazard.

Their land was in an area where marauding Comanches were known to travel. So, the Parkers researched this potential problem, and they concluded that it was worth the risk.

To mitigate the potential threat, they didn't just build houses, they established a fortified safe-haven community. These savvy people trusted God, but they also understood personal responsibility.

Their walled one-acre base camp consisted of a cabin for each family, plus two, 2-story blockhouses for security and storage. These were positioned at opposite corners of the compound. The addition of a water tank and a stock pen for animals made the compound entirely self-sufficient, even if subjected to a long siege.

The entire encampment was surrounded by a wall made of thick cedar log posts. Each post was 15-feet (4.5 meters) in length, with one end buried solidly in the ground to a depth of 3-feet, the top end chiseled to a sharp point. Each post was tightly positioned side-by-side without any gaps to ensure that it blocked observation, and provided a solid, unyielding wall for defense. It was essentially an impregnatable security zone.

There was only one obvious way into the compound, an opening in the wall which was broad enough to accommodate the width of a horse-drawn wagon. To secure this entrance, they fabricated a well-designed armored gate. With admirable foresight in design, they also installed a small emergency exit in the back wall, on the opposite side of the compound from the main entrance. This escape hatch was concealed and well secured.

They also built gunports all around the wall's perimeter. These were accessed by standing on a small platform which was secured to the wall below the opening. This gave the defenders both a height and bench-rest advantage for shooting, while at the same time denying an attacker access to the gunports because they were too high for them to reach.[19]

At 10:00 o'clock in the morning of May 19, 1836, this family of settlers was approached by a group of more than 100 Indians on horseback. One of the Indians in the forefront was carrying a white flag, indicating their peaceful intentions. This band of Indians was greeted by the sixteen unarmed adult men and older boys who were working in the cornfield just outside the compound's open gate. The other six men, along with eight women and the older girls, were working inside the compound, where the community's nine children were playing.

The attack came suddenly with overwhelming violence of action. As Ben Parker was warily conversing with the Indian leader, and in

---

[19] A replica of the old fort Parker encampment has been built in Groesbeck, Texas, as part of the Texas Heritage Trails Program.

spite of his demonstration of Christian hospitality which included offering the Indians baskets of food, he was killed without any provocation.

The troop of unarmed men was immediately cut down by a withering barrage of arrows and gunfire. Then the attacking force rode unhindered, past the open armored gate and security walls, to overwhelm the fortified encampment. The settlers inside the compound rushed to get their nearby guns and supply of ammunition, but all of them were shot before they could reach a firearm.

In less than 30-minutes, most of the residents were dead. Some of the victims were scalped while they were still alive. Many were tortured for no purpose other than the entertainment of their assailants.

Both the elderly women and young girls were sexually abused and disfigured. Infant and toddler children were beaten until they stopped crying. Several of the women and girls were also kidnapped and sold, or taken with Rachel Parker Plummer, 750 miles north to the base camp of the Comanche in eastern Colorado.

Bloodied and brutalized, a few of the inhabitants did manage to escape by hiding in the cornfield. These silently slipped away during the Comanche orgy of violence, and made their way on foot to Fort Houston, a Texas Ranger stockade. Their destination was 75⁺ miles distant, near to what is today Palestine, Texas. Impressively, they made this journey without provisions.

Like flagellated novitiates on a pilgrimage to the Promised Land, it took the battered survivors four days to reach the constabulary protection of the Texas Rangers. A month later, they were able to return home and bury their dead.

We know many of these details because one of the captives, 17-year old Rachel Parker Plummer, was able to chronicle[20] the unprovoked attack, and how she and the other prisoners had been sexually abused and sadistically tortured. Unlike most of the other survivors, Rachel was one of the ones kidnapped. This group of prisoners didn't just experience a day of horror, they were viciously brutalized by the Comanches for the 21-months they were held captive.

---

[20] Rachel Plummer, "Rachel Plummer's Narrative of Twenty-One Months Servitude as a Prisoner Among the Comanche Indians."

That was the outcome. But on the tranquil, bright spring morning when this saga began, none of the settlers were greatly worried. It seemed like an ordinary day.

How did this tragedy happen? It occurred because their extensive preparations and defenses were rendered useless. They had enjoyed many months of peaceful living and had let themselves be lulled into a *normalcy bias*. Nothing had happened; no encounters of any kind, so they had become sloppy in their thinking and lackadaisical with their security measures.

Their complacency eclipsed the insightful design of their safe-haven, their self-defense abilities (two of the men had been Texas Rangers and had previously fought Indians), adequate staffing, as well as their hard work constructing fortifications, building up an arsenal, and the stockpiling of supplies. They had become lax and comfortable. They had neglected the basic tenets of readiness and situation awareness.

These people were devout Christians with a strong Faith in God, but that didn't protect them. They were good people, charitable, and lived righteously. Yet, despite the dangers on their doorstep, they had failed to do their part.

They were not vigilant. [Absence of 'situation awareness.'] And, they were not able to differentiate between peaceful Indians and the vicious Comanche. [Lack of adequate intelligence gathering.] Wanting to be polite and give their visitors the benefit of the doubt, they failed to move into a defensive mode in advance of the Indian's initial act of aggression. {Failure to act in a timely fashion.] The ruse of the white flag further delayed their defensive actions. [Lack of a scenario-based defense plan.] They were surprised and caught unaware because they didn't have a lookout on duty. [No early warning alarms.] And, they had left the security gate wide open, and they were not carrying guns. [Failure to follow security procedures.] [21]

If asked the day prior if they were "prepared," the residents of the Parker safe-haven would have probably said they were thoroughly

---

[21] For a positive example of being prepared and ready, read the Bible's account of rebuilding the city of Jerusalem as described in Nehemiah. In that situation, the people maintained lookouts, had armed guards, used watchmen to sound the alarm if a threat was observed, and they made sure that every able-bodied person, including those engaged in hard labor, carried a weapon. Night and day, they were all armed; they lived in a constant state of readiness.

prepared. Nonetheless, they were obviously not "ready" to defend themselves. They were not *prepared* **and** *ready to roll*.

We may not be able to build an elaborate safe-haven fortification like the Parker family, but we can, in effect, be better prepared than they were if we combine our preparations with being alert, vigilant, and ready to act. Planning and well-rounded preparations are necessary, but vigilance is equally essential. Just as with the Parker family, danger can strike us suddenly when we aren't expecting it.

We should not live in fear, but we should live in a constant state of readiness. The key to this is…

Situation Awareness

White	• Unaware / Clueless
Yellow	• Relaxed but Alert ★
Orange	• Heightened Awareness
Red	• Something is Wrong (Action)
Black	• Caught Unaware (Panic)

To live in the White Zone (above chart) is always dangerous, regardless of circumstances. Conversely, when we live in the Yellow Zone, we can still relax and enjoy life, but we are alert and aware of our surroundings and what is happening. Then, if something seems amiss, we mentally transition to the Orange Zone which is a state of heightened awareness and closer scrutiny. If the situation warrants it, we jump into the Red Zone of reasoned and appropriate action.

The last zone color in the chart is black, and it represents what happens when we live in the White Zone and are suddenly surprised. This emotion often produces panic, which can provoke us to inappropriate or unhelpful action, or it can lead to debilitating fear and inaction. Both the White and Black Zones represent a dangerous mental state.

During times of peace as well as times of danger, we need to be vigilant, aware of our surroundings, and of the changes in the world around us. We need to be relaxed, yet alert. We need to live in the Yellow Zone.

We need to be aware, perceptive, and discerning. We need to live fearlessly, tuned-in to the world around us, and be always vigilant. We need to be Prepared; Ready to Roll.

Chapter 19

Medical Emergencies:
You Will Need More Than a First Aid Kit

First aid and CPR training offered by the Red Cross and hospitals, is an excellent place to start. However, "first aid" is only the first level of care. In a major disaster or extended emergency situation, you will need more. Much more.

Standard first aid kits and popular first aid training programs assume that you can quickly get the injured person to a hospital for treatment. Unfortunately, this may not be the case.

In a disaster or protracted emergency situation, you may not have access to a doctor or hospital. Therefore, it is essential to obtain first aid training, PLUS some additional instruction in "wilderness" medicine or specialized training in disaster-related emergency medical care. Likewise, a traditional first aid kit is a useful place to start, but it is necessary to augment it with additional supplies.

It is worth noting that most medical doctors are also not equipped to deal with the lack of access to a hospital, or at least the medical equipment of a clinic and the drugs of a pharmacy. Hopefully, doctors, nurses, and other medical professionals will take the necessary steps to prepare to serve in an emergency environment, but don't count on it. It may be the ordinary person who gains the skills and assembles the necessary medical equipment, medicines, and reference materials, which will literally become a lifesaver in an emergency situation.

Many aid organizations, particularly those operated by Christians, provide training for short-term mission teams who do volunteer work in developing countries. These agencies can be a great help to you, too. Through them, you may be able to acquire practical medical and health training, reference materials, and advice on supplies. Remember, in a long-drawn-out emergency situation, your area may become like a Third World community. These people are the experts.

Christian aid organizations and socially responsible publishers such as "Hesperian Health Guides" offer free PDF downloads of some of their most sought-after medical and health-care books and booklets. Purchase these materials now, or, download and print them now, as you may not have access to a computer during an emergency situation.

If you plan to download free resources, please make a donation if you are able. Either way, don't miss this opportunity to secure these valuable resource materials. Visit the Hesperian website to order books, as well as to download free materials such as these PDF books. These are essential, so if you don't print them (recommended), at least download them onto a USB flash drive (Chapter-23):

- "Where There is No Doctor"
- "Where There Is No Dentist"
- "A Book for Midwives"
- "Sanitation and Cleanliness"
- "Water for Life"

Free Source: http://hesperian.org/books-and-resources/

Other worthwhile books include:

- "Wilderness and Rescue Medicine," 2012 (6th Edition), by Jeffrey Isaac and David E. Johnson
- "Field Guide of Wilderness and Rescue Medicine," 2012 (7th Edition), by Jim Morrissey
- "Field Guide to Wilderness Medicine," 2013 (4th Edition), by Auerbach, Donner, and Weiss
- "Emergency War Surgery," 2013 (4th U.S. Revision), by U.S. Dept. of Defense
- "First Aid – Responding to Emergencies," 2007
  (4th Edition), by American Red Cross

Note: Especially with medical books, be sure to purchase the most recent editions. As of the time of printing, I have listed the latest version, but check this detail before you order your book(s).

If it is not practical for you to sign-up for an emergency medical class right now, or buy these reference books, at least purchase the Red Cross manual, "First Aid–Responding to Emergencies." Plus, one of the two books mentioned above, and start building your Emergency Medical Supplies Kit.

As previously mentioned, a standard first aid kit is not enough. You need a good first aid kit, but that is only one part of your Emergency Medical Supplies Kit. However, purchasing a first aid kit designed for backpackers who hike into remote wilderness areas, is an excellent place to start.

These first aid kits for wilderness backpackers, such as the 'Adventure Medical' kits available from backpacking stores, are also perfect for inclusion in your GO-Bag (Get-Out) evacuation kit. However, you will still need to add some additional medical and health supplies. Responding to a disaster involves more than backwoods hiking.

Specialty stores such as Recreational Equipment (www.REI.com) offer an assortment of 'Adventure Medical' wilderness first aid kits. These are often far superior to drug store first aid kits, and a better place to start when assembling your own kit.

Companies such as Con10gency (www.con10gency.com) which cater to First Responders, stock the specialty items needed to expand on these basic kits. Many of the businesses which supply police, fire department, and paramedic/EMT personnel, will sell medical supplies to the general public. Their products and prices are often better than storefront retailers, but it's worth checking Amazon.com and other online sources to make sure you're paying a fair price.

Gunshot wounds and injuries involving severe bleeding, whether caused by accident or because of violence, require specialized supplies for effective treatment.

The "QuikClot ACS Advanced Clotting Sponge TraumaPak," made by Z-Medica, has saved many lives because they are so effective in stopping bleeding. Every emergency medical kit should contain at least two of these QuikClot bandages, and at least one chest-wound sealing bandage.

Military surplus stores sometimes sell genuine government-issue "medic" kits, and they may include these items at a reduced price. However, beware of damaged supplies and counterfeit knock-off kits which contain inferior products.

Another disaster-situation injury to prepare for is dog bites. In a protracted emergency situation, abandoned pets will assemble into packs, and they will attack people, especially small children, in an attempt to secure food.

Dog bites will become common, along with more common injuries such as broken bones, cuts, scrapes, twisted ankles, blisters, insect bites, and eye injuries. Expect to encounter these medical problems often during natural and human-made disasters, so stock-up on supplies to match these and other routine medical conditions that you are likely to face.

Keep this in mind: The contents of a typical first aid kit were selected based on the assumption that the injured person will quickly receive paramedic care, or they will be rapidly evacuated to a hospital's emergency department or trauma center. So, though buying a first aid kit may be a great place to start your emergency medical preparations, it is only a place to start. A standard first aid kit is wholly inadequate.

In addition to specialized medical products such as QuikClot, in an extended emergency situation expect to encounter contaminated water and infection-breeding sanitation problems. This development requires different supplies and training. Wound and other infections will likely claim more lives than the injuries themselves.

Be sure to do what you can to avoid injury and illness. Don't take unnecessary chances. Be proactive regarding injury and disease treatment, including the treatment of small cuts and abrasions, minor injuries, and ailments which would ordinarily be considered routine. Poor health also leads to poor decision making, which often causes additional medical and safety dangers.

Make sanitation a top priority. Don't just filter water, purify it. If possible, drink water throughout the day, consuming at least 1-ounce of water for each pound of body weight. (A 150-pound person should consume at least 150-ounces of water, daily). Proper hydration (electrolyte balance) is essential for maintaining health.

If possible, wear dry and clean socks and underwear to minimize the growth of bacteria. Don't hike in wet shoes or boots, as this can result in blisters which can burst and quickly become infected.

Blisters can also develop due to friction between your foot and footwear as well as wet feet, and these problems are further aggravated by thin socks or inadequate shoes or boots. Use moleskin or tape to protect the areas of your feet where blisters tend to form. Without proper treatment, a simple blister can develop into a debilitating injury.

Take what steps you can to avoid becoming chilled or overheated, and force yourself to eat, even when you do not feel like it. When possible, eat nutritious and balanced food, which includes protein, carbohydrates, fruit, roughage, and fats. Each meal probably won't be balanced, but try to achieve balance in your day's consumption of food.

When possible, wash your hands frequently, and maintain proper health standards in your environment, especially before eating and after relieving yourself. Bury waste to minimize contamination, and to reduce the transmission of disease by flies and other insects. Establish a habit of not touching your mouth with your hands, and not mopping the mouth area of your face with a rag or handkerchief.

If you are with other people, watch each other closely for signs of health and emotional problems; talk with each other about health issues. Prevention is better than the best treatment.

Develop an emergency medical kit which includes medical equipment (tools) as well as supplies for treatment. It needs to also include sanitation and water purification supplies, along with a lightweight medical reference book, and an ample supply of often-used items such as Band-Aids and antibacterial soap.

If you encounter even a small cut, abrasion, or blister, we've found it worthwhile to be extremely aggressive in treatment. As soon as possible, scrub the affected area thoroughly with soap and clean water, apply an antibacterial treatment, and protect the injured area from dirt and contamination. Replace soiled bandages and re-clean the wound whenever it becomes necessary. Check the injury frequently for indicators of infection.

You may need to splint broken bones initially so that you can move the patient, but the bone needs to be set within a few hours. Deep wounds need to be scrubbed thoroughly, ideally with a small sterile brush made for that purpose.

> **The most important** first steps to be ready for potential medical problems during a disaster...
>
> **1.** Avoid injury and illness by utilizing prevention techniques, and by using appropriate protection gear such as safety glasses and filter masks.
>
> **2.** Wash often with soap and *lots* of water.
>
> Handwashing should be accomplished before putting anything in your mouth, in advance of purifying water, and before touching even a small cut, open blister, skin abrasion or rash, as well as periodically during the day.
>
> If skin is cut, abraded or inflamed, wash the area, use nonirritating soap. Even for ordinary handwashing, use the "Happy Birthday" method in which you sing to yourself the "Happy Birthday" song. Sing it twice while you wash, to help you be more thorough.
>
> This may seem excessive, but these two simple steps can save you from major problems, later.
>
> -- Marcos Mavromaras, M.D. (Emergency Medicine), and a PRTR Medical Advisor

Severe bleeding needs to be stopped quickly, and measures taken to mitigate potential infection, as blood loss and even a minor infection will multiply health risks and delay recovery. These risks are viable even when the injury itself does not appear to be severe.

You may not have access to professional medical help for a very long time. Be prepared to accomplish wound treatment, suturing, and bone-setting. Your life, or the life of another, may depend on you, your training, and your supplies.

Though most antibiotics only have a shelf life of a year, it is worth asking your doctor for a prescription for a wide-spectrum antibiotic such as Cipro (Ciprofloxacin) or Doxycycline. Purchase it and keep it in your GO-Bag, along with the instructions and the pharmacy label. Take note of the expiration date and replace as needed to maintain potency. (Store medicine and all dangerous items away from children.) Get instructions from your doctor, but in some situations, you may want to administer an antibiotic regimen as part of the initial treatment before the victim demonstrates symptoms of infection.

If you or a family member need other medications, such as for a heart condition or diabetes, be sure to maintain a supply of these medicines in both your GO-Bag and your Emergency Supply Kit. Keep a copy of prescription documents, and other relevant medical records in your kits.

If it is not practical to store these medications in your GO-Bag and

Emergency Medical Kit, be sure to attach a note to your bag, to remind you to retrieve the medicine from your refrigerator before leaving home. Use "Blue Ice" and an insulated container to store medications which require refrigeration, and keep the bag out of direct sunlight. In a vehicle, keep the drugs in the vehicle's trunk, rather than the interior of the car which will super-heat if it is parked outside.

Also, don't discount the value of naturopathic remedies. Everyday food items such as cinnamon, honey, sea salt and baking soda have many medical and health-improving uses. Also, worth noting is that some organic Essential Oils have a reputation for aiding the body's natural healing processes for both injury and disease, as well as for other practical purposes.

For example, Tea Tree Essential Oil and Lavender Essential Oil can be used as an antiseptic, and for antimicrobial and antifungal treatments. Peppermint Essential Oil is touted as useful as both an antiseptic and for antibacterial use. Clove Bud Essential Oil is sometimes used as an anti-inflammatory, insect repellent, and even for replacing a lost filling in a tooth. (1-2 drops of Clove Bud Essential Oil, added to Zinc Oxide, will form a paste that can be used to fill a broken tooth. Bite down and hold for 10-minutes to give the compound a chance to harden.)

Various natural foods, spices, and Essential Oils have historically been used for medicinal and health-enhancing purposes. A modern medicine such as Neosporin may be a useful antibiotic for cuts and abrasions, but a single essential oil can serve a dozen different needs.

Since stress and changes in eating habits often result in stomach upset, heartburn, constipation, or nausea, be sure to include remedies for these problems in your medical kit, too.

Changes in your natural environment may call for the use of products which you infrequently use in your life today, so there is a tendency to forget to add these to your medical kits. Yet, these everyday products may become treasures when you must face a disaster. Ordinary items such as sunscreen lotion, insect repellent (100% DEET), tick removal tweezers, medical filtration-masks (particulate respirators), safety glasses, a small magnifying glass and flashlight, a scrub brush for cleaning wounds, skin lotion, disinfectant and sanitation products, HikeGoo and Moleskin for blisters, and water purification devices or tablets, may become invaluable.

Stockpile quantities of often-used consumables such as antibacterial soap, disinfectants, aspirin, ibuprofen, band-aids, lotions, digestive aids, and medical gloves.

Animals get injured and sick as well as humans, so don't forget these creatures as you prepare for medical emergencies and health needs. Your veterinarian, online vet supply store, or farm/ranch supply co-op can help you get ready for the health needs of your pet or other animals in your care.

Medical kits for use by medical professionals are different than kits for non-professionals

To complete this chapter, I asked a military Special Operations (spec-ops) combat medic to give me a list of the medical supplies he personally carries into harm's way. And, I also asked my own medical team for their recommendations as to what should be included in a GO-Bag medical kit designed to be used by those who are *not* medical professionals.

The objective was to identify those items which are actually needed, and those supplies which are routinely used, rather than what is typically found in the first aid kits sold in stores.

Our emergency medical team not only has impressive credentials, but they also have extensive experience in emergency situations, so these recommendations need to be taken seriously. To be more specific, our medical team includes the following: A hospital emergency department physician who works in a major trauma center, a spec-ops police officer who worked in one of the largest cities in the U.S. who is also a TacMed instructor, a medevac helicopter flight nurse, a Wilderness Medicine instructor, and several paramedics and EMTs. With these credentials and their experience in mind, I heartily recommend that you take their advice seriously. They have provided this information to help you assemble a no-nonsense GO-Bag emergency medical kit.

The following pages include the recommendations of these top professionals. To be clear, the first part of the next section is for use by those who are themselves, medical professionals. The second portion, "GO-Bag Medical Supplies for Those Who are Not Medical Professionals," is for those who do not have a lot of medical training.

As I consulted with these top professionals, there was a recurring theme: "Don't bother to carry gear you don't know how to use." When it comes to the gear list for professionals and non-professionals alike, this may mean you need to get additional training. Whichever category you fit into, you need to know how to use these supplies.

GO-Bag Medical Supplies for Use by Medical Professionals

This and the following 2-pages are for medical professionals.

Note: This list of gear is not for a full military medical kit. Rather, it is the medical supplies carried by one battle-seasoned medic when he is operating in a combat zone or high-danger environment.

As you will quickly conclude, his medical kit is far more elaborate than what most of us will carry. It is also more than we could possibly fit in our GO-Bag. Yet, the following information can nevertheless be helpful, especially for those readers who are medical professionals. It can help the rest of us, too, as we consider what medical gear to include in our own at-home and retreat-location medical kits—which should consist of, and expand on, the contents of our individual GO-Bag medical kits.

For non-medical people, you won't have a clue as to what some of these items are, or what purpose they fulfill. Don't let that concern you. Keep in mind the advice of our team of professionals:

a) *If you don't know what it is, don't include it in your medical kit.*

b) *If it's included in the list for non-professionals, and you don't know what it is or how to use it, learn.*

Of course, if you're preparing a kit in anticipation of having on-hand a medical professional who has the skill to use these items, that's a different story. But otherwise, it is useless to carry Advanced Life Support gear in your personal GO-Bag if you don't know how to use it.

Contents of a Spec-Ops Medic's Personal Kit

In his own words: *"My first-in bag supplements what I carry in pouches on my combat vest, which includes tourniquets, combat gauze, 14g 3" Angio, King LTD size 4, chest seals, and a couple of NAR ETD dressings. Gloves (medical and tactical), headlamp, surveyor's tape, sharpie, grease pencil, medical shears, small binoculars, ChemLights, and a Mark 1 autoinjector.*

"Individually, all team members carry an NAR ETD, NPA, combat gauze, mechanical tourniquet, and gloves, so I can draw from that pool as well.

"I use the North American Rescue NAR4 bag (19x15x7-inches). It clips directly to my vest; its design is fairly ergonomic. The TSSI M9 bag is also good. ATS Tactical Gear took the M9 and improved it, making it slightly larger and ditching the drawstring pouches, replacing that closure method with zipper pouches. These bags are solid, well made, and low profile."

His list is included here to help _medical professionals_ build their kit.

- 2 Mechanical Tourniquets
- 2 Chest seals
- Gloves
- 2 NAR ETD dressings
- 2 Combat gauze
- 8 4x4 gauze
- Z-folded gauze
- 2AA laryngoscope handle, fiberoptic
- Fiberoptic disposable metal blades: Mac 4, Miller 4, Miller 1.
- ET tubes, whole sizes only, and stylets (one pediatric, one adult)
- Bougie
- Suction-Easy
- Nonin fingertip pulse ox
- NPAs
- 10cc syringe
- 100+ cc syringe for flushing wounds with pure water
- Cric hook and scalpel
- Pocket BVM
- Sam Junctional Tourniquet
- Saran wrap roll
- Sam Splint
- Space blanket
- IV start kits, again NAR

- Small pouch of misc. syringes and needles
- 250cc bag LR
- Drug box, lockable
- Epi 1:1000
- Benadryl
- Solumedrol
- Scopolamine
- Etomidate
- Tranexamic acid
- Zofran
- Rocephin or Invanz
- Lidocaine 1% (for IO)
- Kit also includes several other controlled substances and narcotics not listed here.

"Shears and drug box are dummy corded to the inside. Everything not in a pouch has sticky Velcro on it to keep it from falling out when opened and moved."

Truck Bag

"My large truck bag contains stuff for more extended care. IV fluids, wound repair (sutures, staples, glue, SteriStrips), ace wraps, hypothermia kit, snivel care (sniffles, pain, diarrhea, vomiting), SAM splints, ziplock bags for ice. Lots of gauze and dressings for MASCAL. Extra critical care stuff for split team ops. Kendrick Traction Device for when I'm doing airborne jumps. It's big and heavy, so that's why it stays in the truck. Blackhawk STOMP 2, LBT 1562, or Camelbak BFM with Medbak insert is fine for this. I use a SO Tech Mission Pack-Medical.

"I have no financial interest in any of these recommendations."

Commentary on the Previous Section

Though informative, we should not confuse the role of a Combat Medic with that of a civilian medical professional who is working in a post-disaster environment. Nonetheless, this information may be helpful to prepare for a situation when there isn't timely access to ambulances, hospital trauma centers, and other medical care facilities.

The preceding list is included only as a point of reference. It is *not* a "recommended list" of gear to be carried by every medical doctor and medical professional.

GO-Bag Medical Supplies Kit
Gear for those who are __not__ medical professionals

Package your medical supplies in three soft-sided small nylon pouches. Be sure to assemble the following supplies *before* selecting the size bag you need. There are three components to this GO-Bag medical kit (part-A, B, and C). All three contain essential gear.

Medical Kit - Part-A: Trauma Kit, a small nylon pouch containing the self-treatment supplies needed for handling a major injury.

Medical Kit - Part-B: Medicine Kit, a small kit containing both non-prescription and prescription drugs.

Medical Kit - Part-C: Main Medical Kit, details follow.

Medical Kit - Part-D: Dental Kit (see Chapter-20 for details)

Medical Kit - __PART-A__: Trauma Kit for GO-Bag

This kit must be readily accessible, so carry it either: a) On your belt, or b) on the strap of your GO-Bag knapsack, or c) on a chest rig. The pouch you select for your Trauma Kit should be: waterproof, have a zipper closure, and belt loops or PALS/MOLLE-style (military) attachment straps. It should contain:

- [ ] Mechanical tourniquets (2) [Recommendations can be found on the Resources page of the author's website: SIGSWANSTROM.com]
- [ ] Combat gauze – 3 x 48 inches (2) [aka Clotting Gauze, brand name: *QuikClot EMS Rolled Gauze*, or equivalent]

    The U.S. military and law enforcement officers who are also tactical medics (TacMed), often use *QuikClot Combat Gauze LE*. It is the same product as the EMS version, but in a compact z-fold packet rather than a roll of gauze. It's also twice the price.

- [ ] Chest Seal bandage – vented (2)
- [ ] NAR ETD dressings, or Israeli Battle Dressing (1)
- [ ] Medical gloves - not black, as it doesn't show blood contact (2 pr)
- [ ] CPR face shield (1) [optional]
- [ ] Filtration mask – paper – N95 rating (2)
- [ ] Medical shears (1)
- [ ] Sharpie pen (1) for marking treatment info on arm or near injury.

Medical Kit - PART-B: Medicine Kit for GO-Bag
Note: This is in addition to the *Trauma Kit* and *Main Medical Kit*

Since even a mild illness can limit your ability to travel, reduce your stamina, or distract you from the urgent business at hand, your kit needs to include various medications. This is not just a matter of comfort; these are included to help restore your operational health.

Carried in a clear plastic, Hefty Slider bag in your GO-Bag, your medicine kit should contain a small quantity of a wide assortment of medications. It should also include any prescription drugs you need for maintaining health, in addition to over-the-counter medicines.

Over-the-counter medications for your kit should contain products you don't usually use but might discover are necessary, especially if you find yourself traveling on foot, experiencing a change in diet, suffering from unusual stress, or other maladies which surface during an emergency situation.

This kit should not resemble your medicine cabinet. It should be small in size, with medications removed from packaging. However, retain instructions whenever appropriate by cutting that section out of the packaging or copying the relevant details from the label.

The quantities stored in this kit should only be sufficient for a few days of treatment. If a drug is not packaged in 1-dose foil packets, you may want to remove the needed quantity of pills and combine them in an air-tight water-tight plastic pill bottle. If medicines are combined, be sure to label the container with the details of its contents, including a description of each type of pill. Create your own inventory of products; the following list is just to help you get started.

Medical Kit – Part-B Supplies List

Include your favorite over-the-counter medications for...

- [ ] Nausea due to flu, minor food poisoning, & non-serious ailments
- [ ] Allergic reactions to foods, pollen, insect stings, etc.
- [ ] Diarrhea
- [ ] Constipation
- [ ] Upset stomach due to diet change, nerves, etc.
- [ ] Headache and minor pains
- [ ] Sore muscles and/or cramps due to exertion
- [ ] Eye cleansing / Relief from eye irritation
- [ ] Electrolyte imbalance (see Chapters 10 and 14)
- [ ] Nasal congestion, runny nose, cough suppression
- [ ] Sore throat due to cold, or exposure to smoke, bad air, etc.
- [ ] Antibiotic gel for minor cuts and abrasions
- [ ] Burn treatment / relief
- [ ] Poison Oak / Poison Ivy
- [ ] Something to help stay awake
- [ ] Menstrual cramps and discomfort (if applicable)

*** To save space and weight, remove the above medicines from bulky packaging and combine them in airtight plastic bottles. Include a description of the drug and dosage details. For example, "Bright Pink Tablet – Benadryl, for allergies and allergic reactions. For adults, 1-2 every 4 hrs." If you are unfamiliar with the medicine, include the directions from the manufacturer's packaging.

Optional Medication (Can be purchased online without prescription)

- [ ] Potassium Iodide (KI) Tablets, 130 mg, 14 tablets. For nuclear radiation exposure. The brand used by the U.S. military is iOSAT; shelf life 7 yrs, but it can be extended by eliminating light and moisture.

Prescription Medications

- [ ] Add at least a 2-week supply of any prescription medicines you are taking, or think you might need. Be sure to include a copy of your doctor's prescription or the label from the medicine bottle.
- [ ] EpiPen, if needed for severe allergic reactions.

Medical Kit - <u>Part-C</u>: Main Medical Kit for GO-Bag
(Note: This is in *addition* to the "Trauma Kit" and "Medicine Kit.")

- [ ] NAR ETD dressings, or Israeli Battle Dressing (2 minimum)
- [ ] Trauma Pad – 5 x 9 (2 minimum)
- [ ] 4 x 4 gauze bandages (4 minimum)
- [ ] Bandage – Self-Adherent Wrap (aka Coban) – 4-inch x 5 yards
- [ ] Medical adhesive tape - waterproof – 1-inch x 10 yards
- [ ] Butterfly bandages – Medium (12) [Or use Super Glue]
- [ ] Triangular bandage (1-2)
- [ ] Band-Aids – waterproof/sports or flexible fabric (Large) (6)
- [ ] Band-Aids – waterproof/sports or flexible fabric (Medium) (6)
- [ ] Band-Aids – waterproof/sports or flexible fabric (Knuckle) (2)
- [ ] Gauze, roll, 2-inch
- [ ] Medical tape, waterproof, 1-inch
- [ ] Elastic bandage, self-adhering, 3-inch
- [ ] Antibiotic cream
- [ ] Moleskin – Blister treatment and prevention (Keep feet dry, use Moleskin or a similar product to eliminate chafing and diminish pain, keep the area clean to prevent infection. Inspect feet often.)
- [ ] Eyewash, saline only – not medicated. This product is often sold alongside products for contact lense users. 1-oz. plastic bottle (1)
- [ ] Hand sanitizer liquid, 1-oz. (1)
- [ ] Medical gloves, any color except black (as it hides blood) (3 Pair)
- [ ] Medical shears (1)
- [ ] Filtration mask – paper, N95 filtration (2)
- [ ] Fingernail brush for cleaning wounds, small, soft-bristle (1)
- [ ] Surgical soap – Chlorhexidine Gluconate 4% (2⁺oz plastic bottle). Use this soap and the fingernail brush to clean wounds and abrasions.
- [ ] Tweezers (1)

- [ ] Magnifying glass – Small (1)
- [ ] Small flashlight or headlamp (1) [For details, see Chapter 23]
- [ ] ChemLight – yellow, green, or blue color (1) [For details, see Chapter 21 on flashlights and emergency lighting]
- [ ] Space blanket – lightweight version (1)
- [ ] Trash sack – white – 13-15 gallon-size plastic bag (1) [Use under the injury during treatment, or for spreading out the contents of your medical kit.]
- [ ] Safety pins – large (3)
- [ ] Sharpie pen – black (1)
- [ ] Super glue – to seal minor cuts and skin tears. [optional]

The medical version of super glue was developed as a topical skin adhesive to replace sutures (stitches). It is sold under the brand names such as: Dermabond, SurgiSeal. Histoacryl, Indermil, Glu-Stitch, GluSeal, PeriAcryl, LiquiBand, and Epiglu.

Those who are not medical professionals, and those who want to save money, often use an industrial-grade super glue product such as those sold in hardware stores. If this is your intention, a major brand may provide greater purity.

Some eliminate butterfly bandages from their kit altogether and routinely use super glue to bring together the edges of cut or torn skin. If this is your intention, be sure to include multiple small tubes as the shelf life is very short for an opened tube.

Use: After cleaning the injured area, apply *a thin layer* of glue to the cut or torn edges of the skin, and press them together until the skin bonds. The skin does not need to be completely dry.

Storage: Shelf life is one year on an *unopened* tube, but this can be extended by sealing the super glue tubes in a Mylar bag with a desiccant, such as silica gel, to eliminate the damaging effect of moisture on the product.

Note: The items listed on these two pages are in addition to those in the *Trauma Kit* (Part-A of your GO-Bag medical kit), and your *Medicine Kit* (Part-B), and *Dental Kit* (Part-D, Chapter-20). There are four component parts to the recommended medical kit.

General information about your GO-Bag Medical Kit, Part-C

Part-C of your medical kit needs to be small and compact like the rest of your GO-Bag's contents. When parts A, B, and C are combined, this first aid kit is far smaller than a medical kit you might keep at home or in your vehicle.

Like the other two segments, Part-C of your medical kit needs to be small-in-size and lightweight. These are essential attributes as the GO-Bag itself, by necessity, must also be compact and lightweight.

A more elaborate medical kit should be kept in your home, office, and each vehicle. The GO-Bag medical kit is more than a first aid kit. It is a "specialty" kit designed specifically for traveling on foot and in different environments and hazards, including injuries due to traffic accidents, flying debris, collapsed buildings, and violence. This is a basic kit; those with special needs, as well as medical professionals, will likely want to carry a more elaborate kit.

Rather than buy a container and fill it, start by assembling the items listed on the prior two pages, then find a brightly-colored nylon bag with a zipper closure. Or, use a heavy duty (or freezer) Hefty Slider plastic bag. Select the size of the bag to fit the kit contents loosely. Do not use a plastic box. This bag needs to be lightweight but sufficiently durable that it won't break open if you need to throw it to an injured person.

Organize the contents of this durable outer bag by using several waterproof clear plastic bags, such as smaller Hefty Slider bags. These plastic bags can be removed quickly, and the needed items can be easily located since the bag is transparent. Organize these plastic bags to correspond to specific medical problems, such as: cuts and abrasions, severe bleeding, blisters and foot problems, etc.

Pet First Aid

According to the American Veterinary Medicine Association, emergency medical kits for a dog or cat are essentially the same with a few exceptions. A digital 'fever' thermometer should be used as 'normal' temperatures for animals are higher. Also, a soft cloth is needed to wrap the mouth, to keep an injured animal from biting. Sticky tape or Band-Aids should not be used on the fur of a pet.

PetMD says that various human medications can be used for dogs and cats. Aspirin (but *not* other painkillers), Pepcid or Pepto Bismol (stomach), Lomotil (diarrhea & cough), MiraLAX (constipation), and Benadryl (allergic reactions & emotional distress) are all human medicines which can be used for dogs and cats. Adjust the dosage to their weight. Antibiotic gels such as Neosporin can be used on cuts and abrasions, and saline on eyes.

Vehicle-based First Aid Kits

An evacuation-oriented first aid kit to carry in your vehicle should be the same as the Part-A Trauma Kit, and Part-C Main Medical Kit, but add extra quantities of the items which might be needed to treat traffic accident injuries.

At-Home and Retreat-Location Medical Kits

Duplicate the contents of the "GO-Bag Medical Supplies" kit, but add additional quantities to accommodate the number of people in your group or household, the circumstances for which you are preparing, and the duration of the emergency you anticipate. Then, add additional items from the Military Medic kit as may be appropriate, and other medical supplies and gear that correspond to the health needs of your individual family/group members.

Simple items such as a 100cc or larger syringe (or a 3-oz. stainless-steel marinade injector as used for cooking meat), may be very helpful for wound care as copious amounts of fast-moving water can dislodge dirt and debris from a wound. Stock up on versatile supplies such as medical tape and sterile gauze, or even individually wrapped disposable menstrual pads, as these can be used to make an assortment of bandage types and sizes.

In addition to extra quantities of the previous supplies, add:

- ☐ Hydrogen Peroxide, 3%, unopened plastic bottles, (3 or more)
- ☐ Cotton balls or 2-inch gauze pads for cleaning wounds (25)
- ☐ Gauze roll. 4-inch (2 or more)
- ☐ Additional sizes of gauze pads and bandages
- ☐ Thermometer (2 or more), oral, glass, with protective case (Non-electronic)
- ☐ Fever thermometer, electronic (1) [optional]
- ☐ Alcohol pads, individual foil pouches [optional]
- ☐ Instant Cold Packs (2 or more)
- ☐ Instant Heat Packs (2 or more) [optional]
- ☐ Eye pads (2 or more)
- ☐ Eye wash with eye cup
- ☐ Eye drops, medicated
- ☐ Blood pressure cuff (non-electronic)
- ☐ Stethoscope
- ☐ _____
- ☐ _____
- ☐ _____
- ☐ _____
- ☐ _____
- ☐ _____
- ☐ _____

Medicine: Medicines for diarrhea, constipation and upset stomach are essential because a change in diet often upsets your body systems. When possible, use natural products rather than drug-based chemical products. For example, a natural laxative such as Metamucil may be a better choice than a pill designed to accomplish the same purpose. Due to convenience and space limitations, it's important to include various medicines for ailments such as diarrhea, constipation, and upset stomach in your GO-Bag, but natural products are better for long-term use.

> In Appendix-B of this book you will find specifics on what the U.S. military has determined to be the ideal Calorie count, nutritional balance, and vitamin & mineral intake for an adult who is operating in a high-stress emergency situation.

Vitamins: Most multivitamins are actually a waste of money as they are not digested before being expelled, so don't bother with anything other than a quality vitamin. To test your vitamin tablet, put it in a clear drinking glass with a cup of tepid water. Stir for a few seconds, and then let it sit for 30-minutes. If the vitamin pill has not dissolved after half an hour, stir or shake the water again. If the vitamin has not completely melted after 60-minutes, it is unlikely that this brand of vitamin will be helpful to your health. It probably won't dissolve in your stomach, either.

Unfortunately, quality vitamins generally have a short shelf life, but they are nevertheless worth including with your emergency supplies. Just as with your food, rotate them to keep the supply fresh.

Certain vitamins also have additional uses or benefits, so you may want to include extra quantities of these. For example, Vitamin C is useful to accelerate healing after an injury.

Confusion Over 'Self-Sacrifice'

When is it appropriate to stop and render aid as in the well-known Good Samaritan story? And, when is it the right choice to pass by, without stopping to help? Or, provide limited or quick help?

Do we have a responsibility to help people we don't know? If so, when does this responsibility end? What are our "Good Samaritan"[22] moral responsibilities for rendering medical and other forms of aid?

Each of us needs to come to our own conclusions. But we can't afford to wait until the situation is upon us to establish our own Good Samaritan guidelines.

Emergency situations are jam-packed with people who need medical and other forms of assistance. When we are bugging-out and time is of the essence, or our resources are meager, do we help others? How much aid do we provide? When should we stop helping? Do we use our meager supply of medicine or medical supplies to assist others? Do we share our limited water and food stockpile with those who had the opportunity to prepare, but didn't?

These are topics that are rarely discussed, and are rife with confusion. Television shows and movies add to the mental fog, but we can't expect morally bankrupt Hollywood to provide sage guidance. Even so, it is valuable to work through these questions with the benefit of external input. Still, where do we get wise counsel on a topic that others don't want to talk about?

Regardless of your spiritual beliefs, a book like the Holy Bible is an invaluable source of time-tested advice. In its book of Proverbs, we find a collection of short, pithy precepts for practical living. The life of Jesus[23] as related in the Bible is also ripe with concrete examples that are fruitful for us, which we can use to guide our actions. Jesus' parable of the Good Samaritan is a well-known example that is respected not just by Christians, but by all thoughtful people.

If we are interested in time-tested counsel, we need to be careful to get this guidance from the reliable source itself, not from a paraphrase or other people's teaching on the subject. For example, an often-cited Bible verse that relates to this topic is often misquoted as, "There is no greater example of love than for a person to sacrifice his

---

[22] Jesus' parable of the Good Samaritan is found in the Holy Bible, Luke 10:25-37.

[23] Contained in the Bible books of: Matthew, Mark, Luke, and John.

life to save another." However, this sweet sounding pseudo-quote isn't what the Bible actually says. An accurate translation of Jesus' teaching on this subject is phrased slightly different, and it ends with the words, "for a friend." He didn't say, "for another." When it comes to the subjects we are dealing with in this book, these seemingly minor changes can make a life-or-death world of difference.

This is a poignant reminder. Jesus teaches that family and friends are generally worthy of our selfless sacrifice, including, perhaps, even the sacrifice of our own life. However, even Jesus, who is respected as the most loving man who ever lived, does not suggest that we have an obligation to give this same level of consideration to everyone.

In fact, it is foolish and inappropriate to risk our own life and well-being, if that sacrifice is likely to harm our family or friends. With this in mind, giving medical care to an injured person is typically appropriate, and is often even our responsibility. It is a commendable labor of love.

However, it is not an act of loving kindness to provide aid to a stranger if that action may result in harm, abuse, or increased risk to a loved one. This is an important distinction.

As discussed in Chapter-1, *running scenarios* can help us with our medical triage. It can also assist us with our decision making.

"When do we render aid?" "How much help should we give?" The answers to these enigmatic questions are clouded by shades of gray, so we need to keep our thoughts practical and based on something external; a source that bypasses our natural tendency of self-centeredness. It's easy to get trapped on a rabbit trail of confusing thoughts, or become absorbed with straw-man arguments which we are unlikely to encounter in the real world.

These questions are not just the subject of academic or theological debate. They are real-world issues that each of us must consider. We need to talk about these matters with our family and friends, too.

When we encounter a protracted emergency situation, we will be forced to answer these questions with either action or inaction. Therefore, it is far better to consider these issues now, when we have the time to apply rational thought and contemplation.

Self-sacrifice can be noble and is sometimes even heroic. Self-sacrifice can also be foolish, or an act of selfishness if the cost of our decision will be paid, even in part, by family and friends. They are our responsibility. Our answers to these questions must keep this responsibility not just in mind, but addressed first, with primacy.

Chapter 20

Preparing for a Dental Emergency
Medical Kit – Part-D
(See Chapter-19 for Parts A-C of this medical kit)

Emergency situations can become an even more significant disaster if you are coping with the pain of a broken tooth, particularly if it is a severe pain such as is caused by a broken tooth with an exposed root. Since a trip to the dentist may not be feasible during an emergency, it is a good idea to include a dental repair kit in your at-home emergency supplies.

You may also want to add a small 1-tooth repair kit to your GO-Bag, and to your vacation or business travel bags, too. Since dental problems often happen at inopportune times, be prepared for this potential problem now. It may also be a godsend when traveling, or on an ordinary weekend when your dentist's office is closed.

Since dental emergencies take various forms; a broken tooth, a

> You have two basic options for acquiring Part-D of your medical kit.
>
> Option-1: You can purchase the component parts and assemble your own kit. These products can be found online. You might want to use the contents of the Dental Kit made by 'Adventure Medical Kit' to inform your shopping. The purchase price of these parts will cost about the same as a dozen donuts at your favorite bakery. Or,
>
> Option-2: You can buy a prepackaged 1-tooth kit for price of two boxes of donuts. (Though I'm a retired police officer, I still think about donuts.)
>
> Whichever method you choose, you may want to be equipped to repair more than one tooth.

lost filling, or a crown (cap) that has fallen out, your emergency dental kit needs to be both universal and reasonably complete. At a minimum, it should include:

- ☐ Painkiller tablets,
- ☐ dental glue,
- ☐ Dental cotton balls (pellets) or gauze,
- ☐ Round toothpicks,
- ☐ Dental floss,
- ☐ Dental wax, and
- ☐ Tooth-filling material.

Optional but valuable additions include:

- ☐ Medical gloves,
- ☐ Small mirror like the ones dentists use,
- ☐ Magnifying glass, ideally illuminaed; and a
- ☐ Flashlight, small, lightweight penlight.

Tooth pain, or any other pain, will drain your body's energy reserves at a much faster rate. You may be able to cope with the pain, but it can nevertheless become a serious impediment to safety because you need to be 100% focused and attentive to problem-solving. If you are in pain, do what you can to alleviate it.

Note: In a bind, you can use Super Glue to reattach a crown. First, try to fit the crown back into place, to make sure it fits and there are no missing pieces. Then, dry the base of the crown and the area where it belongs. Add a drop of glue to each surface and wait a few seconds. Put the crown in place and press the crown to hold it in place for 2 minutes. Only use this method in a true emergency, when you don't have a dental repair kit and you can't get to a dentist.

Inexpensive dental repair kits may not have all of the above supplies, but they can be a great place to start. Augment your pre-packaged dental kit as necessary. Emergency repairs of dentures and partials require additional materials made specifically for this purpose.

At a minimum, GO-Bags should include dental wax which can be used to cover a broken tooth that has an exposed root. Tooth pain is not just inconvenient; it can create a life-threatening distraction.

Pre-packaged dental repair kits are not all the same, and professional-grade repair materials are a must, but you do not need to purchase an expensive kit to get what you need.

A "DenTemp Custom" kit can be purchased online for under $5, but it is definitely a minimalist kit. Far from complete, yet it does contain two essential items, so it can be used as the foundation for building your own low-cost kit.

The DenTemp package contains zinc oxide and Eugenol putty, materials you can use to repair or replace a missing filling, or to cover the void of a broken tooth. The zinc oxide forms the putty, and the Eugenol reduces inflammation and protects the nerve of the tooth. These are the same materials that many dentists use to bring temporary relief to their patients.

Thankfully, application of these tooth repair materials not only doesn't require a dental degree; it doesn't even require any experience. A good kit will include diagrams and all the instructions needed, so being trained by your dentist in how to use the kit is helpful, but not necessary.

If you are assembling your own do-it-yourself kit, make sure to include printed instructions which relate to the materials contained in your kit. These instructions are typically available on the product manufacturer's website.

Since it is hard to accomplish dental repairs when you cannot see what you are doing, in most dental emergencies, it is far easier to have someone else do the work on a damaged tooth. However, it is certainly possible to do it yourself. Many people have accomplished the task alone with excellent results.

Most dental repairs can be achieved by touch and feel, even if you don't have a mirror and can't see what you are doing. Nevertheless, even a small signal mirror is very helpful if you find yourself alone.

If you have the benefit of having the help of another person, you will find that a lightweight, small flashlight and magnifying glass (or a magnifying glass with a built-in light) will be a great help. Since these items can be useful for other, non-dental purposes as well, they are a good addition to any emergency kit.

Pre-packaged Dental Repair Kits

Dental repair kits are not all the same. Some have additional components, higher quality materials, or additional quantities which make them useful for repairing more than one tooth. Therefore, check the contents before you make your purchase.

The inexpensive dental repair kits found in many drugstores are typically inferior for emergency use, especially when you may not have access to a dentist for many days or weeks. We applaud being frugal and appreciate convenience, but this may not be the place to cut corners.

Just as the first aid kits made by "Adventure Medical Kits" (AMK) are more comprehensive (and more expensive), so are their dental kits. If you are looking for a quick and easy solution, purchase their kit. For many, the AMK *Dental Medic Kit* is well worth the price. (Note: This kit is included in several of their complete medical kits, so you may not need a stand-alone kit if you have already purchased one of their more elaborate first aid kits.)

Whichever kit you choose, be sure to check the Contents List before you make your purchase decision. Just because the package is large, or expensive, does not mean that it contains a greater quantity of useful supplies.

Instructions on how to use your dental repair kit

* Most of the better kits use a process which is similar to that which is included here. If the directions which came with your kit are different, use them.

Step 1: First, dry the tooth area as much as possible. Accomplish this by using the dental cotton pellets or gauze included in the kit. Or, if you have electricity and a hairdryer, consider using it on the lowest setting. Either way, thoroughly dry the tooth which is in need of repair. (If you plan to use a hairdryer, test it first to make sure the air is not too hot or forceful. Keep the hairdryer at least two feet away from the mouth to help avoid problems.)

The damaged tooth area needs to be completely dry. This advance-prep work is necessary for achieving a stable bond between the broken tooth and the tooth repair material. Therefore, take the time needed to dry the affected area thoroughly.

Before you start the repair work, have all your supplies at hand and containers open, so everything is ready before you start working on the tooth. If possible, wash your hands with disinfecting soap before starting, or at least use hand sanitizer. Medical gloves are best, but many people end up removing the gloves once they get into the task; dental repair work requires all the dexterity you can muster.

Step 2: Once the tooth is dry, the tooth putty from the kit is applied. Using a cotton dental-pellet dampened with pure drinking water, use it to gently tamp the putty into the damaged area of the tooth. Alternately, a rounded toothpick can sometimes be an even better way to tamp the material into place—as long as you have first cut off the sharp tip of the toothpick. The tamping surface needs to be flat, not sharp.

If you intend to use a toothpick, rather than break the toothpick's tip, which will splinter the wood, use a knife to carefully cut the sharp tip from one end of the toothpick. Next, remove any wood debris from the toothpick surface before proceeding. Now you can use the flat, non-pointed end of the toothpick as a tool to tamp the tooth repair material firmly into place.

To fill the void of a lost filling, or to fix a broken tooth, keep the putty-mixture fairly dry. This somewhat dry putty material can then be rolled into a little ball. Because the repair material is dry, it will not stick to your fingers, so accurate placement of the putty is easier.

Step 3: Place the ball of repair material onto the broken (dry) area of the tooth, and then shape it to cover the entire region of the break, being careful to keep it off the smooth, undamaged area of the tooth. (Since the tooth repair material will not bind as well to the smooth, undamaged surface of the tooth, extending excess repair material onto this area can make the repair less durable, and it will not last as long.)

Step 4: The filling material can be shaped using rolling action on the little cotton ball or gauze roll, or with a round toothpick or even your finger. Make sure that the filling material is level or lower than the tooth above or below it, as even after the material is cured, you do not want chewing to add unnecessary pressure on the temporary filling. When in doubt, make the filling lower than the surrounding teeth. The filler material does taste bitter, but it is not toxic in these small quantities. The bad taste will go away in less than an hour.

It is important to keep excess pressure off of the repair for the first 20-minutes. With most of these kits, it takes 60-minutes to achieve a complete "cure" of the filler material, after which you can resume drinking and eating.

Note: Instructions incorporated into this chapter are generic. They are provided to illustrate how easy it is to use a do-it-yourself dental repair kit. In your situation, refer to the manufacturer's directions on how to use their product, as they might be different from those included here.

The dental repair materials contained in kits such as the ones described here are for temporary dental repairs.

The repair materials are intentionally designed to not fully bond to the tooth, so that a dentist can easily remove the temporary repair. With this objective in mind, it is easy to understand why these kits do not provide a durable, long-lasting, long-term repair.

Keep this in mind as you plan and assemble your supplies. You may want to have additional dental supplies on hand if you are preparing for a family, or for an extended "grid-down" situation. Keep in mind, too, that though these temporary repairs may not be long lasting, you can repeatedly make temporary repairs—if you have a sufficient quantity of materials.

Emergency dental repair kits are actually designed for those who will be traveling to remote parts of the world, or to regions which lack competent dental care. Therefore, the manufacturer's objective is to help you temporarily solve common emergency dental problems. They expect you to be able to return home to your dentist within a few weeks, or to at least get to an area where professional dental care is available, so these repairs are not permanent. If you want to be able to accomplish more permanent solutions to dental needs, you will need the guidance of a qualified dental professional.

The temporary dental repair materials discussed in this chapter do not provide for a permanent bond with the tooth. These materials may soon fall out if there are no undercuts on the tooth, or if the broken tooth does not have a rough surface to help the materials adhere.

In optimal conditions, these temporary dental repairs can last 3-months or longer. Yet, for most repairs accomplished on yourself, when you are only equipped with a basic kit and you have no training or experience, don't expect the repair to last more than a week or two.

Longevity of the repair is best achieved by completely drying the tooth before making the repair, by proper mixing of the repair material, and after the repair is made, by cautious eating. Avoid chewing on ice, foods which contain seeds, hard or sticky candy or other hard or sticky foods, and other abuses of the repaired area.

If you are preparing emergency supplies for a family or group, it is a good idea to have a more elaborate emergency dental kit, or at least several of the smaller kits. Keep in mind that an inexperienced user can easily need two of the small, basic kits to accomplish the repair if the initial effort was not successful.

For those wanting to prepare for longer-term emergencies, sailing adventures, jungle treks and other activities which may prevent you from visiting a dentist for an extended period, more kits or a larger kit is needed. If longer-term care is your preparedness goal, it is best to consult with your dentist and get their help in preparing a kit designed specifically for your purpose, and the duration you expect.

Consider explaining to your dentist that you are anticipating spending an extended time in a Third World setting, as this may be helpful in orienting them to your need. In reality, these Third World-like conditions are what we need to be prepared to encounter.

A 2-week GO-Bag and all in-home emergency supply kits, need to both contain at least one dental repair kit, per person. These kits are small, lightweight and the DIY version is inexpensive.

Still, since space in a GO-Bag is at a premium, some may be tempted to ignore the need to include a dental kit. This is a risky decision. If you opt to ignore our recommendation to include a dental kit, at least include a small piece of dental wax. Like duct tape, dental wax is useful for many repair purposes, in addition to providing relief to a painful, broken tooth.

For additional details on products, links to manufacturer's websites, and other details which are periodically updated to keep them current, visit the author's website. On the "Resources" page, look for "Book 2 & 3 Supplemental Information."

www.SigSwanstrom.com

Chapter 21

Flashlights, Emergency Lighting, and Batteries

"Two is one; one is none."
-- Old Military Adage

Whether thinking about emergency lighting for your home, car, or GO-Bag, the first thing to understand is that one source of illumination is not enough. Two is a minimum. Three is better. In an emergency situation, Murphy's Law is something you can depend on...

"Anything that can go wrong, will go wrong."

Recommendation: GO-Bags and Emergency Kits should contain at least three sources of light: 1) flashlight, 2) headlamp, 3) chemical light. These three light sources and others, will be discussed in this chapter.

Flashlights, as well as anything else which requires batteries; anything electronic, or anything mechanical, it is essential that you plan for a malfunction. When it comes to flashlights, Murphy's Law teaches us...

"When you need your flashlight most, it probably won't work."

So, what do you do about this potential problem? You anticipate it, and you plan for it.

Typical problems such as dead batteries can be offset by packing spare batteries with your flashlight. Leaking batteries which can easily ruin a flashlight (or any electronics), is a potential problem which can be remedied by removing the batteries before the item is stored.

However, the main set of batteries for a flashlight or any electronics, should always be stored attached to it. Consider wrapping the batteries in 3-5 layers of Cling Wrap, and then attach them directly to your flashlight with a Velcro strap, duct tape, or two heavy-duty rubber bands.

Use the same storage process for anything which requires a battery. To keep the battery from accidentally draining or shorting, protect the positive ("+") end of the battery from directly touching the other batteries, and from touching anything metallic. Do not wrap uninsulated (unprotected) batteries in aluminum foil or Mylar bags.

Suggestion: Since disaster may strike during nighttime hours, it may be a problem to not have batteries installed in your flashlight. To solve this potential problem, keep either a chemical light (ChemLight) or a small flashlight that does have batteries, readily available. This secondary flashlight should utilize Lithium-ion batteries as this type of battery is less likely to leak and has a longer shelf life.

Flashlights

What many people don't realize is that most modern flashlights, and all LED flashlights, are run by a battery AND an electronic circuit. This makes them susceptible to damage from dropping, corrosion, and electromagnetic pulse.

A LED "bulb" may be rated as having an impressive useful life of 50,000 hours, and the LED itself may be far more durable than an incandescent flashlight bulb, but the electronics which run the flashlight are often not as impressive when it comes to durability.

LED flashlights can be easily damaged. This is one of the reasons why there is such a wide range in purchase price among modern flashlights. Durability and reliability are the reason police officers and firefighters often purchase flashlights which cost more than a hundred dollars. (Brands most popular with professionals are flashlights made by SureFire and Streamlight.)

Yet, old-style flashlights are not necessarily a better choice. The incandescent bulbs used in old-fashioned flashlights are easily broken, they are not as bright, and they require more power, so batteries do not last as long. Their only durability attribute is that they do not use low-quality electronic circuitry. This makes these old-style flashlights still useful, particularly for those who want to prepare for events such as a solar flare (coronal mass ejection from the sun), nuclear blast, or EMP detonation.

"Two is one, one is none."

As you select your two (or more) emergency lights, here are a few things to consider:

1. Brand Name: A quality name brand may be worth the added money. (On the Resources page of the author's website, you will find a list of manufacturers of quality flashlights that are popular with those who use these lights as an essential tool for their job.)

There are quality flashlights made in China, and there are garbage flashlights that come out of China, but lower-cost quality lights are often produced by a Chinese manufacturer. On average, lights made in the U.S.A. may be better quality, but they are not always better. The country of manufacture is not synonymous with "quality" or "junk." If your budget necessitates the purchase of a low-cost light, also purchase a backup light which uses the same size battery.

2. LED or Conventional Bulb: Since LED flashlights are generally much more energy efficient and more durable, they are usually the best choice. However, it is helpful to have at least one, old-fashioned style flashlight that uses a filament bulb, such as Krypton or Xenon. As mentioned previously, these are not as susceptible to damage from solar flares and EMP events.

3. Choosing Battery Size: Old style flashlights often used "C" or "D" cell batteries, whereas most modern flashlights use either "AA" or "AAA," or the far more expensive CR123 and similar batteries. Flashlights which use 9-volt, or "coin" or "button" batteries such as the CR2032, should be avoided unless you have other electronics which require the same size battery.

Recommendation: *Select a flashlight which uses the same size battery as your other electronics.* If all, or at least most of your other battery-powered gear, such as your emergency radio, walkie-talkies, mobile phone charger, all use the same size battery, this is a huge plus.

By using the same size battery in all your electronic gear, especially a size that is commonly found in local stores, gives you a distinct logistical advantage. Not only are you more likely to be able to purchase batteries when you need them, you will also only need to stockpile one size battery. This attribute saves space, weight, and cost. Plus, if you exhaust all your spares, you can cannibalize batteries from your other, less essential electronic gear.

4. Selecting Battery Type: Batteries labeled as "Heavy-Duty" or "Industrial Grade" tend to be much cheaper but they should not be considered for your emergency gear. Irrespective of the promise implied by the label, these do not offer the long-life of a battery which utilizes more modern technology.

"Alkaline" batteries provide long life and a low purchase price. The most popular brands are Duracell, Energizer, and Kirkland. Fresh Alkaline batteries from these manufacturers can have a shelf life of 10 years.

If you can afford them, Lithium-ion batteries can provide the highest power output and the longest life among the battery options you can typically find in local retail stores. However, purchasing them online may be your best bet, especially if you select a vendor who offers free shipping.

Importantly, Lithium batteries are also less likely to leak and cause damage to your flashlights and electronics. If purchased at a favorable price, these high-performance batteries generally offer the best light output, the longest shelf life, and the lowest cost-per-hour of light.

Before you purchase a Lithium-ion battery, make sure its voltage matches the requirements of your flashlight (or electronics). Today there are various batteries which look to be the same size but produce different voltage.

Some of the newer flashlights are designed to be "dual fuel" flashlights capable of using both *disposable* Alkaline and Lithium AA batteries *and* rechargeable Lithium-ion batteries such as the highly-efficient rechargeable versions of the CR123a battery. This, too, is a logistic advantage.

However, other than dual-fuel flashlights, most electronic gear will not accept these higher voltage dual-fuel size Lithium-ion batteries. Again, check voltage requirements for the products you have selected.

The advantage of a dual-fuel flashlight is that in a pinch, when you can't recharge the flashlight battery, you can switch to using Alkaline AA batteries in your light. Don't expect to use these specialized batteries in all your electronics.

5. Rechargeable vs. Disposable. Ni-MH and Ni-Cd batteries are the most commonly found rechargeable batteries. Unfortunately, they won't accept many charges and often won't fully recharge, unless you are using a smart-recharger that drains the battery before it starts the recharging cycle.

If Ni-MH and Ni-Cd batteries are not fully discharged before recharging, they have a "memory" effect which limits their operating life. This is problematic in an emergency situation where you want to recharge your electronics whenever possible, to make sure you always have fully charged batteries ready for use.

If you want the advantage of rechargeable batteries, a far better choice is to select Rechargeable Lithium-ion batteries. These last longer and they don't have the "memory" problem of the Ni-MH and Ni-Cd batteries. Again, check the battery voltage before making a purchase.

Rechargeable Lithium-ion batteries are a lot more expensive than Alkaline batteries, but they are well worth the investment. To maintain maximum battery life and cycles of recharging, use a 'smart charger.' This type of battery charger is available in 110/240 volt, and 12-volt versions; combo units are the most versatile choice.

The new *dual-carbon* batteries might be an even better choice as they have a faster recharge time, but they are hard to find.

Disposable Chemical-Light Sticks

As a back-up, store a chemical-light stick with your vital battery-powered gear, fire starting tools, and first aid kits. If the disposable flashlight stored with these items doesn't work, the chemical-light is a backup source of light. (Remember: Two is one, one is none.)

Chemical light sticks are useful for installing batteries, checking gear, marking trails, during storms, in wet or windy conditions, flammable environments, and for delivering emergency first aid at night. These lights will even float if dropped in water, and they are so durable that they can be attached to a rock and thrown, or launched by a slingshot into a tree or hillside to mark a location for rescue or an equipment drop.

Chemical-lights are not subject to damage from solar flares and EMP events, so they are additionally valuable as a secondary light source. However, since they are not as bright as a flashlight and *cannot be reused once activated*, they don't take the place of a flashlight or headlamp.

A standard-size chemical-light stick, also known as a "chem-light," "glow-stick," "light stick" or "snap-light," is a lightweight, waterproof, and durable, polyethylene plastic tube containing light-producing chemicals. Once activated, it will glow for a limited period of time.

Lightweight and small-in-size, standard size ChemLights are 6 x ¾-inch tubes. These disposable lights are packaged in a thick foil envelope and have a shelf life of 4-5 years, so be sure to check the packaging to ensure that you are buying a fresh product. Properly stored, these chemical-lights can last much longer than the indicated shelf life.

Each "stick" contains a non-toxic, non-flammable combination of liquid chemicals. Therefore, chemical-lights are perhaps the safest and most durable form of portable, emergency lighting. In fact, they are so safe that they can be used by children, and even around flammable or explosive materials such as gasoline.

Activated by bending the stick until you hear an internal crack, the stick is then shaken to mix the internal chemicals, which in turn transforms the entire tube into a glowing 360-degree light source. The shorter the operating time indicated on the package, the brighter the light. However, even the brightest chemical light (5-min) does not deliver the light output of an ordinary flashlight. Nevertheless, these are valuable emergency lights that are suitable for localized lighting needs.

Caution: When storing chemical lights, make sure they cannot be accidently bent and the internal tube broken. Once the inner tube of chemical is broken, the light is activated, so be sure to store your them in a manner that prevents unintentional bending.

The inner tube of chemicals is quite durable. An unopened chem-light package can often be thrown off a cliff without breaking it. But since they are designed to be activated by bending the plastic tube to break the internal glass tube, store your chem-lights so that they will not be inadvertently bent.

Limitations: The 5-min to 8-hour models (and 12-hour military-grade model) chem-lights provide enough illumination to install batteries into electronics, operate radios, for sorting gear or setting up an emergency shelter, for reading a map or for changing a tire. However, even the brightest models (5-min to 15-min) have limited value for tasks such as hiking at night.

On the downside, to avoid premature activation, chemical-lights must be transported and packed to prevent undue flexing of the plastic tube. Also, the light produced by a chemical-light, and the duration of its light output, is significantly affected by ambient temperature.

When the operating temperature is 72-degrees (22-degrees C), the light-generating time listed on the chemical lights foil package (30-min, 8-hour, etc.) is reasonably accurate. However, when the ambient temperature is much higher or lower, the amount of illumination and the duration of the light-generating time of a chemical-light will change radically.

For example, if the operating temperature is 57-degrees F (14-degrees C), a chemical-light will only be half as bright as it would be at 72-degrees. On the plus side, it will continue to glow for twice as long as indicated on the package. Similarly, when a chemical-light is activated at 93-degrees F (34-degrees C), it will glow twice as bright, but it will only last half as long as indicated on the package's label.

Once activated, a chemical-light will continue to glow until the chemical reaction stops. It cannot be reused and it cannot be turned off. These are a disposable light source.

A package of 10 industrial-grade or military-grade chemical-lights costs about the same as a pound of gourmet coffee. These lights are available in an assortment of colors.

White Chem-Lights: Conventional wisdom would suggest that "white" would be the brightest, but this is not the case with chem-lights. "White" is the only chem-light model which offers anything close to an accurate color rendition of the things illuminated, but it is not the brightest.

Colored Chem-Lights: In practice, green or yellow chem-lights provide more illumination than any of the others. However, if you want to be able to discern colors, such as the color codes on a topographic map, a white chem-light is a better choice. Other colors can nevertheless be useful.

For industrial use and for hunters and warriors, the green is the most popular as it is substantially brighter than red, and yet it has minimal effect on night vision. UV chemical-lights are also available for providing illumination that can only be seen by those who are equipped with night vision equipment.

Chem-Light Brand Selection: Since the quality of chemical-lights varies widely among manufacturers, the "industrial-grade" (SNAPLIGHT) or "military-grade" (CHEMLIGHT) made by Cyalume Technologies, may be the most reliable brand to purchase. These can be found online and in some sporting goods stores.

Since the price isn't much different from that of low-quality chemical-lights and the *industrial-grade* SNAPLIGHT made by Cyalume Technologies, these are the ones usually stocked by police departments and emergency services. Oddly, "Industrial-Grade" SNAPLIGHTS are more durable, brighter, and have a longer shelf life than the military-grade CHEMLIGHT, but the military-grade product is still a viable alternative.

Headlamps & Hat/Helmet Lights

A headlamp should be considered essential equipment. Designed to be worn on the forehead and attached using an elastic headband, a headlamp is the best light source for walking at night, and for making repairs or working around a campsite at night. Why? Because it leaves your hands free for other activities.

Sure, you can put a small flashlight in your mouth (as long as you had the foresight to encase the tail end of your flashlight in rubber tubing or you have wrapped the end with rubber bands to protect your teeth), but it's far safer, and better, to just put your headlamp on like a cap, and flip the "on" switch. Voila, light wherever you look.

Headlamps are an essential tool, but in my experience, you need a headlamp *and* a flashlight. You need both.

Even a modern high-power LED headlamp does not take the place of a flashlight if you are searching for someone in the dark, or for something that is at a considerable distance away from you. For this purpose, a flashlight works better.

Conversely, if you are walking at night or working on a project, a headlamp is a better choice because the field of illumination changes with your head movements. Since you need the redundancy of two lights anyway, why not make one a headlamp?

Note: Some miniature flashlights such as those which use a single AAA-battery, have a pocket clip. On some models, this clip can be reversed, which makes it possible to clip the light to the bill of a cap, transforming it into a makeshift headlamp.

Headlamp Disadvantages: With a headlamp, the light tracks wherever you look. Oddly, this may not be helpful when you are searching for someone or something at night. In this situation, moving your light while your head remains stationary, is often better for finding someone or something.

Headlamps are also *undesirable* when you are using a firearm. If you use a headlamp with a handgun, or long gun, the light will brightly illuminate your firearm. This makes sighting at night more difficult; far more difficult than using a flashlight held in your off-hand, under the gun. Plus, if you are searching for a bad guy at night, a headlamp illuminates the wearer, making you an illuminated target. So, using a headlamp when holding a gun, can be dangerous thing to do.

These drawbacks acknowledged, a headlamp is invaluable for practically everything else. In your Go-Bag, and when operating at night in a disaster or emergency situation, you need both a flashlight *and* a headlamp. One of each. Minimum.

Murphey's Law: As a volunteer firefighter, I was recently involved in fighting a house fire, and was using a large D-cell LED flashlight. I had it tucked under my arm to illuminate a leaking hose coupling. In the wet conditions, my industrial-grade flashlight slipped and dropped to the concrete. Since I was kneeling, the flashlight only fell about two feet, but it nevertheless broke.

Constructed of aircraft-grade aluminum, my flashlight was rated as being able to withstand a 6-foot drop onto concrete. Nevertheless, my light apparently had a weak spot in its circuitry, and it broke. Suddenly, I was in complete darkness.

The manufacturer will doubtless replace my expensive flashlight, but that warranty was useless to me that night. Fortunately, I had a headlamp on my helmet, and a small, spare flashlight in my pocket. Problem solved.

Moral of the story: Expect electrical, electronic, and mechanical devices to fail. Plan for it. *One is none, two is one, and three—even better.*

What to look for in a headlamp: If you don't already have a headlamp, look for an LED model that incorporates several levels of light output, both spotlight and floodlight beams, plus a red-only or green-only beam for retaining night vision. With my headlamp, most of the time I prefer using a green-color floodlight rather than a red light. I use a red light for tactical operations, but green for everything that is less critical. I've found green-light to be a worthy compromise between retaining night vision, better illumination, and the ability to discern color such as on a topographic map.

Budget-Conscious Headlamp Specifications: Even if you are on a tight budget, it is worth getting a LED headlamp that has these three features:

At least two white-light brightness settings; one at least 90-lumens, and a low setting of no less than 4-lumens. And third, a second LED in red or green to maintain night vision.

Having the ability to switch to a low-lumen output that will extend battery life to *at least* 24-hours, has obvious benefits, especially when you are bugging-out or when you only have a limited supply of replacement batteries. Ideally, your headlamp should get you through three nights of on-foot travel on just one set of batteries.

An example of a well-designed headlamp: As a point of reference, here are the specifications for one of the most popular medium-price LED headlamps, the redesigned "Storm," made by Black Diamond:

With this headlamp the user has the option of a white-light flood beam with 2 LEDs to illuminate a wide area, or a spotlight beam to search for distant objects. Light output is infinitely variable in all three colors of light, from a bright 250 lumens down to 4 lumens. This low-light option is ideal for in-hand tasks such as adjusting a radio, reading a map, or viewing a compass.

When loaded with Alkaline batteries, this headlamp provides the user with an operating duration of 80-hours on the brightest setting, and an astounding 250-hours on the 4-lumen setting.

If you load it with 1.5-volt disposable Lithium batteries rather than Alkaline, you can conservatively double the useful run-time. Depending on use, run-time with disposable Lithium batteries can be as much as 7x longer. And with a 20-year shelf life, this makes disposable Lithium batteries a top choice for use in emergency gear.

Importantly, the "Storm" has dimmable red and green LEDs to maintain night vision. Thankfully, these colored lights can be turned on without cycling through a white light, so night vision remains unaffected. This headlamp also has a variable intensity strobe mode for signaling in either green, red, or white-light.

The polycarbonate waterproof/dustproof case is rated to IP67. So, this light can not only survive a torrential rain storm, but also submersion in 1-meter of water for 30-minutes. Practical experience indicates that it will survive underwater much longer, but it should not be considered a swim or dive light.

Even though the "Storm" is feature packed, it is still reasonably lightweight. The light itself weighs only 2.2 ounces (62 g), and a modest 3.9 ounces (110 g) when combined with the batteries. The included foam pad incorporated into the strap, combined with the modest weight, makes this light comfortable to wear during all-night treks.

This headlamp uses four easy-to-find AAA batteries, an important feature when batteries are in short supply, or when you need to cannibalize batteries from another device. The battery compartment is even self-heating, which provides better cold weather operation. As a precaution, if one battery is inserted backward in this headlamp, it will still work (though not as bright). It has a circuitry design which protects the headlamp from damage, an important feature if replacing the batteries in the dark.

It also has a "lock" mode to reduce the chance of the headlamp turning "on" when it is in your GO-Bag or pocket. This is a beneficial feature when you have a limited number of spares. Cost: $50 MSRP, $30 online.

5 Key features of a headlamp

1. White Light: If you are searching for something in the distance, or signaling, nothing beats a white-light spotlight (spot-beam), as the narrow beam projects further. However, if you are walking, or looking for something close to you, the broad beam of a floodlight is ideal. The better headlamps will provide both types of light.

When used at a campsite, a headlamp can be attached to the trunk of a small tree, or even a Nalgene water bottle, resulting in the hands-free illumination of a wider area. If the light is aimed at a light-colored object, like the interior wall of a tent, it can bathe the entire interior with soft light.

2. Light Output Options: Having at least three power settings is essential. Though some have additional or even variable settings, being able to switch output from a low setting (4-10 lumens) to extend battery life, to medium (around 50 lumens) for walking on a trail, to bright (100+) is adequate for most uses.

You might want a flashlight that has the capability of producing an ultra-bright energy-sucking 1,000+ lumen spotlight beam. However, most people don't use that feature on a headlamp, even if their light includes that feature.

When selecting a headlamp, remember to pick one which uses *only* LED bulbs. Your batteries will last longer with an LED light, plus LEDs are far more durable.

3. Weight: Lightweight is an important consideration, as wearing a heavy headlamp will increase discomfort and fatigue. Some headlamps utilize a large, heavy battery pack, which can make wearing the light bothersome for infrequent users. With traditional flashlight bulbs this was unavoidable, but with the newer LED headlamps, this is not necessary unless you are looking for a headlamp to use for caving or in continuous darkness for an extended period of time.

4. Battery Choice: Be sure to select a headlamp which uses the same type of batteries as your other electronics. The option to share the same type of battery between your different lights and electronic devices makes logistics much simpler. And, it makes using rechargable batteries a more viable option, too.

5. Quality: There are a lot of poor-quality headlamps on the market. If you are unfamiliar with brands, purchase your headlamp from a reliable vendor such as REI.com. You don't want your headlamp to fail when you are depending on it during a storm or another emergency situation.

The dangers of ultra-bright LED lights: When used on their "bright" settings, some LED flashlights and headlamps are so bright that they can cause eye damage. Therefore, when possible, use a lower setting when operating near other people. Be intentional; when using a headlamp, do not look into the eyes of another person. This harmful effect is more pronounced when operating in a rural or totally-dark environment.

Special-purpose headlight options: Some LED flashlights and headlamps include a blue or ultraviolet light that is designed to make fresh blood glow in the dark. Some hunters swear by these blood lights, whereas others have found them to be useless.

LEDs in both flashlights and headlamps will often reflect the eyes of animals at night. This can be helpful as it gives you forewarning, perhaps additionally useful if you are walking with a dog that might run off after a wild animal. In a survival situation, this makes night-hunting easier. Certain green LEDs are outside of the visible wavelength of some animals. For example, when I'm using the green LED on my headlamp, I can walk up to a deer without it seeing me.

Camping Lanterns for Emergency Lighting

Camp Lanterns: Battery powered lanterns or fuel-run Coleman-style lights are useful for illuminating a room or campsite, but they are generally too large to be included with your bug-out gear, including vehicle kits. Yet, they do have a place in your at-home preparations and with the set-up of your safe-haven retreat location.

For either of these places, it is best to pick a camp-light which uses a readily available fuel. This might be batteries if you have a way to recharge them during a power outage, but battery powered lanterns are generally impractical for emergency situations lasting more than 2-3 days.

Solar Rechargers: The solar panels which are included in some models of camp lights are typically inadequate, even if you are blessed by having bright sunlight during the day. If you intend to use the sun to recharge your batteries or your camp light, it is better to use a small solar panel designed for this purpose.

Note: The batteries which come with lanterns are usually Ni-MH or Ni-Cd, and these are inadequate for long-term emergency use. In the flashlight section of this chapter, review section 5 which deals with rechargeable batteries. You may want to replace the "included" batteries with Lithium-ion rechargeable batteries.

Wind Turbine Rechargers: With the right technical know-how, this can be a viable option if you live in a windy location. Unfortunately, the small wind-turbines often marketed for this purpose are inadequate, so the choice is to purchase an expensive unit or undertake a do-it-yourself project.

Crank-Powered Rechargers: Hand-crank rechargers such as found on many multipurpose emergency radios, are only a short-term solution for power generation. It is labor intensive to use these manual hand-crank rechargers. And, the manufacturing quality is usually poor, so they break easily.

If you are interested in a human-powered recharging method, there are various devices which can be attached to an ordinary bicycle. This device is a more reasonable "crank" solution, but it is still questionable if the energy created is worth the energy expended.

For those who are interested in pedal-crank chargers, there are various devices available which can be added to a bicycle. For these, the bike is held in a stationary mount, so that the pedaling action turns a generator which, in turn, charges batteries. For those interested in a do-it-yourself project, an automotive generator can be adapted for this purpose.

Liquid Fuel Lanterns: Lanterns which require cloth mantles and use either liquid fuel or propane can be a long-term solution, but they do require the stockpiling of a sufficient quantity of operating supplies and fuel.

If you favor liquid fuel, be sure to select a lantern (and camp stove) which is "multifuel" as they are much more versatile. Some multifuel camp lights and stoves can even burn automotive gasoline. If you are limited to using White Gas, the traditional fuel used in camping lanterns, there is a good chance you will be out of fuel before the emergency situation is over.

If you favor liquid fuel, there are many options. This ranges from the Coleman multifuel which burns either camp fuel (White Gas) or unleaded auto gasoline, to the Britelyt multifuel lantern which will operate on kerosene, biodiesel, diesel, gasoline, mineral spirits, lamp oil, and even lighter fluid.

Propane Lanterns: If you prefer clean-burning propane, purchase a 5-gallon propane bottle (aka / 20-pound tank) and the attachment hoses and adapters needed for connecting your lantern (and other appliances) to this bulk fuel bottle. This combination makes it possible to use the long-lasting and more economical big bottle/tank rather than the small disposable cylinders.

The fuel in a full 5-gallon bottle (20-pound tank) equates to approximately 16 disposable cylinders, so the savings can be considerable, and the convenience-factor should not be discounted, either.

If you opt for using a 5-gallon (20-pound) or larger bulk tank, make sure you get it filled to its maximum capacity. While it's true that federal law limits filling the tank to 80% of its capacity, some vendors sell a "full" tank that has not been filled to the legal limit. This slight-of-hand transaction can be a problem if you are depending on having a full tank(s) for use during an emergency.

Purchasing Pre-Filled Tanks: Partially-full vs. full tank may be an unnoticed problem when purchasing propane from a store that uses an "exchange" company. This convenient service makes it possible to buy propane at grocery stores and other retailers not set-up to fill bulk tanks, but it comes at a hefty cost beyond the purchase price. These "exchange" tanks are often only filled to 75% of their legal capacity.

Check the weight. An honestly filled 5-gallon bottle (20-pound tank) should weigh about 37-pounds when filled to its legal capacity. If you purchase a pre-filled tank, weigh it when you get home to see if the vendor has sold you a full tank.

Filling your own tank at a "bulk fuel" facility: Since a filled 5-gallon tank only holds about 4-gallons of propane due to legal restrictions, the *fuel* in a tank filled to the legal limit, will weigh approximately 16.8-pounds (7.6 kg). So, it's a simple calculation to add the weight of the empty tank to the weight of the fuel, to see if your bulk-fuel vendor has filled the tank.

Connection Adapters and Hoses: If you already have a large propane tank at your home or retreat location, make sure you have the hoses and adapters for attaching your camp lantern, camp stove, portable propane heater, RV propane refrigerator, and other appliances to your 5-gallon (20-pound) bottle and/or outdoor tank. Stores selling recreational vehicle supplies are good place to find adapters, advice, and propane-fuel appliances.

To make your camp lantern and stove more versatile, consider buying the adapters needed to refill a 5-gallon (20-pound) bottle from your large tank rather than limiting yourself to running a long gas hose between your appliance and your bulk propane tank.

Natural Gas: If your home or retreat location is connected to a natural gas pipeline, that may work, but do not expect natural gas to continue to flow from your local utility during a disaster. It might, but it might not. Since you can't control this fuel source, don't depend on it. Have a backup plan.

At the very least, be prepared to adapt your natural gas appliances to propane, and buy a bulk-fuel tank. This adaptation is easily accomplished.

For natural-gas appliances, purchase what you need to switch the fuel orifice with the smaller one designed for propane. These conversion kits are readily available since there are more than eight million U.S. households using propane.

Along with the conversion of your appliances, be prepared to use a bulk-fuel tank(s), either the 5-gallon (20-pound) size often used on barbeque grills, or a larger one such as those used in rural locations. Then if natural gas stops flowing during a protracted emergency, these can become your gas source. Be sure to check local regulations on propane tank storage.

I was near the epicenter, participating in a SWAT training exercise at Fort Ord when the 6.9 magnitude San Francisco (Loma Prieta) earthquake hit. It was a warm, pleasant October afternoon when life suddenly changed for millions of people, including the families of the 67-people killed and the 3,757 who were injured.

In the aftermath of that quake, 1.4 million households lost electric power and natural gas service. Few were prepared for this development, and most grocery and emergency supply stores were empty within three hours.

Not only were local radio and television stations off the air, so was the State emergency communication system. Large crowds of people milled around in a daze, not knowing what to do.

Our response can be different—*if we are prepared.*

Weapon Lights

Designed specifically for mounting on a firearm, a 'weapons light' can look like a flashlight, but that is where the similarity ends. A true *weapons light* is an extra rugged flashlight-like device which can withstand the repeated sharp, punishing recoil of a firearm.

Off a gun, these lights can be used as a flashlight, but unless you have a need for an unusually durable flashlight, they may not be a great choice for someone who just wants a flashlight. If flashlight durability is your primary concern, consider a LED flashlight made by SureFire or Streamlight.

There are many after-market mounting devices which make it possible to attach an ordinary flashlight to a gun. However, this combination does not transform a flashlight into a weapons light.

A weapons light is designed to keep the batteries from bouncing inside the light, and uses a bulb assembly and circuitry that can withstand the sharp recoil of a gun. These are incredibly durable single-function lights which utilize either a tail cap on/off switch, or a pressure-pad on/off switch designed to be attached to the firearm.

Those looking for a less expensive weapons light alternative, are often disappointed by mounting a standard flashlight to their firearm. After a shot or two, many flashlights will fail—or the mount will fail. It's true that some quality flashlights will work like a champion, but don't assume an ordinary flashlight will work—*and continue to work*.

If you opt to mount a standard flashlight on a gun, be sure to practice with the light mounted and turned "on" to simulate an actual nighttime situation. To test the light and its mount, rapid-fire a full magazine of ammunition and note the effect. If the light fails, blinks, or fades, or if the mount does not retain a rigid hold on both the light and the gun, it isn't going to be reliable.

Strobe Effect: Law enforcement professionals tend to select a weapons light with only one setting; a room-flooding bright white light. However, lights which produce a disorienting strobe effect are becoming increasingly popular among police officers. This is because it is difficult for an assailant to shoot at a bright, strobing light, plus the strobe can alter the depth perception of the attacker.

Notwithstanding, slow strobes tend to conceal furtive actions, making the situation even more dangerous for the law enforcement officer. So, if you are opting for a strobe light, pick one that has a rapid pulse rate.

Research indicates that the ideal strobe rate is 18-21 Hz. If you don't have access to this technical data, avoid choosing a strobe light which has a pulse rate that you can count, or even attempt to count. On the other hand, if the light flashes so quickly that it seems almost continuous, that strobe is flashing too fast.

Beam Brightness and Intensity: In an urban setting where the weapons light will be used for searching a home or office, brightness in the 200-lumens range is ideal. Any brighter and white walls can reflect the beam and temporarily blind the user. Conversely, in a rural environment or for searching a warehouse or manufacturing building, a much brighter light may be advantageous. So, consider your intended use before selecting your weapons light.

The intensity of the beam can be weighted to be brighter in the center, but a beam pattern which is flat and provides uniform intensity, works better for most people. A beam that has nearly uniform brightness, makes it easier to find a hiding assailant who is located on the periphery of the beam.

Also, if you do need to fire your gun, the mind infers that the bright center of the beam is where the bullet will strike, and this is not necessarily the case. Since a weapons light is repeatedly put-on and taken-off a gun, it cannot be accurately sighted-in like a weapon-mounted laser. Therefore, a light which produces a beam of nearly uniform intensity, is a better choice.

Multifunction Lights: Worth noting is that most law enforcement professionals do not choose ordinary multifunction lights, nor lights with variable brightness that are adjusted using the same tail-cap switch that turns on the light. The reasoning is simple. In high-stress situations, you don't have mindshare to select options, nor do you want to cycle through various options. You want a light that works. You want a light that instantly provides the illumination you need.

A weapons light or tactical flashlight, must be operated using a silent tail-cap button. Or, by activating a pressure switch attached to the gun's grip, that is connected to the light by a thin electrical wire.

On/off should be the only function of this switch. However, it is advantageous if a partial depression of the button will activate the light until the finger/thumb is removed from the button, whereas a full depression (click) of the button, turns on the light and it remains 'on' until it is clicked again. If you want a two-function (strobe and bright white light) or multifunction weapons light (various brightness levels or colors), make sure those features are changed by a mechanism that is entirely separate from the tail-cap switch.

Buyer Beware: Some manufacturers and advertisers use the word "tactical" or "military-grade" to describe an ordinary flashlight. Their goal is to capitalize on the "cool" factor (aka, tacti-cool). Be wary of the use of these terms on any piece of equipment. It may, or may not be tactical gear.

Note: Many police officers carry a weapons light, but they also carry a flashlight. They use the weapons light mounted on their gun to search for dangerous people, and the flashlight for routine tasks such as writing traffic tickets and searhing for trespassers.

Weapon lights are single purpose lights. The purpose is to illuminate and correctly identify bad guys, and stop their acts of violence. They are not ideal as an all-purpose light—especially when they are attached to a gun. Off the gun, use it, no problem. But since a gun should not be pointed at anything, or anyone, you don't intend to destroy, a light that is currently mounted on a gun should not be used for any other purpose until it is removed from the firearm.

Pistols: If you are considering a weapons light for a pistol, choose one with a simple on/off switch on the tail cap. With a two-hand grip on the handgun, you should be able to toggle the switch with your off hand (left-hand thumb, for a right-handed person).

Long Guns: If you are selecting a weapons light for a rifle or shotgun, select a model which uses a separate pressure switch connected to the light by a short length of wire. Use zip-ties to secure the wire to the gun, eliminating the possibility of the wire snagging on something when you are moving. Inadvertently snagging a branch, clothing, doorframe, or other object can easily create an accidental-discharge situation.

Mounting Location: When you mount your weapons light, don't let the lens of the light extend beyond the end of the gun's muzzle. Yet, you *do* want to mount it as far forward as is practical. Otherwise the barrel will create a blind spot in the beam.

There isn't a right answer as to if you should mount the light on the left or right side of the rifle or shotgun, except as it relates to making sure it doesn't interfere with the operation of the firearm. When selecting a weapons light, be sure to consider a light which uses the same size battery as your flashlight.

Wax Candles

Don't forget low-tech options when it comes to preparing for a disaster. Wax candles are a good example of a low-tech option that can be a lifesaver. Even if you have battery-powered and propane gear, having long-burning candles is still useful. Long-burn emergency candles are a valuable addition to at-home emergency supply kits, and for preparing your retreat-location.

Summary

Short-term, having several different types of battery powered lights is the best solution. Plus, an ample supply of batteries is required if you find it necessary to live your life using battery powered devices. These lights and electronics will consume a lot of batteries.

When recharging batteries is not an option, *disposable* Lithium-ion batteries are usually the most cost-efficient power solution. These, combined with the use of propane lanterns (and camp stoves) which are attached to a bulk supply of fuel such as a 5-gallon propane bottle, provide a longer-term solution.

To depend solely on battery-powered devices during a long-term disaster is problematic. Using *rechargeable* Lithium-ion batteries and a viable off-grid method to recharge them, will become essential for long-term emergency situations.

In long-term disaster scenarios, most people should plan to use propane-powered lighting or candles to produce general illumination, and flashlights and electronic devices only sparingly to conserve batteries. Recharging batteries is difficult without suitable equipment.

Outfitting GO-Bags and preparing for evacuation, represents different equipment needs than at-home and retreat location preparedness. Don't confuse the two. Portability, compactness, and lightweight are essential for on-the-move situations.

With the proper smart-charger adapter, flashlight batteries can be recharged from 12-volt car batteries. Multiple recharging methods, and having multiple smart-chargers is essential. The adage, *"Two is one, and one is none"* applies to batteries, electronic devices—and battery charging equipment.

Caution: Keep in mind that fuel-powered lights and stoves require ventilation. Death can occur from improper use.

For additional details on products, links to manufacturer's websites, and other details which are periodically updated to keep them current, visit the author's website. On the "Resources" page, look for "Book 2 – Supplemental Information."

www.SigSwanstrom.com

Chapter 22

Fuel Transport, Stabilization, and Safe Storage

In a bug-out situation, you may not be able to purchase gasoline or diesel fuel while driving to your retreat location. Even if fuel is available, there may be very long lines at gas stations, and waiting may create new, serious problems for you. Therefore, you need to carry extra fuel with you.

As a safety measure, in daily life, do not let your vehicle's fuel tank get lower than ½ full. This is not only a benefit for bugging-out; it may also be a lifesaver for a run to the hospital or some other urgent situation.

Keep in mind: Whether you are evacuating in the middle of the night and gas stations are closed, or, increased demand has emptied the gas station tanks, created long wait times, or restrictions on the quantity they are willing to sell, or, there is a power outage which renders the gas station's pumps unusable so you can't pump gas, any of these conditions can make it impossible to get the fuel you need. These are additional reasons why it is essential to get out early.

With these potential problems in mind, your bug-out preparations need to include enough fuel for the entire trip. Plus, another 50% in case you find it necessary to detour. An alternate route may force you to drive many additional miles to reach your safe-haven location.

If you bug-out and find that gas stations are open and lines are short, buy gas. But whether filled at a gas station or from fuel cans you have with you, keep your vehicle's fuel tank at least half full. Something may happen which will make it difficult to refuel.

If you are able to purchase fuel along the way, great. Buy it. If this is the situation you encounter, keep your extra fuel for a future emergency, or for bartering.

Fuel Storage Containers for Gasoline and Diesel

If you've been in the U.S. military, chances are you have seen the Scepter fuel can. In our experience, these are the best and safest fuel containers available in the general-use market. They are far superior to both the red plastic and red metal gas cans widely in use.

In the last decade, plastic gas cans are almost the only type of gas container you can find in retail stores. The old-style steel "Jerry-can" has become too costly to produce. Chinese made Jerry-can knock-offs are available, but these are often substandard in quality—*and you don't want to skimp when it comes to the storage of an explosive liquid such as gasoline.*

In addition to lower manufacturing cost for plastic fuel containers, they have also become popular because they are less prone to leak over time and exposure to abuse. The red plastic fuel cans available today, with semi-rigid sides, are generally better than the old Jerry-cans for this reason.

Scepter aka/ Military Fuel Cans (Gas Transport Containers)

In our experience, fuel containers made by "Scepter" are by far the best choice. New ones are available, but military surplus containers are generally significantly less expensive. You may be able to negotiate a lower price on a scuffed or junky-looking can that is still in good condition.

Note: This is the version made for the military, which is available to the general public, not the standard consumer-version found in auto supply stores.

Positive Characteristics of the *Scepter* fuel can:

1. Far more durable than consumer-grade fuel containers;

2. They don't leak fuel or fumes, even when exposed to ambient temperature fluctuation;

3. They are reasonably lightweight;

4. They have an internal vent mechanism which provides a smooth flow when fuel is poured from the container;

5. They are far safer in a house fire, vehicle fire, or traffic accident, than consumer-grade fuel storage containers.

The U.S. military gas cans are made by Scepter, a company based in Canada. Genuine Scepter fuel containers have the "Scepter" brand name, and "Made in Canada," molded into the plastic on the side of the can. It may also say "U.S. Government Property" or "Military Use Only," but don't let that put you off. With the end of the Iraq and Afghanistan wars, the U.S. Government auctioned thousands of these cans.

Scepter Military Fuel Containers (Gas Cans) are made of durable injection molded polyethylene, not just plastic. Though Scepter fuel containers look substantial, they are actually relatively lightweight. The advanced materials and the manufacturing method makes them both lightweight and durable.

U.S. military surplus Scepter fuel cans are usually sand-color (tan) or olive drab (green), but occasionally you will find them in yellow. The Scepter cans made for the civilian market are similar in appearance but have a high-visibility yellow check-strap attached to the lid.

Caution: *Blue plastic containers (cans), including those made by Scepter, are for water, only.* They do not have the same safety features as a fuel can.

Note: Scepter WATER CANS can be found in the same colors as the fuel cans, so check the embossed information on the can before making your purchase. These water containers are great, but they do not offer the same design features and safety as the containers made for transporting fuel. *You can quickly tell the difference between a Scepter military* FUEL *can and a Scepter* WATER *can by the distinctive small-spout built into the large cap of the water can.*

Negative Characteristics of the *Scepter* fuel can:

The only downside of purchasing Scepter fuel containers is that it may be difficult to find a pour spout designed to transfer the fuel from the can to your vehicle. And, these spouts are apparently illegal for use in California and New York. Go figure.

In any case, it's easy enough to make a pour-spout for the Scepter if you can't find one to purchase. Another option is to buy a flexible metal gas-can spout at an auto supply store which may fit the INSIDE threads of the Scepter can. (Unfortunately, this is a trial and error process).

If you find a good deal on Scepter fuel cans, but can't get a spout from the same vendor, it is still worth buying the fuel can(s). They are extremely popular and getting hard to find, so don't delay.

If you purchase a used U.S. military surplus fuel can, be sure to rinse it with gasoline before filling it with fuel. Let it sit outside for a couple of days with the lid off so the contents can fully evaporate, before you fill it. Diesel and gasoline cans are made in all three military colors, so if it is important to you to get a container that has only held the right type of fuel/liquid, visit the manufacturer's website (www.ScepterMilitary.com) to find a look-up table of model numbers.

Other Fuel Storage Containers

If you can't find a Scepter fuel can, NATO fuel cans can be an acceptable alternative. However, these other "mil-spec" gas cans are a mixed bag, and in our experience, none of them come even close to the quality of Scepter military cans.

Whether you select a mil-spec NATO can or a genuine Scepter, be sure to inspect it before making your purchase. These containers are extremely durable, but they aren't indestructible. A fuel container that leaks is not a bargain.

Used steel NATO fuel cans are often repainted to make them appear to be new. Repainted or not, open the cap and look inside for rust. If it's rusty it may not be serviceable.

Keep in mind, too, that a painted, faded or scratched Scepter fuel container may still be serviceable. If you want to restore the faded exterior of a Scepter can, use 'rubbing compound' which can be found in the auto wax section of any auto supply store.

Caution #1: Most of the surplus mil-spec NATO fuel cans are metal, and used metal cans have a tendency to leak due to internal corrosion, or paint-covered rust along the seams. With this in mind, it's best to buy them from a store which will let you return the can if it is defective. After you fill a used fuel can, keep an eye on it for several days to be sure it isn't leaking. Even after an extended period of exposure to sunlight, it should not leak.

The NATO fuel cans are a risky buy if they are second-hand (used) and purchased online from a no-name vendor. Military gear is sometimes sold because of excess quantities, or because the item has been replaced by a newer design, or, because it is worn or damaged and is no longer serviceable.

Caution #2: Though you may be able to mend a torn army tent, repairing a damaged fuel container is not worth the effort.

Recommendation: Whenever possible, purchase a fuel can spout from the same vendor as the fuel can, as it can be nearly impossible to find the military-style pour spout for Scepter and NATO fuel cans. The California and New York-compliant child-resistant and flow-restricted pour spout, including the one made by Scepter, are not durable like the military version. A big funnel may work, but it's messy.

Health and Fire Hazards

Never transport fuel inside the cab of a vehicle. The fumes can be deadly. Only transport gasoline or diesel fuel in a container made for this purpose. It is dangerous to store or transport fuel in a container that is not specifically made for fuel. To reduce fire and explosion hazard, always place a fuel container on the ground before filling it. Never fill a fuel can when it is in a vehicle, or in the bed of a truck or in a trailer, as non-grounded fuel transfer is much more susceptible to dangerous sparks created by static electricity. Always have a fire extinguisher nearby when filling a fuel container, and also when transferring gas from a fuel can to a vehicle. If a fire extinguisher is needed, stand back and sweep the base of the fire with the spray as per instructions on the fire extinguisher's label.

Before Storing Gasoline or Diesel Fuel: Add Fuel Stabilizer

Whether in a vehicle or in a storage tank, fuel that will be stored for more than a couple of months needs to be conditioned with fuel stabilizer. The performance of stored gasoline noticeably degrades after only four months and is generally unusable after one year. Diesel fuel lasts longer, but is also subject to degradation.

***"STA-BIL"* vs. *"PRI"* Fuel Stabilizer:** The most commonly found fuel stabilizer is "STA-BIL," but in our tests, we found "PRI" to be a far superior product. Therefore, even if it is a bother to obtain PRI, we recommend expending the extra effort.

A different fuel stabilizer formula is used for gasoline and diesel fuels. Order **PRI-*G*** for gasoline, **PRI-*D*** for diesel fuel. Be sure to purchase the right PRI product for the type of fuel you are storing. They are not interchangeable products.

With PRI, even old fuel can sometimes be brought back to life. Just give it a double-dose of the appropriate PRI product, mix it thoroughly into the fuel, then use it. If the fuel is in a vehicle, the fuel lines and injectors may need to be flushed to remove old fuel before the motor will start.

As to the PRI fuel-treatment product itself, it will remain fresh for decades, as long as it is properly stored and the container remains unopened. Once opened, PRI should be used within three years.

To properly mix the fuel stabilizer with the fuel, add it to the container BEFORE you fill it with fuel. The filling action will help mix the fuel treatment additive with the fuel.

Similarly, if you plan to store a vehicle or fuel-powered equipment, add the PRI to the tank and then top it off with additional fresh fuel. This will not only help the PRI mix with the fuel that was already in the tank, it is also a safer way to store the equipment.

Run the engine for several minutes after adding the fuel/PRI mixture to the tank. This will add treated fuel to the fuel lines.

* *Even treated fuel needs to be either used or re-treated annually.* If you are using PRI brand fuel stabilizer, the fuel can remain fresh for 12 years (or longer) if treated with PRI annually.

Treat every piece of equipment that uses gasoline or diesel. Add PRI to fuel storage cans, fuel tanks of stored vehicles, as well as to the fuel tanks of generators, tractors, lawn mowers, gardening equipment, and all gas and diesel engines before they are stored.

Fire Hazard: With gasoline, it is the fuel vapors at the top of the can/tank which are combustible. Therefore, an undamaged, full, tank of gasoline is generally less of a fire hazard than a partially-filled gas tank. A full tank of fuel will also diminish destructive moisture condensation that tends to build-up in a partially filled gas can/tank.

Quality, undamaged, fully intact fuel containers can be surprisingly safe for fuel storage. For example, we threw a full can of gasoline into a bonfire fueled by wooden pallets, and left it there for two minutes before removing it. The fuel container swelled, but it did not rupture. Since there was no leakage of fuel, nor gasoline vapor, the container did not burn or explode.

Of course, if a gas container is exposed to fire long enough, the fuel will expand due to the fire's heat. Eventually, this will cause the container to rupture, resulting in a ball of fire.

Stored gas is not safe. But it is safer than many people think.

The first step in safe fuel storage is to make sure gas vapors are not escaping from the container. If you can still smell the odor of gasoline after a day or two subsequent to it being filled, the container is probably leaking. It may not be leaking enough to see a rivulet of gas flowing out of the can, but since the smell is created by escaping vapors, these same vapors are flammable and therefore a fire hazard.

Fuel should not be stored in an area occupied by people or animals, nor in a place where open flames are present in the same room, nor near spark-producing equipment including electric motors. Fuel storage containers should not be kept in an area that gets warmer than 85-degrees, nor where they can be hit by direct sunlight, including sunlight filtered through a window.

Gas-can explosions are rare. Fortunately, it's not like on television or the movies. For example, a bullet hitting a full gas can will generally not cause an instant explosion. During testing, we shot rifle bullets, including incendiary "tracer" rounds, through a full can of gasoline. In our tests, we not only couldn't replicate an explosion such as seen in television shows and movies, we actually had difficulty trying to start a fire.

After we repeatedly shot holes in the gas can, causing it to leak for more than a minute, we were eventually able to set the surrounding area on fire. However, shooting into the can, even with tracer bullets, never did create a fire. It was only after repeatedly shooting at nearby rocks, which generated sparks, were we finally able to ignite the leaking gasoline. After repeated attempts, we were unable to replicate an explosion such as those seen in action movies.

Note: Diesel fuel is less flammable than gasoline, but it can still be dangerous. Treat diesel fuel with the same safety precautions as used for storing gasoline.

Fuel Transport and Dispensing

Remember, if you are transporting fuel, the container needs to be tightly and strongly secured. Bungee cord attachment is not enough. The fuel can must be held securely, so that even in a traffic accident it cannot become dislodged. (This is so dangerous, that traffic citations are routinely issued to drivers who are transporting a fuel container that is not adequately secured.) But securing these containers is even more important in a bug-out situation, since you may find yourself on bumpy roads, or even driving off-road.

Fuel Weight: Gasoline weighs around 6.6 pounds (3.9 kg) per gallon (.74 kg per liter), diesel fuel 7.1 pounds per gallon (.85 kg per liter) so a 5-gallon gas can that is full of fuel will weigh 35-pounds (16 kg) or more. Therefore, in a traffic accident, a dislodged can of gasoline can be more dangerous than a duffer swinging a sledgehammer.

Weight is an issue. This is why some people are utilizing multiple 2 ½ gallon fuel cans rather than the traditional 5-gallon containers. Even if you are strong enough to tote a 5-gallon can which is full of fuel, and you are able to hold it in position above the fuel port so that you can pour that fuel into a vehicle, you may still want to use a fuel siphon, instead. It's a lot easier, and fuel-wasting spills are less likely.

Self-Priming Siphons: Made for use with fuel (with no-spark fittings and an anti-static hose), are an easy solution for fuel transfer. With minimal training, even a young child can manage this task, although they should be supervised as fuel transfer can be dangerous. For the siphoning process to work, remember that the fuel container needs to be higher than the tank of the vehicle.

Funnels: In addition to a self-priming siphon hose, a plastic funnel with a long neck (tube) is a handy addition to your fuel-transfer kit. The long neck of the funnel works like a gas station's fuel pump nozzle, and this can help un-restrict the flow of fuel during the transfer process. This is noteworthy because modern cars have a device in the neck of the filler pipe which makes it more difficult for thieves to steal fuel from your vehicle. Though some siphon hoses may be rigid enough to bypass this anti-theft device on your vehicle, it may worth having one of these long-neck funnels, just in case.

*Be sure to test your fuel transfer method
and equipment, before you need to use it.*

Fuel Siphon and Fuel Funnel Specifications: Only use a siphon device which is made for the transfer of gasoline, as other siphons may have parts which can cause a fire-creating spark. Not all self-priming siphons perform the same. We recommend that you purchase a siphon with a semi-rigid hose that has a large diameter (3/4 - 1" / 2 – 2 ½ cm), as it will transfer fuel much faster.

Fuel funnels which have a corrugated, flexible tube attached may be less durable than a solid, plastic funnel which has a long, tube-like neck. Do not use siphons with steel fittings or screws, funnels made of metal, or pumps made for uses other than fuel transfer. These items may contain spark-inducing metal parts which can cause a fire.

Scavenging Gasoline or Diesel Fuel: An abandoned parked car as opposed to a vehicle abandoned along a roadway, will likely still contain fuel. In a true emergency when there are no other options, and when you are confident that it is abandoned by the owner and you won't be stealing from another evacuee, you may find it necessary to scavenge its fuel. For this task, a siphon hose and simple tools to open the car's fuel door, are all that you need to fill an empty gas can or container. Remember, to siphon the fuel, the destination container needs to be lower than the source of fuel.

Scavenging fuel from a gas station's fuel tank is far more difficult. The fuel in these tanks is usually 23-feet under the ground, or deeper, so a siphon hose will not work. To accomplish this fuel-removal task, you will need bolt cutters to remove the padlock from the lid, and an electric submersible pump that is safe for use with flammable substances such as gasoline. The size of the pump with hose and wires attached needs to be no larger than 2-3/4-inches in diameter. Adding it to the end of a long pole is desirable to facilitate easy removal of the pump.

Propane Fuel (aka/ Liquefied Propane Gas – LPG)

Propane gas will last indefinitely if the valve on the container successfully prevents leaking, and rust or physical damage has not compromised the tank. When not in regular use, detach the appliance from the tank since stoves, lanterns, and other devices are prone to leaking fuel. A full 5-gallon (20-pound) tank only contains 4-gallons of fuel. It should be stored away from humans and animals.

Caution: Since a filled 5-gallon propane tank weighs approximately 37-pounds, it must be strongly secured before transport to prevent injury in the event of a traffic accident. See the chapter on *Emergency Lighting* for additional details on propane fuel.

Chapter 23

Backup ID, Encryption, Micro Data Storage for Mobility, Useful PDF Reference Documents

Copies of ID & personal documents, medical records, photos of loved ones *("Have you seen?")*, and important reference materials that may be needed during an emergency.

Having access to personal records, medical information, and even reference materials is one aspect of preparation which never seems to get any attention. Yet, some of this data

may be urgently needed during a time of disaster or emergency. However, without advanced planning, you may not have what you need when you urgently it.

On the practical side, we can't slip a file cabinet into our GO-Bag, but we can bring along digital copies—*if they have been securely encrypted*. True, you may not have access to a computer to read or copy these digital files, but having digital copies is still your best bet. In fact, it's probably the only viable option. Even if you have backup paper copies in a safe, kept at your safe-haven retreat location, you may find yourself someplace else when you need access.

Personal records which are essential include identification such as a scanned copy of your driver's license, vehicle registration, passport, medical history and drug prescription data, proof of insurance, property deeds and contracts, access codes and passwords, and emergency contact information for family and friends—and their photos.

Since data storage is now so compact and inexpensive, you can even bring a library of medical reference and "how-to" books in PDF form, in your GO-Bag. Much of this 'reference' and 'instruction' information is available free online, so it's worth downloading it now, while it is easy to get.

Storage Locations

Copies of critical records should be kept in four places:

1. Secure protection in your home or place of business;

2. Off-site in a safe deposit box of a financial institution; or, encrypted, and after it is encrypted, stored in a 'cloud' storage company that has its servers in a different state (don't depend on their encryption);

3. An ultra-small portable data-storage device which is always kept in your wallet, pocket or purse. Since most people are aware of the need for storage in the first two locations, this chapter focuses on the third category which is essential, but often overlooked; plus…

4. A few pages of frequently needed information stored in your GO-Bag.

Most people want to have paper copies of at least some of their "wallet" information stored in their GO-Bag. Consider also having this same information for your spouse, children, and others who may be in your care. For pets, you need to have copies of their inoculation records.

GO-Bag Data Storage: Consider including a scanned copy of your driver's license and vehicle registration, proof of insurance and medical cards, copies of medical prescriptions including eyeglass prescription, passport and business ID. This is a good start to data preservation.

If you are nervous about identity theft and the possibility of someone getting their hands on these copies of documents, that is understandable. As a minimum, consider having a photocopy of your driver's license and medical insurance card. The other items can be contained in secure storage as described later in this chapter.

Since we live in a data-dependent society, we do need a digital data storage solution which makes it possible to safely carry dozens or even hundreds of pages, of genuinely vital confidential records. To do this, we need an ultra-small and durable mobile storage device that is secure (encrypted).

For many people, low-cost is also necessary, so this chapter provides both our recommendation as to the best security option, as well as inexpensive data storage solutions.

Whatever data is essential to your everyday life and well-being, needs to be backed up and securely stored on a portable device which you always keep with you. Since size and weight are factors which limit practical implementation, this chapter explains how to meet this need with minimal inconvenience.

The previously mentioned documents, and more, should be kept in a safety deposit box or uploaded to cloud storage in a different state or country, but it is still advisable to keep a copy of essential information with you always. Compact digital storage is the answer.

Disaster often strikes unexpectedly, so access to stored data can be terminally interrupted. For example, if a bank is destroyed in the same storm as your home or place of business, the documents kept at those locations might be gone forever. Similarly, cloud (Internet) storage of data can be damaged or lost, hacked or compromised, or it can be inaccessible when you need it because the Internet is down, or you don't have access to it.

Thankfully, the miniaturization and low-cost of data storage and advances in data security, now make it possible to carry this essential information with you. Even if your house or office is burned in a fire or damaged by a flood or storm, or otherwise inaccessible because you have fled the area to escape from turmoil, or just because you are on vacation, relevant records can still be retrieved if you have access to a computer. And, if you don't currently have access to a computer, it's likely that you will at a later date. Even after a massive EMP event, 3-5% of computers may still work.

Beginning the Storage Process

The process starts by using a scanner to copy your relevant records and transform them into PDF documents. This format is recommended since PDF files can be opened by most computers. Be sure to assign file names which make specific records easy to find. Current versions of Microsoft Office also make saving a document to PDF format as simple as saving it to Word format.

Ultra-Small Data Storage Options

For many, they see their laptop computer or smartphone as the place to store this vital information. That's fine, but since these tools are prone to theft and damage, and security of the data is dubious even if you use security apps, this isn't sufficient. Keeping this data on an encrypted memory card or USB device is far more secure and even more portable.

Option #1 - Memory Card (Approx. Cost, $10-25): Memory cards such as those used in digital cameras are relatively inexpensive, and ideal for data storage as well as photo storage. Card readers for these memory cards are abundant, but adding an extra-small USB card reader ($10) to your GO-Bag is nevertheless a good idea. In an emergency situation, the data contained on your memory card can be accessed using almost any computer—as long as you have a card reader along.

At little more than ½-inch and less than the weight of two aspirin, these ultra-small memory cards like the SanDisk 'micro SD card' (15 mm x 11 mm x 1.0 mm, 0.5 grams), are a portable data marvel. These tiny, inexpensive cards can store from 8 GB to 32 GB, or up to several Terabits (TB) if you're willing to spend the money. This makes them ideal for this purpose. Be sure to buy a quality card made by a company known for reliable products, such as ScanDisk.

Transport and Packaging of Your Memory Card: Before adding data to your memory card you need to protect it. You'll need two levels of protection: encryption to keep your information private, and physical protection of the memory device itself.

To protect the card from moisture and damage, and still maintain its diminutive size, insert the card into a tiny Hefty Slider bag such as those used for electronic components or jewelry, or wrap it in 4-5 layers of Cling Wrap. For added protection, consider adding a thin piece of rigid plastic to keep the memory card from flexing. Next, wrap it in 4+ layers of tinfoil to help protect it from data intrusion and electromagnetic pulses. When you are finished, this little package can still be smaller, and weigh less, than a stick of gum.

For security, use a piece of duct tape to secure this tiny package to the inside of your wallet, or to the underside of your wristwatch, or in a locket, or in some other item you always have with you.

The total cost of this project (depending on the storage capacity of the memory card you select), can be as little as $20 (USD) for the memory card and a card reader. Note: The card reader should be stored in your GO-Bag. It is not necessary to carry it on your person. Remember, *always encrypt confidential data*. The section in this chapter, "Data Security is Essential" will help you accomplish this requirement.

Option #2 – *"IronKey"* (brand) Encrypted Flash Drive (Cost $40-200+): This brand of compact flash drive was designed from the ground up for data security. IronKey flash drives were initially made for the U.S. government, defense contractors, and to meet the needs of those who transport secret corporate data. Now available to the public online as well as in some retail outlets, an IronKey flash drive (aka/ 'USB drive,' or 'thumb drive') is reportedly the most secure portable data storage method available to the general public. And, it's small enough to carry on your key ring!

An *IronKey* data storage device requires a password to open it, and the data stored on the drive is fully encrypted. Even the least expensive IronKey model, which can store 4GB of confidential data, automatically encrypts anything you add to it. Since this level of encryption is not needed for most documents, the small IronKey is sufficient for most people.

Since it uses the high industry standard of 256-bit AES hardware-based encryption, it is very secure. At only 3 x 3/4 x 3/8-inch (75mm x 19mm x 9mm) in size, and designed to 'plug and play,' you can insert it into the USB drive of any computer and quickly access your password-protected information.

If you want an even higher level of protection, select the IronKey S250 or D250 USB drives (capacities range from 2GB-64GB). These have an even higher level of encryption, 256-bit AES Cipher-Block, chained-mode (government-grade) encryption, plus an impressive tamper-proof design of the drive itself, which prevents disassembly.

For routine daily use of your personal computer, as well as during a disaster situation when you are using someone else's computer, these models include the IronKey 'Identity Manager.' This provides a safe and quick method to store and retrieve all of your passwords.

These IronKey drives are durable, too. The *IronKey* USB drives are *water resistant*, but the S250 and D250 drives are extra durable, tamper-proof, and completely *waterproof*.

When kept on your keyring, your IronKey USB device is available for daily tasks such as routine data transfer between computers, as well as for recovery of your personal records after a disaster. Though not as compact as a Micro SD card, the IronKey USB data drive (models S250 or D250) is the option which reportedly provides the most durable, secure, portable data storage.

Summary: If convenience, ease of use, and easy setup are important attributes for you, an 'IronKey' flash drive is probably your best choice. If cost or an extra-small (concealable) size is your most important consideration, then use a Micro SD Card.

Encryption: Data Security is Essential

If you are storing your personal data on a memory card or anything other than an IronKey USB drive, confidential data needs to be encrypted. This is essential for keeping your data secure even if your storage device becomes lost or stolen. Identity thieves would have a field day if they got their hands on your personal records, so all confidential data needs to be password protected *and* encrypted before you make it portable.

Some manufacturers of memory cards and USB drives have models which password-protect the data. In our experience this is inadequate, but it is far superior to no encryption.

At the very least, use the encryption software which probably came with your computer. With both Microsoft and Apple computer operating systems, there is an encryption option built into the software. Though far from ideal, this software can be used to encrypt the data on a memory card or generic portable drive. This low-level encryption-protection is far better than nothing, but there are better alternatives.

To learn more about the software that is built into your computer's operating system, use the "help" feature of your operating system to find the software tool and its tutorial. On PC's running the various versions of Microsoft Windows operating system, the file encryption feature is referred to as 'EFS' (Encrypting File System). If you are using a Mac computer, you will find the encryption software by searching for the term "FileVault" or the word "encryption."

Keep in mind that if you utilize either of these methods to encrypt data on your portable drive, you will only be able to access your data by using the same type of computer (PC or Apple), and in some cases, the same version of the operating system. This might severely limit your ability to access your data after a disastrous event.

To achieve a much higher degree of data security, use the free program, "TrueCrypt," to encrypt the data on your memory card or portable storage device. This free software provides true 256-bit encryption, and it will also run on nearly all desktop and laptop computers. For more information and to download TrueCrypt encryption software, visit: www.truecrypt.org

TrueCrypt encryption software provides a very high level of encryption, plus it makes it possible to hide encrypted files. On the TrueCrypt website, be sure to read the "Beginner's Tutorial," which is part of the TrueCrypt User's Guide. In it, you will find instructions on how to set-up the software in *portable mode*.

This *portable mode* method loads the TrueCrypt encryption software onto the memory card (or flash drive) and lets you partition the drive. This makes it possible for you to run the encryption program on nearly any computer and allows you to store both encrypted and unencrypted data on the same drive. The minimum size for a memory card used for this purpose is 8MB, but a larger memory card will be needed if you plan to store much data.

Whether you use a memory card such as the SD MicroDrive or a flash drive (aka/ 'USB drive,' or 'thumb drive'), remember that you must routinely have it with you, so that your data is available to you when disaster strikes. An encrypted drive that is left behind may not be a security risk, but the work of preparing it will have been wasted if you don't have the drive when you need it.

What Records to Store: Encrypted and Unencrypted

Even the most basic personal data such as your driver's license should be encrypted. However, you may want to make some information, such as photos and your address book, accessible without entering a password. At the very least, an unencrypted text file which includes your contact information may make it possible for a lost or stolen drive to be returned to you, *and* emergency contact information will be readily available to authorities if they need to contact your loved ones after you have been seriously injured.

Remember to add PDF 'reader' software to your memory card or USB device, too. You may need to borrow a computer which does not have this software installed (see links at the end of this article), and the owner of the machine may not want you to download software onto their computer. Or, the Internet may be down making a download impossible.

It's up to you to decide what records you store, and what you encrypt, but don't let a lengthy list delay implementation. It is much better to have an encrypted drive with just a little information stored on it, than to have nothing at all at a time when it's needed.

What Records to Include

The following list isn't *your* list, it's included to stimulate your thinking. It's added here to help you develop your own list of essential documents.

If your list is long, don't let the enormity of the task prevent you from beginning right now. Scan and store your wallet documents on your personal computer today, buy a micro or flash drive tomorrow, encrypt it, and add additional data as soon as you can.

Consider, too, that you might want to include the personal records of your spouse, children, or other close family members or trusted friends on your drive, as well. It's a simple task to make multiple identical sets of emergency records so that each family member has the documents they may need. You might even use the same password on each drive so that you and your spouse can both access one of the other drives if yours is lost. And, if you are separated from your spouse by circumstances, you will both have what you need.

A Check-List to Help You Get Started

1. Driver's License
2. Company or Employee ID
3. Gun license (CHL-Concealed Handgun License, LTC-License to Carry, ATF tax stamp docs, etc.) and firearm records
4. Passport (The two-page spread which includes your photo)
5. Social Security Card
6. Medical Insurance Cards
7. Dental Insurance Cards
8. Organ Donor Card
9. Pharmaceutical Prescriptions or Prescription Medicine Labels
10. Medical History & Immunization Records
11. Copy of your Last Will and Testament
12. Vehicle Insurance
13. House/Office Insurance Documents
14. Titles for Vehicles and Property
15. Property Descriptions with Serial Numbers
16. Professional Licenses or Certification Documents
17. Credit Card Numbers & Contact Info for Card Companies
18. Banking Information, Including Account Numbers and Passwords
19. List of Other Access Codes and Passwords
20. Membership, Affiliation or ID Cards (Particularly those which give you permission to occupy facilities and property which you might want to access during an emergency)
21. Letters of Permission to Occupy Land or Facilities
22. Address Book (Contact information for family, friends and colleagues)
23. Photos (Be sure to include close-up, passport-like images of yourself, family members, key friends and colleagues that you might want to find during an emergency situation.)
24. Physical Description (Yourself, family, friends, and colleagues)
25. Fingerprints and copies of dental x-rays
26. Maps and Directions

Summary

Having access to identification and other personal records may prove to be invaluable in the aftermath of a disaster or during an emergency situation. Start by preparing a micro memory card or USB drive with encryption. Then, use a scanner to make copies of your most important identification cards and documents, starting with what you carry in your wallet. Store these records in PDF format so that this data can be read, and even printed if necessary, using any computer.

Include a physical description and close-up photographs of each of your family members and close friends. If any of these people (or even pets) become missing, these photos will help others, help you.

If there is room, don't forget to add PDF books, instructions on relevant topics, and maps to your data storage. Or, prepare a flash drive for this purpose, and keep it with your GO-Bag. This data needn't be encrypted, but you may find it invaluable to have with you.

For example, data on water purification or first aid might be urgently needed. Books and documents can be stored at home or at your safe-haven retreat location, but you may find yourself needing this information when you don't have access to reference materials. So, scan what you think you might need, and keep it with you, or in your GO-Bag.

For additional details on products, links to manufacturer's websites, and other details which are periodically updated to keep them current, visit the author's website. On the "Resources" page, look for "Book 2 – Supplemental Information."
www.SigSwanstrom.com

Chapter 24

Dogs and Pets: Turning a Problem into an Asset

Whether you love or just tolerate your pet, now is the time to consider what you will do with them when you are facing an emergency situation. It is irresponsible to leave a pet behind except in the direst of circumstances. (And, by the way, your convenience never qualifies as a 'dire' circumstance.) So, you need to formulate a plan. You need to decide how you will handle it.

Unfortunately, most pets, except some dogs and a few other animals, increase your problems during an emergency situation. But if you leave them behind to fend for themselves, a domesticated animal, like a pet dog, will probably either starve, become injured and die a horrible death, or join a pack and become dangerous to people, especially children.

On the other hand, if you take them with you, you will need to feed and care for them. This can make evacuation more difficult, but it is a responsibility of ownership to care for your pet during both times of ease and periods of hardship.

As mentioned earlier in this book, when facing a disaster or emergency situation, don't plan on leaving your animal at your favorite pet boarding kennel, veterinarian, animal care services center, or with a family member or friend, either. You are just handing off your problem to them, and that isn't fair. You can't shirk your responsibility.

Furthermore, in the U.S., if you take your pet with you to a federal or State sponsored shelter, they will likely separate you from your pet, and though they may not tell you, the official protocol calls for euthanasia. They will kill your pet. Do you think I must be wrong? Read the confidential (but not Classified) U.S. Government document, FM-39.40 "Internment and Resettlement Operations."

Of course, you may encounter a shelter operator who loves animals and ignores this directive, but are you willing to gamble with your pet's life? If not, what are your options? In my view, you have three choices.

1. Either keep your pet with you and stockpile/carry the food and water they will need, and hope for the best; or,

2. When that time comes, humanely euthanize your pet(s); or

3. If your pet is a dog, turn them into an asset. These benefits can be enjoyed today, and you will be ready to face tomorrow with your loyal companion as a valuable partner.

Unfortunately, the third choice is not available to owners of cats and most other pets, but it is an excellent option if your pet is a healthy dog. If you're up for 20-minutes of training 3-days a week for four months, Option #3 is the best choice. I heartily recommend it.

In any case, we can't avoid facing the truth. Dogs tend to be either a security problem or a security asset, and they require extra work and supplies that may be difficult to provide.

If you unleash your dog and it runs off, or it barks without sufficient provocation, the animal represents a security risk during an emergency situation. This problem is most glaring with yappy little dogs.

During an emergency, a barking dog attracts attention. If your dog is small or undisciplined, criminals will probably not perceive your dog to be a threat. As a result, the animal can create unnecessary risks for you, the owner. More to the point, this unwelcomed attention may make you a target for crime, additionally so if you are trying to hide or remain inconspicuous.

One of my former firearms students is a dog trainer for FEMA, and I talked to her about this issue. In the conversation, I asked her, "Why are little dogs so often barkers?" Her answer, "Because their owners allow it."

Yes, a barking dog may be an unrivaled asset, but only if you are the one controlling that response. A well-trained dog that barks in accord with your training can give valuable early warning to a problem, but a dog that uncontrollably barks may create added risks for you and your companions.

A dog's fine-tuned hearing and sense of smell can provide far better early warning than the most sophisticated electronic alarm system.

Yet, these amazing attributes are only helpful if the animal is properly trained.

When I was a police officer, I had the opportunity to periodically work alongside K9 dogs and their handlers. It was a beautiful thing to watch. The partnership between a well-trained dog and its well-trained handler is an impressive partnership. Whether the purpose is defense, security patrol, detection, tracking, or search and rescue, a dog can be a tremendous asset. I've even seen a police dog save the life of his handler.

Unfortunately, most people do not know how to turn their pet into a service dog; an asset which can be valuable during ordinary times as well as during a crisis. Thankfully, this lack of knowledge can be overcome.

The first-step for transforming your dog from liability to asset is obedience training. Yes, it is easier to train a young dog than an old one, but both can be taught if you are patient and know what you are doing. You need to teach your dog to not bark without provocation and to obey immediately. Basic training must include both voice and signal commands for "heel," "come," "stay," "off," and "down."

Barking or growling on command is useful, but at the very least, train your dog to only bark as a result of actual provocation. If you fail to teach your dog not to bark indiscriminately, your undisciplined animal may attract the kind of attention that brings serious heartache.

Once problem-erasing basics have been handled, you are ready to start transforming your dog into a working-dog asset; a partner. This will require the professional help of an experienced dog trainer who has done this for the military, a government agency, or a private security firm.

Or, use an online training program produced by a company that uses these same highly-credentialed trainers, and also provides telephone support as part of their fee. You will need someone to answer questions, as a video training course will not address all the questions you will have.

An ordinary dog trainer cannot take the place of one who has extensive experience in the behavior you are trying to model. My recommendation is to not waste time with YouTube videos produced by self-promoting people without serious credentials (or credentials you can't verify), nor kindly dog-trainers who are well-meaning but lack the specific skills necessary for this task. Use an expert. In the long run, you will not only save time and money, but you will also be far more successful.

Whether evacuating due to an emergency, or living at your safe-haven retreat location, or leaving a place of safety to help a friend or family member who is in need, don't discount the benefits that a well-trained dog can provide. If you live in a place where you cannot carry a gun, a well-trained medium or large-size dog that is properly trained can be both a reliable low-tech security system and a source of unparalleled defense. Even if you do have a gun, and even if you know how to use it, a dog can still be an indispensable partner.

Chapter 25

Bartering, Sustainability & Opportunities

Whether it be an economic downturn, a shortage of food or goods that are unavailable, or the need to supplement your income, or recruiting people for a safe-haven community, there are specific skills and related supplies which will be useful to have during hard times. Some of these will be valuable, while others simply useful, but all will be needed in a post-disaster environment.

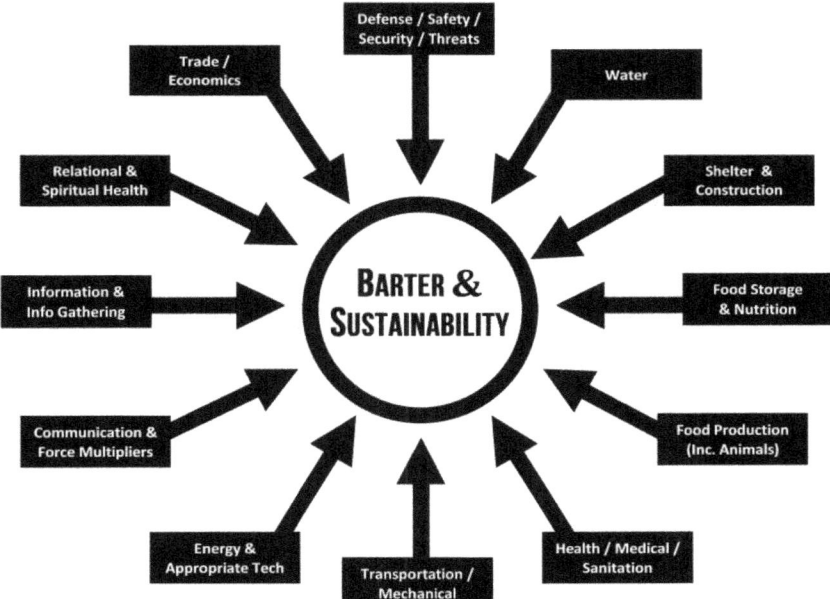

The above chart not only identifies these skills, but it also illustrates their codependent interrelationship for sustainability and community health. It identifies areas of need, and also service, barter and other opportunities in both a disaster and recovery environment. Whereas selling goods is limited by available inventory, these skills and services are unlimited; essentially a renewable resource.

During periods of affluence people buy new products, but during hard times the demand is for quality *used* goods, or for the repair of items which have broken or become worn. As a result, during extended periods of hardship or disaster, underground economies develop. These are often based on trading goods and services rather than purchasing with fiat cash which does not have an inherent value. What is valuable, are the skills which are needed for independent living during difficult times. These also represent post-disaster opportunities for service and trade.

The following list is tied to the pathways identified in the chart. These skills, gained either through a profession, job, vocation or hobby, will be in higher demand during a protracted emergency situation. So, *it is to our advantage to develop at least one of these skills*.

During the early years of the United States when growth was so robust and society healthy, the Founders believed that even professionals such as doctors, lawyers, accountants, and shopkeepers, also needed to have expertise in a "manual labor" skill. They considered this to be a hedge against adversity, and selected a 'trade' to teach their children. Discerning parents made this selection based on three things; aptitude, interest, and anticipated demand and usefulness.

The following list of categories is included to help stimulate your thinking. If you already have one or more of these skillsets, consider developing them further, tailoring them to the needs of a barter economy. And, purchase the supplies now, which you will need in the future when re-supply is costly or impossible.

For example, a medical doctor will need to develop skills and purchase low-tech equipment to compensate for the lack of laboratory resources and limited ancillary services and referral opportunities, and focus their education on the treatment of all the injuries and ailments which will be commonplace in a post-disaster environment.

Additionally, consider reviving the "apprentice" model used in prior generations to train others. Young people need mentors to teach them these skills today, and many will need to have these skills in the future.

Apprentice or mentoring relationships can be informal and based on a two-way street where the novice is a helper who receives training in the process. Or, it can be formal or semi-formal with compensation or barter-benefits going to either the teacher or the individual who is able to provide noteworthy assistance to the expert. These relationships often become friendships, too, and this can exert positive influences and benefits which go far beyond the task at hand.

Listed in alphabetical order.

1. Communication and Force Multipliers

Skills and practical knowledge in: Emergency radios, 2-way radios, ham (amateur) radios, antennas, field-expedient antennas, computer-aided amateur radios and PDF transmission, ham (amateur radio) certification for FCC license; radio stations, podcasts and vodcasts. Also, batteries, alternative power, and recharging options; force multipliers, early-warning devices and portable alarms, surveillance and observation aids, night vision and thermal scopes, sensors, cameras; navigation and map use; communicating with light; non-mechanical communication methods, etc.

2. Defense, Safety, Security, Threat Analysis

Skills and practical knowledge in: firearm repair, gun selection, gun use and carry methods, weapon accessories; safe storage and long-term storage; specialty guns for defense and other purposes; less-lethal weapons; self-defense, home, and community defense; situation and threat analysis; defensive and offensive tactics; vehicle defense and assault; creation of fire teams, team movement; developing a security force, training guards; security for travel; scouting and tracking; concealment; selection of animals for defense and early warning, training animals for a security role, security skill development for volunteers; selection of defensible sites, designing defensible space, barricades, perimeter defenses and structures, etc.

3. Energy and Appropriate Technologies

Skills and practical knowledge in: Solar and alternative fuels, alternative fuel retrofitting, power generation options, electrical and electronic jerry-rigging, mechanical labor-saving devices, energy storage, heating/cooling.

4. Food Production

Skills and practical knowledge in: Agronomy, soil augmentation, site selection, irrigation, gardening and growing methods, heirloom seeds, seed selection and preservation, fertilizers and composting; growing seasons and scheduling plantings to extend harvest; hidden gardens, foraging; beekeeping and pollination; pest control, protecting food sources from predators; vegetable gardening; growing spices, herbs and medicinal herbs; orchards and fruit trees; trees and vegetation grown for fuel. Protein and fats: aquaponics, hydroponics, fish farming, Trans-Farming; raising birds and small animals for food, raising medium-to-large animals for food. Veterinary: medical skills relating to animals; insemination and birthing of animals. Processing animals: butchering animals; storage; hunting and stalking.

5. Food Storage, Cooking, and Nutrition

Skills and practical knowledge in: Long-term food storage, selecting long shelf-life foods, trail foods, canning, drying, smoking, cheese making and preserving, creating prepackaged meals; rodent and insect control, and storage methods; preparing savory food, coaxing kids to eat unfamiliar foods; cooking for groups; nutrition for high-stress high-energy-demand situations; DIY Mylar packaging, and the use of oxygen absorbers and desiccants; cooking methods and creative stoves and ovens, etc.

6. Health, Medical, and Sanitation

Skills and practical knowledge in: First aid skills, wilderness medicine, foot care, TacMed (Tactical Medicine; gunshot and stab wounds, catastrophic injuries); transport of the injured; midwifery, medical care when there is no hospital or clinic; triage; isolation; emergency dentistry for the layman; probiotics and health enhancement methods; injury prevention; physical therapy; vitamin and mineral supplements; electrolyte imbalance; sterilizing medical equipment; what to stockpile and how to store it; creating saline, disinfectants, and other useful products; low-tech medical devices and their maintenance; dealing with pandemics; diagnosis and treatment of nuclear, biological and chemical injuries; naturopathic and alternative treatment methods; community health and sanitation; sewage treatment; safe and respectful burial and cremation; contaminated waste disposal, etc.

7. Information, Info Gathering, and Education

Skills and practical knowledge in: Tools and techniques for information gathering; information analysis and validation; misinformation and recognizing false flags; finding alternative news sources; dealing with cyber-attacks; old-school skills; secure storage and transfer of data; encryption; homeschooling, community education; library development and maintenance, etc.

8. Shelter and Construction

Skills and practical knowledge in: Emergency shelter; site selection and building a safe-haven; construction methods (concrete, papercrete, stone, metal, log, cordwood, adobe block, rammed earth, straw bale, tires, and other geographically available materials); repurposed intermodal (Conex box) shipping containers; defensible space and concealment; basic engineering skills and reference materials; heating, cooling and ventilation; constructing WMD defensive measures and medical quarantine areas; salvaging and construction using salvaged and re-purposed materials.

9. Spiritual and Relational Health

Skills and practical knowledge in: Fearless living; dealing with spiritual crisis and unbiblical expectations; spiritual warfare; developing a chaplaincy program, ministry of encouragement, victorious life, grief and death counseling, suicide prevention, fear and anger management, coping mechanisms, marriage counseling, parenting, dispute resolution; worship, music, the arts, things of beauty and creating times of respite; team building and coaching, building upon gifting; evangelism, discipleship, home-church development, portable Bible study resources, dealing with heresies; community/relational health, representative, governance, fiduciary responsibilities of membership, tithing and giving gifts, town hall meetings; law, criminal conduct, and judicial processes; discipline, redemption and forgiveness; community administration, record keeping, inventory control. Note: Leadership and administration are a subset of community health.

10. Trade, Barter, Business and Economics

Skills and practical knowledge in: How to become an entrepreneur, business strategies, business planning and start-up; legal issues; pro forma financial projections and budgeting; analysis of trends and tipping points, finding opportunities in problems, problem solving techniques, identifying niche markets, market and risk analysis, win-win negotiating; marketing and sales; back-pocket businesses, developing a public market, bartering techniques for goods and services; establishing the value of "things," creating "money" in a cashless society; developing a cadre of morale-boosting solution-oriented business advisers, etc.

11. Transportation and Mechanical

Skills and practical knowledge in: Repair and repurposing of vehicles and equipment; welding, metal cutting and fabrication; tire repair; fuel creation, fuel storage; conversion of engines/motors to alternative fuels, mechanical labor-saving devices, tool making, windmills, pumps, hydraulics; equipment maintenance; repurposing of appliances and machinery, equipment and appliance repair, MacGyver solutions, etc.

12. Water

Skills and practical knowledge in: Water sourcing, water wells; rainwater collection and water storage; water diversion; hydration needs of humans and animals; purification techniques, water filtration, bio and sand filters; avoiding contamination, decontamination of water; water transport, pumping and pipe; creative PVC solutions for water,+ as well as miscellaneous devices and construction; irrigation methods; hydrology; and human waste processing.

Chapter 26

Author's Personal Reflections

Except for the reference information contained in the Appendix, this book is finished. You needn't read further. The publisher has assigned a purchase price based on the book up to this point, so the cost of adding this chapter will be deducted from my royalties. Since you didn't pay for it, I have the liberty to tell you more about what I'm thinking. Therefore, only read it if you are interested. What follows are my personal reflections on several topics which relate to the subject of this book. I am including them here in the hope that you will find them useful.

Postscript

Our best "Early Warning System" for emergency situations is to keep abreast of noteworthy events in real time. In Book-1 of this *PREPARED: Ready to Roll* guidebook series, I chronicled what the U.S. Government is doing to prepare for the period of adversity their experts predict. And in it, I explain how to use alternative news sources and apps to tap into perceptive analysis and facts not addressed by the mainstream media. But in addition to monitoring these signs-of-the-times and the forecasts of credentialed experts, there is a bedrock topic which is undervalued but essential.

Thinking that it is a dull topic, many people are not interested in history. Most of our schools have cut back on their traditional history and civics classes, replacing them with politically correct froth. This trend is hazardous to our health.

Thankfully, many private schools, some charter schools, and Christian homeschool curriculums are counteracting this trend. These educators understand that we can save ourselves a lot of pain if we are willing to learn from the past and diligently develop analysis and critical-thinking skills. For those of us who are no longer attending school, we need to peruse this education on our own.

Unlike some popular slogans, history is not a loop, and we are not forced to repeat it, but we can nevertheless learn valuable lessons and gain perspective by looking into the past. As in the business world of manufacturing where a prototype is used to help guide future product development, we can use history as our prototype. It, too, can help us get ready for the future we are manufacturing.

If we want to reduce hardship and live without regrets, we need to learn from the past and apply what we learn to get ready for the changes that are coming. We need to know about current events, of course, but we also need a working knowledge of history if we want to evaluate what's happening and put it into a helpful context.

The future will not look like today, nor will it look exactly like any past era. This is a given. But the past can still give us additional insights which can be used to help us make better decisions today.

Momentous changes are just around the corner. This is obvious to anyone who takes the time to study our various current predicaments. There are severe dangers on our doorstep. So, gaining an understanding of relevant current affairs, plus the lessons taught by history, can help us get ready for what is coming.

Practical planning isn't an academic exercise. When winter is coming, we bring out our warm clothing and make sure our furnace is working. If we don't have enough fuel, we get more. This is a lesson learned from history, either our own or one gained from the experiences of others. This mundane example is an illustration of practical, useful history. It is the bedrock on which prudent people will build their future.

Likewise, when the weather moderates and an anticipated storm passes uneventfully, history teaches us that winter isn't over just because a storm petered out. Just the opposite. Our past experiences (history) helps us appreciate that we were fortunate, and we have a little more time to prepare for the coming winter storms. The next time we may not be so lucky. As we are reminded by the adage...

"Hope for the best. Prepare for the worst."

Today, I want to add another line to this familiar saying...
"Be resilient and adapt to surprises."

Valuable lessons from history are not only of monumental importance to a history professor. These can be essential for us, too, if we learn how to separate what is actually useful from the mind-numbing litany of facts.

If we take the time to read-between-the-lines of history, particularly those periods of social upheaval, disastrous changes, economic crisis, and other times of radical change, we can glean valuable lessons which we can apply to our world today.

> When we lived in Guatemala, my resilient and adaptable wife added a new beatitude for our family, *"Blessed are the flexible, for they shall not be bent out of shape."* Her humorous quip is good advice for us all.

It is not the names and dates of the historical events which are vital to us, but rather the backstory. The story behind the story. This is where we will find the gems which lead to a deeper understanding of our current circumstances.

For critically important topics such as preparing for severe emergency situations, we can unearth life-lesson treasures if we look for similarities between history and current events. Colossal changes, and the study of what caused the rise and fall of nations is foundational if we are to gain big-picture understanding. Similarly, we need to investigate less epic but more recent events which involve disasters.

For Example: As we learn about the Hurricane Katrina disaster, and what transpired before and immediately afterward, we can learn some important things about our society and human nature that can help inform our decision making in the future.

With Katrina, when we delve into what happened in 2005 at the Superdome when 20,000 people fled to this government-sponsored shelter, we can learn some valuable lessons. We note that emergency supplies were pre-staged at this sports stadium, and it had been used several times previously as an Evacuation Center. So, the government knew what to expect. And, since these same results have happened several times since, a pattern emerges. Therefore, we can deduce what we can expect from the government in the future.

The Superdome Evacuation Center became like a gang-controlled prison. The evacuees were confined and not allowed to leave even when conditions became deplorable. For these people, it became a second disaster, one that was man-made and preventable.

The problem wasn't a lack of supplies, or that government workers weren't on hand to help. Nor was it a lack of security staff. There were 550 National Guard soldiers stationed at the Superdome, and they did commendable work.

It's not politically correct to say it, but the truth is that the problem was the evacuees; their entitlement attitudes, their lack of initiative, and the absence of self-reliance. And, that the evacuee population included gang members and criminals of all sorts. These preyed on the ordinary, good people who were just seeking refuge.

Mostly unreported outside of New Orleans, the severity remains unknown except to those who are willing to dig for specifics. The fact is this: There were two back-to-back disasters. The first was caused by a storm. The second catastrophe was even more significant. It was created by people.

It was in this second disaster where the government's premier shelter, the Superdome, became a hellhole of tragedy. Yet, it was a predictable outcome. And the authorities did predict it; they just couldn't cope with it.

Recent history teaches us that this tragic New Orleans "refugee camp" situation was not unusual. So, when possible, I will personally avoid evacuating to a big government shelter. That's one of my take-away lessons after studying the history of hurricane Katrina.

There are many strategic lessons which can be learned from this same disaster. In just a few minutes of reading news articles from those dark days, we can arrive at various conclusions. We can use these to give us valuable insights. This discernment is invaluable as we develop our personal plans and preparations.

Studying events like this one, which occurred relatively recently, is perhaps even more important than studying ancient history. Yet, both are worthwhile.

As we distill cause-and-effect principles from both recent events and distant history, this can help us navigate the changes that are coming. This isn't rocket science, it just a simple method for using the past experiences of others, to help us better understand our present circumstances and our future. This gives us the opportunity to be more insightful in our preparations for the days ahead.

As explained in Chapter-1, *running scenarios* is an enormously useful tool. When we use past events to help us develop these scenarios, they become even more valuable and relevant.

History gives us a basis for asking questions such as: "What would I do if I found myself in that situation?" "How would my neighbors and community respond?" "What can I do now, to make sure I don't suffer the same fate?" "How can I avoid becoming a victim?" And, "What can I do now, to make sure I am ready to help myself and others when the world turns upside down?"

You may not be able to avoid a disastrous situation, but you can prepare for it. You can fare better than those who were unprepared and caught by surprise.

> Morality is not situational. Those who steal the provisions of another are not justified by the circumstance.
>
> To scavenge abandoned property may be reasonable. However, to deprive someone of their supplies is never warranted—even if our children are hungry. Our failure to adequately prepare doesn't justify theft.[17]

After we distill relevant current-event details from sources of reliable first-hand information (rather than from talking-head newscasters), we ask ourselves, "Is there a legitimate threat?" If so, "What is the true nature of the threat and its ramifications to me?" Then we ask, "Based on my past experiences and the experiences of others (history), what should I do to weather the coming storm?"

Oddly, historians are rarely great planners. To flourish in the future, we need to do more than just study the past.

We need to be selective about what materials we study, which experts we esteem, and what we conclude from our efforts. As we learn, we need to concentrate on the practical, real-world applications we can glean from what we have learned.

---

[24] The enormously popular post-disaster novel, "Lights Out" by David Crawford, was followed by "Collison Course." Yet, Crawford's second novel was not as popular. Why? Because it addresses an uncomfortable topic—the slippery slope of post-disaster moral failure. This is a book worth reading, and a topic worthy of contemplation.

Moreover, learning from the past does not mean we should try to return to the past, especially an idealized past that never actually existed. Since Adam and Eve left the Garden of Eden, there has never been a Golden Era when life was perfect for everyone. Yet, learning what worked in the past is still useful.

If we want to gain a strategic advantage for the future, we must learn from the past. And this study needs to be not only practical, but cause-and-effect *outcome* oriented.

We need to learn how to encapsulate significant events in history: "This is what happened…, this is the backstory…, this is what they did…, and the outcome was…" We shouldn't oversimplify, but we do need to reach conclusions which can be used to inform our present-day actions.

We need to make our study of history not just diligent, but accurate, too. "Revisionist history" is widespread in modern society. Not concerned with truth or accuracy, it is fabricated to advance a particular political agenda. This is not the fact-based history we need for decision-making. Therefore, we need to check our sources to make sure they are reliable. Often it is the old sources of information, recorded closer to the event itself, which are more trustworthy.

Next, we need to concentrate on historical events which initiated sweeping change. When these events are considered together with current events, our conclusions become more reliable and our planning efforts more fruitful.

The useful information needed to answer these questions is rarely included in Wikipedia-like summaries; it's found in the details and first-hand accounts. For example, despite the fact that the French Revolution and American Revolution occurred in the same timeframe, why was the conduct of the participants so different in the two wars? Why was the outcome so different?

Reliable Sources of Information

The more crucial the decisions we face, the more critical it is to dig deep for information. Contemporaneous, original sources are best. Thankfully, when it comes to events such as the revolutionary wars of the past four centuries, we have access to an abundance of information written by those who were eyewitnesses. This is where we will find our most useful facts.[25]

Character + Strategy: Virtue, justice, truth, optimism, sacrifice, and a spirit of hope, all add power to a movement, even when only a small percentage of the population is committed. However, it is the addition of shrewd, insightful strategies which bring victory, and these come from studying the details.

For those who take the "I don't have time," "it's fate" or "God is in control" shortcuts to personal responsibility, they are exposing dangerous laziness. While it is true that we may not be able to change the world, and that the eventual outcome is in God's hands, that's not the end of the discussion. Moreover, these statements are not an excuse for escapism. We need to do our part, too. God doesn't reward foolishness; we need to use the brain our Creator gave us.[26]

The classic novel by Charles Dickens, "A Tale of Two Cities," opens with an insightful sentence. It reads, *"It was the best of times, it was the worst of times, it was the age of wisdom, it was the age of foolishness…"* Similarly, our modern era has both rosy and cancerous attributes. We need to look at both if we are to find valuable insights.

Regrettably, in our era, most of the mainstream media, politicians, and self-proclaimed experts think of themselves as wise and enlightened, yet most are so consumed by their own agendas that they fail to embrace the obvious. With this in mind, we need to be very careful about where we get our information and analysis.

Moreover, we need to be solution oriented and work at advancing the positive things which are happening in our society. Yet, we also need to acknowledge the adverse developments and prepare for their damaging effects.

Unfortunately, most of us allow our lives to be so busy that we don't have time to think about the world around us. As a result, we are plagued with baseless optimism and have surrendered to a self-imposed normalcy bias. We've learned that staying busy and living in denial is more comfortable than the work of hiking on the road less traveled. But if we love our families, and care about others, this must change.

---

[25] If you are interested in learning about the Founders of the United States and the history of American Revolution, David Barton and his colleagues at Wall Builders, are a good source for materials. www.WallBuilders.org.

[26] Holy Bible; Proverbs 6:6-11, 13:14, 22:3.

Most people are optimistic about the future, especially when their favorite politician has been elected to office, or the stock market is trending upward, or there hasn't been a terrorist incident for a while, and especially when their life is stable and reasonably comfortable. Yet, these are fleeting improvements.

Moreover, trends are unreliable. They can swing up or down in a heartbeat. When underlying problems have not been fixed, constructive developments, at best, only buy us more time to prepare.

The Western world is inexcusably self-indulgent, and the underlying problems are myriad. In response, some people are busy trying to make the world a better place, and we need to applaud and participate in these efforts. But at this point, we can't let these good works wholly supplant the priority of other future-oriented tasks. We are too far behind where we need to be, to continue to allow that to happen.

Few have learned the valuable lessons taught by ancient and recent history, combined them with the current strategic indicators of change, and then applied them to get ready for the future. If you have read this book, you are apparently a member of this rarefied, small group of discerning individuals.

This guidebook was written for you and this group of perceptive people. If you feel somewhat alone in your quest to get ready, don't be discouraged. You are in the top 3% of society, so it's no wonder you feel alone.

Together, we need to do what we can to help others awaken. Yet, most will refuse. We need to anticipate this; history also teaches us to expect resistance to uncomfortable truth. Not that we shouldn't try, it's just that we can't assume that revival will automatically come as a result of our efforts. Only God can bring meaningful revival.

Yet, as the Founders of America learned, a successful revolution only needs 3% of the population to be active in seeking substantive change. This is true for peaceful revolutions, too—but the word "active" is operative.

Peaceful or violent, substantial change is coming. We don't know what it will look like. It might be real improvements brought about by a renaissance or revival. Or, it might be the natural progression of increasingly difficult and life-harming developments which follow the current trends. Or, the change might be in the form of a sudden catastrophe. Only God knows.

What we do know is that regardless of the path we take to the coming changes, the status quo we have enjoyed is coming to an end. Radical change is the road we are now traveling. It is unavoidable. Positive or negative, the coming changes will have a profound effect on each of our lives and the lives of our children.

So, we need to work for positive change, but we also need to be ready for a negative turn. To do less is irresponsible.

As we consider the future, we need to keep in mind that challenges such as food and water problems, national debt, terrorism and threats of war, are not the only dangers on our doorstep. We are also facing a foundational threat that is even more deadly than these. It is represented in the "Cycle of Nations," and it is yet another valuable lesson from history that we cannot afford to ignore.

Often attributed to Scottish historian Alexander Fraser Tyler (1747-1813), the "Cycle of Nations" sequences the rise and fall of nations. This diagram is based on the insights of Tyler and other historians over the past 200 years. It illustrates the progression of a country, particularly a democracy, from its optimistic origin to its eventual fall. I've included it here as an example of yet another useful lesson which can be gleaned from the study of history.

I've also included it as a challenge. I encourage you to identify the position your nation holds in this 8-step progression.

Difficulties will arise during each of the eight eras of national health that are depicted in the chart, and the duration of each will vary. However, history teaches that the rate of decline often accelerates before the return to bondage.

Sudden Shock: "Surprise" often accompanies the stages of rapid decline. Despite the insights that some leaders and self-proclaimed experts now claim, none of the high-profile pundits anticipated the rapid collapse of East Germany and the end of the Cold War.

When the Berlin Wall suddenly came down, almost everyone was surprised. Many had observed the signs-of-the-times which were harbingers of dramatic change, but no one grasped that it would happen suddenly, with a burst of unanticipated speed.

One of the founders of the United States had this to say about sudden catastrophes, and what we can expect in the future...

> *"**If we abide by the principles** taught in the Bible, our country will go on prospering and to prosper; but if we and our posterity neglect its instructions and authority, no man can tell how sudden a catastrophe may overwhelm us and bury all our glory in profound obscurity."*
>
> - Daniel Webster (1782-1852)
> U.S. Congressman, Senator, and
> Secretary of State

The collapse of East Germany was the result of many factors, so Tyler's *"Cycle of Nations"* does not provide the basis for every national collapse, but rather a nation that implodes due to internal forces.

The Cycle of Nations is more akin to an unrelenting rainstorm. Rainfall may cause the level of a lake to rise, but it is the water-swollen streams which feed into that lake, which create a destructive flood. It's the same with nations that self-destruct.

As various problems and issues grow in magnitude, though they may not be devastating individually, if unchecked, they become like flooding streams which wreak havoc when they pool together. The combined effect will either stimulate a peaceful revolution that ushers in a new era of positive change or one that brings calamity. Absent a true revival, it's calamity.

Though a lake rises as a direct result of rainwater landing in it, the destructive flood is due to the many surging streams which flow into it. As we apply this to national disasters, this is regarded as a confluence event. For us, as we consider the future of our own nation, this *confluence* model is useful to us.

What can we expect in our future? The United States, as well as many other Western nations, are nearing the end of Tyler's Cycle of Nations. As we get closer to this tipping point, what will happen if a confluence of simmering problems suddenly heat-up and begin to boil?

The answer is probably obvious to you. It will accelerate the pace of coming change. Once this *confluence* of events starts (which it already has), even a small increase in temperature can bring society to a rolling boil.

It's like a pressure cooker. Without substantive changes in the circumstances, the lid will eventually blow off like a bomb. The pot and lid which currently keep these boiling problems under control will ultimately blow off. When that happens, scalding water and pot fragments will be thrown everywhere. Including on us.

> *As a nation*, we need to fix the damage which is causing us to sink. But *as individuals*, we need to grab a life preserver, put it on, and get ready to spend some time in the water.

It's like a speedboat that has traveled over a reef, tearing a hole in the bow of the boat. It immediately starts to sink. In this circumstance, a skilled captain will hit the throttle, adding maximum power. His response is designed to use speed to lift the damaged area out of the water, a move that he hopes will buy time so that he can get the boat and passengers to safety before it sinks.

For a brief time, the boat may leap across the water as if the damage has been repaired, but the reprieve is only temporary. Unless the hole in the hull is fixed, the boat will founder and eventually sink. It's the same with nations.

Effective leaders and improved policies may use momentum to buy time and delay the inevitable, but without structural repairs, the ship of state will eventually sink.

This is the situation of the U.S., the UK, and most of our European allies. If we don't make the required underwater repairs, adding more power to the engines won't be enough to keep us skipping over the crest of the waves for much longer. The damaged nation will not be able to escape its current predicament. At best, we will only stay afloat long enough to hand over the problem to our children.

In the days ahead, we can expect a crisis, probably more than one. This may happen because we have reached the final stage of the Cycle of Nations. Or, it may be the result of a catastrophic event or a confluence of events which become increasingly destructive due to our weakened condition. Either way, when the time comes, the progression of events can quickly escalate into catastrophe. The dangers on our doorstep will become present dangers.

Today, there are scores of highly-credentialed economists, social scientists, and experts in various fields who are all sounding the alarm. Unfortunately, few are listening. Yet, at this point, we don't need new experts and additional research. We need common sense.

For those of us who are willing to look, we must intensify our focus, step out of our complacency, and dare to be different. Importantly, as we endeavor to fix the Ship of State, we need to be wearing our life preservers. We need to live our lives as a Lookout, ready to warn family and friends, and ready to roll—so that we can instantly swim to safety.

We can expect the political and economic landscape to continue to go up and down, but short-term changes are not to be feared—nor excessively praised. We cannot afford to diminish our intensity even when positive changes are occurring. At best, Band-Aid improvements will only conceal and temporarily ebb the flow of the nation's hemorrhage.

---

[27] Jefferson Memorial, Washington, DC. Notes, ed. Peden, 163. Manuscript available at Massachusetts Historical Society. www.monticello.org; Graham, Billy (July 19, 2012), "My Heart Aches for America," Charlotte, NC: Billy Graham Evangelistic Association.

As a nation, if we are to avoid Tyler's category of national bondage (collapse or succumbing to tyranny), *"we the people"* need to make some changes, personally. The heart of the nation needs to change. And, as individuals, our hearts need to change, too.

Political maneuvering and new policies are not going to solve our national or personal problems. At the core, it is a heart issue. Thankfully, the "inevitable" can still be thwarted, but only if we accept a heart transplant and live transformed lives.

Fundamental, foundational change is necessary to avoid the slide that is taking us toward the *Cycle of Nations* category of "bondage." In one form or another, that bondage is now inevitable unless we reestablish relational and family health, economic responsibility, moral character, respect for our Creator, and the spiritual vitality which separated the Founders of the United States from their counterparts in France.

With these Americans who grew a fledgling nation into the most prosperous one on earth, these characteristics cultivated a spirit of personal vitality. This, in turn, produced the national outcomes represented on the uplifting side of Tyler's *Cycle of Nations*.

Whether the U.S. and Europe make the necessary changes or not, individually, we can personify these characteristics. If we do, the future needn't be gloomy.

"God who gave us life gave us liberty." *"Can the liberties of a nation be secure when we have removed a conviction that these liberties are the gift of God?" "Indeed, I tremble for my country when I reflect that God is just; that his justice cannot sleep forever."* [27]

- Thomas Jefferson
  3rd U.S. President
  First Author of the U.S. Declaration of Independence

"If God doesn't *punish America, He'll have to apologize to Sodom and Gomorrah."* [27]

- Billy Graham, Evangelist
  Ruth Graham, Billy's wife

"If my people, *which are called by my name, shall humble themselves, and pray, and seek my face, and turn from their wicked ways; then will I hear from heaven and will forgive their sin, and will heal their land."*

Holy Bible
2 Chronicles 7:14

As individuals, we can anticipate a new era replete with the most exceptional opportunities of our lifetime—*if we are prepared and ready to embrace them.*

We will not be able to avoid the national and worldwide changes that are coming. However, we can control how we respond to them.

Personally, I'm a pragmatic person. I have spent my professional life pursuing facts and evaluating evidence. My university degree is in the science of criminology, and after graduation, this interest was further formalized through the practical experiences and training I received as a Crime Scene Investigator (CSI) and a police detective, and more recently as an entrepreneur.

I have spent my life dealing with facts and empirical research, and rubber-meets-the-road hardcore experiences. But one night a few years ago, I was awakened by a dream that was different from any I had previously experienced. It was so unusual that upon awakening, I immediately got out of bed and wrote down the details.

You can come to your own conclusions as to what stimulated this dream. I'm including it here merely as a story to illustrate the message of this chapter:

We need to be ready for sudden change because unparalleled change is now inevitable. If we are surprised and unprepared, we are destined to be victims when we could have been victors.

There are numerous latent messages buried in the storyline of my dream. I hope you'll look for them. Here is what I wrote. This is what I typed into my computer immediately after awakening from this strange dream...

"My Odd Dream the Morning of November 20, 2014"

"The setting of my dream was an eerily normal sunny day after a few days of unprecedented storm, the first morning when the sun had again shone brightly after the horrendous event. My dream was in vibrant high-definition color, incredibly realistic, and without any of the fanciful or impossible aspects usually associated with dreams.

"I was standing on the manicured green lawn of a gently sloping little valley; a greenbelt which had previously separated two neighborhoods of an American city. But now, overnight, this previously tranquil setting had morphed into a fast-flowing river. Where no river had previously flowed, there was now a fast-moving body of water that had brought destruction to many, many people.

As I watched the scene in front of me, I saw remnants of houses flowing with the new river, along with cars and trucks and business buildings. Occasionally, steel girders of a bridge fragment or part of large concrete building would tumble through, pushed by the fast-flowing water and detritus.

Along the banks of this newly formed river-of-disaster, were a few dozen people; just me and a few small clusters of men, women and children, hugging couples, and lone individuals, all silently watching. Mesmerized by the mêlée in front of them, their shocked uncomprehending eyes were riveted on the destruction which flowed past us.

In this new river, human remains were so common that they didn't rate a glance; floating bodies were routine and plentiful, like a blanket of dead Fall leaves after a Spring rain. Rather, the focus of every person's attention was on the structures that had only days before seemed secure and safe; pieces of buildings, spans of bridges, and seemingly, entire communities which had suddenly been wiped away. A constant parade of these artifacts was sweeping past where we were standing.

Yet, the danger wasn't over. The threat of collateral damage from the storm was still very real. Any thinking, watchful person would know this, yet a father and his young son were standing at river's edge. Perhaps the dad wanted a better view, or wanted to see if he could salvage something valuable, or maybe just because he was clueless. Or, arrogant, imagining that his survival was due to his prowess. In any case, the two stood together, the father with his arm over his son's shoulder, posture erect, both standing tall in their invincibility.

They had beaten the odds. They were not only alive, but they were also completely unscathed.

Suddenly, a massive steel bridge, seemingly intact, came into view. It careened and rolled in the center of the river as it approached our location. After catching on some submerged obstruction, the bridge suddenly swung in a new direction. Without fanfare or notice, the end of the bridge changed course. In an instant, it turned toward us, and lifting out of the water as if targeting the pair, the man and his son were suddenly gone. The slippery slope was empty.

No one seemed to notice. But as my eyes searched for them, a moment later they reappeared, floating in the choppy water. The dad's abnormal movement betrayed his fatal injuries, but he was still alive, clawing at the water in a futile attempt to reach his drowning son. As I watched them struggle in the rapidly moving water, they were swept out of sight, the grip of the current drawing them to the center of the river where they disappeared from my view.

Heartbroken by this unnecessary loss, I forced myself to look up-river. What I saw was initially so surprising that I didn't recognize what it was. It was unbelievable. A massive wall of water was rapidly advancing toward us. As far as I knew there wasn't a dam in the area, but a wall of water was somehow descending on us as if a swollen lake had suddenly emptied its entire contents.

The danger was imminent, so I screamed at the people around me and pointed toward the coming onslaught. No one moved. No one looked. They were all fixated on the carnage that was in front of them. So, I quickly ran in front of those who were nearby. I yelled and pointed, my face must have been contorted in terror and concern. More lives were about to be needlessly lost.

These people had all been surprised and caught unawares by the storm itself, but that didn't need to happen now. Even if they weren't before, now they should be alert and awake to danger. Yet, all of them remained trance-like, as if hypnotized by the results of the unexpected storm. They were like sheep, oblivious, unaware that they were facing slaughter.

Turning away, I was alone as I quickly ran up the embankment to a place of safety."

"At this point, I awoke from my dream."

"I got out of bed but still I couldn't shake away these images. They seemed indelibly imprinted on my mind, so I sat down at my computer and wrote this transcript while the images were still fresh in my mind.

Rarely am I aware of my dreams. After I awake from a dream, rarely do I recall anything but dream fragments or nonsensical events, so this unsettling dream was unusual for me, so much so that I felt compelled to write it down immediately. Proverbs 22:3; Matthew 16:2-4; Psalm 73."

— — — — — — —

Recap of this Book

Since the step-by-step guidance contained in "PREPARED: Ready to Roll—Book-2" may seem dry and antiseptic, I have included the dream-story on the previous pages to transition from fact-oriented information that may feel somewhat abstract, to the intended purpose—*to help you get ready for the changes that are coming.*

It isn't productive to debate the source of my dream, but we can all agree that it contains several valuable lessons. Disaster can strike suddenly. It can surprise us if we don't live our life like a Watchman.

Any honest and aware person knows that various dangers are lurking on our doorstep. Yet, most remain oblivious and ill-prepared. Still fewer, are getting ready.

> Don't be so hypnotized by living life that you are afraid to face the future. Adversity and eventual death are inevitable. Deal with it. Our decisions can change our route, but we can't alter the terrain.

Even though there is an abundance of flashing warning signals, when society founders, most people will not only be physically unprepared, they will be mentally dumbstruck. It is to their own peril when they ignore these warnings, yet few are physically and emotionally preparing for the changes that are coming.

Still, you and I have a choice. At least we do today. We can choose a different route to the future. This road-less-traveled will require three things; insight, informed planning, and resolute effort.

Yet, the United States and the Western world generally, will stagger, express shock, and respond poorly. Federal and local governments, and those individuals who live in major cities, and most ordinary people, will be unable to cope with the coming changes.

There is a lesson here for all of us. Difficulties are coming. That's a given. We may be forced to cope with an unprecedented natural disaster or one that is manmade, but either way, we cannot expect to overcome these adversities successfully if we refuse to prepare.

Within the ranks of our governments and citizenry, when faced with the coming widespread crisis, many will be needlessly swept away, some will survive by dumb luck, while yet others will become opportunistic predators. And, a select few, will be okay because they prepared for a time such as this. Even a cursory study of history makes this four-part scenario clear.

History also teaches us that many will suffer from neglect or be exploited, become victims of malevolent violence, or just give up. For these individuals, the world will suddenly tilt, throwing them off balance. Then it will turn upside down.

Some of the victors will step out from anonymous corners of society, and out of their comfort zone, to become leaders who inspire, bring hope, and provide guidance. These will be able to help because they were discerning Watchman, and were prepared for the dangers that were on their doorstep.

> Having endurance is an important character trait. However, it is not itself a solution to our problems. For success, our objective needs to be victory for a purpose, not simply survival. This requires deliberate thought, strategic planning, and preparation.

During the coming era of hardship, leaders and citizens alike will not know how to regain equilibrium. Absent effective planning, when surprised, most people will react based on emotion rather than reason. Poor decisions will lead to anger and desperation. Survivors will play the blame-game to excuse their own unlawful conduct. "The greater good" will be used to justify all sorts of injustices.

We need to expect these developments. We need to take these responses into account as we make our own, personal plans.

As in the storyline of my dream, some of the unprepared people will initially be spared. However, when the situation becomes protracted and luck fades, these unprepared people will also succumb to the forces of calamity. The storyline of my dream matches what we can expect in our future.

If the disaster is widespread, for those who ride out the initial turbulence, the aftermath will not consist of temporary inconvenience. Unlike the disasters which we have experienced in the past, it will *not* be followed by a time of quick recovery. It will not be followed by a wave of outside aid.

What will emerge is a new normal. Life will be different.

My Analysis:

We need to be honest with ourselves. Based on a pragmatic risk analysis of the dangers on our doorstep, I am forced to conclude that we will eventually encounter one of these three scenarios:

1) Either a widespread catastrophe of unprecedented magnitude which produces long-term profoundly adverse effects; or,

2) A substantial degradation in quality of life, which progressively declines to dire levels over a several year period. Genetic manipulation of humans will become mainstream, and the expansion of robotics plus other factors will shrink the middle class. We will experience a shortage of healthy foods, new health problems, and widespread suffering. The poor will become enslaved by their dependency on government largess.

As a ruse to improve safety and economic health, there will be a dramatic loss of freedom and privacy. This will enable the subversion of justice, redefining the Constitution, and spark a revisionist history movement to help justify actions. Blatant public corruption will flourish, we will see the emergence of an elite who are above the law.

> Effective planning and preparations require sound analysis. Sound analysis requires the acquisition of truth. And yet truth is elusive because it requires effort, and it often forces us to face unpleasant realities, and make decisions and take action that is uncomfortable. Yet, this is necessary for our well-being.
>
> Truth is the intersection where the paths of reality, perception, and words merge. So now, as we move forward, let's commit to being honest with ourselves. Let's defeat our normalcy bias. Let's overcome fear. Let's take the high road to where the evidence and sound thinking lead us. And, let's do it now, while we still can.

This will be celebrated by manipulated public opinion and emboldened by an everpresent military and paramilitary police presence on America's streets. These *'security forces'* will frequently engage in public displays of frightening force.

In addition to this intimidation, the public will be further distracted by manufactured strife and destabilizing conflicts, fake news repeated until it is accepted as fact, and the silencing of truth-tellers. Also, acts designed to discredit opposition, especially those who dissent based on traditional values, the Bible, or on anything that does not align with the "enlightened" progressive agenda; or,

3) A refreshing new era of revival will emerge, which leads to national recovery.[28]

Whichever path our future takes, a very different landscape will surround the route. The environment of the "new normal" will look vastly different from the world which surrounds us today.

Whatever path we take, the future isn't something to fear. Those who prepare for the coming momentous changes will also encounter unprecedented opportunities. They will not only have the capacity to overcome the difficulties; they will face extraordinary opportunities of all sorts. *It will be the worst of times; it will be the best of times.* We will see these extraordinary opportunities exploited for personal gain, and also to help others during their time of greatest need. We can choose either path or deadly inaction.

Now is the time for decisive, insightful, constructive action. If you feel overwhelmed, go back to Chapter-1 of this guidebook, and methodically follow the step-by-step instructions. As you think and prepare physically, you will also have the chance to get ready mentally, relationally, and spiritually. Don't let fear or indecision cripple you.

Many tasks need to be accomplished with a sense of urgency, but don't let this become a source of stress. Don't live in fear.[29] Turn off the TV, discard purposeless activities, and use the time to get ready.

It's time for us to help each other, too. It's time for all of us to step out of the delusions of fairy-book land and into the future.

The future will not follow a natural progression from the past. We can't graph the specifics like a trendline. We cannot control the future. But thankfully, we can influence it. We have free will, and that gives us choices. This includes making today a day of new beginnings.

If we choose to tread the road to the future as if life is an accident controlled by fate, or walk the streets that are paved with fictions

---

[28] Holy Bible, 2 Chronicles 7:14.

[29] If you struggle with fear, read or watch the video, "The Kingdom, Power, and Glory: The Overcomer's Handbook," by Dr. Chuck & Nancy Missler. https://resources.khouse.org Or, read or view the DVD of Max Lucado's "Fearless: Imagine your life without fear" available at Amazon and bookstores.

such as fake news, false science and manipulated accounts of history, we will experience debilitating hopelessness.

On the other hand, those who are willing to be trailblazers during this time of change, can forge their future with truth and discernment, and enjoy hope and savvy optimism.

The deceptions of "fate" and "fiction" lead to being perpetually lost and uncertain, selfishness, depression, depravity, gratuitous violence, greed, corruption, and being emotionally reactive and withdrawn. The effects include loss of liberty, loss of dignity, loss of justice, and the abandonment of hope.

> **Radical Change is Inevitable**
>
> Those who have 'pleasure' as their goal in life will have a future filled with anger. But those with a passion for 'service' are destined to enjoy an exciting life, filled with hope and purpose.

Tyler in his *Cycle of Nations* identifies these as willing victims who fall into "Bondage" because they deny their Creator and are enchanted by self-centered living. They avoid spiritual truth, and have turned their back on seeking other truths, as well. Nonpartisan justice, personal integrity, courage, honor and liberty, are no longer virtues to be pursued or even enshrined.

At this point, you and I can choose a different path. Thankfully, we have a choice. We can chart a different course if we decide to accept our Creator's guidance and help. His assistance leads to guaranteed success because His pathway for us is *designed* [30] for our well-being, to help us grasp and enjoy our life purpose and find meaning in life. It's the ultimate strategic plan.

As I have done throughout this book, I am speaking from personal, not theoretical knowledge. And with this final chapter, I have maintained this practical approach. In my experience, when I have opted to follow my Creator's map and His destination-oriented strategic plan, triumph has followed.

It's the route to clarity and purpose-filled real-world fearless living. Still, it is up to us to choose this path.

By design, our Creator does not force us to be an obedient robot. He lets us choose our path. The truth is, He does not punish us for our failures, but He does hold us accountable if we refuse to let him fix our predicament.

---

[30] Holy Bible, Ephesians 2:10

Let's be "Big Picture" and "Solution" Oriented

If we race behind our Creator and alongside His wisdom, we can have confidence that our footing is sure, irrespective of the circumstances we encounter. No matter what punctuates our journey, we can have rock-solid confidence that we are on the right road, and that we will eventually reach the crème de la crème of destinations. If we choose wisely, sooner or later, we will reach the ultimate safe-haven. There we will find the peerless Intentional Community that our Maker designed for us.

When we choose this path and accept the role of being a positive change-agent rather than a change-victim, our future will be bright with justifiable hope. This remains true even when the mud of life temporarily hides our feet.

As I emphasized earlier in this chapter, if we fail to learn from true-history we are harming ourselves. We are shackling our future.

As we consider the lessons learned from our study of the past, I would be remiss if I failed to draw attention to the best-selling history book of all time—the Holy Bible. It is much more than a history book, but it does tell the story of people who were successes or failures due to the choices they made.

More than that, it also chronicles the 4,000-year period when the entire nation of Israel alternately suffered or flourished. They suffered when they chose to live their lives separated from God, but they thrived when they decided to follow the path of life constructed by our Creator. Tyler's *Cycle of Nations* was operable in those days, too.

Some readers may find it odd that my list of GO-Bag supplies in Chapter 11 includes a Bible (New Testament with Psalms and Proverbs). However, this addition is not an abstraction generated by personal bias or proselytizing.

Based on my personal experience and that of others, I have found that reading the New Testament, Psalms, and Proverbs, can be therapeutic, especially during a period of prolonged adversity or when alone during a crisis.

Moreover, I have observed that even non-religious people have found this Book to be of transcendent value during a time of upheaval or adversity. If you don't agree with my conclusions now, at least give yourself the option to change your mind in the future.

As William Paley[31] reminds us,

> *"There is a principle which is a bar against all information, which is proof against all argument, and which cannot fail to keep man in everlasting ignorance. That principle is contempt before investigation."*

Today we still have a choice.[32]
Indecision is a hollow choice, but it is still a decision.

Our future will be filled with many changes. Some of these will be very difficult to handle; many will be difficult to overcome.

Self-reliance is essential, but at some point, that's not enough. What are you going to do? What is your anchor, your foundation that can't be moved by the derecho winds of time and circumstance? Are you prepared physically, mentally, relationally and spiritually? Are you fully prepared? If not, are you going to get ready? When it's time to act, will you be PREPARED: Ready to Roll?

---

[31] William Paley (1743-1805) was a philosopher and outspoken clergyman in England during the period of conflict between the King of England and the Colonies in America.

[32] For those who are not acquainted with the contents of the Holy Bible, it is the most widely circulated and most influential book of all history. To ignore it is foolish. It is consistent in message even though it was penned by 40 authors over a period of nearly 4,000 years. The most recent portion, written 2,000 years ago, is known as the New Testament. It chronicles the life of Jesus, how to become reconciled with our Creator, and Jesus' guidance on how to live life with hope and purpose.

Though ancient, the Holy Bible is relevant for today. It addresses topics such as right living, persecution, facing opposition, overcoming fear and adversity, good and evil, dealing with poverty and affluence, and most importantly, our Creator's plan to fix humanity's problem of being separated from Him. It's not about religion; it's about restoring relationship.

Presented in a very different format from that of the New Testament and its focus on Jesus and practical living, the Bible books of Psalms and Proverbs, which are a portion of the Old Testament, concentrate on the same practical issues but convey these truths using history, poetry, and proverbs. As a result, both portions are particularly helpful during periods of crisis. The entire Bible is valuable reading for all stages of life, but the New Testament, Psalms, and Proverbs are especially valued by those who seek guidance and comfort during times of upheaval or confusion.

Appendix

Appendix – A

GO-Bag for Extended Duration Use
(Heavy)

Food for Your GO-Bag

For important details on food types and selection, nutrition and Calorie needs, and food preparation, read Chapter 10, "GO-Bag Food and Water."

Military MRE (Meal, Ready-to-Eat) meal entrées, plus a MRE water-activated heater for each.

Not the full MRE meal; just the entrée portion, as the full MRE meal is too bulky for use in a GO-Bag. These entrées can be purchased separately. The use of the entrée only, will reduce weight and bulk while still providing a hot 'normal' meal – an important consideration in a high-stress environment. If water is in short supply, use any water to activate the MRE heater. For more about MREs, read the chapter on "GO-Bag Food and Water."

Food Bars: Energy / Protein / Nutrition / Meal-Replacement Bars

Check shelf life on packaging. Select bars which contain at least 3+ grams of protein, 15+ grams of sugar, 3+ grams of fiber, some healthy fats and carbohydrates. A variety of flavors is important, but make sure that each bar contains at least 150 Calories and some fiber. Selecting several brands will minimize digestive problems. Unlike our goals for normal healthy eating, in a bug-out emergency situation we want to increase our intake of Calories because we need energy.

Top brands to consider: CLIF (best meal replacement bar), LUNA (high in protein), Kashi ROLL (high in protein), marathon by Snickers (high in both protein and carbs), Fruits of Life (contains probiotics; fruit flavors are a nice departure from candy-like bars), Pure (100% organic, minimal processing), OATMEGA (high in protein and carbs; high in Omega 3), Zing (top rated for flavor; also have gluten-free, dairy-free, and soy-free options), Fruition (high in carbs), CLIF Mojo (for older kids and adults), Z Bar (for young kids).

- **Metal Cup** (Suitable for boiling water over a fire)
- **Spork** – *Light-My-Fire Titanium* Spork (spoon/fork), or silverware designed for backpacking
- **Metal Spoon** (heat safe)
- **Disposable Utensils** - plastic knife, fork, spoon
- **Magnesium Fire-Starting Tool**
- **Lighter** – BIC or major brand (3)
- **Storm Matches** in watertight container
- **Waxed Tinder** – *Zippo Waxed Tinder Sticks* or equivalent
- **Can and Bottle Opener** (P-51 Military-style can opener, or equivalent)

Water for Your GO-Bag

For important details on water storage and purification, read Chapter 10, "GO-Bag Food and Water."

On average, an adult needs 100 oz. / 3.0 L per day of pure drinking water (not distilled water). If the temperature is high, or if the day involves significant physical exertion, the amount needed can be considerably more.

- **Water Purification Tablets**
- **Water Purification Filter**
- **Water Pre-Filter**
- **Plastic Water Bottles**
- **Sport Drink Powder that is high in electrolytes.**

At least two hard-plastic wide-mouth bottles which will fit into a pocket on your knapsack, or into a pouch that can be worn on your belt. Examples: Nalgene *'Wide Mouth,'* Camelbak *'eddy'* or *'Chute,'* or Kleen Kanteeen *'Wide Mouth Stainless.'*

To save space, put other supplies such as energy bars, inside these empty bottles. Store your bottles inside your GO-Bag, at the top of your supplies, so that they can be quickly retrieved and filled with fresh water before you evacuate (bug-out).

Store pre-bottled drinking water with your GO-Bag, but not inside it. When your GO-Bag is needed, then empty your supply of bottled water into your reusable plastic water bottles (or water bladders, or pouches). By utilizing this method, you can conveniently replace your stored water bottles every three months, thereby insuring that your emergency supply of water is healthy and fresh.

Collapsible Canteens / Water Bladders

Collapsible water bottles such as the Nalgene *'Contene'* are lightweight and take little space. Be sure to select water transport products which have a wide mouth, so that cleaning is easier.

Water bladders, such as those made by *Camelbak* (www.Camelbak.com) and *Source WXP* (www.Source-Military.com), make drinking-on-the-go simple. These collapsible water bladders have a drinking tube which runs from the water bladder, over the wearer's shoulder, and secured to the shoulder strap of the knapsack.

To drink, the wearer places the end of the drinking tube in the mouth, gently squeezing the end of the tube with the teeth to release the flow of water. Then, sucking as on a drinking straw, water flows from the water pouch/bladder which is stored in your GO-Bag knapsack. Most quality knapsacks have a pocket designed to hold this bladder, but caution still needs to be used to keep sharp objects from puncturing this soft-sided, collapsible water container.

* *Plan for hands-free carry of a minimum of 1-gallon (128 oz/4 Liters) of water per person. It is not enough to have containers, you also need to plan for how you will carry these containers once they have been filled with water.*

GO-Bag Emergency Shelter

For extended duration GO-Bags, rather than the SOL Emergency Bivvy, use a Single-Person Bivy Shelter or a Freedom Shelter. Both are made by Wiggys.com, supplier to spec-ops units. They also make components for USAF survival kits. Their military-grade sleeping bags use synthetic insulation rather than the moisture absorbing down found in many lightweight-but-warm backpacking bags.

GO-Bag Medical / Dental Supplies

For more details, read Chapters 21 & 22

- **First Aid Kit**, including care for serious bleeding and gunshot wounds.
- **Dental Kit,** including repair kit for crowns, and care for broken teeth with exposed roots.
- **Medicine**, personal prescription drugs, as well as over-the-counter drugs for: diarrhea, nausea, allergies, constipation, pain, etc.

GO-Bag Communications

For important details on mobile phones, AM-FM-SW radios, and 2-way communication, read Chapter 7, "Communication During Emergency Situations."

- **Radio Receiver AM/FM/NOAA** (see chapter, "Emergency Radios, NOAA Receivers")
- **Walkie Talkies** (2) - GMRS or Ham Radios (see chapter on 2-Way Radios)
- **Extra Batteries**
- **Notepad** (waterproof paper) *Rite-in-the-Rain Outdoor Journal*
- **Ballpoint Pen** (Write-anywhere "*Space*" pen)
- **Indelible Marker Pen** – Black Ink (*Sharpie*)

GO-Bag Signaling

- **Signal Mirror** – Small
- **Whistle** on Lanyard
- **Contractor's Ribbon** (Bright color plastic ribbon for trail marking and messaging)

GO-Bag Navigation

For important details on route selection, navigation, and maps, read Chapters 5, 6 and 7.

- **Local Maps** (see chapter, "Evacuation: Pre-Planning is Essential")
- **Compass** - 3H Military Compass, SUUNTO A-30, or equivalent quality

GO-Bag Flashlights and Emergency Lights

For important information of flashlights, headlamps, and emergency lighting, read Chapter 21, "Flashlights, Emergency Lights, and Batteries."

- **LED Flashlight**
- **LED Headlamp**, adjustable brightness to extend battery flashlight
- **Micro Flashlight** (attach to main zipper-pull on knapsack)
- **Extra Batteries or Rechargeable Batteries & Charger**
  (Quantity of batteries should provide for 3-5 days/night of use for each device. When feasible, select battery powered devices which use the same size battery.)
- **Recharging method for your mobile phone**
- **ChemLights** (2) – chemical powered disposable lights (*Cyalume Light Sticks*); one 30-min, and one 8-hr stick, in white or yellow)

GO-Bag Miscellaneous Gear

- **Pocket Knife**, Stainless Steel – Swiss Army '*Explorer*' model or equivalent
- **Collapsible Limb-Cutting Saw**, Stainless Steel Blade (as used for gardening) [optional]
- **Scarf or Shemagh** (multipurpose; face protection, bandage, towel, sweat band, etc.) – earth tone color
- **Large Handkerchief**, bright color (for personal use or signaling)
- **Work Gloves** – Leather
- **550 Paracord** – 25-50 feet (military grade braded cord, break strength 550 lbs.)
- **Duct Tape** – 10 ft.
- **Super Glue**

- **Insect Protection Head-net** [optional]
- **Insect Repellent** – 90+% DEET (liquid, not aerosol) - Sawyer *Jungle Juice'* 2 oz., pump spray
- **Sunglasses**
- **Spare Prescription or Reading Glasses** (if used)
- **Compact Binoculars** – 8x
- **Mini Survival Kit**
- **Cash** (Keep in mind that credit and debit cards cannot be used without electrical power, so having cash is essential. Lower denomination bills are best since vendors may not be able to make change.
- **Firearm(s) and Ammo,** where legal. (See the various chapters on guns for more on this topic.)
- **Identification and Reference Docs** – (See Chapter 26, "Backup ID and Safe Data Storage.")
- **Bible** – New Testament with Psalms and Proverbs (to provide comfort; valuable even for people who are not religious)

* Not including water, the above GO-Bag items, together with a quality knapsack, will weigh approximately 20 pounds (9 kg). Don't thoughtlessly add additional items. Your GO-Bag needs to be lightweight and compact, so that you are agile and can move quickly.

* Use *Hefty Slider* or *Ziploc Slider* heavy-duty or freezer type, clear plastic bags to organize your supplies by category, and to protect items from water and dust. Add corrugated cardboard as padding, if needed. This is especially important if cushioning is needed to protect your back from the contents of the bag. This layer of corrugated cardboard can help protect the water bladder (if you have one) from damage, too. If needed, this corrugated cardboard can also be used to help start a fire.

* Do not fill your GO-Bag so tightly with gear that it is difficult to repack it in a hurry.

*** *Reminder: Do not store batteries in flashlights or electronics. Frequently replace batteries, water, and other items susceptible to quality or safety degradation. Check your GO-Bag and emergency supplies each change of season.*

GO-Bag Cooking Equipment for Extended-Duration Operations

This is optional gear. Only include it if you are assembling a GO-Bag backpack designed for 5+ days of travel, or for ongoing use beyond the period of evacuation.

- *"MSR DragonFly"* multi-fuel stove, plus extra fuel bottle and repair kit. (Replace fuel at least annually.)
- Cook Pot, lightweight backpacking-style with lid, and heat exchanger (store stove inside).
- Windscreen and heat reflector for cooking. (MSR brand or equivalent)
- Insulated mug with lid and handle (Size: 16+ oz.).
- Stainless steel spoon, plus sturdy plastic or aluminum spork (fork/spoon combination).
- Dish/pot scraper and brush.

Food Supplies for Extended Duration Travel or Field Operations

* For long-duration bug-out situations, include several pounds of rice and beans, sealed in single-serving Mylar bags with oxygen absorbers. These can be self-packaged at low cost.

For more about this do-it-yourself Mylar bag storage method, download the PDF instructions from the 'Resources' page of the author's website: www.SIGSWANSTROM.com

This Mylar Bag food-storage method is a lighter weight alternative, and provides a storage shelf life of 20+ years.

By personal experimentation, identify the food-portion size that is best for you. Keep in mind that you will likely be very hungry if you have been traveling on foot, or if you have been engaged in physical labor. Based on this information, purchase heavy duty Mylar bags in the size which matches either single-meal portion size, or per-day portion size.

To improve nutrition and taste, mix $1/8^{th}$ to $1/16^{th}$ pound of freeze dried vegetables per pound of rice and/or beans, plus salt. A lower-cost and less flavorful alternative, is to use dehydrated vegetables rather than freeze-dried. Add this mixture to your Mylar bags.

With your food supplies, include a collection of your favorite spices, as variety is important. During an emergency situation, some people do not feel like eating, so do what you can to make eating desirable, and preparation simple.

For improved nutrition and variety, augment your meals by adding freeze dried, dehydrated, or canned meats. (If purchasing canned meats, select small cans or small foil retort packages as safe storage of opened containers will not be impossible.) Add a small portion of beef, chicken, pork, or fish to meals, and foraged food when available, to further improve these meals.

However, *do not* add these meats to your rice/beans and vegetable mixture. Meats contain oils and fats, which reduce their shelf life, so they spoil more quickly. This includes lean meats, and freeze dried, dehydrated, and smoked meats. Therefore, never include them in the rice or beans and vegetable mixture as this can result in the contamination of your primary source of food. You can do without meat, but you can't survive without food.

If you want the convenience of being able to cook your food in this same Mylar bag, select a bag size that will also easily accommodate the necessary amount of water. If you opt for this method, do the best you can to remove air before dealing, and add extra oxygen absorbers to the bag. Be sure to remove the oxygen absorber packets before adding hot water to the Mylar bag.

Using this do-it-yourself method, you can carry many days of healthy food in a very lightweight and compact package.

Appendix - B
Nutritional Standards for Emergency Food
U.S. Military Food Rations

This information is included as a reference, to help guide our own nutritional standards for meals during emergency situations.

Nutrient	Unit	Operational Rations	Restricted Rations [1,3]
Energy	Kcal / Cal	3600	1100–1500
Protein	gm	100	50–70
Carbohydrate	gm	440	100–200
Fat	gm	160 (maximum)	50–70
Vitamin A	mcg RE	1000	500
Vitamin D	mcg	10	5
Vitamin E	mg TE	10	5
Ascorbic Acid	mg	60	30
Thiamin	mg	1.8	1.0
Riboflavin	mg	2.2	1.2
Niacin	mg NE	24	13
Vitamin B_6	mg	2.2	1.2
Folacin	mcg	400	200
Vitamin B_{12}	mcg	3	1.5
Calcium	mg	800	400
Phosphorus	mg	800	400
Magnesium	mg	800	400
Iron	mg	18	9
Zinc	mg	15	7.5
Sodium	mg	5000–7000 [4]	2500–3500 [4]
Potassium	mg	1875–5625	950–2800

1. Values are minimum standards at the time of consumption unless shown as a range or a maximum level.
2. The operational ration includes the MCI, MRE, A, B, and T rations.
3. Restricted rations are for use under certain operational scenarios such as long-range patrol, assault, and reconnaissance when troops are required to subsist for short periods (up to 10 days) on an energy restricted ration.
4. These values do not include salt packets.

For more information, see Army Regulation 40–25. It incorporates the nutritional requirements of all branches of the U.S. military.

MRE Manufacturing Date-Codes

Shelf life is 3-years from the date of manufacture if the MRE or HDR is stored at 80-degrees or less. Responsible manufacturers are now clearly printing the date of manufacture on each case of MREs, and on the individual meals, as well, but some are still using confusing date codes.

If you encounter a four-number code, the first number generally refers to the year of manufacture, followed by the day of the year. For example, a date code of "7240" indicates the 240th day of 2017, or August 28, 2017. Similarly, a five-digit code of "17240" would indicate the same date.

A similar method is often used on each component of the MRE such as the entrée pouch, crackers, peanut butter, etc., but additional numbers are added to identify other production details. Therefore, a code of "72401234" or "172401234" probably indicates a manufacturing date of August 28, 2017. (Same as the previous example.)

Military MREs sold online, at gun shows, and by unscrupulous sellers, are often old. Sometimes very old. An old MRE meal may still be safe to eat, but the nutritional value starts to degrade 3-years after the date of manufacture. If there is no date code on the MRE bag itself, that MRE was likely manufactured before 2003. MREs packaged in a dark brown bag were manufactured before 1996.

*** More info on MREs can be found in Chapters 10 and 15 ***

Appendix - C

"Black Sky" Events: Protecting Electronics and Essential Gear from EMP, Solar Flare/CME, Nuclear, and Other Grid-Down Events.

D-I-Y Protection Containers & Faraday Cages
Three Do-It-Yourself Protection Methods:[33]

Steel buildings are helpful and do afford a modest level of protection, but alone, they are not adequate. A steel trash can, steel drum or steel ammo can, prepared as described in this Appendix, and stored in a metal building, provides the best EMP/CME protection that most of us can afford. If you don't have a steel building, these precautions are nevertheless useful.

Commercially available Faraday Cages costing less than $1,000 are generally not as effective as these three do-it-yourself methods.

---

[33] EMP is an acronym for Electro-Magnetic Pulse, which is a manmade effect caused by a nuclear or electronic device. CME is an acronym for Coronal Mass Ejection, which is a naturally occurring electromagnetic pulse produced by the sun. These are dangers on our doorstep.

EMP and CME pulses can destroy anything electric or electronic, and can even ignite electrical wires and cause fires. Depending on the magnitude and proximity, these pulses can fry electrical devices such as the simple motor which moves the blades of your house fan, to the more advanced microcircuits in our modern cars, cell phones, and computers. You will find more on this subject in several other parts of this book.

Though this topic is widely ignored, an EMP and several CME pulses, have struck the U.S. in the past. What makes this a much greater threat today is that we have become dependent on technology.

These past occurrences were before the advent of micro-circuitry, so the damage was minimal. If identical events occurred today, they would cause catastrophic damage. Modern society is wholly unprepared.

Even though EMPs and CMEs do not typically harm human and animal life directly, the damage to modern society would be devastating. To reduce this threat, we need to do what we can to protect essential electrical and electronic devices and components.

Don't be duped by advertising rhetoric; these simple techniques can produce far better results than many devices and containers which claim to provide EMP/CME protection.

But if you aren't concerned with protection from EMP, solar flare, nuclear, and other electromagnetic pulse incidents, and just want water, dust, and durability protection for electronics, firearms, documents, and other valuables, the task is much simpler.

For these simpler needs, use either steel ammo cans, steel drums, or plastic drums such as those used to transport ingredients for food.

If your need is for basic protection while maintaining mobility, use a U.S. military ammo can (box). The most common sizes are designed for 5.56mm or 7.62mm ammunition, but ammo cans are also made to fit rockets and other larger munitions, so almost any size object can be accommodated if you will search for the appropriate size ammo can.

These containers are easily found for sale online, at gun shows, or from a military surplus store, but be sure the can is undamaged, rust free, and that the lid's rubber seal is not cracked or damaged. Caution: There are many similar boxes sold that are not made according to military specifications. Don't be fooled. If you are concerned with durability and that the container is waterproof, you will want to use a genuine military ammo can (container).

Before sealing the can, smear a thick layer of Vaseline on the gasket. If the container will be buried in the ground or submerged in water, paint the can inside and out with zinc spray paint, but be sure to keep paint off the rubber gasket.

An ammo can and seal in good condition that has been properly prepared, can withstand submersion in 10-feet of water for a year or longer. (We only tested for 1-year.) To ratchet up the protection a step further, pack a desiccant packet in the box before it is sealed. These moisture-absorbing packets are available from any large gun store and many sporting goods stores.

Less waterproof but often more economical, is a 35-55-gallon (or similar) steel drum, or a similar size plastic barrel such as those used to transport ingredients for food. These can be found online or locally through specialty shops, or purchased used from manufacturers such as those who bottle soft drinks.

If you plan to use this barrel/drum storage method, select a container that has a removeable lid, and a rubber gasket designed to make the lid watertight, even if you don't plan to store the drum outside. The barrel/drum should have a steel clamp designed to provide a uniformly tight seal around the entire rim of the lid. If your barrel/drum does not have a rubber gasket, a makeshift gasket can be made using either outdoor caulking or liquid gasket purchased from an automotive parts store. Be sure to select a product which does not act like glue.

The advantage of a steel container is durability, whereas plastic barrels are not easily found by metal detectors. Don't forget to include a hoist or roller base to the barrel/drum before packing it, as they can be heavy and awkward once filled.

EMP/Solar Flare/CME/Nuclear: Protected Storage

Trash-Can Method: To achieve at least a minimal level of EMP protection, store electrical and electronic equipment in a new galvanized steel trash can. This container should be stored in a location that protects it from inclement weather and water. And, it should be set directly on the ground, not on wood or rubber, as it needs to be grounded to the earth.

The trash can should *not* be kept on a shelf, nor on wood or carpeted floor, nor on any other material which might act as an electrical insulator. The EMP "pulse" needs to flow around the surface of the can and into the ground.

A tight-fitting lid is also necessary. This provides an electrical connection between the trash can's lid and the rest of the can.

Though a Faraday Cage[34] or copper container would offer far better protection, this isn't practical for most of us. So, to achieve this minimal defensive measure against an EMP pulse or solar flare (CME) inexpensively, the storage container needs to be constructed wholly of highly conductive material such as steel. *Not* plastic or aluminum.

---

[34] Invented by English scientist Michael Faraday, these cages are made of highly conductive wire mesh, designed to shield electrical devices from EMPs and CME events. They are used extensively by militaries and government intelligence agencies and are now being installed on critical civilian infrastructures such as national power grids. The DIY instructions contained in this Appendix are not a true Faraday Cage, but they do provide a basic level of protection based on the same scientific principles.

Steel Drum/Barrel Method: An undamaged 55-gallon (or any size) steel barrel or steel drum that has a tight-fitting steel lid that clamps shut, is more expensive but an even better choice. It will also hold more than a large trash can. Irrespective of the gallon-to-gallon similarities in size, in my experience, a 55-gallon steel drum will often hold 2-3x more electronics than a 31-gallon steel trash can.

Note: If your steel drum has a rubber gasket to make the lid watertight, be sure to remove it so that the steel surface of the barrel is in direct contact with the steel lid. To further improve the electrical connection between the lid and the barrel, use a wire-wheel connected to a drill motor, to remove all the paint from the areas where the lid and the steel barrel touch. Then, coat the bare steel with a liquid metal protector that is *conductive*, such as Armor-Shield Rust-Proofing manufactured by Watson Coatings.

Steel Ammo-Can Method (military-surplus ammunition box): Though even a large military-surplus ammo can is far smaller than a trash can, it can still be a good choice, especially for small high-value items like radios that need to be transportable. But if you intend to use a steel ammo can, be sure to remove the rubber gasket from the lid and replace it with conductive material.

It is necessary to remove the rubber gasket so the electric current of the pulse can flow from the edges of the lid to the box itself. Unfortunately, this means the ammo can will no longer be watertight.

To further improve EMP protection, use a wire wheel attached to a drill motor to remove all the paint from the area where the lid and the can come into contact. In the gap between the lid and the can, stuff copper wool or copper mesh. These products are available from Rogue River Tools and other manufactures, but be sure that the product is actually made from copper and is not just copper color.

General Instructions: Whatever container you select, the edges of its base need to be flat on the ground. This helps "ground" it, directing the fast-moving electromagnetic pulse around the steel container and into the ground.

Next, to keep the damaging pulse from flowing into the items stored inside the trash can, use layers of corrugated cardboard to pad the bottom of the can, and to line its interior walls. The layers of corrugated cardboard need to be at least 2-3 inches thick on the bottom, and 1-2 inches thick on the walls.

A loose fitting 1-2 inch blanket of corrugated cardboard should be put on top of the stored items. This is to prevent the stored items from coming into contact with the steel lid.

There can be gaps in the cardboard; a perfect fit isn't necessary. The purpose of the cardboard is only to keep your stored items from getting close to the steel can when it is hit by the pulse.

Without insulation, even items which are still in their original, padded packaging, can be damaged. If even one of the stored items is allowed to touch the steel container, everything inside the container becomes vulnerable. Just one item stored too close to the skin of the steel trash can, may be enough to open a pathway for the pulse's electric current to flow inside the can, damaging its entire contents.

An insulation material other than corrugated cardboard can be used, as long as you are sure it is non-conductive. However, since most styrofoam and plastic is somewhat conductive, corrugated cardboard is often the safest choice. Stick with using corrugated cardboard unless you are knowledgeable on this subject.

This thick layer of cardboard is an important component. The corrugated cardboard must be on the bottom, sides, and the top. This is to reduce the chance of an electrical arc occurring inside the can.

As a physicist will be quick to point out, these methods only provide a modest level of protection. They are not 100% effective, but they do provide a reasonable first-level protective measure that is much better than no protection.

Utilizing a true Faraday Cage will provide better protection, but a genuine EMP-defeating Faraday Cage is extremely expensive. It's what governments and major corporations build, and the cost makes them an inaccessible purchase for most of the general public.

If you are using your makeshift Faraday Cage to store replacement electrical parts for a vehicle, you'll need to learn how to replace these parts yourself, too. Just having them isn't enough. So, don't forget to purchase a repair manual written for your particular vehicles, such as those published by Haynes or Chilton. For convenience, you might want to store these reference materials inside the container, too.

If you don't have a mechanic to serve as your mentor, get a recommendation from a friend who can endorse the work of a mechanic who does repair work out of his home, or owns a small shop. Then, before you put him to work on your vehicle, get him to agree on a fixed price, and make sure he is willing to let you watch and teach you as he does the work.

Caution: There are retailers who sell what they purport to be "Faraday Cages" built into backpacks and other types of containers. Personally, I've never seen one of these that is even close to as effective as an inexpensive, ordinary, steel trash can or ammo box prepared as described in this appendix.

Appendix - D

Summary of Radio Options and 'Quick-Reference' Frequency and Radio Guides

AM & FM Radios

AM/FM radio receivers are what is generally found in vehicles, clock radios, home stereos, and inexpensive portable radios. They are not used for 2-way communication, but they are essential for obtaining news updates during an emergency. AM/FM radios which can also receive Weather Band (WB) emergency broadcasts are particularly useful.

The AM band is 535-1605 kHz. AM radio broadcasts can be received from greater distances than FM broadcasts. Since the AM broadcast distance extends even further at night, some commercial AM stations are required to reduce power at sunset. Still, in an emergency, scanning AM is often where you will find useful info.

The FM band is between 88-108 MHz, and is used for commercial radio broadcasts. Unless authorized by the station holding the license for a specific broadcast frequency, it is illegal to transmit in either the AM or FM radio frequency bands.

---

* A radio operator's license or base-station license is not required to *listen* to any of the radio frequencies listed on the following pages, but a license is required for transmitting (talking, or data transmission) on any of the frequencies listed here—unless specifically mentioned as permitted without a license.

* Having a radio operator's license in one of these categories does not automatically authorize you to use frequencies allocated for a different type of radio. Even a licensed Amateur (Ham) radio operator is not automatically authorized to transmit on every frequency that can be dialed into his/her shortwave radio. Life-saving emergency transmissions may not be penalized, but these exceptions are only made for serious, true emergencies.

FRS / GMRS 2-Way Radios
Family Radio Service / General Mobile Radio Service
For non-commercial use by civilians sending brief 2-way voice transmissions. (Channels 1-22: 462.5625 - 462.7250 MHz) Unlike CB and Marine, none of these frequencies are monitored for emergency calls. FRS and FRS/GMRS radio frequencies are what is frequently used in the most popular, inexpensive, walkie-talkie type radios. Transmission distance is greatly diminished by terrain and obstructions, and despite advertising hype, is generally limited to line-of-sight. Larger antennas and higher-wattage radios can have greater range. A combination radio which can use both FRS and GMRS frequencies is more desirable and usually costs only a few dollars more. An FCC operator's license is required but enforcement is rare, see www.fcc.gov.

CB Radio 2-Way Radios
Citizen Band
For non-commercial use by civilians sending brief 2-way voice transmissions (Channels 1-40; 26.965 – 27.405 MHz; emergencies: Chanel 9). Commonly used in private cars and commercial trucks for driver-to-driver communication. Transmission distance is diminished by terrain and obstructions, and is generally limited to not much more than line-of-sight. An FCC operator's license is required but enforcement is sporadic. For licensing info, visit: www.fcc.gov.

MURS 2-Way Radios
Multi-Use Radio Service
For non-commercial use by civilians sending brief 2-way voice transmissions (151.820 – 154.600 MHz). No license is required, nor is there an age limit for operators. MURS radios are suitable for short-distance, two-way communications, and are typically hand-held radios similar to walkie-talkies. Not as popular as FRS/GMRS and CB, these radios only have 5 channels and are limited to a maximum of 2-watts transmitting power, so these radios have limited value. However, their lack of popularity is itself a positive feature as the channels are rarely crowded.

Marine Radios
For both commercial and non-commercial use by boaters and mariners, these restricted-use radios typically use the *VHF maritime mobile* band frequencies (156.000 – 162.025 MHz). However, commercial ships and yachts operating on the ocean, use shortwave *MF/HF-SSB maritime band* frequencies (1.6 - 30 MHz) as these radios are capable of longer-range operation. Licenses are absolutely required to transmit on these frequencies except in a life-or-death emergency situation. See FCC.gov.

Aviation Radios
For both commercial and non-commercial use by pilots, aircrews, airports, FBOs, and commercial airline companies, these restricted-use radios use frequencies set-aside for this purpose. Operating frequencies: HF – 2,100-28,000 kHz; VHF – 118-137 MHz; and UHF – 225-328.6. Military aircraft have additional frequencies available to them which are encrypted in war zones: UHF – 225-328.6 and 335.4-400MHz. Licenses or military authorization is absolutely required to transmit on any of these frequencies except in a true life-or-death emergency situation. See FCC.gov.

Amateur Radio (aka / Ham Radio, Shortwave Radio)
Capable of worldwide communication, these 2-way radios can be fixed-base radio stations, mobile (in a vehicle or carried in a backpack), or in a hand-held walkie talkie. Generally, a small lightweight radio coupled to a small antenna, will have little range. Conversely, a high-power radio with a good antenna is, under the right conditions, capable of worldwide communication.

These radios can be used to communicate via voice transmission, Morse code, or data (computer-to-computer). HF model radios have the greatest range.

Models which operate using the 70cm and 2-meter bands have far less transmitting range, but they are lighter in weight and are considerably less expensive. With these radios in particular, a well-designed antenna is as important as the radio itself. However, an inexpensive, simple, homemade antenna can still be effective for long range communication.

Passing a FCC test is required to obtain an operator's license. There are three levels of licenses issued: Technician, General, and Amateur Extra. The higher the license, the more frequencies are available to the operator. See FCC.gov for licensing details, and ARRL.com to view a "Band Plan" of frequencies, and articles explaining operating details and capabilities. License enforcement is strict and fines are levied for improper use.

NOAA Weather Radio (NWR) – All Hazards Radio Frequencies

Reception is limited to approximately 40 miles from a government NWR transmitter, so it is advisable to scan each of these frequencies to find one which can be received clearly, and then confirm by listening that the station is transmitting information on your location.	Frequency (MHz)
	162.400
	162.425
	162.450
	162.475
	162.500
	162.525
	162.550

Time Standard Frequencies

The following frequencies announce the exact time of day at specified intervals.

WWV in Colorado
2500 kHz
5000 kHz
10,000 kHz
15,000 kHz
20,000 kHz

CHU in Canada
7335 kHz

VGN in Australia
4500 kHz
12,000 kHz

CB Radio Frequencies

The 40 CB channels can be listened to on a CB radio and on most shortwave radio receivers. Transmitting on these frequencies requires a license, and is subject to various power restrictions.

1 26.965 MHz	9 * 27.065 MHz	17 27.165 MHz	25 27.245 MHz	33 27.335 MHz
2 26.975 MHz	10 27.075 MHz	18 27.175 MHz	26 27.265 MHz	34 27.345 MHz
3 26.985 MHz	11 27.085 MHz	19 27.185 MHz	27 27.275 MHz	35 27.355 MHz
4 27.005 MHz	12 27.105 MHz	20 27.205 MHz	28 27.285 MHz	36 27.365 MHz
5 27.015 MHz	13 27.115 MHz	21 27.215 MHz	29 27.295 MHz	37 27.375 MHz
6 27.025 MHz	14 27.125 MHz	22 27.225 MHz	30 27.305 MHz	38 27.385 MHz
7 27.035 MHz	15 27.135 MHz	23 27.255 MHz	31 27.315 MHz	39 27.395 MHz
8 27.055 MHz	16 27.155 MHz	24 27.235 MHz	32 27.325 MHz	40 27.405 MHz

* **Channel 9 is reserved for emergency use.** It is monitored by some State police agencies and county sheriff's departments, and by civilians who relay emergency transmissions to police and fire departments.

FRS & GMRS Radios

FRS radios only have channels 8-14, but depending on brand, a walkie-talkie radio might use numbers 1-7 on the radio's dial. Nevertheless, the actual frequencies in use are those listed on the right.

GMRS radios generally include both FRS and GMRS frequencies (channels 1-22).

Channel	Type	Frequency
1	FRS / GMRS	462.5625
2	FRS / GMRS	462.5875
3	FRS / GMRS	462.6125
4	FRS / GMRS	462.6375
5	FRS / GMRS	462.6625
6	FRS / GMRS	462.6875
7	FRS / GMRS	462.7125
8	FRS	467.5625
9	FRS	467.5875
10	FRS	467.6125
11	FRS	467.6375
12	FRS	467.6625
13	FRS	467.6875
14	FRS	467.7125
15	GMRS	462.5500
16	GMRS	462.5750
17	GMRS	462.6000
18	GMRS	462.6250
19	GMRS	462.6500
20	GMRS	462.6750
21	GMRS	462.7000
22	GMRS	462.7250

Amateur (Ham) Radio Frequencies

This is included to help you understand the span of shortwave frequencies.

* In the United States, amateur radio operators (Hams) typically operate using LSB (aka / Lower Side Band) mode.
* Though not required, Morse Code operators are usually found in the lower frequencies of each band grouping.
* Amateur radio operators with the highest license rating tend to use the upper areas of each band.
* During disasters and emergency situations, amateur radio operators (Hams) are known for voluntarily broadcasting emergency information when other means er means of communication breakdown.

Portions of these bands are set aside for continuous wave (CW) Morse code communication, single sideband (SSB) voice communications as indicated in the below chart, and for other purposes.
NOTE: 100,000 kHz = 100 MHz

Band	CW (Morse code)	SSB (voice)
160 meters	1800 to 1840 kHz	1840 to 2000 kHz
80 meters	3500 to 3800	3800 to 4000
40 meters	7000 to 7150	7150 to 7300
30 meters	10,100 to 10,150	N/A
20 meters	14,000 to 14,200	14,200 to 14,350
17 meters	18,068 to 18,110	18,110 to 18,168
15 meters	21,000 to 21,250	21,250 to 21,450
12 meters	24,890 to 24,930	24,930 to 24,990
10 meters	25,000 to 28,300	28,300 to 29,700
6 meters	50,000 to 51,000	50,100 to 50,125
2 meters	144,000 to 144,100	144,200 to 144,275
1.25 meters	222,100 to 222,150	222,100 to 222,150
70 cm	432,070 to 432,100	432,100 to 432,300
33 cm	902,075 to 902,125 903,100 to 903,400	902,075 to 902,125 903,100 to 903,400
23 cm	1296,080 to 1296,200	1296,080 to 1296,200

Note: These band-use restrictions are international, but they are not strictly observed in every country.

U.S. Amateur Radio Bands

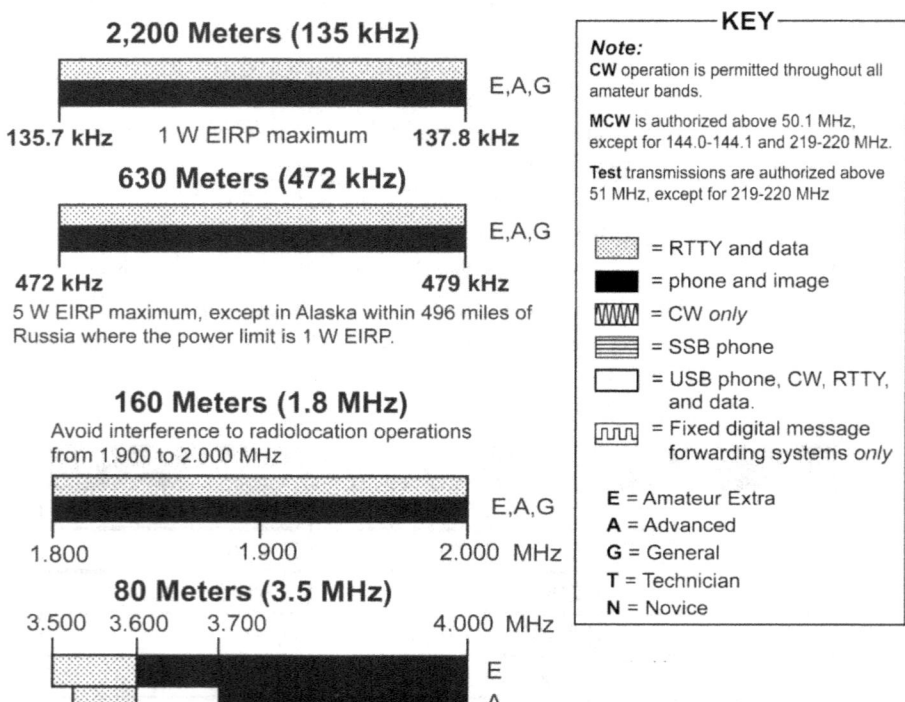

For more about Amateur (Ham) Radio, including detailed band plan charts, visit www.ARRL.org

Graphics and data courtesy of ARRL.

40 Meters (7 MHz)

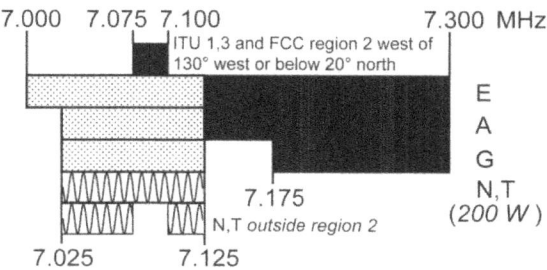

See Sections 97.305(c), 97.307(f)(11) and 97.301(e). These exemptions do not apply to stations in the continental US.

KEY
- ▨ = RTTY and data
- ■ = phone and image
- ⋀⋀ = CW *only*
- ☰ = SSB phone
- ☐ = USB phone, CW, RTTY, and data.
- ⨅⨅ = Fixed digital message forwarding systems *only*

E = Amateur Extra
A = Advanced
G = General
T = Technician
N = Novice

30 Meters (10.1 MHz)
Avoid interference to fixed services outside the US.

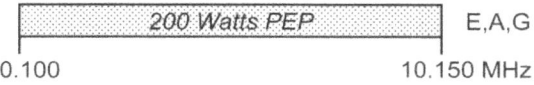

20 Meters (14 MHz)

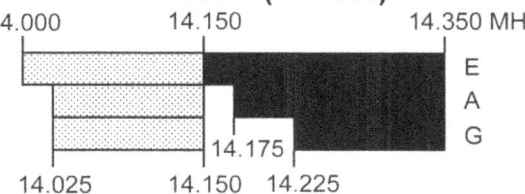

17 Meters (18 MHz)

15 Meters (21 MHz)

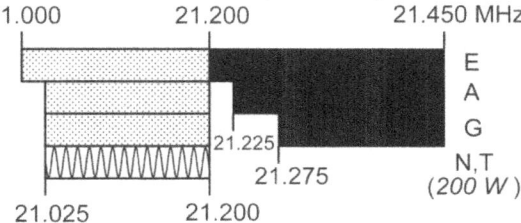

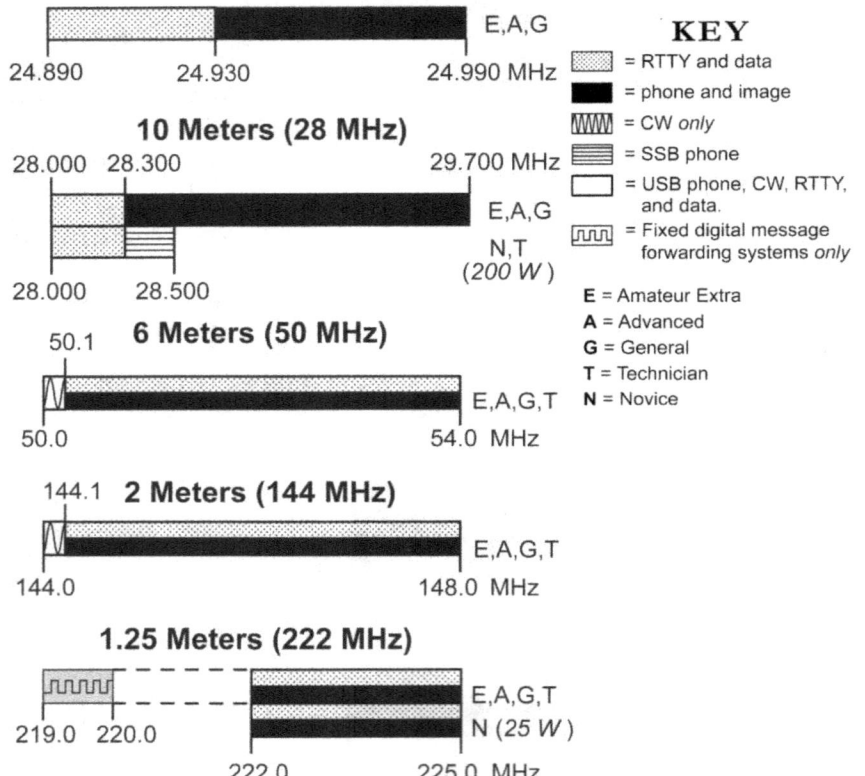

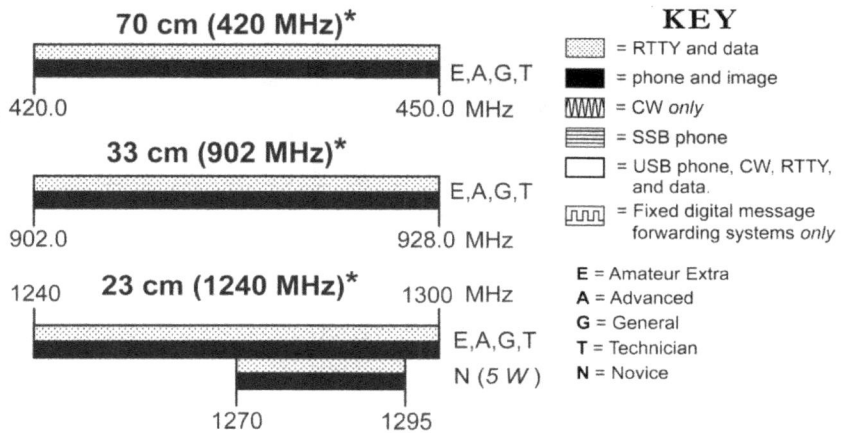

To learn more about Amateur (Ham) Radios, radio selection and use, FCC licensing tests, antennas, and to find a local radio club, visit: www.ARRL.org.

International Commercial-Radio Frequencies

International commercial broadcasts are found in the following shortwave bands. Programs (often in English) usually contain news, commentaries, music, and special features reflecting the culture of the broadcasting country. Reception for this range is best between 6:00 PM and midnight (your time).

Amateur (Ham) Bands		Frequencies (kHz)
120 meters	*	2300 to 2495
90 meters	*	3200 to 3400
75 meters	*	3850 to 4000
60 meters	*	4750 to 5060
49 meters		5900 to 6200
41 meters	**	7100 to 7350
31 meters		9400 to 9990
25 meters		11,600 to 12,100
21 meters		13,500 to 13,870
19 meters		15,100 to 15,800
16 meters		17,480 to 17,900
13 meters		21,450 to 21,750
11 meters		25,600 to 26,100

* These frequencies are reserved for stations in tropical areas.
** There is heavy interference in the 41-meter band since amateur radio operators and international radio stations share the frequency range: 7100 to 7300 kHz.

U.S. Marine Channels and Frequencies

New Channel Number	Old Channel Number	Ship Transmit MHz	Ship Receive MHz	Use
1001	01A	156.050	156.050	Port Operations and Commercial, VTS. Available only in New Orleans / Lower Mississippi area.
1005	05A	156.250	156.250	Port Operations or VTS in the Houston, New Orleans and Seattle areas.
06	06	156.300	156.300	Inter-ship Safety
1007	07A	156.350	156.350	Commercial. VDSMS
08	08	156.400	156.400	Commercial (Inter-ship only). VDSMS
09	09	156.450	156.450	Boater Calling. Commercial and Non-Commercial. VDSMS
10	10	156.500	156.500	Commercial. VDSMS
11	11	156.550	156.550	Commercial. VTS in selected areas. VDSMS
12	12	156.600	156.600	Port Operations. VTS in selected areas.
13	13	156.650	156.650	Inter-ship Navigation Safety (Bridge-to-bridge). Ships >20m length maintain a listening watch on this channel in US waters.
14	14	156.700	156.700	Port Operations. VTS in selected areas.
15	15	--	156.750	Environmental (Receive only). Used by Class C EPIRBs.
16	16	156.800	156.800	International Distress, Safety and Calling. Ships required to carry radio, USCG, and most coast stations maintain a listening watch on this channel.
17	17	156.850	156.850	State & local govt maritime control
1018	18A	156.900	156.900	Commercial. VDSMS
1019	19A	156.950	156.950	Commercial. VDSMS
20	20	157.000	161.600	Port Operations (duplex)
1020	20A	157.000	157.000	Port Operations

1021	21A	157.050	157.050	U.S. Coast Guard only
1022	22A	157.100	157.100	Coast Guard Liaison and Maritime Safety Information Broadcasts. Broadcasts announced on channel 16.
1023	23A	157.150	157.150	U.S. Coast Guard only
24	24	157.200	161.800	Public Correspondence (Marine Operator). VDSMS
25	25	157.250	161.850	Public Correspondence (Marine Operator). VDSMS
26	26	157.300	161.900	Public Correspondence (Marine Operator). VDSMS
27	27	157.350	161.950	Public Correspondence (Marine Operator). VDSMS
28	28	157.400	162.000	Public Correspondence (Marine Operator). VDSMS
1063	63A	156.175	156.175	Port Operations and Commercial, VTS. Available only in New Orleans / Lower Mississippi area.
1065	65A	156.275	156.275	Port Operations
1066	66A	156.325	156.325	Port Operations
67	67	156.375	156.375	Commercial. Used for Bridge-to-bridge communications in lower Mississippi River. Inter-ship only.
68	68	156.425	156.425	Non-Commercial. VDSMS
69	69	156.475	156.475	Non-Commercial. VDSMS
70	70	156.525	156.525	Digital Selective Calling (voice communications not allowed)
71	71	156.575	156.575	Non-Commercial. VDSMS
72	72	156.625	156.625	Non-Commercial (Inter-ship only). VDSMS
73	73	156.675	156.675	Port Operations
74	74	156.725	156.725	Port Operations
77	77	156.875	156.875	Port Operations (Inter-ship only)
1078	78A	156.925	156.925	Non-Commercial. VDSMS
1079	79A	156.975	156.975	Commercial. Non-Commercial in Great Lakes only. VDSMS
1080	80A	157.025	157.025	Commercial. Non-Commercial in Great Lakes only. VDSMS

1081	81A	157.075	157.075	U.S. Government only - Environmental protection operations.
1082	82A	157.125	157.125	U.S. Government only
1083	83A	157.175	157.175	U.S. Coast Guard only
84	84	157.225	161.825	Public Correspondence (Marine Operator). VDSMS
85	85	157.275	161.875	Public Correspondence (Marine Operator). VDSMS
86	86	157.325	161.925	Public Correspondence (Marine Operator). VDSMS
87	87	157.375	157.375	Public Correspondence (Marine Operator). VDSMS
88	88	157.425	157.425	Commercial, Inter-ship only. VDSMS
AIS 1	AIS 1	161.975	161.975	Automatic Identification System (AIS)
AIS 2	AIS 2	162.025	162.025	Automatic Identification System (AIS)

Note: VDSMS (VHF Digital Small Message Services). Transmissions of short digital messages in accordance with RTCM Standard 12301.1 is allowed.

Frequencies are in MHz Modulation is 16KF3E or 16KG3E.

Note that the four-digit channel number beginning with the digits "10" indicates simplex use of the ship station transmit side of what had been an international duplex channel. These new channel numbers, now recognized internationally, were previously designated in the US by the two-digit channel number ending with the letter "A". That is, the international channel 1005 has been designated in the US by channel 05A, and the US Coast Guard channel 1022 has been designated in the US as channel 22A. Four-digit channels beginning with "20", sometimes shown by the two-digit channel number ending with the letter "B", indicates simplex use of the coast station transmit side of what normally was an international duplex channel. The U.S. does not currently use "B" or "20NN" channels in the VHF maritime band. Some VHF transceivers are equipped with an "International - U.S." switch to avoid conflicting use of these channels. See ITU Radio Regulation Appendix 18 and ITU-R M.1084-5 Annex 4.

Partial List of Shortwave Radio Stations Transmitting in English

Freq.	GMT Time	Station	Country	Days	Location
3195.00	2200-0100	WNQM, Inc.	United States	1234567	Nashville, TN
3915.00	2100-2359	BBC World Service	Singapore	1234567	Kranji (Merlin)
4835.00	2130-0830	ABC-Radio Australia	Australia	1234567	Alice Springs
4910.00	2130-0830	ABC-Radio Australia	Australia	1234567	Tennant Greek
5025.00	2130-0830	ABC-Radio Australia	Australia	1234567	Katherine
5110.00	0000-2359	Allan H. Weiner	United States	1234567	Monticello, ME
5875.00	2200-2300	BBC World Service	Thailand	1234567	Nakhon Sawan
5895.00	2200-2300	VOA - Voice of America	Philippines	12345	Tinang 1
5905.00	2100-2300	BBC World Service	Oman	1234567	A'Seela
5915.00	2200-2300	VOA - Voice of America	Thailand	12345	Udorn
5935.00	2200-2300	BBC World Service	South Africa	1234567	Meyerton
5960.00	2200-2300	Radio Romania International	Romania	1234567	Galbeni
6090.00	2200-1000	Caribbean Beacon	United Kingdom	1234567	Anguilla
6195.00	2200-0100	BBC World Service	Singapore	1234567	Kranji (Merlin)
7295.00	0000-2359	Radio Television Malaysia	Malaysia	1234567	Kajang
7355.00	2200-0400	WRNO Worldwide, Inc.	United States	1234567	New Orleans, LA
7415.00	2200-1400	Allan H. Weiner	United States	1234567	Monticello, ME
7435.00	2200-2300	Radio Romania International	Romania	1234567	Galbeni
7460.00	2230-2359	VOA - Voice of America	Philippines	1234567	Tinang 1
7465.00	2100-0100	WNQM, Inc.	United States	1234567	Nashville, TN

7480.00	2200-2300	VOA - Voice of America	Kuwait	12345	Kuwait
7490.00	2200-2359	BBC World Service	Thailand	1234567	Nakhon Sawan
7505.00	2200-1600	WRNO Worldwide, Inc.	United States	1234567	New Orleans, LA
7555.00	2030-2359	VOA - Voice of America	Kuwait	1234567	Kuwait
7575.00	2200-2300	VOA - Voice of America	Philippines	12345	Tinang 1
9330.00	1200-0600	Allan H. Weiner	United States	1234567	Monticello, ME
9350.00	2100-2359	WNQM, Inc.	United States	1234567	Nashville, TN
9570.00	1900-2300	Radio Exterior de Espana	Spain	7	Noblejas
9570.00	2230-2359	VOA - Voice of America	Thailand	1234567	Udorn
9580.00	2200-2359	BBC World Service	Korea (Rep. of)	1234567	Kimjae
9590.00	2200-2300	China Radio International	China	1234567	Beijing
9590.00	2200-2359	ABC-Radio Australia	United Arab Emirates	1234567	Dhabayya
9660.00	2100-2359	ABC-Radio Australia	Australia	1234567	Brandon
9730.00	2230-2300	Far East Broadcast Company	Philippines	1234567	Bocaue
9740.00	2200-2300	BBC World Service	Thailand	1234567	Nakhon Sawan
9740.00	2200-2300	BBC World Service	Oman	1234567	A'Seela
9790.00	2200-2300	Radio Romania International	Romania	1234567	Tiganesti
9830.00	2200-2300	Turkish Radio-TV Corp	Turkey	1234567	Emirler
9850.00	2200-2359	LeSea Broadcasting Corp	United States	7	Furman, SC
9850.00	2200-2359	LeSea Broadcasting Corp	United States	123456	Furman, SC
9915.00	2100-2300	BBC World Service	United Kingdom	1234567	Ascension
9980.00	1200-0200	WNQM, Inc.	United States	1234567	Nashville, TN

11695.00	2200-2330	ABC-Radio Australia	Australia	1234567	Shepperton
11840.00	2230-2359	VOA - Voice of America	Philippines	1234567	Tinang 1
11870.00	2200-2359	Republic of Palau	United States	1234567	Rep. of Palau
11940.00	2200-2300	Radio Romania International	Romania	1234567	Tiganesti
11955.00	2200-2300	VOA - Voice of America	United States	12345	Tinian Islands
12080.00	2000-2359	ABC-Radio Australia	Australia	1234567	Brandon
12095.00	2100-2300	BBC World Service	United Kingdom	1234567	Ascension
13620.00	2200-2300	LeSea Broadcasting Corp	United States	6	Furman, SC
13630.00	2100-2300	ABC-Radio Australia	Australia	1234567	Shepperton
13845.00	1200-2359	WNQM, Inc.	United States	1234567	Nashville, TN
15230.00	2200-2359	ABC-Radio Australia	Australia	1234567	Shepperton
15320.00	2230-2300	Adventist Broadcasting Svs	United States	1234567	Agat, Guam
15340.00	2230-2359	VOA - Voice of America	United States	1234567	Agingan Pt, Saipan
15415.00	2200-2359	ABC-Radio Australia	Australia	1234567	Shepperton
15515.00	2100-2300	ABC-Radio Australia	Australia	1234567	Shepperton
15560.00	2200-2359	ABC-Radio Australia	Australia	1234567	Shepperton
15590.00	1400-0100	WRNO Worldwide, Inc.	United States	1234567	New Orleans, LA
15610.00	2200-2359	Eternal Word Television Network, Inc.	United States	1234567	Vandiver, AL
15720.00	2145-0500	Radio New Zealand	New Zealand	1234567	Rangitaiki

Phonetic Alphabet and Morse Code

LETTER	PHONETIC	MORSE CODE	NUMBER	MORSE
A	Alpha	· —	1	· — — — —
B	Bravo	— · · ·	2	· · — — —
C	Charlie	— · — ·	3	· · · — —
D	Delta	— · ·	4	· · · · —
E	Echo	·	5	· · · · ·
F	Foxtrot	· · — ·	6	— · · · ·
G	Golf	— — ·	7	— — · · ·
H	Hotel	· · · ·	8	— — — · ·
I	India	· ·	9	— — — — ·
J	Juliet	· — — —	0	— — — — —
K	Kilo	— · —		
L	Lima	· — · ·		
M	Mike	— —		
N	November	— ·		
O	Oscar	— — —		
P	Papa	· — — ·		
Q	Quebec	— — · —		
R	Romeo	· — ·		
S	Sierra	· · ·		
T	Tango	—		
U	Uniform	· · —		
V	Victor	· · · —		
W	Whiskey	· — —		
X	X-ray	— · · —		
Y	Yankee	— · — —		
Z	Zulu	— — · ·		

For More Information, Visit
WWW.SIGSWANSTROM.COM

In the movie "The Matrix," the main character was given a choice to take a blue pill to continue living a life of delusion, or a red pill which would strip away falseness and let him embrace the truth. Today, as we consider preparing for a future that will likely look very different, we face a similar decision. For us, our blue pill is to either ignore the signs of the times or to minimally prepare and pretend we have done all that we can reasonably accomplish.

Or, we can figuratively take the red pill, and literally embrace truth and the real-world in which we are now living. We can prepare and be ready to roll into our future fearlessly, with the knowledge that hardship will be accompanied by rich relationships, opportunities, and fulfilling purpose.

Which pill will you choose?

Footnote from page 250: These are examples of Bible verses found in Psalms, Proverbs, and the New Testament, and the three different translations mentioned on that page.

Old Testament

Psalm 55:22 (New Living Translation)

"Give your burdens [concerns] to the Lord [Jesus in prayer and resolve], and He will take care of you. He will not permit the godly to slip and fall."

Psalm 34:19 (New Living Translation)

"The righteous person faces many trials, but the Lord [Jesus] comes to the rescue each time."

Proverbs 11:14 (New American Standard Version)

"Where there is no guideance the people fall, but in abundance of counselors there is victory."

Proverbs 25:26 (New American Standard Version)

"Like a trampled spring and a polluted well is a righteous man [person] who gives way before the wicked."

New Testament

Luke 22:36 (King James Version)

"Then said He [Jesus] unto them, but now, he who hath a purse, let him take it, and likewise his scrip, and he that hath no sword, let him sell his garment, and buy one."

Romans 15:4 (King James Version)

"For whatsoever things were written aforetime were written for our learning, that we through patience and comfort of the Scriptures [Bible] might have hope."

Note: Bible verses must be considered in context. "Cherry-picking" individual verses or phrases and applying a meaning other than that which is evident by the context, is specious and dishonest.

Notes:

www.ingramcontent.com/pod-product-compliance
Lightning Source LLC
Chambersburg PA
CBHW071327190426
43193CB00041B/893